MODERN MORTGAGE LAW
AND PRACTICE

MODERN MORTGAGE LAW
AND PRACTICE

Robert Kratovil, J.D.

Member American Bar Association,
Illinois State Bar Association, and
Chicago Bar Association

Prentice-Hall, Inc.
Englewood Cliffs, N.J.

Prentice-Hall International, Inc., *London*
Prentice-Hall of Australia, Pty., Ltd., *Sydney*
Prentice-Hall of Canada, Ltd., *Toronto*
Prentice-Hall of India Private Ltd., *New Delhi*
Prentice-Hall of Japan, inc., *Tokyo*

Library of Congress
Catalog Card Number: 77-172276

Third Printing . . . . . January, 1973

PRINTED IN THE UNITED STATES OF AMERICA
ISBN-0-13-595702-8
B&P

A Word from the Author

Every book exists to meet some need. Out of my daily contact through many years with mortgage men and their attorneys there has emerged comprehension of the great breadth and diversity of the problems that confront them. All these problems, however, have a theme in common. Working within a complex framework of shifting laws and court decisions these men must struggle constantly to so conduct their affairs that disastrous loss is avoided. To make it possible to achieve this goal, illumination is needed on the law and practice applicable to every phase of the mortgage transaction, beginning with the little-understood application and commitment, through the disbursement of construction loans, the preparation of dependable leases that will provide the cash-flow needed for debt service, and concluding with the problems and mechanics of foreclosure. The cast of characters in these loan transactions must be understood. The general partnership as a lender poses problems different from those of a limited partnership. The foreign corporation lender poses problems in a judicial foreclosure state different from those in a power of sale foreclosure state. Bankruptcy marshalls a host of problems that must be anticipated even before the loan commitment is signed. For example, lease options to renew, lease clauses, security deposits by tenants, and guarantees of rent must be so drafted and manipulated that the reefs and shoals of bankruptcy are skirted or withstood. The point here is, of course, that bankruptcy law, partnership law, and corporation law, to take some illustrations, are not traditionally regarded as "mortgage law," but one cannot make mortgage loans with safety unless this "non-mortgage law" is understood. Again, possible vulnerability to mechanic's liens left by a construction lender's procedures must be brought to light before his first multi-million dollar commitment is given. Even some experienced attorneys seem unfamiliar, for example, with the dangers inherent in the Los Angeles clause and the absence of adequate lien coverage on tenant work.

Since the end of World War II the real estate business has skyrocketed into multi-million dollar projects, and attractive innovations like the shopping center, the planned unit development, and the condominium have become part of the familiar American scene. Phrases like "mortgage warehousing" have crept into our jargon. The Uniform Commercial Code, which most real property lawyers ignored in the mistaken belief that chattel financing did not concern their clients, has suddenly burgeoned into a real property problem of major proportions, as lenders fret over the possibility of removal of stoves, refrigerators, dishwashers, heaters, and air-conditioners from apartments they have financed. Tight money, with its usury consequences, has had even the best-informed lawyers and lenders "kicking the sheets" at night, while they brood over possible invalidity of "points," "service changes," and "stand-by commitments." The automatic sub-ordination flowered in California, only to be followed by a flowering of hostile court decisions that resulted in millions of dollars of loss. The sale and leaseback, the sale and buy back, the wrap-around mortgage offer opportunities for good return and pose problems the courts have not grappled with. Yet lenders and their lawyers must grapple with them and with other problems simply because they are here to be grappled with.

The circle of those concerned, of course, includes the mortgagor, his tenants, the assignee or pledgee of the mortgage, the mortgage broker, the title company, the builder, the architect, countless government officials, and attorneys representing all these diverse interests.

Enough has been said to make it clear that the effort here is to illuminate recurring problems and offer suggestions as to law and procedure to cope with them. When litigation occurs, the resourceful advocate will find his authorities elsewhere. My major premise is that the chief concern of mortgage lenders must always be to see all the problems in advance and to avoid litigation through procedures that skirt or solve the problems. The magnitude of real estate transactions today leaves the lender no alternative. All losses today come in jumbo sizes. Even in the case of residential construction, large-scale developments and modular construction have assigned the small builder a role of dwindling importance. Everything, including risk of loss, is on a large scale today.

I am aware, of course, that laws and court decisions vary from state to state. However, care has been taken to point out the significant differences in point of view, for example, in the material on possession and rents. Carefully researched representative selections of local laws and decisions have been included with a view to flagging the major traps for the unwary.

I gratefully acknowledge the kind permission of the *American Banker* to reprint my article on "Interest Escalation Clauses"; the kind permission of the American Bar Association to reprint my article on "Problems of the Title Examiner under the UCC" that appeared in the *Real Property, Probate and Trust Journal* of that Association; the kind permission of the Chicago Title and Trust

Company to reprint various articles that appeared in that Company's *Lawyers' Supplement to the Guarantor,* including the article on "Subordinations," by John P. Turner, General Counsel of Chicago Title and Trust Company and Chicago Title Insurance Company, and articles by me on "Mortgage Draftsmanship and Conveyancing," "The Mortgagee Looks at Leases and Lease Draftsmanship: Problems of Lessees and Their Lenders"; the kind permission of the *De Paul Law Review* to reprint portions of my articles on "Mortgages—Problems in Possession, Rents and Mortgagee Liability"; and "The Uniform Commercial Code and The Real Property Lawyer"; also the kind permission of the *University of Pennsylvania Law Review* to reprint portions of my article on "Fixtures and the Real Estate Mortgagee." I also wish to express my thanks to Abert Marks of Chicago for many helpful suggestions.

A thought or two on the manner of presentation in this text. Many, many lawyers who have read my book on Real Estate Law have been enthusiastic in commenting on the simplicity of statement and generous use of examples. Over and over I have heard it said that simplicity and clarity are cardinal virtues in all books, including legal books. Obviously, I concur in this view.

Robert Kratovil

Table of Contents

§ 372. Liability of leasehold mortgagee. § 373. Acceleration clause. § 374. Landlord's cooperation where he refuses to join in leasehold mortgage. § 375. Economic disadvantages. § 376. Joinder by fee owner in tenant's leasehold mortgage. § 377. Marshalling of assets.

§ 378. In the sale and buy-back.

§ 379. In general. § 380. Sale and leaseback as a disguised mortgage. § 381. Usury aspects. § 382. Junior and other financing. § 383. Recording. § 384. Title requirements of the investor.

§ 385. In general. § 386. Sale and leaseback. § 387. Leasehold mortgage—ground lease. § 388. Marshalling of assets—fee and leasehold in one mortgage. § 389. Leasehold mortgages—subleaseholds. § 390. Non-disturbance clauses. § 391. Holding companies. § 392. Joint ventures—the unanticipated joint adventure. § 393. Wrap-around mortgage. § 394. UCC filings. § 395. Sale or reservation of building combined with lease of land.

§ 396. In general. § 397. Filing a claim. § 398. Foreclosure. § 399. Foreclosure of fee mortgage where junior lessee is in bankruptcy. § 400. Trustee's deed in lieu of foreclosure. § 401. Notice of the bankruptcy as affecting the mortgagee. § 402. Sale by trustee—subject to or free and clear of mortgages. § 403. Sale free and clear—objections by the mortgagee. § 404. Sale free and clear—encumbrances other than liens. § 405. Sale by trustee—protection of mortgagee. § 406. Leases —security deposits. § 407. Lease terminations by bankruptcy. § 408. Lease subordinate to mortgage—bankruptcy of fee owner.

§ 451. Mortgagee in possession. § 452. Statutes extinguishing mortgage lien. § 453. Marketable title acts.

§ 454. In general.

§ 455. Necessity for release. § 456. Who signs the release deed. § 457. Recording. § 458. Release on margin of record. § 459. Defective releases. § 460. Penalty for failure to release. § 461. Release of part of mortgage land. § 462. Release of mortgage as automatic release of assignment of rents. § 463. Title standards. § 464. Wrongful release—protection given an innocent purchaser.

§ 465. Trustee executes release. § 466. Recording of release. § 467. Wrongful release. § 468. Bona fide purchaser or lienor after recording of wrongful release. § 469. Missing notes. § 470. Future advances. § 471. Provisions of deed of trust. § 472. Recitals.

§ 473. In general—information to be furnished the foreclosing attorney. § 474. Defects in proceedings—nonjurisdictional defects. § 475. Jurisdiction of the subject matter. § 476. Jurisdiction of the parties—necessary parties—omitted parties. § 477. Omitted parties—foreclosure as an assignment of the mortgage. § 478. Omitted parties—mortgagee in possession. § 479. Lis pendens. § 480. Exceeding jurisdiction. § 481. Jurisdiction of the land. § 482. Multi-state mortgages. § 483. Multi-county foreclosures. § 484. Filing of the foreclosure suit. § 485. Hearing and judgment or decree. § 486. Appraisal statutes. § 487. Upset price. § 488. Sale. § 489. Cash bids—holder of mortgage debt. § 490. Title acquired. § 491. Sale en masse. § 492. Marshalling of assets.

Text References

References herein to texts refer to the following editions thereof:

Basye, *Clearing Land Titles* (2d ed. 1970)
Collier, *Bankruptcy* (14th ed.)
Gilmore, *Security Interests in Personal Property* (1965)
Glenn, *Mortgages* (1943)
Jones, *Mortgages* (8th ed. 1928)
Kratovil, *Real Estate Law* (5th ed. 1969)
Osborne, *Morgages* (2d ed. 1970)
Patton, *Titles* (2d ed. 1957)
Powell, *Law of Real Property* (1970) (Footnotes are more extensive in 1952 edition.)
Scott, *Trusts* (3rd ed. 1967)
Sherman, Malcolm C., *Mortgage and Real Estate Investment Guide* (Marshfield, Mass. 02050) (State-by-State loose-leaf service)
Simes and Smith, *Law of Future Interests* (2d ed. 1966)
Thompson, *Real Property* (Grimes edition)
Tiffany, *Real Property* (3rd ed. 1939)
Wiltsie, *Mortgage Foreclosures* (5th ed. 1939)

1

History of Mortgage Law

§ 1. **Mortgage defined.** A mortgage may be defined as a conveyance of land given as security for the payment of a debt. On analysis, this definition discloses the existence of two elements: (1) Like a deed, a mortgage is a conveyance of land. (2) However, the object of the document is not, as in the case of a deed, to effect a sale of land, but to provide security for the payment of a debt.

§ 2. **History of mortgage law.** The history of mortgage law is the history of hundreds of years of ceaseless struggle for advantage between borrowers and lenders, and the lawbooks reflect the constantly shifting fortunes of this war. Occasionally the battle has gone in favor of the lenders. More recently, however, many laws favorable to the borrowers have been passed, and the battle has usually gone in their favor. To understand how the modern mortgage developed out of these centuries of struggle is to take a long step forward toward understanding modern mortgage law.

Much of our mortgage law comes to us from England. In that country, mortgage arrangements of various kinds existed even in the Anglo-Saxon times before the conquest of England by William the Conqueror in 1066. However, it will suffice for our purposes to begin with the mortgage of the fourteenth century. This document was a simple deed of the land, running from the borrower (mortgagor) to the lender (mortgagee). All the ceremonies needed for a full transfer of ownership took place when the mortgage was made. The mortgagee became the owner of the land just as if a sale had taken place. However, this ownership was subject to two qualifications:

> 1. The mortgagee, as owner, could oust the mortgagor, take immediate possession of the property, and collect the rents. However,

the rents so collected had to be applied on the mortgage debt. For this reason, the mortgagee often permitted the mortgagor to remain in possession.

2. The mortgage described the debt it secured and stated a date of payment, known as the *law day*. The mortgage gave the mortgagor the right to pay the debt on the law day. If he did so, the mortgage provided that it was thereby to become void. This provision was known as the *defeasance clause,* for payment of the debt on the law day defeated the mortgage and put ownership back in the mortgagor.

In early times, the courts enforced the mortgage as it was written. Foreclosure proceedings did not exist. Failure to pay the mortgage debt when due, termed a *default,* automatically extinguished all the mortgagor's interest in the land.

§ 3. **The equity of redemption.** For many years no one dreamed of questioning this scheme of things. Then slowly at first, and later in greater numbers, borrowers who had lost their property through default began to seek the assistance of the king by presenting *petitions* to him. A typical petition by such a borrower would set forth the borrowing of the money, the making of the mortgage, the default in payment, and the resulting loss of the land. The petition would continue with the statement that the borrower now had funds and offered to pay the mortgage debt in full, with interest. The petition would then ask that the king order the mortgagee, who now owned the land, to accept the proffered money and to convey the land back to the borrower. The king had little time or inclination to tend to these petitions personally, and so he habitually referred them to a high official, the Lord Chancellor. Since the king was the fountain of all justice, it was the Chancellor's duty to dispose of these petitions justly and equitably, according to good conscience, and this he did. In cases of hardship or accident, for example, where the mortgagor had been robbed while on his way to pay the debt, the Chancellor would order the mortgagee to accept payment of the debt from the borrower and to convey the land back to the borrower. A mortgagee who refused to do as he was told was sent to jail. In time, by about the year 1625, what had begun as a matter of grace on the part of the king had developed into the purest routine. Borrowers filed their petitions directly with the Chancellor, who was now functioning as the judge of a court, and with routine regularity his order was issued commanding the mortgagee to reconvey. Thus a new and very important right was born, the right of the mortgagor to pay his debt even after default and in this manner to recover his property. This right came to be known as the *equitable right of redemption,* or the *equity of redemption.* Later the courts held that the mortgagor could sell this equitable right of redemption, that he could dispose of it by his will, and that if he died leaving no will, the right could be exercised by his heirs. You will perceive that as a result of these developments, the mortgagor, even after default, retained very important rights in the land. Technically the mortgagee became full owner of the land upon default, but practically the mortgagor could now be regarded as the owner even after default, since he could reacquire ownership by exercising his equitable right of redemption.

§ 4. **Waiver of equitable right of redemption.** The mortgagees reacted to the development of the equitable right of redemption by inserting in their mortgages clauses reciting that the mortgagor waived and surrendered all his equitable rights of redemption. The courts, however, nipped this idea in the bud by holding that all such clauses were void, since a needy borrower will sign anything and it is up to the courts to protect him. This rule flourished and exists in full vigor today. Any provision in the mortgage purporting to terminate the mortgagor's ownership in case of failure to make payments when due is against public policy and is void. *Once a mortgage, always a mortgage.* It cannot be converted into an outright deed by the mere default of the mortgagor. And no matter how the mortgagee seeks to disguise an attempted waiver of the equitable right of redemption, the courts will strike it down.

EXAMPLE: At the time the mortgage was made the mortgagor signed a deed conveying the property to the mortgagee as grantee. He then delivered the deed to a third person in escrow with directions to deliver the deed to the mortgagee in case of default in the mortgage payments. This deed and escrow were held invalid as an attempted waiver of the equitable right of redemption. *Plummer v. Ilse,* 41 Wash. 5,82 P1009; *Hamod v. Hawthorne,* 52 Cal.2d 78, 338 P2d 387.

§ 5. **Development of foreclosure.** The efforts of the courts to rescue the mortgagor in turn placed the mortgagee at a disadvantage. The mortgagee, it is true, became the owner of the land when the mortgagor defaulted, but he could not be certain he would remain the owner, for the mortgagor might choose to redeem. To remedy this situation a new practice sprang up. Immediately upon default in payment of the mortgage debt, the mortgagee would file a petition in court, and the judge would enter an order, called a decree, allowing the mortgagor additional time to pay the debt. If he failed to pay within this time, usually six months or a year, the decree provided that his equitable right of redemption was thereby barred and foreclosed. Thereafter he could not redeem his property. Thus developed the *foreclosure suit,* a suit to bar or terminate the equitable right of redemption.

The method of foreclosure just described is known today as *strict foreclosure.* It is still used in Connecticut and Vermont and occasionally elsewhere.

The next development was foreclosure through public sale. The idea emerged that in mortgage foreclosures justice would best be served by offering the land for sale at public auction, for if at such sale the property sold for more than the mortgage debt, the mortgagee would be paid his debt in full and the surplus proceeds of the sale would be salvaged for the mortgagor. This method of *foreclosure by sale* is the most common method of foreclosure in America today. This development constituted another major victory for the mortgagor. More important still, it led to another and even greater victory for the borrowers. As the practice of foreclosure by sale grew more common, the view began to emerge that *the mortgage, despite its superficial similarity to a deed, was really not a deed of conveyance but only a lien on the land—that is, merely a means of bringing about a public sale to raise money for the payment of the mortgage debt.*[1]

§ 6. Title and lien theories. The relatively recent view that the mortgage is not really a conveyance of land but only a lien, has reached its fullest development in the agricultural and western states. Certain states, called title theory states, still take the older view that a mortgage gives the mortgagee some sort of legal title to the land. In other states, called lien theory states, the view that the mortgagee has the legal title is entirely superseded by the view that he has merely a lien to secure his debt. Some states take a position midway between these two views. These are called intermediate states.

It is not possible, however, to draw any hard and fast line between these groups of states, since vestiges of title theory will be found in lien theory states, and many title theory states have adopted rules developed by lien theory courts.

Even in title states the "title" that is vested in the mortgagee tends to be rather shadowy for most purposes. For example, no one but the mortgagee can avail himself of the "title" vested in the mortgagee.

EXAMPLE: R, a landowner, mortgages his land to E. T, a stranger, takes possession of the land, and R sues to oust him. T will not be permitted to contend that title is really vested in E. *Allen v. Kellam,* 69 Ala. 442; *Porter v. Seeley,* 13 Conn. 564; *Harlow Realty Co. v. Cotter,* 284 Mass. 68, 187 NE 118.

And even in title states the mortgagor may sell, lease or mortgage the land, subject, of course, to the paramount rights of the first mortgagee. One might say that the mortgagee's "title" exists primarily for the purpose of giving the mortgagee the right to take possession and collect rents after default. *See* Chapter 27.

§ 7. Statutory redemption. When a mortgage foreclosure sale is held, the equitable right of redemption ends. Indeed, the whole object of the foreclosure suit is to put an end to the mortgagor's equitable right of redemption. In the last hundred years, however, laws have been enacted giving the mortgagor an additional concession. Under these laws, the mortgagor is given one last change to get his property back.

---

[1] Kratovil, *Real Estate Law*, 5th ed. (Englewood Cliffs, N.J.: Prentice-Hall, Inc., 1969), pp. 203–206, © 1969.

EXPLANATION: Suppose, for example, that a farmer whose farm is mortgaged has a bad crop year. He cannot meet his mortgage payments, and the mortgage is foreclosed. Perhaps next year the weather and crops will be good, and he will have enough to pay all of his debts. To afford farmers and other mortgagors one last opportunity to salvage their properties, many legislatures have passed laws allowing additional time, often one year, after the foreclosure sale during which the mortgagor can, by paying the amount of the foreclosure sale price, get his property back from the mortgagee. This right is called the statutory right of redemption. Thus the equitable right of redemption ends and the statutory right of redemption begins with the holding of the foreclosure sale. See Chapter 46.

Whether the statutory right of redemption may be waived is a question discussed elsewhere. *See* § 542.

§ 8. The title and lien theories today. The notion of the mortgage as a conveyance of title to land has all but vanished today. It retains importance with respect to problems of rents and possession and problems involving the deed absolute. But today's mortgage litigation is resolved mainly in terms of the mortgage as a lien, even in title states. Priority of lien is the main concern. The rule that *prior in time is prior in right,* with its numerous exceptions, is one of the principal battlegrounds in mortgage litigation. As a necessary corollary, the problem of *inception of lien* is one that frequently recurs both as to the mortgage and competing liens.

EXAMPLE: In 1968 R mortgages land to E for $10,000 but E advances only $5,000. R gives a mortgage to E-2 in 1969 for $4,000. Both mortgages are recorded. In 1970 E advances the remaining $5,000 to R. A question of competing priorities will arise as between E and E-2 with respect to the advance made in 1970. See §§ 115, 116.

EXAMPLE: R hires X to grade his vacant land in Arkansas and this is done in 1968. R puts on a construction loan in 1969 to E. R hires Y to construct a building, and construction begins in 1970. X and his subcontractors contend that their liens have their inception in 1968, when the grading was done, and therefore they have priority over E. See § 214.

ADDITIONAL REFERENCES: 7 U.C.L.A. L. Rev. 83; 50 Minn. L. Rev. 331; 6 Mo. L. Rev. 200; 40 Neb. L. Rev. 261; 47 N.C. L. Rev. 464; 18 Western Res. L. Rev. 765 (Ohio); 12 So. Tex. L. J. 129; 8 Utah L. Rev. 125; Rudolph, *Wyoming Law of Real Mortgages;* 3 Powell, *Real Property,* § 439 (listing statutes expositive of title or lien theory).

2

Types of Mortgages

§ 9. **Types of mortgages.** There are several different types of mortgage instruments. Those commonly encountered are the *regular mortgage,* the *deed of trust,* the *equitable mortgage,* and the *deed absolute given as security for a debt.*

§ 10. **Regular mortgage.** The ordinary printed form of mortgage encountered in most states today is referred to herein as the *regular mortgage.* It is, in form, a deed or conveyance of the land by the borrower to the lender followed or preceded by a description of the debt and usually including a provision to the effect that such mortgage shall be void on full payment of such debt. The content of the additional paragraphs of "fine print" varies considerably. *See* Chapter 6.

§ 11. **Deeds of trust.** The regular mortgage involves only two parties, the borrower and the lender. In the *deed of trust,* also known as the *trust deed,* the borrower conveys the land, not to the lender, but to a third party, in trust for the benefit of the holder of the note or notes that represent the mortgage debt.

The deed of trust form of mortgage has certain advantages, the chief one being that in a number of states it can be foreclosed by trustee's sale under the power of sale clause without any court proceedings. *See* Chapter 8.

§ 12. **Equitable mortgages.** As a general rule, any instrument in writing by which the parties show their intention that real estate be held as security for the payment of a debt will constitute an *equitable mortgage,* which can be foreclosed in a court of equity.

EXAMPLE: *R,* a landowner, borrowed money from *E* and gave *E* a promissory note to evidence the debt. On this note *R* placed the following recital:

28

"This note is secured by a real estate mortgage on" (here followed a description of the land). Actually no separate mortgage was executed. The court held that the note itself, with the quoted endorsement, constituted an equitable mortgage on the land, for it clearly expressed an intention that the land should stand as security for the debt. *Trustees of Zion Methodist Church v. Smith*, 335 Ill. App. 233, 81 NE2d 233. See Chapter 4.

§ 13. **Deed absolute given as security.** Quite often a landowner will give an ordinary warranty deed or quitclaim deed when he has no intention of selling his land and his only purpose is to provide security for a loan.

EXAMPLE: *R* owns a home on which he has a large first mortgage. Because of illness in the family, he is compelled to borrow money, but no one will give him money on the security of a second mortgage. *R* goes to *E*, a relative, who loans *R* the money but insists that *R* give *E* a quitclaim deed to the land, hoping thereby to avoid the trouble and expense of foreclosure if *R* fails to pays the loan off. The deed is nothing but a mortgage. Such a deed is called a *deed absolute given as security* or simply a *deed absolute*. See Chapter 3.

§ 14. **Conditional sale.** The phrase *conditional sale,* as it is used in mortgage law, has a meaning wholly different from the meaning given it in security transactions involving chattels. In mortgage law, a conditional sale is a sale in which the seller reserves an option to re-purchase the land. If the parties really intend a sale, there is nothing objectionable in such a transaction. 44 ALR2d 345.

EXAMPLE: *R* owns some land worth $100,000. He needs to raise some money. He could, of course, borrow money on a note and mortgage, but *R* does not wish to incur the personal liability involved in such a transaction. *R* offers to sell the land to *E* for $100,000, but insists on reserving an option to re-purchase the land within a year for $110,000. The transaction is consummated in this form. One advantage to *R*, if he is a businessman, is that he need not show the option as a liability in his financial statements furnished bankers in connection with his borrowings. Indeed, he will show it as an asset. A mortgage and note would have to be shown as a liability.

Obviously, however, this situation lends itself to other uses. It can hide a disguised loan. It can be used to conceal usury.

EXAMPLE: *R* owns a home worth $20,000 in a state where the maximum interest rate is 6%. *R* makes application to *E* for a loan of $10,000. Few loans to individuals are being made in the state because interest rates generally are in the neighborhood of 9%. *E* insists that *R* give *E* a deed to the land. *E* gives *R* $10,000 in "payment" for the deed. *E* gives *R* an option to re-purchase the land within one year for $11,000. Clearly this is nothing but a disguised loan at 10% interest. *R* has no choice but to exercise the option. Otherwise he would lose a home worth $20,000 in return for only $10,000. Moreover, *R* never wanted to "sell" his home. He wanted to mortgage it. Thus the deed here is a deed absolute. See Chapters 3 and 14.

§ 15. Deed to secure a debt. In Georgia, under a special law, a deed made to secure a debt, where such deed shows on its fact that it is given to secure a debt, passes the title of the property to the grantee until the debt is paid. An ordinary warranty deed form is used, with various clauses added. Thus, whereas a regular mortgage in this state creates only a lien, a warranty deed given to secure a debt gives the grantee legal title and enables him to take possession of the land on the borrower's default. *Wiley v. Martin,* 163 Ga. 381, 136 SE 151. This "loan deed" is used in Georgia instead of a mortgage.

§ 16. Vendor's lien reserved by deed. In some states, a seller, in lieu of taking back a mortgage from the buyer, expressly reserves in his deed to the buyer a lien on the land to secure payment of the balance of the purchase prcie. Such a lien is called a vendor's lien. It is really a mortgage.

EXAMPLE: *A, a landowner, conveyed to B by a warranty deed which warranted that title was free from all encumbrances excepting three certain notes executed by B, for which a vendor's lien was retained until said notes and the interest thereon should be fully paid. The court held that this clause created a lien on the land. Such a lien is regarded as partaking of the nature of an equitable mortgage. It is really a mortgage. It is governed by the same rules as a mortgage and must be foreclosed as such. Crabtree v. Davis, 237 Ala. 264, 186 So 734.*

Such a lien enjoys priority over subsequent liens and encumbrances and, like a purchase money mortgage, has priority over prior judgments against the purchaser. The grantee under such deed does not become personally liable for the purchase money unless, as in the example given, he has signed a promissory note or otherwise obligated himself personally to pay the debt. And a purchaser from such grantee does not become personally liable to the holder of the vendor's lien unless by his deed he assumes and agrees to pay the unpaid balance of the debt. The debt may be assigned, and the assignee will have the right to foreclose the lien.[1]

---

[1] Kratovil, *Real Estate Law*, 4th ed. (Englewood Cliffs, N.J.: Prentice-Hall, Inc., 1964), pp. 210–211, © 1964.

3

Deed Absolute Given as Security

§ 17. **In general.** Often when a landowner borrows money he gives as security an absolute deed to the land. By absolute deed is meant an ordinary quitclaim or warranty deed such as is used in sales of land. On its face the transaction looks like a sale and conveyance of the land. Nevertheless the courts treat such a deed as a mortgage, although they require convincing evidence that the deed was really intended only as security for a debt. But if such proof is available, the borrower is entitled to pay the debt and to demand a reconveyance from the lender, just as in the case of an ordinary mortgage; whereas if the debt is not paid, the grantee must foreclose just as if a regular mortgage had been made. *See* § 13.

Ordinarily when one person gives a deed to another, he intends to transfer ownership of the property to the grantee. However, the *deed absolute rule* teaches us that a deed may not be intended as an absolute transfer of ownership. It may be intended merely to provide the grantee with security for repayment of the debt. It is a disguised mortgage in such case. Complicating the problem somewhat is the fact that such transactions are often accomplished without benefit of legal advice, and the parties are not at all clear as to what they really intended.

In principle, the test is quite a simple one. Did the parties *intend* an actual sale of the land or did they merely *intend* to provide the grantee with security for the repayment of a debt? As a corollary question, was it the *intention* of the parties that if the grantor could repay the grantee, the grantor would get his property back?

§ 18. **Parol evidence.** In nearly all states parol (that is, oral) evidence is admissible to show that a deed was merely intended as a mortgage. Osborne,

31

Mortgages § 72. More than a preponderance of the evidence is required to show that the deed is nothing but a mortgage. Usually, the courts call for evidence that is "clear and convincing." *Walker v. Struter,* 191 Ark. 604, 87 SW2d 43; Osborne, *Mortgages* § 74. The courts have been able to sweep aside both the parol evidence rule and the Statute of Frauds in order to establish the mortgage character of the deed. 34 *Ill. L. Rev.* 189.

§ 19. **Deviations from the rule permitting parol evidence.** In a number of states there are deviations from the rules given above with respect to deed absolute given as security. For example, in North Carolina and Louisiana it takes something approaching fraud or undue influence to convert a deed into a mortgage. In Georgia if possession of the land is delivered to the grantee, parol evidence is inadmissible to establish the transaction as the mortgage unless there is fraud. A similar rule prevails in Mississippi. In Pennsylvania oral evidence is not admissible to contradict the deed. 1 Wiltsie, *Mortgages and Mortgage Foreclosures,* 45; 59 CJS *Mortgages* § 50.

§ 20. **Circumstances bearing on the question of character of transaction.** In determining whether a transaction is a sale or a mortgage, the following circumstances are considered:

1. Adequacy of consideration—necessity of personal obligation. If *R* deeds to *E* land worth $10,000 and receives only $5,000, this tends to indicate that the transaction is a mortgage, for normally land will sell for its full value. Here is a situation where the technical absence of a "debt" does not preclude a court from holding that the transaction is a mortgage. *Bailey v. Poe,* 142 Md. 57, 120 A 242. *Contra: Maxey v. Citizens Nat. Bank,* 432 SW2d 722 (Tex. Civ.App.) Clearly the true rule is that personal liability on *R*'s part is not necessary since it is not necessary in the case of a regular mortgage. 1 Glenn, *Mortgages* 25, 61. Moreover, the economic compulsion to repay the money in order to procure a reconveyance of the land creates an "obligation" quite as compelling as the signing of a promissory note. *Campbell v. Dearborn,* 109 Mass. 130.

2. Prior and contemporaneous negotiations between the parties. If *R* applies to *E* for a loan and the transaction is consummated by *R* giving *E* a deed to the land, this tends to show that the transaction is a mortgage. It is as if *E* had said: "I will loan you the money, but give me a deed as security." Of course if it appears that *E* rejected the application for a loan, this tends to show that the transaction is a sale. It is as if *E* had said: "I will not loan you any money, but I am willing to buy your land." *Blue River Saw Mills v. Gates,* 225 Ore. 439, 358 P2d 239. Likewise if some contemporaneous document talks about the grantor's right to "redeem," this language tends to show that a mortgage was intended. *Matthews v. Sheehan* 69 N.Y. 585.

3. Subsequent conduct of the parties. If *R* receives money from *E* and gives *E* a deed to *R*'s land, but *R* thereafter remains in possession, paying taxes,

insurance premiums, and so on, this tends to show that the transaction is a mortgage, for in a normal land sale the buyer takes possession. *Morton v. Allen,* 180 Ala. 279, 60 So 866.

4. Equality of bargaining power. If the grantee in the deed is a sophisticated person or corporation having substantial financial resources and the grantor is unsophisticated and in financial distress, there will be a tendency to hold that the deed is a security transaction. *Morton v. Allen,* 180 Ala. 279, 60 So 866. At times this problem appears in usury law. If an actual sale is involved, usury is not present, for the parties can agree on any price they choose. But if a disguised loan is discovered, and the transaction is held to be a security transaction, it may be that usury will be present. Oddly enough, the courts sometimes reverse the theoretically logical procedure. They find that the so-called borrower was a sophisticated person enjoying independent legal advice. Having thus ascertained equality of bargaining power, they find that usury was not present, for the usury laws were not intended to protect the sophisticated. *Meridian Bowling Lanes v. Brown,* 30 Ida. 403, 412 P2d 586. Having found that usury was not present, the court can then conclude that the deal was a sale rather than a loan. *See* Chapter 14. Where usury is claimed by the mortgagor, the courts resolve doubtful cases in favor of holding the transaction a true sale rather than a mortgage. *Brown v. Dewey,* 2 Barb. 28, 32; *Vincent v. Walker,* 86 Ala. 333, 5 So 465. Where the grantor is simply seeking to get the land back by offering payment, doubtful cases will be resolved for the grantor.

5. Whether the "borrower" acquires ownership of the land contemporaneously with the supposed security transaction. This is more fully discussed hereafter. *See* § 27.

§ 21. Character of title acquired by grantee in deed absolute. As is observed elsewhere, in discussing title and lien theories, there are differences in viewpoint as to the nature of the interest acquired by a mortgagee in a mortgage. *See* § 6. This question grows somewhat more complex when we are dealing with a deed absolute in the nature of a mortgage. Even in lien states the document looks more substantial than a mere mortgage.

Except, perhaps, in a few lien states, it is the general rule even in lien theory states that a deed absolute passes the legal title to the grantee. In other words, while a mortgage in a lien state creates only a *lien* on the land, leaving the legal title in the mortgagor, a mortgage transaction that takes the form of a deed absolute given as security vests the *legal title* in the grantee. 71 *U.Pa.L.Rev.* 284; 32 *Yale L.J.* 611. The significance of this rule lies in the fact that a mere cancellation of a written defeasance or even a verbal surrender of the equity of redemption will serve to extinguish the mortgagor's rights, leaving a good clear title in the grantee in the security deed. *Stall v. Jones,* 47 Neb. 706, 56 NW 653.

At all events, in both title and lien states, the situation gives courts a chance to give more emphasis to considerations of justice and practicality than is true in the typical formal mortgage situation.

EXAMPLE: R borrowed money from time to time from E and gave E an absolute deed by way of security. Finally, when it became apparent that R could not repay the debt, E gave R a lease and both parties signed a four-line paper stating that the accounts between them were settled. Observe that if we still regard R as being the real owner of the property and E as being a mere mortgagee, this would be much too informal a way of transferring ownership of land, which, as is well understood, requires a deed. Nevertheless the courts can say in this situation that the absolute deed gave E ownership (not a mortgage interest) in the land, and that relinquishment of R's interest can be accomplished informally. *West v. Reed,* 55 Ill. 242; *Williams v. Williams,* 270 Ill. 552, 110 NE 876.

§ 22. Escrow. Another illustration of the courts' readiness to regard a deed as a mortgage and to hold invalid any device that fetters the mortgagor's equitable right of redemption is their attitude toward deeds delivered in escrow where the sole purpose of the escrow is to provide a lender a quick remedy where default is made in payment of a debt.

EXAMPLE: R borrows $10,000 from E and gives E his note due one year after date. He signs a quitclaim deed to E as grantee. Both the note and deed are delivered to X in escrow. The terms of the escrow are that if the debt is paid when due, X is to deliver the note and deed to R cancelled. If the debt is not then paid, X is to record the deed. The debt is not paid. X records the deed. E has not acquired good ownership of the property. The deed is nothing but a mortgage, since it was intended only as security. *Hamod v. Hawthorne,* 52 Cal2d 78, 338 P2d 387; *Plummer v. Ilse,* 41 Wash. 5, 82 P1009; 1 Glenn, *Mortgages,* 281.

§ 23. Bona fide purchaser. Normally, in the deed absolute situation the grantor in the deed remains in possession of the property. Indeed, this is one of the criteria by means of which the court adjudges the transaction a loan rather than true sale. In nearly all states possession imparts constructive notice. Kratovil, *Real Estate Law* (5th ed. 1969) § 127. In other words, all the world must take notice of the rights of the person in possession of the land. Since inquiry from him would reveal his rights in the property, there will rarely be a bona fide purchaser in these cases. However, where the land is vacant it is possible for the grantee in the security deed to convey good ownership of the land to an innocent purchaser of the land.

EXAMPLE: R borrows $10,000 from E and gives E a quitclaim deed of certain vacant land as security. R fails to pay the debt when it falls due. E, being unaware that he should foreclose the deed absolute as though it were a mortgage, sells and conveys the land to P, who has no knowledge of the facts of the case. P is a bona fide purchaser. He takes free of any title or rights of R.

§ 24. Deed absolute as a fraudulent conveyance. There is danger that an absolute deed given as security for a debt will be held void as a fraud upon creditors. The theory is this: As far as the public records show, the grantor in such a deed apparently has sold the land to the grantee. Actually he remains the owner of the land, and the grantee is only a mortgagee. Other creditors of the mortgagor are deceived and fail to pursue the land, thinking that the mortgagor has parted with all his interest in it. If this is actually the purpose of the transaction, the deed will be set aside when the creditors discover the fraud, and the courts will punish the grantee by holding that as against such creditors he does not even have a mortgage. Also, if the transaction was intended as a fraud on creditors, and if the grantor attempts to pay his debt but the grantee refuses to reconvey the land to him, most courts will not help the grantor get his property back. *Svalina v. Saravana,* 341 Ill. 236, 172 NE 281; Osborne, *Mortgages,* 120.

§ 25. Recordability. A deed absolute, by its very nature, misrepresents its nature. It purports to be a conveyance of the land. Actually it is nothing but a security transaction. It tends to mislead creditors. Moreover, it lacks the honesty of a true mortgage in that it does not describe the mortgage debt. For this reason there are decisions that, although it has been recorded, the deed absolute has only the status of an unrecorded mortgage. *Machez v. Homer Harmon Inc.,* 146 Conn. 523, 152 A2d 629; Osborne, *Mortgages,* 121.

§ 26. Conditional sales—validity. It is not uncommon for a vendor to sell land but to reserve in his deed an option to repurchase the property. Such options, if made in good faith, are valid. *See* § 14. However, such transactions are occasionally nothing but disguised loans. The deed, in that event, is a deed absolute, that is, a security deed that is nothing more than a mortgage. Courts can readily detect the true nature of a transaction, for example, where it is nothing but a cloak for usury. 154 ALR 1065.

§ 27. Conditional sale—sale and resale between different persons. If the sale and resale are between an existing owner and his "purchaser" there is more tendency to hold the transaction a disguised loan than where a new purchaser is coming into the picture. 154 ALR 1079. *See also* Chapter 31; *also* § 181.

EXAMPLE: *R* has owned a farm for several years. Needing money he seeks out *E. E* demands a deed, which *R* gives him. *E* gives *R* $50,000 and an option to repurchase the farm within one year at $55,000. The farm is worth $100,000. *E* also gives *R* a lease for one year, at a nominal rent. Obviously this is a disguised loan at something over 10% interest. If this exceeds the maximum rate, usury is present. Obviously a sale was not intended. Intention is important. A farm worth $100,000 does not "sell" for $50,000. See § 104.

EXAMPLE: *R* wishes to buy a farm owned by *X*. He lacks the funds. He seeks out *E. E* buys the farm from *X* for $100,000. He now contracts to sell the farm to *R* over a five-year period at a price of $110,000 and interest at the maximum rate. This is a genuine sale and resale. It is not a mortgage. There is no usury. **Cf.** § 45.

A conditional sale can involve either an option or a contract to repurchase. And in either case the transaction can be a true sale or a disguised mortgage. Where there is a contract to repurchase, the courts, if so disposed, can point to the legal obligation of the contract purchaser as creating something like a mortgage debt. *See* Chapter 10. In an option this legal obligation is lacking. This, however, is but one circumstance. As pointed out in the first example in this section, the economic compulsion to exercise an option to purchase can be quite as compelling as a legal obligation created by a document. *See also* § 32.

§ 28. Conditional sales—options and contracts of sale—effect of holding the transaction to be a mortgage. If a deed with option to repurchase is later held by the courts to be a mortgage transaction, expiration of the option period does not cut off the optionee's rights. In an ordinary option transaction, when the option period has expired the option is dead. But if the transaction is a mortgage, even after the option has expired the optionee has the right to pay his debt and redeem his property. Powell, *Real Property* § 578. And if the transaction was, in form, a deed and installment contract of repurchase, the vendor cannot declare a forfeiture of the contract when default occurs. The purchaser still has his right to pay the mortgage debt and redeem his property. *Albright v. Henry,* 174 NW 106.

§ 29. Lieu of foreclosure transactions—in general. A special type of deed absolute problem arises when a mortgagor (or his grantee) makes a deed to the mortgagee. Such transactions are common enough. When a default first occurs, a typical mortgagee endeavors to work out the problem with the mortgagor. Payments will be reduced in amount. Often the mortgagee will be content to collect interest only while the mortgagor recovers from an illness or looks for a new job. However, a time may come when the mortgagee can no longer wait for his money. He will cooperate with the mortgagor in endeavoring to find a purchaser for the property. When all such efforts turn out to be in vain, the mortgagor and mortgagee may, to avoid the time and expense of foreclosure, come to an agreement.

EXAMPLE: *R,* a mortgagor, being in default, makes a quitclaim deed of the mortgaged land to *E,* the mortgagee. The mortgage and the mortgage note are cancelled. *E* gives a lease to *R* for a period of one year. Thus the deal is "sweetened" by permitting the mortgagor to remain in possession with his family for another year. Moreover, *E* pays *R* $300 for the quitclaim deed. *R* winds up with his debt cancelled and with $300 in his pocket. In most states the courts sanction such transactions. Such a deed is called a *deed in lieu of foreclosure.*

§ 30. Lieu of foreclosure—debt cancellation. It is of the utmost importance that, as part of the lieu of foreclosure transaction, the mortgage debt be cancelled. 129 ALR 1487. If the mortgage note is not cancelled, the courts will treat the new deed as merely a deed absolute given as security for a debt, or, in other words, another mortgage, or they will hold the deed to be invalid. In other words, the courts look to see that the parties intended the deed to operate as an extinguishment of the mortgage debt. *Smith v. Farmers & Merchants Bank,* 398 Ill. 239, 75 NE2d 299; 129 ALR 1455. This is sensible, since in return for giving up his property the mortgagor has the burden of debt lifted from his shoulders. It probably suffices to cancel the mortgage note only. A mortgagee who wishes to buy a deed from the mortgagor may wish to keep the *mortgage* alive. He may fear the presence of junior liens. But he must cancel the *mortgage note* and release any personal liability created by the mortgage (*Tripp v. Vincent,* 3 Barb.Ch. 613) to prevent the deed from being held to be merely a security deed.

There is a danger here in that a deed given where the only consideration is cancellation of an existing debt is, in some states, not such a deed as will constitute the grantee, a bona fide purchaser. Hence, there is danger that the grantee will take title subject to unrecorded mortgages or other unrecorded interests in the land. Only a bona fide purchaser *for value* is protected against such matters. In some states cancellation of an antecedent debt is not *value. Zackary Veneer Co. v. Engelken,* 136 Fla. 89, 186 So 813; 92 CJS *Vendor & Purchaser* §323-b (6)(a). *Contra: Bunn v. Schnellbacher,* 163 Ill. 328, 45 NE 227. For this reason it is best for the mortgagee to pay some cash consideration for the deed.

Finally if there is an equity value in the property over and above the mortgage debt, the transaction may be attacked within four months as a preference under the Bankruptcy Act. *See* § 416.

§ 31. Lieu of foreclosure—freedom from coercion. The courts are also likely to scrutinize the transaction to make sure that it was voluntarily entered into by the mortgagor and that it was free from coercion or unfairness by the mortgage. 129 ALR 1438. If litigation over the validity of the deed arises, the burden is on the mortgagee to show the transaction was fair. 129 ALR 1451. In general, it may be said that there are three lines of decisions on this problem. In one line, it is assumed that the deed is valid unless the contrary is shown. In the second line, the mortgagee has the burden of proving freedom from fraud and oppression. And in the third line the courts indulge in a presumption of fraud until the contrary is shown. Basye, *Clearing Land Titles* § 281.

§ 32. Lieu of foreclosure—option or contract to repurchase. The mere fact that the mortgagee, on receiving a deed from the mortgagor, grants an option to the mortgagor to repurchase the property does not invalidate the deed. 129 ALR 1473. An option imposes no obligation on the optionee to buy the property and the transaction retains its advantage to the mortgagor of lifting the burden of debt from his shoulders.

If, however, the mortgagee, on receiving a deed from the mortgagor, enters into a contract to sell the land back to the mortgagor, this, according to some decisions, simply changes the form of the mortgagor's debt from one form to another. Instead of being obligated on the mortgage note the mortgagor is now obligated on the contract to repurchase. This is enough, in some states, to invalidate the deed. 129 ALR 1480. However, some states take the practical view that a contract to repurchase is likely to be more a benefit than a burden to the mortgagor and hold that the deed is valid. *Kimmel v. Bundy,* 302 Ill. 514, 135 NE 56.

§ **33. Lieu of foreclosure—unfairness.** It has often been said that a mortgagee obtaining a deed from the mortgagor must not treat the mortgagor unfairly. What this means is not entirely clear. The fact that the mortgagee has threatened foreclosure does not vitiate the deed. The mortgagee can threaten what he legally has the right to do. 129 ALR 1521. But if there is inequality between the parties, as where a lawyer-mortgagee is pitted against an unsophisticated mortgagor, there may be a duty on the lawyer's part to explain the mortgagee's redemption rights. 129 ALR 1522, 1523. Even where there is no disparity between the parties, the mortgagee must not misrepresent that "this is your last chance" if there is a redemption right. The mortgagee must not take advantage of the mortgagor's fears. 129 ALR 1534. Gross inadequacy of consideration may vitiate the deed. 129 ALR 1528. Poverty and illness of the mortgagor have also carried weight with the courts. 129 ALR 1533, 1534.

§ **34. Lieu of foreclosure—provision in deed.** Some mortgagees like the public records to show that the deed was taken in full satisfaction of the mortgage debt:

SUGGESTED CLAUSE: This deed is an absolute conveyance of title in effect as well as in form and is not intended as a mortgage, trust conveyance, or security of any kind. The consideration therefore is full release of all debts, notes, obligations, costs and charges heretofore subsisting on account and by the terms of that certain mortgage (or trust deed) heretofore existing on the property herein conveyed, executed by _____ to _____, recorded in Book ___, page ___, of the Official Records of _____ County, _____, this conveyance completely satisfying said obligation and terminating said mortgage (or trust deed) and the notes or bonds secured thereby and any effect thereof in all respects.

§ **35. Lieu of foreclosure—affidavit.** Other mortgagees prefer to take an affidavit from the mortgagor to the effect that his deed to the mortgagee was given voluntarily, that it was intended as a conveyance of complete title and not as a security, and that the land has no value over and above the amount of the mortgage debt. At times this document is couched in the form of an "estoppel certificate," rather than an affidavit. In such case it is addressed "to all whom it may concern."

§ **36. Lieu of foreclosure—contract in lieu of foreclosure.** Still other mortgagees prefer to sign a contract with the mortgagor which recites that the transaction was initiated by the mortgagor. All these devices (clause in deed, affidavit, contract) are helpful. Some courts hold that the Parol Evidence Rule prevents introduction of evidence that the deed was merely intended as security. 111 ALR 448. But some courts will still take the view that if the mortgagee can force the mortgagor to sign a deed, he can also force him to sign other documents. If property rises sharply in value after the deed is given, some courts will be tempted to set it aside, reasoning that the mortgagee can't be hurt if he gets his money back with interest.

§ 37. **Lieu of foreclosure—title search.** Obviously before any deed in lieu of foreclosure is given a search must be made for intervening liens.

EXAMPLE: *R makes a mortgage to E in 1968. R defaults in 1970. E has the title searched and finds that R gave X a second mortgage in 1969, which remains unpaid. R must foreclose his mortgage in order to cut X. A lieu of foreclosure transaction cannot be employed.*

Likewise possible defects in title other than liens may make a lieu of foreclosure deal impossible.

EXAMPLE: *R makes a mortgage to E in 1968. R dies in 1970 leaving no will. The estate is not probated. In addition to the problem of determining who R's heirs are, the claims of creditors of R will be a cloud on the title to the land for a period of time, depending on local law. E must foreclose.*

§ 38. **Lieu of foreclosure—bankruptcy.** If the mortgagee does not pay the mortgagor a consideration for the deed approximating the value of the mortgagor's equity, the deed is vulnerable to an attack for four months after its date if the mortgagor goes into bankruptcy. *See* § 416. Hence an adequate consideration should be paid for the deed or the documents should recite that no value exists above the amount of the mortgage debt.

§ 39. **Lieu of foreclosure transactions—statutes and title standards.** In a few states statutes and title standards adopted by bar associations are in effect that have as their objective protecting purchasers from the mortgagee against any attack on the title by the mortgagor. Basye, *Clearing Land Titles* § 281.

ADDITIONAL REFERENCES: 8 U. Fla. L. Rev. 132; 18 Drake L. Rev. 197; 31 Mo. L. Rev. 312; 32 Fordham L. Rev. 299 (N.Y.); 40 N.C. L. Rev. 516, 817; 3 Powell, *Real Property* § 447 (discussing various state statutes providing that deed absolute is to be treated as mortgage if intended as security and other statutes providing that deed absolute is not notice of its security nature unless defeasance is recorded).

4

Equitable Mortgages

§ 40. In general. As has already been indicated, any document that indicates an intention that land shall stand as security for the repayment of a debt is an equitable mortgage. *See* § 12. Thus, an agreement in writing that certain land will be mortgaged is, if supported by consideration, an equitable mortgage. *Owens v. Continental Supply Co.,* 71 F2d 862.

§ 41. Defective instrument intended to operate as regular mortgage. An instrument intended as a regular mortgage, but which contains some defect, may operate as an equitable mortgage. Jones, *Mortgages* § 232.

EXAMPLE: Through inadvertence a deed of trust securing a debt altogether omitted the name of a trustee. It obviously was ineffective to transfer title, since it lacked a grantee. However, it was sustained as an equitable mortgage, which could be foreclosed by means of a foreclosure suit. *Dulany v. Willis,* 95 Va. 606, 29 SE 324.

§ 42. Agreement to sell to pay debt distinguished. Where a landowner agrees in writing that certain debts will be paid out of the proceeds of a land sale, when the land is sold, this is not a mortgage.

EXAMPLE: A executed a document to B, stating that A acknowledged that B held A's promissory note in the sum of $10,000 and that in case A sold Lot 1 in a certain subdivision this note would be paid out of the proceeds of the sale. B filed a foreclosure suit on this document. The court held it was not a mortgage and could not be foreclosed. *Hibernian Banking Assn. v. Davis,* 295 Ill. 537, 129 NE 540.

§ 43. Trust for sale distinguished. If a person having a number of creditors conveys his land under a trust instrument requiring the trustee to sell, pay the creditors, and hold any surplus for such grantor, this is not a mortgage. It is an assignment for the benefit of creditors. 5 Tiffany, *Real Property* § 1400.

§ **44. Negative pledge.** A lender may exact of the borrower an agreement that until the loan is repaid the borrower will not further mortgage the land. Or the agreement may forbid the sale or mortgaging of the land before full repayment of the debt.

EXAMPLE: *R* borrowed money from *E* and signed an agreement not to transfer or encumber certain land without *E's* consent until the loan was repaid. The court held that this was an equitable mortgage. *Coast Bank v. Minderhout,* 61 Cal. 2d 311, 392 P2d 265.

Before the *Minderhout* decision there was some tendency to hold that an equitable mortgage was not created by these negative covenants not to mortgage or sell. This is the *negative pledge* problem. After *Minderhout,* the view found some acceptance that these negative covenants created equitable mortgages. 2 Gilmore, *Security Interests in Personal Property,* 1010. In *Tahoe National Bank v. Phillips,* 92 Cal.Rptr. 704 (1971), the Supreme Court of California, quite inexplicably, held in a case involving a document virtually identical with that in *Minderhout* that no equitable mortgage was created. As nearly as one can make out this unusual opinion, the court has chosen to return to the view of the older cases that a purely negative covenant (that is, one not to convey or mortgage the property until a debt has been paid) does not create an equitable mortgage.

The negative pledge type of document such as was involved in *Minderhout* occurs with some frequency where institutional lenders are involved in home improvement loans. There are two reasons why this occurs: (1) Most institutional lenders are forbidden to loan on junior mortgages, and this pushes lenders toward use of documents that do not resemble the traditional junior mortgage. (2) In overcoming sales resistance of borrowers, the lender avoids the distasteful term "second mortgage" and simply asks the borrower not to sell his property until the debt is paid.

The uncertainty created by *Minderhout* and *Tahoe National Bank* seems to indicate the desirability of avoiding use of such ambiguous documents.

§ **45. Money loaned for the purchase of land.** This is best explained by an illustration.

EXAMPLE: *P,* who wishes to buy Lot 1, which is owned by *V,* lacks funds for this purpose. *P* approaches *E* and explains that he would like to enter into a contract for the purchase of the land but needs money. *E* loans *P* the funds on *P's* verbal promise to give him a mortgage on the land. *P* buys and obtains a deed from *V,* but refuses to sign a mortgage. Most cases will allow *E* to file a suit to impress an equitable lien on the land. 18 ALR 1100. Cf § 27.

A variant of the above occurs in the following situation.

EXAMPLE: The facts of the transaction are as in the preceding example, down to the executing of the deed. However, in this instance E insists that V make the deed to E, and this is done. Now P obtains funds, offers them to E, who refuses to convey. P files a suit against E and will prevail. The courts will treat this as essentially a mortgage transaction coupled with a resulting trust. 5 Scott, *Trusts* § 448. In a resulting trust P buys land from V and has title taken in some third party without any intention to make a gift to that party. The facts of the example meet these requirements. But P encounters difficulties in a few states that have abolished resulting trusts. Osborne, *Mortgages*, 137, 141. But even in this group of states a number will allow P to prevail. The fact that P has entered into a written contract to buy the land from V before he makes his contract with E does not prevent application of the rule, and, indeed, that fact is often present. If the injured party is E he also will be given his remedy in court. Suppose for example, that after E has acquired title, P refuses to pay him and take the property off his hands. E may file suit to foreclose his lien. This will be necessary because the presence of P's rights makes E's title unmarketable.

Another variant of the situation occurs where a judicial or execution sale is involved.

EXAMPLE: R's mortgaged land is about to be sold at a foreclosure sale. R persuades E-2 to loan R funds and to use the funds to bid in at the sale, the parties agreeing that R will reimburse E-2 as soon as he has the funds. E-2 is the successful bidder. R can compel him to carry out his promise and convey the land to R on being reimbursed for his expenditures. 5 Scott, *Trusts* § 448.

Suppose we assume a situation where P has no contract to buy the land when he makes his contract with E.

EXAMPLE: P wishes to buy Lot 1 from V, but has no contract with V; P approaches E and states that if E buys the land from V at $20,000 (V's asking price), P will buy the land from E on an installment contract at $25,000 repayable in one year. E does buy the land and the installment contract is executed. P now claims that this was nothing but a mortgage. He will do this in order to claim usury. Obviously the return to E ($5,000 on an investment of $20,000 over a period of one year) is greatly in excess of normal usury limits. In general, the courts are disposed to hold for E. *Stark v. Bauer Cooperage Co.,* 3 F2d 214. However, if P can actually establish by convincing oral testimony that the discussions between P and E were in *mortgage* terms rather than sale terms, he may prevail. The trouble is that these are usually transactions between laymen acting without legal advice, and they are unlikely to be precise in their formulation of legal concepts.

Obviously none of these transactions offers any attraction to institutional lenders.

5

Application and Commitment

§ 46. **In general,** a mortgage transaction usually begins with an application for a loan. The application serves a double purpose: (1) It is a source of information on which the lender will base his decision as to making the loan, and (2) it defines the terms of the loan contract. The application is usually a printed form prepared by the mortgagee and signed by the prospective borrower. After investigating the prospective borrower's financial circumstances and appraising the real estate, the prospective mortgagee may write the prospective borrower a letter stating that his application for a loan has been accepted. This letter is sometimes referred to as a *commitment*. The result is to create a contract for the making of the mortgage loan. *St. Paul Corp. v. Manufacturers Life Ins. Co.,* 278 A2d 12; 12 *U.Cinc.L.Rev.* 5.

From the discussion later in this text relating to the time when the mortgage becomes a lien of the land, it will become obvious to you that *it is desirable from the mortgagee's standpoint that he be obligated to make the loan.* If the application and commitment, taken together, are to constitute a binding contract for a loan, the application should state in detail all the terms of the mortgage loan, and the commitment should simply say, in effect, "Yes, we will make the loan on the terms stated in the application." Technically, the application is an *offer* by the mortgagor to accept a mortgage loan on the terms specified in the application. *See* Chapter 10. The commitment is an *acceptance* of the offer. *Burns v. Washington S. & L. Ass'n,* 251 Miss. 789, 171 So2d 322. Under basic contract law the acceptance of an offer creates a contract. If the letter of commitment makes any changes in the terms, it is technically a *counter-offer,* which legally is a rejection of the offer. There is no contract unless the landowner agrees to the new terms, which he may do by writing the word *accepted* and his signature on the mortgagee's letter of commitment. Since the application and commitment define the terms on which the loan is to be made and constitute a contract that neither party can change or add to without the other's consent, the application should state the terms in detail, including agreement of borrower to sign note and mortgage in a certain specified form; his agreement to furnish evidence of title and plat of survey at his expense; his agreement to sign chattel mortgage and assignment of leases and rents; provisions for deducting title charges and other charges from proceeds of loan; provisions that lender shall have possession of fire insurance policies and abstracts; the amount, premium and character of insurance to be carried on the property; and so forth.[1]

While it is best for the borrower to make a formal acceptance of the loan commitment, courts have sometimes held that the conduct of the parties showed their understanding that a loan agreement was in existence. *Dovenmuehle Inc. v. K-Way Associates,* 388 F2d 840.

§ 47. **Commitment.** In modern mortgage practice the application has diminished in importance. After looking over the situation, the lender decides on what terms he is willing to make the loan and sets forth all his requirements in the commitment. This varies so greatly from the application that it is obviously a counter-offer, which the mortgagor can accept or reject. The commitment tends to be rather detailed. 86 *Banking L. J.* 597. Since, when accepted, the commitment constitutes the loan contract, it should, like any other contract, be complete and certain. It should outline the following:

1. Amount of loan, interest rate, dates and amounts of payments, prepayment privileges and penalties.
2. Documents to be signed by mortgagor, including mortgage, note, waiver of defenses, assignment of permanent loan commitment, assignment of leases and rents, chattel liens, with special mention of the form thereof, so as to avoid controversy as to provisions like waiver of right of redemption where state law permits.
3. Documents to be furnished by mortgagor, such as contract for construction, principal subcontracts, architect's certificates, waivers of lien, building and other permits, contractor's bonds, insurance policies and endorsements thereon to protect mortgagee. Time limits are imposed on furnishing documentation.
4. Charges to be paid by mortgagor, such as points, commission, origination fees, title insurance fees including fees for bringing title to date as construction disbursements are made, recording fees, credit report fees, survey costs, and the like.

---

[1] Kratovil, *Real Estate Law,* 5th ed. (Englewood Cliffs, N.J.: Prentice-Hall, Inc., 1969), pp. 210–211, © 1969.

5. Statement of pre-conditions to payment of construction disbursements, which should be in some detail. If there are several general contractors, each doing part of the construction, each should be treated separately. Note that each disbursement will involve documentation, e.g., (a) architect's certificates; (b) title insurance reports covering disbursements; (c) survey bring-downs to show whether construction is staying within lines established by ordinances and building restrictions; (d) contractor's affidavits; (e) lien waivers; (f) architect's certification that balance of loan funds is adequate to complete building.

6. How extras and change orders are to be handled.

7. Provision for *retentions,* e.g., holdbacks of part of each disbursement to insure completion of construction.

8. Schedule of disbursements, detailing what work must be in place to warrant disbursement, and tying this into plans and specifications approved or to be approved by lender. The pre-conditions to the first disbursement require extra care. Some lenders want the mortgagor's contribution toward construction to be deposited with lender in cash, whereas others will take lien waivers for work done, if supported by architect's certificates and lender's inspection to determine that work is in place. Manner of disbursement should be covered. In a given case a lender may be willing to trust the general contractor and disburse to him. In other cases he may wish to pay the subcontractors directly.

9. Requirement that borrower sign construction loan agreement, attaching form thereof, with any modifications required by particular job.

10. Acceptance by borrower of commitment within time specified.

§ 48. Acceptance of commitment. If the borrower fails to accept a commitment which varies from the application, there is no loan contract. However, if the mortgagee intends for the commitment to be binding, and the borrower changes position in reliance on the commitment, the mortgagee may be liable to the borrower.

EXAMPLE: *R* obtained a loan commitment from *E*, but did not accept the commitment. Relying on the commitment, he sold his house. *E* refused to go forward with the loan. *E* is liable to *R* for damages. The basis here was *promissory estoppel. Morrison v. Home S & L Assn.,* 175 Cal.App.2d 765, 346 P2d 917.

If the borrower pays the lender a fee for giving the commitment, he forfeits the fee if he fails to go forward with the loan.

EXAMPLE: *R* paid *E* $22,000 for a loan commitment, but failed to go forward with the loan. He forfeits his fee. *Boston Road Shopping Center v. Teachers Ins.* Assn., 11 NY2d 831.

§ 49. Rights of third parties. Third parties, for example, the borrower's general contractor, if a construction loan is involved, have no rights against the lender, as third party beneficiaries, or otherwise. *Burns v. Washington S & L Assn.*, 251 Miss. 789, 171 So2d 322.

However, a commitment is assignable, and quite commonly assignments take place.

EXAMPLE: *R*, who is about to construct a building in his land, goes to *E-1* for the construction loan and to *E-2* for the permanent loan. *E-1* insists that *E-2* give *R* a commitment to make the permanent loan. *E-2* does so. *R* assigns this commitment to *E-1*. In reliance on this assignment, and being certain that the construction loan will be paid off by *E-2*, *E-1* gives his commitment to make the construction loan.

§ **50. Truth in Lending.** The federal Truth in Lending Act has given new and increased importance to the loan contract. The "time of consummation" of the loan contract is a key concept under this law. Reg. Z § 226.8(a) provides that disclosures under the Act must be made before "the transaction is consummated." Where a commitment is given, the Act views the transaction as being consummated at that time.

6

Validity, Form and Contents
of Mortgage

§ 51. **In general.** The basic structure of the mortgage is like that of a deed. It has a mortgagor (grantor) who, if an individual, is usually joined by his spouse, a mortgagee (grantee), words of grant (often *mortgage and warrant*) and a description of the mortgage land. In addition, it contains a description of the debt and sundry provisions deemed necessary for the protection of the mortgagee.

Where the mortgagor is a corporation, trustee, partnership, etc., the document again parallels the deed in its form.

Forms sold by stationers or found in statutes or form books seem universally inadequate. Local mortgage houses who do a large volume of lending usually have excellent forms.

Contests over the validity of the mortgage are rare where institutional lenders are involved. A valid debt is always present in these cases. A title search is made. The mortgagors are checked out through credit reports and their signatures are attested by a notary public. In those instances where a forgery or mistaken identity occurs, the loss usually falls on the title insurance company, since the typical loan policy demanded by the mortgage lender (ALTA form) specifically insures the validity and enforceability of the mortgage. In areas where abstracts are common, notably in the agricultural Midwest, the communities are smaller, the people involved are known to the lender, and the possibility of forgery or mistaken identity reduced. Nevertheless, lenders, especially out-of-state lenders, who are less familiar with the community, increasingly demand the ALTA policy.

§ 52. **Fraud, duress and mistake.** The defenses of fraud, duress and mistake are available to the mortgagor, as they are in other transactions. However, fraud of a husband in inducing his wife to sign will not, as a rule, invalidate the mortgage if the mortgagee has no knowledge of it. *Lesser v. Strobe,* 67 N.J.Sup. 537, 171 A2d. 114. And where the mortgage secures a negotiable note or where the mortgagors sign a waiver of defenses, an innocent assignee of the mortgage may take free of the fraud.

§ 53. **Payment of taxes and other prior liens—hazard insurance.** Mortgage law permits the mortgagee to pay prior liens in order to protect his lien and to add amounts so paid to the mortgage debt. 60 ALR 425; 84 *id.* 1366, 1371, 1393, 1397; 123 *id.* 1248. *See also* § 259. However, it is customary and, indeed, necessary to spell these rights out in detail in the mortgage. For example, it is customary to permit the mortgagor to contest, in good faith, the validity of part or all of his real estate tax bill if he supplies satisfactory indemnity to the mortgagee. Payment of special assessments that are a prior lien is not required as long as installment payments thereon are kept current. The mortgagee is permitted to pay delinquent real estate taxes without inquiring into their validity.

Every mortgage should contain a covenant by the mortgagor to provide fire and extended coverage with a standard mortgage clause attached in companies and in form satisfactory to the mortgagee, policy to be lodged with mortgagee. *See* Kratovil, *Real Estate Law* (5th ed. 1969), Chapter 15. There are some strange decisions to the effect that a covenant to insure does not run with the land. By way of precaution it is best to phrase this clause in such terms that where the hazard coverage is lacking or inadequate, in the mortgagee's judgment, he may take out such insurance as he deems necessary for his protection and add the expense to the mortgage debt. This portion is not a covenant imposing liability on the mortgagor, but a right given the mortgagee to procure coverage. In some states the mortgagee does not have this right if the mortgage is silent. The existence of fire or other damage to the property, the mortgagee may argue, should also give the mortgagee the right to accelerate. The mortgagor, understandably, will resist this. The mortgagee ought not resist any arrangement that ensures proper rebuilding with the proceeds of the insurance.

Typically, modern mortgages require the mortgagor to deposit with each monthly payment 1/12th of the sum needed (in the morgagee's judgment) to pay the annual real estate taxes and insurance premiums. *See* § 225. Because the bookkeeping expense is significant it is customary to provide that these "escrow deposits" may be commingled with the mortgagee's general funds and do not draw interest.

§ 54. **Prepayment privilege.** In the absence of an agreement to the contrary, the mortgagee has a contractual right to have his money out earning the stipulated interest. Unless there is an agreement to that effect, the mortgagor has no right to insist upon making payment before maturity, even by offering to pay the principal and all interest to the maturity date. *Fuller v. Manchester Bank*, 102 NH 117, 152 A2d 179. The mortgagee's attorney must be prepared to bargain with the mortgagor's attorney on this score. Obviously, it is to the mortgagor's advantage to have the mortgage and mortgage note provide that the debt is payable *on or before* the due date, or that the debt is payable in monthly payments of a stated sum *or more*; or a specific clause may be inserted conferring on the mortgagor the privilege of prepaying the mortgage debt. This is known as a *prepayment privilege*. In trust deeds securing issues of bonds, the comparable provision is that providing for redemption of bonds prior to their stated maturity dates. Such provisions enable the mortgagor to refinance when money is cheaper (which is why the mortgagee resists inclusion of such provisions) or to retire the mortgage where he has entered into a contract of sale that requires him to deliver title free and clear of any mortgage. A good compromise permits prepayment in case of a sale of the property but not to effect a mere refinancing. The amount of *prepayment premium* charged for the privilege of prepaying the debt depends on the mortgage market at the time the mortgage is made.

Suppose that *A* is a mortgagor in a mortgage which allows him to make prepayments on any monthly payment date and that he then makes several payments of two or three times the amount specified in the mortgage. Suddenly a time arrives when he is pinched for money. He now contends that he has the right to skip several payments until the amount he has prepaid is exhausted. This contention will not prevail. In effect, the prepayments are applied on the last payments falling due. *Smith v. Renz*, 122 Cal. App2d 535, 265 P2d 160. However, for the benefit of the mortgagor who is confronted with a personal emergency, such as illness or unemployment, we can expect to see increasing use of a clause now found in some mortgages to the effect that prepayments build up a right to skip principal payments for a period of time equal to the number of prepayments made, although it is customary to require the mortgagor to pay interest during that period.[1]

§ 55. Eminent domain. There are various views as to the right of the mortgagee in a condemnation award and as to the necessity of including the mortgagee as a necessary party to the condemnation proceeding. Obviously this is a matter that can and should be controlled by a provision in the mortgage. Among the provisions the mortgagee will argue for are the following: (1) A covenant by the mortgagor to notify the mortgagee of any condemnation suit that comes to his attention. (2) A covenant by the mortgagor to pay as part of the mortgage debt, the mortgagee's attorney's fees in defending the condem-

---

[1] Kratovil, *The Guarantor* (Chicago, Ill.: Chicago Title & Trust Co., April, 1969) 3. © 1969.

nation. (3) The right to accelerate the debt where all or a substantial part of the premises are taken. (4) The right to receive the condemnation award and apply it in reduction of the mortgage debt.

SUGGESTED CLAUSE: TOGETHER with any and all awards heretofore and hereafter made to the present and all subsequent owners of the mortgaged premises by any governmental or other lawful authorities for taking or damaging by eminent domain the whole or any part of the mortgaged premises or any easement therein, including any awards for any changes of grade of streets, which said awards are hereby assigned to the Mortgagee, who is hereby authorized to collect and receive the proceeds of any such awards from such authorities and to give proper receipts and acquittances therefor, and to apply the same toward the payment of the amount owing on account of this mortgage and its accompanying note or bond, notwithstanding the fact that the amount owing thereon may not then be due and payable; and the Mortgagor hereby covenants and agrees, upon request, to make, execute and deliver any and all assignments and other instruments sufficient for the purpose of assigning the aforesaid awards to the Mortgagee, free, clear and discharged of any and all encumbrances of any kind or nature whatsoever.

§ **56. Oil development.** Where there is any possibility of oil development involving the mortgaged premises, some thought ought to be given this aspect. For example, the mortgagee may wish to have the right to accelerate if oil development is initiated on the premises. A dry hole or even a well that is a poor producer can certainly depreciate the value of mortgaged premises. An improperly capped well can be completely disastrous. In some cities the zoning ordinances forbid such development, but the suggested clause puts control of the situation in the mortgagee's hands.

§ **57. Bankruptcy and condemnation expenses.** Every mortgage should contain a clause giving the mortgagee the right to add to the mortgage debt all expenses, including attorney's fees, incurred for the protection of the mortgagee in any litigation, including proceedings initiated under the Bankruptcy Act, proceedings to condemn part or all of the mortgaged premises or some interest therein, and probate estates of deceased mortgagors.

§ **58. Master mortgage.** Fine print provisions in mortgages tend to become more elaborate as lenders strive to overcome adverse decisions regarding their rights. This runs up recording fees, which are based on the length of the document. To overcome this many states have enacted laws permitting a mortgagee to record a form of mortgage in his standard form. Actual mortgages thereafter simply refer to the book and page of the record where this master mortgage can be found for all the printed language. Some mortgagees, fearing that the mortgagor might claim he was imposed upon by this device, print all of their standard form on the back of the mortgage with instructions thereon "Not to be recorded." In time virtually all states will adopt this excellent measure. The public records are too complex as it is. Anything that shortens or simplifies these records should be encouraged. The following states are among these that have adopted *master mortgage statutes*: Ohio, Pennsylvania, Virginia, North Carolina, Nevada, Maine, Arkansas, Arizona, California, Florida, and Idaho.

There have been, and still are, statutes that set forth forms of various mortgage clauses, and a mortgagee can incorporate these statutory clauses by a simple reference in the mortgage to the appropriate number of the statutory clause. The difficulty is that this method is inflexible. Times change and experience teaches the need for revision, but the legislature is slow to act. Moreover, mortgagees have their own preferences as to the clauses that go into the mortgage, based, in large part, on their experiences. This indicates that statutory clauses are likely to wane in importance and the master mortgage is likely to increase in importance.

§ 59. Miscellaneous statutory requirements. Recent years have seen a spate of state laws (in Florida and New Jersey, for example) forbidding recording of a mortgage unless it shows the name of the draftsman (designed to prevent practice of law by laymen) and also shows the addresses of both parties. Other requirements are proof that the local mortgage tax and local real estate taxes were paid. Evidently little thought has gone into draftsmanship of a number of these statutes. Unsophisticated people are involved in many such transactions, including recorders of deeds. If the law declares the mortgage unrecordable if it fails to comply with law (as in Minnesota and New Jersey, for example), it is legally an unrecorded document even if the recorder records it on his books. Some laws declare a mortgage not enforceable if it fails to comply, as is true in New York if the tax is not paid. All junior mortgages that comply with the law would be senior to such mortgage. One questions the wisdom of such legislation. Undeniably, however, mortgagees must be aware of such laws and comply with them.

Statutes are beginning to appear that prescribe the size of the mortgage page, the type size, margins, etc., to make the instrument eligible for recording.

§ 60. Successor in trust. It is prudent to insert in deeds of trust a clause designating a successor trustee to act in the event of the death or other inability to act of the original trustee.

§ 61. Waiver of homestead and dower. In some states, a mortgage on homestead land must include a clause releasing and waiving homestead rights. Again, in some states, a mortgage signed by the spouse of the mortgagor should contain a clause stating that such spouse thereby waives all dower as against the mortgagee.

§ 62. Signature. The signature of the mortgagor is, of course, absolutely essential. His spouse should also sign. If the mortgagor's signature is a forgery, the mortgage is completely void. However, a forged mortgage, although initially void, may become valid if the mortgagor subsequently recognizes it as a valid lien, as for example, by making payments on it. *Rothschild v. Title Guarantee and Trust Co.,* 204 N.Y. 458, 97 NE 879. Ratification often occurs in family situations, as where a son has forged his father's name on a mortgage. The father ratifies to keep his son out of jail.

§ **63. Seal.** In states that require deeds to be sealed, a mortgage should have the mortgagor's seal affixed thereto. A corporate mortgage should always have the corporate seal affixed.

§ **64. Witnesses.** As in the case of deeds, some states require the mortgagor's signature to be witnessed, two witnesses being the number usually required.

§ **65. Acknowledgment.** Laws in many states require the mortgage to be acknowledged, and in the case of a mortgage on a homestead, failure to obtain an acknowledgement may render the mortgage void. *American S & L Assn v. Burghardt,* 19 Mont. 323, 48 P 391. In any event, mortgages should always be acknowledged. In nearly all states a mortgage that is not acknowledged is treated as an unrecorded mortgage. 50 ALR2d 1299. The local requirements as to acknowledgements should be followed. 25 ALR2d 1124.

§ **66. Delivery.** Like a deed, a mortgage must be delivered. Delivery becomes effective when the mortgagor surrenders the completed mortgage with the intention of making it operative.

§ **67. Recording.** As a practical matter, a mortgage must be recorded, since an unrecorded mortgage is void as to subsequent purchasers, mortgagees, or judgment creditors who are ignorant of the existence of such mortgage. It is important that the mortgage be filed or recorded as soon after its execution as possible.

§ **68. Miscellaneous.** Scattered throughout the text there will be found numerous suggestions as to the form and contents of the mortgage as relevant to particular problems discussed in the text.[2]

---

[2] Kratovil, *Real Estate Law*, 4th ed. (Englewood Cliffs, N.J.: Prentice-Hall, Inc., 1964), pp. 225–226, © 1964.

7

Parties to Mortgage

§ 69. In general. The problems of parties to the mortgage are, to some extent, like those found in the law of deeds. All owners should be named in the body of the deed as mortgagors, their spouses should join where this is required by local law, single persons should recite their marital status with technical accuracy (*spinster, bachelor, widow, widower, divorced and not remarried*), the proper name should be used in a corporate mortgage, and so on. There are, of course, many problems not encountered in deed law.

§ 70. Mortgagor—married women. There are some remnants still of the old disabilities of married women; for example, in some states a mortgage of the wife's land to secure the sole debt of the husband is void. *Sansom v. Sturkie,* 245 Ala. 514, 18 So2d 267. Institutional lenders will take a loan application from both husband and wife, have both sign the mortgage and note, and make the disbursement check payable to both.

§ 71. Mortgagor—corporations. Where the mortgagor is a corporation the loan should be one for corporate purposes. *Ultra vires,* however, is not as frightening as it was in earlier times when courts were prone to declare ultra vires transactions void.

Proper corporate action is needed for corporate mortgages, usually a resolution of the corporation's board of directors.

Where the mortgaged asset constitutes all or substantially all of the assets of the corporation, a vote of two-thirds of the shareholders is a common requirement of state law. This requirement should be complied with where the mortgaged plant is the mortgagor's only operating plant, even though stock in trade exceeds the plant in value. *McDonald v. First Nat. Bank,* 70 F2d 69. Foreclosure

53

of the mortgage closes down the operation. Hence, courts feel that this is a decision on which shareholders should vote.

So far as the details of statutory requirements for the execution of a corporate mortgage are concerned, they are set forth in Shoerri, *Statutory Requirements for Authorization of Corporate Mortgage,* 18 Bus. Law. 731. Only in Wisconsin is a corporate mortgage possible without action of directors or shareholders. The requirements as to directors' or shareholders' authorization vary considerably, as one might expect. Moreover, the requirements change often enough to make any detailed statement at this point relatively useless. However, the references in the above article to statutory sections will remain o 'alue for some time.

In the case of a close corporation, it is convenient to call a joint meeting of *all* shareholders and *all* directors and obtain a *unanimous* vote authorizing the loan and mortgage. The secretary of the corporation certifies to this fact, and the paper work is reduced to a minimum.

The cases occasionally deal with the question of the effect on a bona fide mortgage of a failure on the part of a mortgagor corporation to observe the statutory requirements in making the mortgage. Typically, the mortgagee demands that he be furnished a certified copy of the corporate resolution authorizing the transaction. It is clear that if he does so, and is furnished a duly certified copy of what appears to be a proper resolution, the mortgagee is protected. Corporate records import verity. *Ashley Wire Co. v. Ill. Steel Co.,* 164 Ill. 149, 45 NE 410; *In re Norcor,* 97 F2d 208. The fact that the secretary's certificate is false and that the proper directors or stockholders did not vote for the transaction is immaterial. Any other rule would be disastrous. People dealing with corporations must have some place to go to find out what corporate action took place. The corporate secretary's office is that place. If the secretary bears false witness, the loss must fall on the corporation.

The picture becomes more cloudy when the mortgage is regular on its face and recites that proper corporate action took place, but the mortgagee fails to demand certified copies of resolutions. For example, if the corporate officers execute a mortgage on all of the corporate property despite the failure of two-thirds of the shareholders to vote therefor, as required by statute, the better rule regards the mortgage as nevertheless valid. *Prefix Radiator Co. v. Goetz,* 179 Wis. 338, 191 NW 755; *Beaufort Transfer Co. v. Fisher Trucking Co.,* 451 SW2d 40 (Mo). At all events, junior lienors cannot raise this point. *Dillon v. Myers,* 58 Colo. 492, 146 P 268. The philosophy of the decisions denying the shareholders the right to attack the mortgage is that shareholders elect directors and directors elect officers. Strangers who elect neither should not be compelled to bear losses occasioned by breach of trust by the officers. But there are occasional statements that would indicate that the corporation, when sued in a foreclosure suit, could defend on the ground that proper corporate action did not take place. *Petroleum Anchor Equipment Inc. v. Tyra,* 419 SW2d 820, 45 *Mich. L. Rev.* 341. Even then, if the corporation receives the benefit of the transaction, the mortgage is perfectly valid. *Dillon v. Myers,* 58 Colo. 492, 146 P 268.

Quite commonly money is borrowed by a corporation to raise funds for a parent or subsidiary. In the earlier law, there was some concern over these situations. It was stated, and is still stated, that as a matter of corporation law a corporation can borrow only "for corporate purposes." This is still true. Modern corporation laws to a very considerable extent have eliminated the defense of ultra vires, but for some purposes the rule still exists. Nevertheless, it is quite obvious that *Corporation X* is borrowing for corporate purposes when it is helping its subsidiary, *Corporation Y,* to produce components for an article *Corporation X* is assembling.

§ 72. **Mortgagor—foreign corporation.** Where the mortgagor is a foreign corporation doing business in the state where the land lies, it should qualify to do business under local foreign corporation laws. If it does not, it will not be able to maintain suits in the local courts. If it cannot do this, it cannot even evict a tenant who is in default in payment of rent. It could not maintain suit on local contracts that it has performed. While failure to qualify does not invalidate the mortgage, it makes the mortgagor vulnerable. The mortgagee typically requires the mortgagor to qualify, and the mortgage allows the mortgagee to accelerate if the mortgagor allows the qualification to lapse.

If a foreign corporation is incorporated in a state where a mortgage of all its assets does not require shareholder approval, and proceeds to mortgage land in a state where shareholder approval is required, the law of its domicile governs and shareholder approval is not needed. *In re Olivit Bros.,* 57 F2d 718; *Muck v. Hitchcock,* 212 N.Y. 283, 106 NE 75.

§ 73. **Mortgagor—partnership.** Partnership law governs the situation where a partnership mortgages its land.

EXAMPLE: In a state where the Uniform Partnership Act is in effect the partnership has taken title in the partnership name. The mortgage should be executed in the partnership name.

§ 74. **Mortgagor—partnership—limited partnership as mortgagor.** Since general partners must not, under the Uniform Limited Partnership Act (Sec. 9), do any act, without the written consent of the limited partners, that would make it impossible to carry on the ordinary business of the partnership, the general partners ought not to mortgage all of the assets of the partnership without such written consent. Obviously, foreclosure of the mortgage would put the partnership out of business. Whether this is a matter that concerns the mortgagee is another question on which there is little or no law. In other words, the mortgagee, it is argued, ought not to be put to the trouble of inquiring whether the general partners are taking advantage of the limited partners.

§ 75. **Mortgagor—trustee.** In a number of statutes the Uniform Powers of Trustee Act has been enacted, or some comparable law is in force. This gives the trustee the power to mortgage the land unless the trust instrument contains some indication of a contrary intention. Such a law may be helpful to a mortgagee who is making a loan to a trustee. In general, however, in the absence of such a law a mortgagee should not loan money to a trustee who has merely a power to sell. A power to sell does not connote a power to mortgage. The reasons are obvious. When a trustee sells, he obtains, one presumes, full value for the property. When he mortgages, he does not obtain full value and yet the risk exists that the property may be lost. See 3 ABA *Real Property, Probate and Trust Journal* 273, 292 for decisions and statutes. In mortgages by a trustee it is customary for the mortgage and note to include provisions exculpating the trustee from personal liability. 1 Glenn, *Mortgages,* 492.

§ 76. **Mortgagor—miscellaneous problems.** Where the mortgagor is a trustee, guardian, executor, or any other entity with limited powers, obviously a check must be made to insure that the power to mortgage exists and was legally exercised. A short cut for the mortgagee is to insist on the ALTA mortgage title policy, which insures that the mortgage is valid and enforceable. This throws all such burdens on the title company. Frequently title to land is placed in a nominee, who signs the mortgage and note. This is done to insulate the real party in interest from personal liability. It is perfectly valid. *Barkausen v. Cont. Ill.Nat. Bank,* 3 Ill. 2d 254, 120 NE2d 649.

§ 77. **Mortgagee—foreign corporation.** Where the mortgagee is a foreign corporation, the problem, of course, relates to *doing business* laws. Today the old-fashioned punitive *doing business* statute that declared void a contract entered into by an unlicensed foreign corporation has just about disappeared. Its place has been taken by a statute that permits the mortgagor to plead in defense of a mortgage foreclosure the fact that the plaintiff-mortgagee was unlawfully doing business in the state without having procured a license to do so. In many cases this simply puts the mortgagee to the expense of qualifying while the foreclosure is pending, thus merely delaying the foreclosure. In a few states, however, the mortgagee cannot foreclose unless it had a *doing business* license at the time the loan was made. *Lake States Corp. v. Lawrence Seaway Corp.,* 15 Mich.App. 637, 167 NW2d 320. And in the case of certain corporations, notably banks, no machinery exists for obtaining a *doing business* license that will enable them to originate loans in a foreign state. In these instances the defense poses substantial danger to the lender. Where foreclosure is by exercise of a power of sale, an unlicensed foreign corporation can foreclose, since court proceedings are not involved. *Flakne v. Metrop. Life Ins. Co.,* 198 Minn. 465, 270 NW 566. And an insurance company need not, as a rule, obtain a general license to do business. Its license to do an insurance business qualifies it to loan money on mortgages. *John Hancock Mut. Life Ins. Co. v. Lookingbill,* 218 Ia. 373, 253 NW 604.

If the statutes of the state where the land is located bar suits by an unlicensed foreign corporation, the lender cannot circumvent this law by going into the federal courts. *Wood v. Interstate Realty,* 337 US 535.

To a constantly increasing extent, statutes are being enacted that define what transactions are to be regarded as "doing business" and what transactions do not fall in that category. Prather, *What Constitutes Doing Business,* 25 Savings and Loan Legal Bulletin, 65, 74. Some states (for example, Hawaii, Iowa, Louisiana, Nebraska, Oregon, Rhode Island, and Washington) have adopted, in whole or in part, the Model Business Corporation Act, which contains a section (§ 99) defining what transactions are not to be regarded as doing business. Unfortunately, this section is somewhat muddy in the area of mortgage loans. It speaks of "creating" mortgages as not constituting the doing of business, but does not make it clear whether it is the mortgagor or the mortgagee who is doing the creating. Some states (notably Pennsylvania) have clarified the section by indicating that it comprehends creation by either the mortgagor or mortgagee. Other states have omitted this portion of the Model Act altogether. One would be inclined to jump to the conclusion that the legislature in this last case intended to put the making of mortgage loans in the "doing business" category. However, there is a decision holding in these circumstances that the legislature intended to leave the prior case law in effect, and if that law permitted the making of mortgage loans without qualifying to do business, that law remains in effect. *Ross Const. Co. Inc. v. U.M. & M. Credit Corp,* 214 So2d 822 (Miss.).

There are quite a number of decisions holding that a corporate lender making one mortgage loan in the state is not "doing business." Doing business connotes a continuity of operation. However, some states now define doing business as including engaging in one transaction. 27 ALR3rd 397. Moreover, lawyers are unwilling to approve a loan on the "isolated transaction" theory. There is no way of guaranteeing that the lender will not engage in other similar transactions after it has made the "isolated loan." Hence, the rule is not particularly useful. Also, in states that have adopted the Model Business Corporation Act it is necessary that the isolated transaction be "completed" within 30 days, which is impossible in the case of a construction loan.

In virtually all states the *insulation theory* is followed. *Equitable Trust Co. v. Central Trust Co.,* 239 SW 171; *Union Savings Bank v. De Marco,* 254 A2d 81 (R.I.).

EXAMPLE: *R* goes to *E* in *State A,* where *E* is incorporated, and there obtains *E*'s commitment to give *R* a mortgage loan. *R* signs the loan documents there and the loan proceeds are distributed there. The mortgage covers land in *State B,* in which *E* has not qualified to do business. *E* can foreclose in *State B.* The loan transaction took place in *State A,* and *State B* will enforce the mortgage. Whatever business has been done, has been done in *State A.* 14a CJ 1283.

It is obvious why this is a necessary rule. A large corporation may own land in 20 or more states. It goes to a New York bank for a loan. The bank cannot even qualify to do business outside of New York. To hold that it cannot make mortgage loans on land located outside of New York would be manifestly absurd. This theory is exhaustively described in Prather, *What Constitutes Doing Business,* 25 Legal Bulletin 65, 80.

The following advice is given to a home state lender seeking to take advantage of the insulation theory:

1. Limit site inspection of properties and subsequent inspections to the absolute minimum.
2. Maintain no offices or employees in any states except the home state.
3. Refrain from instituting or carrying on any negotiations except in the home state and make certain in each instance that all negotiations are consummated in the home state.
4. Commitments and contracts for the purchase of mortgages should by their terms be home state contracts and should be executed by the borrower only in the home state.
5. To the greatest extent possible, avoid or minimize all relationships outside the home state with servicers, brokers, mortgage companies, originators and the like which might give rise to the existence of an agency relationship outside the home state.
6. Close all purchases of mortgages, and disburse all funds, either loan proceeds or purchase price of mortgages, in the home state.
7. Make serious efforts to dispose of foreclosed property as promptly as possible and avoid operation of such properties to the greatest extent possible.
8. To as great an extent as possible use servicing contracts under which the servicer is an independent contractor, rather than the agent of the investor.

Where a mortgage has been originated by a corporation unlawfully engaged in doing business without having qualified, its assignee, as a rule, will likewise suffer from the disability to foreclose if the *doing business* defense is pleaded. *Tornado Southern Inc. v. Harry's Auto Parts,* 222 So2d 29 (Fla.); 6 ALR3rd 326. However, if the suit is filed by the holder in due course of a negotiable note secured by the mortgage, in all but a few states, such holder takes free of the *doing business* defense.

Where the chief business of a corporation is the purchasing of mortgages, it may offend against *doing business* laws by engaging in this practice in a foreign state without obtaining a local license, but a majority of the states now expressly permit the investor to engage in such purchases without a license, though in some states some informal statutory procedure is specified. The philosophy here is that local bankers are protected against competition of corporations that seek to originate mortgage loans without qualifying, but these same bankers are content and, indeed, anxious, to sell to foreign investors mortgages they themselves have originated. However, an investor engaged in purchasing should also endeavor to limit his activities outside its home state to avoid any contention that such activities go beyond the "purchasing" that the statute permits. Some statutes are quite detailed, however, in permitting the investor to renew, modify, or foreclose purchased mortgages, and manage, sell, or otherwise dispose of property acquired by foreclosure. Of course, if an investing corporation remains in its home state, it can at that place buy mortgages on land all over the country and foreclose them, as necessary. Foreclosing a mortgage is not "doing business."

The situation of national banks remains shrouded in some doubt. Formerly these banks were limited by law to making loans within a radius of 100 miles of their home office. This restriction was removed in 1934, and able lawyers feel that this enactment, made in the heart of the Great Depression, was intended to provide banking service across state lines, owing to the fact that many areas were left without banking service due to widespread closing of state banks.

To a less extent the same is true of federal savings and loan associations. A number of decisions have held that such associations are immune from state regulation because federal legislation has "occupied the field." *People v. Coast Fed. S & L Assn.,* 98 F.Supp. 311.

§ 78. **Mortgagee—partnership or general partner as mortgagee.** If the mortgagee is to be a partnership, much thought must be given to the transaction. In states that have adopted the Uniform Partnership Act the partnership by its partnership name may be named as mortgagee. If a corporation is one of the general partners, the state law must be checked to see if it permits a corporation to become a partner. The prevailing point of view seems to be that both the corporation law and the partnership law governing the enterprise must sanction the acceptance of a corporation as a partner. 60 ALR2d 932. If making of the mortgage loan constitutes "doing business" in the state and a foreign corporation is one of the partners, the partnership, it seems, becomes subject to the doing business laws of the state. In other words if the local law requires a foreign corporation to qualify in order to do business, a foreign corporation cannot escape this requirement by forming a partnership. *Ashland Lumber Co. v.*

Detroit Salt Co., 114 Wis. 66, 89 NW 904; *Harris v. Columbia Water & Light Co.,* 108 Tenn. 245, 67 SW 811.

In a few states a foreign partnership must qualify like a foreign corporation in order to do local business. 24 Corporation Journal 267.

Where a partnership borrows money from one of the general partners and gives him a mortgage on partnership land, it seems that if such a mortgage remains unpaid when the partnership becomes insolvent, the general creditors of the partnership will enjoy priority over the mortgage and must be paid in full before anything is paid to the mortgagee. This is an unusual situation, since normally a mortgagee has priority over unsecured creditors. But a general partner has unlimited liability for partnership debts. This produces the result indicated here. 1 Rowley, *Partnerships* § 40(b); 68 CJS *Partnership* § 104. Apparently, however, if the partner-mortgagee sells and assigns the mortgage before insolvency occurs, his assignee is entitled to priority over partnership creditors. *Waterman v. Hunt,* 2 R.I. 298. Since partnership law is quite generally applied to joint ventures, these being partnerships entered into for one specific venture only, the result will be the same in the case of a joint venture.

§ 79. Mortgagee—limited partner as mortgagee. Where a limited partnership borrows money from a limited partner and gives him a mortgage on partnership land, such mortgage is entitled to priority over unsecured creditors and junior liens of the partnership. *Hughes v. Dash,* 309 F2d 1; *A.T.E. Financial Services v. Carson,* 111 N.J.S. 254, 268 A2d 73. 2 Rowley, *Partnerships* § 53.13. This is consistent with the better-reasoned law prior to the Uniform Limited Partnership Act; *Clapp v. Lacey,* 35 Conn. 463.

§ 80. Joint ventures. The problem of the joint venture is omnipresent today. Lenders often participate in the rents or profits of the mortgagor's business, either directly or through corporate affiliates. This sharing of the profits is one of the indicia of partnerships and joint ventures. If the existence of a joint venture is established, serious consequences ensue. The lender may become personally liable to the creditors of the joint venture. In case of insolvency, creditors could argue that the lender, as a joint venturer, must be content with a priority position subordinate to that of firm creditors. However, the courts have shown little disposition to find that a joint venture has been created. Typically, a court might point out that the lender exercises no control over the business, except, perhaps, such control as is customarily exercised by construction lenders. This absence of control indicates no joint venture was intended. *Mortgage Associates Inc. v. Monona Shores,* 47 Wis.2d 171, 177 NW2d 340. A joint venture, the courts observe, presupposes joint control. *Gainesville Carpet Mart v. First Fed. S & L Assn.,* 121 Ga. 450, 174 SE2d 230. *See also* § 392.

8

Deeds of Trust

§ **81. Defined.** A deed of trust (described in § 11) is in the nature of a mortgage and subject to the same rules as a mortgage. *National Acceptance Co. v. Exchange National Bank,* 101 Ill. App2d 396, 243 NE2d 264.

§ **82. Uses and purposes of deeds of trust.** The chief use and purpose of the deed of trust today is the achievement of speed and economy in the process of foreclosure. In quite a number of states the law sanctions foreclosure without court proceedings. The most convenient method of foreclosing in these states is by means of a power of sale contained in a deed of trust. The trustee, being a disinterested third party, is trustee for both the lender and borrower. 3 Jones, *Mortgages,* 798. When a default occurs, the note holder notifies the trustee and the trustee initiates foreclosure proceedings. Usually publication of some sort of notice is required and a public auction is then held by the trustee. Since the sale is being held by a disinterested third party there is no obstacle to the note holder bidding at the sale.

§ **83. Advantages and disadvantages of deed of trust.** Use of the deed of trust has certain advantages:

1. It facilitates the borrowing of large sums of money. For example, if a corporation wishes to borrow money to build an industrial plant, it may obtain the funds by borrowing from a bank. The corporation thereupon executes a deed of trust on the land running to the bank, as trustee. The deed of trust secures a large number of promissory notes or bonds. These bonds are sold to various investors, and the corporation thereby replaces in its till the money it has advanced or will advance for the erection of the building. Obviously it would be impractical to give each bondholder a separate mortgage. If it becomes

61

necessary to foreclose, the bank, as trustee, forecloses for the benefit of all bondholders.

2. A person holding a note secured by a deed of trust may, in many states, sell and transfer the note with a minimum of difficulty and expense. Sale of a note secured by a regular mortgage involves the making and recording of an assignment of the mortgage.

3. A person owning a note or bond secured by a deed of trust may keep the fact of his ownership a secret, if he wishes to do so.

Use of the deed of trust involves certain disadvantages:

1. When the mortgage debt has been paid in full, the mortgagor will want to have the trust deed released, a matter that is more fully discussed later. *See* Chapter 41. The trustee, obviously, will refuse to sign any release of the deed of trust unless all of the notes secured by it are produced and exhibited to him, duly canceled. He does this because he would be personally liable to the note-holder, if he were to sign a release of the trust deed while any of the notes remained unpaid. If the property owner misplaces some of the notes he has paid (which notes are, of course, surrendered to him on his payment of them), he must go to the trouble and expense of procuring a surety-company bond to protect the trustee against liability, should he wish to induce the trustee to sign a release deed.

2. When there are a number of different notes owned by different persons, foreclosure of the deed of trust is an expensive and cumbersome process. The trustee has the power to initiate foreclosure proceedings on behalf of all noteholders, but he does not, in many states, have the power to buy the property at the foreclosure sale on behalf of the noteholders, unless the trust deed specifically confers this power. 88 ALR 1260; 96 ALR 1456; 130 ALR 1349. This means that some committee of noteholders must make arrangements for a joint purchase of the property at the foreclosure sale. Cash must be raised to pay the noteholders who do not wish to participate. A corporation or trust must be formed to acquire title to the property, with shares in the corporation or trust to be distributed to the noteholders who participate in the purchase. Usually the expense of such an arrangement is very substantial. Alternatively, the property may be reorganized under the Bankruptcy Act, which also is very expensive.

§ 84. Deed of trust as a mortgage. There are some curious decisions holding that a document which is in form a deed of trust may nevertheless be a mortgage rather than a deed of trust. Oddly, many such decisions stress the presence or absence of the *defeasance clause,* that obsolete clause declaring the mortgage void when the debt is paid. 5 Tiffany, *Real Property* § 1400. If such a clause is present some cases say the document is a mortgage. Advantages and disadvantages result. A deed of trust in some lien states conveys a legal title.

5 Tiffany, *Real Property* (3rd ed.) § 1400. This gives certain rights as to possession and rents. But a mortgagee may be entitled to resort to strict foreclosure, whereas a trustee in a deed of trust, in some states, may not. Distinctions of this sort tend to become obsolete.

§ 85. **The trustee.** Local legislation should be checked before an individual trustee is selected. For example, Virginia, West Virginia, Missouri, and Indiana (and perhaps other states) have legislation directed against trustees who do not reside in the state. Foreign corporate trustees present a problem far beyond the scope of this text. If the trustee is an individual employed by the lender, it is best, and in some states, necessary, to substitute an impartial third party to hold the sale if default occurs.

§ 86. **Foreclosure provisions.** The deed of trust that contains a power of sale will, of course, recite in some detail the events of default that will give rise to foreclosure and exercise of the trustee's power of sale. Provision will also be made in the deed of trust for publication and posting or mailing of a notice of the public sale that the trustee is to hold. The trustee's deed to the purchaser at the foreclosure sale will, in turn, recite the events of default that occurred and that requisite notices were published, and posted or mailed. The recitals in the trustee's deed normally establish a rebuttable presumption of the truth of the facts recited therein. 32A C.J.S. *Evidence* § 767. However, the deed of trust may contain a clause that such recitals are conclusive evidence of the truth of the statements therein contained, and some decisions sustain the validity of such a provision. *Ibid.* Such provisions, of course, are common in trust instruments. *Eisel v. Miller,* 84 F2d 174 (CCA 8th 1936). Absent such a provision the recitals in the trustee's deed may be effective only as to purchasers subsequent to the original purchase at the foreclosure sale. 59 CJS *Mortgages* § 594. In some states statutes exist concerning the effect of recitals in trustee's deeds, e.g., West's Calif. Civil Code Annot., § 2924 (1967 pocket part); Vernon Mo. Stat. Annot., § 443.380. Obviously the deed of trust should contain a strong clause as to the conclusiveness of the recitals in the trustee's deed. *See* Chapter 43.

§ 87. **Duties of a trustee.** It is well settled that the trustee in a deed of trust owes duties both to the mortgagor and the holder of the debt. Hence he must act with strict impartiality. 117 ALR 1054, 1055. This duty to act fairly extends also to any purchaser from the mortgagor. 117 ALR 1064. He has no duty, however, to investigate the title to see that the mortgagor owns the property or that the title is clear. 57 ALR 472. Nor is the trustee under a duty to record the deed of trust. That duty rests upon the lender. *Bell v. Title Trust & G. Co.,* 292 Pa 228, 140 A 900, 57 ALR 463. *Contra*: *Miles v. Vivian,* 70 F 848. If part of the loan funds is left with the trustee for any purpose, *e.g.,* to apply toward construction of a building, the trustee must faithfully apply the funds toward such purpose. *Wallrath v. Bohnekamp,* 97 Mo.App. 242, 70 SW 1112. A trustee must, at his peril, make certain that the debt is paid before he issues his release deed. He is personally liable to the lender if he issues a release where the debt remains unpaid. 57 ALR 477, 71 ALR 1415.

§ 88. **Death of mortgagor.** Death of the mortgagor has no effect on the power of sale. 57 ALR 224.

§ 89. **Assignment of mortgage.** Where the power of sale is in a mortgage rather than a deed of trust, an assignment of the mortgage passes the power to the assignee. 3 *Jones, Mortgages,* 823.

§ 90. **Note certification by trustee.** Where a deed of trust is involved, it is customary in many areas to use a responsible corporate trustee and to have the trustee certify on the face of the note that it is the true note secured by the deed or trust. 19 Am.Jur.2d *Corporations* § 1063. This prevents fraudulent floating of a number of notes each purporting to be "the" note secured by the deed of trust. It also facilitates release of the deed of trust when the debt has been paid and the cancelled trust deed and note are produced to the trustee for execution of his release of the trust deed. A corporate trustee will not execute a release of the deed of trust unless he is satisfied that the original papers have been produced for his inspection.

§ 91. **Validity of power of sale.** The decisions indicate that a power of sale is valid and foreclosure by exercise of power of sale is proper in the absence of a state statute (as in Illinois, for example) forbidding foreclosure except by judicial proceeding. *Bell Silver & Copper Mining Co. v. First National Bank,* 156 US 470.

EXCEPTION: In Nebraska power of sale foreclosures were outlawed by court decision.

§ 92. **Power of sale in lien theory states.** It seems that the fact that the state follows the lien theory of mortgages (*see* §§ 6, 8) offers no obstacle to the use of the power of sale. 16 Kan. L. Rev. 612, 618. After all, the use of a power of sale by persons who do not own the property (executors under a will granting such a power, for example) is commonplace.

§ 93. **Redemption laws as affecting power of sale.** While the power of sale is used most effectively in states that have no statutory redemption laws, since the purchaser at the sale gets an immediate title to the land, the presence of a redemption law does not prevent use of the power of sale. *In re Fair's Estate,* 132 Cal. 523, 64 P 1000. Of course, the sale extinguishes the equitable right of redemption. This is true of all foreclosure sales. What we are discussing here is a statutory redemption law. *See* Chapters 45 and 46.

§ 94. **Exculpatory clause.** It may be helpful to the trustee to include an exculpatory clause in the deed of trust. The trustee plainly is trustee for both the landowner and the noteholder. At times their interests and contentions are in conflict. The trustee may have personal liability in these circumstances. Hence it is desirable to include an exculpatory clause.

SUGGESTION: Let the clause provide that neither the trustee nor any successor will have any liability for any action taken in the exercise of his discretion, including, without limitation, sale en masse or in separate parcels, any action taken on the advice of counsel or any action taken based on the trustee's reasonable belief as to the existence of relevant facts, including the fact of default or breach of covenant in the part of the landowner.

Reference: *See* Chapter 41.

ADDITIONAL REFERENCES: 26 Calif. L. Rev. 206; 27 *id.* 66; 44 Ore. L. Rev. 149; 8 Utah L. Rev. 125; 41 Wash. L. Rev. 94.

9

Closing Mortgage Loans

§ **95. Closing defined.** Just as a sale is *closed* by delivery of the deed to the buyer and delivery of the balance of the purchase price to the seller after examination of the title and disposition of other details, for the protection of buyer and seller, so a mortgage transaction is *closed* by delivery of the mortgage and note to the lender and disbursement of the mortgage funds to the mortgagor after attending to the details that insure the mortgagee that he has a good first lien on the property.

§ **96. Title defects.** It is, of course, important to the mortgagee to be sure that his mortgage is a first lien on the land and that no title defects exist. Among the precautions he would take in this regard are the following:

1. Check mortgage for errors in filling blanks, signatures, witnesses, acknowledgment, etc. Have mortgage filed or recorded and bring abstract or other evidence of title down to cover the date of the recording of the mortgage before paying out. This will disclose any other liens that have appeared of record prior to the recording of the mortgage. Any such liens should be paid and released or subordinated to the mortgage. The prudent lender will weigh the true worth of the various means of evidencing title. Sophisticated lenders tend to insist on the ALTA mortgage title insurance policy. Among other advantages, it insures that the mortgage is valid and enforceable. It also insures against unfiled mechanics' liens, unrecorded leases, unrecorded easements, encroachments and other questions of survey, and lack of legal access to the mortgaged property. If the lender is forwarding funds to a title company's agent or its approved attorney, the lender should insist on receiving its *insured closing letter,* which insures the mortgagee against embezzlement of loan funds or the agent's failure to follow the mortgagee's directions. This,

66

incidentally, insures the lender that all prior liens shown on the title search will be paid off, for all mortgagee's directions require this, and the insured closing letter insures that this will be done. If the mortgage is being assigned to your company, require the title company to issue its endorsement to the mortgage title policy insuring the validity of the assignment and subtituting the name of your company as the party assured.

2. Analyze all objections to the mortgagor's title disclosed by the examination of title. All defects in title should be cleared. If the title search reveals building restrictions or conditions, ascertain whether existing buildings violate such restrictions.

3. The mortgagee should inquire into the rights of parties in possession for the purpose of discovering unrecorded leases with options to purchase, unrecorded deeds and contracts, unrecorded easements, and so on. He must keep in mind that fact that the mortgagee, in nearly all states, takes his mortgage subject to the interests of all parties in possession of the premises.

4. The mortgagee should: (a) Inspect the building carefully for signs of recent work, and if any appears, demand to see paid bills and demand mechanic's lien waivers for any substantial work, as in construction loans. (b) Get affidavit from mortgagor that all work or materials furnished to premises have been paid in full, which if false, will subject him to criminal prosecution. (c) If the building is occupied by persons other than the mortgagor (tenant, contract purchaser, and so on), see that notice of nonliability for mechanics' liens is posted on the property in the states where such notice is effective.

5. A survey should be obtained to determine whether any encroachments or other survey defects exist.

6. The mortgagee should obtain the usual mortgagor's affidavit to the effect that there are no judgments, divorces, bankruptcies, and so on against such mortgagor.

7. A chattel lien search should be made where the mortgagee is acquiring a lien on valuable chattels.

8. A check should also be made for violations of zoning and building ordinances.

§ 97. Insurance. Existing fire insurance policies should be checked to determine that the amounts thereof are adequate and that the policies are properly written, covering all foreseeable risks in companies satisfactory to the mortgagee, and mortgagee clauses should be attached.

§ 98. Suggestions as to the loan closing statement. Seldom does the borrower receive the full amount of the mortgage loan. Various deductions are made for title searches, surveys, recording fees, and other items. Therefore, on disbursement of the loan, the mortgagee will prepare a loan settlement statement similar to that prepared in sales of land. This form should be used for three reasons: (1) it furnishes the borrower with a complete record of all disbursements made by the mortgagee from the proceeds of the loan; (2) it provides the mortgagee signed authorization by the borrower for all such disbursement and thus eliminates all possibility of any legal action that might be taken if the mortgagor claims improper charges were made against his loan; and (3) in those cases where there is no binding loan commitment, it fixes the date on which the mortgage becomes a lien on the land, since where there is no binding commitment, the mortgage does not become a lien on the land in some states until the date on which the loan is paid out to the mortgagor. In general, this settlement statement shows the full amount of the loan, and beneath that sum shows all deductions from it and their amount. It also shows the net amount available to the mortgagor and contains an acknowledgment by him that he has received that amount. The statement should be dated and signed by both mortgagor and mortgagee. The loan settlement statement is signed when the loan is closed.[1]

§ 99. Survey. The mortgagee's attorney will often find himself examining a survey of the property. One problem here is that surveyors at times omit information vital to the mortgagee, such as the existence of joint or party walks and drives, overhangs of eaves, manhole covers indicating the presence of subsurface installations, and so on. Matters of this sort charge purchasers or mortgagees with notice of easements not revealed by the public records. E.g., *Sievers v. Flynn,* 305 Ky. 325, 204 SW2d 364; *Jones v. Harmon,* 1 Cal. Reptr. 192, 175 Cal.App.2d 869. Title companies tend to insist that the surveyor attach a surveyor's report form to his plat covering a number of such miscellaneous items. Somewhat the same result can be achieved by calling for a survey that conforms to standards set by the local bar association, e.g., 57 Ill. B.J. 327 (1968). The survey must reveal all encroachments, whether of our buildings on adjoining land and streets, whether of adjoining buildings on our land, and whether above, below or at the surface. In this connection it is important to ascertain that the surveyor has plumbed the buildings, for some walls are not truly vertical. The neighbor's building may be within the lot lines at ground level but may project onto the air space of the mortgaged land from the tenth story upward. Worse still, the buildings on the mortgaged land may encroach into the neighbor's air space. The seriousness of an encroachment depends on a variety of factors. Kratovil, *Real Estate Law,* 97 (5th ed. 1969). As new construction goes forward the danger of new encroachments is constantly present. Likewise there is the possibility that the construction will intrude into areas required to be kept open by building restrictions or zoning ordinances. It is therefore desirable to require that the survey be updated with each payout of a construction loan.

Of course, the survey is also the source of information that reveals whether

---

[1] Kratovil, *Real Estate Law,* 5th ed. (Englewood Cliffs, N.J.: Prentice-Hall, Inc., 1969), pp. 248–249, © 1969.

the character of the building violates zoning ordinances or private building restrictions.

§ **100. Mortgage escrows.** Since a mortgage given to secure a debt does not become a lien until a debt exists, mere recording of a mortgage does not create a lien. Liens attaching to the land prior to the time that the mortgage money is disbursed to the mortgagor are sometimes held to be superior to the lien of the mortgage. This would not be true where the mortgagee has given the mortgagor a binding commitment to make the loan, as is discussed in connection with the mortgage debt. *See* Chapter 10. Where a binding commitment to loan money exists, the lien of the mortgage relates back to the date of the recording of the mortgage. Also, if the mortgagee deposits his mortgage money in escrow, with directions to pay the money over to the mortgagor if an examination of title shows the mortgage as a first lien on the date of its recording, then immediately upon the recording of the mortgage its position as a first lien is established. Not only has the mortgagee obligated himself to make the loan, but he has also parted with control over the mortgage money. Indeed, it is certainly arguable that the mortgagee has disbursed the mortgage money by paying it over to the escrowee. In such case the priority of the mortgage over liens accruing after its recording is assured.[2]

§ **101. Documents of the loan file.** The mortgagee's loan file should include the following papers:

1. Application for loan, signed by borrower, and copy of mortgagee's letter of commitment.
2. Plat of survey.
3. If loan is made to finance purchase of property, the mortgagee should have a copy of the contract of sale in his files. This will prove helpful in checking appraisal of property.
4. Appraisal of property.
5. Mortgage, mortgage note, chattel lien on personal property in building, and assignment of rents and leases.
6. Assignment of mortgage and waiver of defenses if loan was purchased from original lender.
7. Operating statement showing borrower's profit and loss figures for last fiscal year, also audited financial statement. These help in determining borrower's financial responsibility on bigger loans.
8. Insurance policies, with mortgagee loss clauses attached.
9. Mortgagee title policy, abstract and opinion, Torrens certificate, or other evidence of title.

---

[2] Kratovil, *The Guarantor* (Chicago, Ill.: Chicago Title & Trust Co., October 1969) 3, © 1969.

10. Mortgagor's affidavit as to judgments, divorces, recent improvements, and other pertinent facts.

11. Copy of escrow agreement, if loan was closed in escrow.

12. Loan closing statement, including receipt for loan proceeds signed by borrowers.

13. If loan was a refinancing loan, the canceled mortgage and note that was taken up by the new loan.

14. Waiver of encroachments by FHA, and all other FHA documents when loan is FHA-insured.

15. Loan guaranty certificate and other documents needed in case of VA insured loans or copies of such documents.

16. Subordination of reverter if one was obtained. If any other prior mortgage or other lien was subordinated to the current mortgage, the subordination agreement, of course, should also be in the loan files.

17. Certified copy of corporate resolutions if mortgage was made by corporation. If property mortgaged is all, or substantially all, of the assets of corporation, resolutions by both directors and stockholders may be necessary.

18. Will, trust indenture, or other trust instrument, or copy of these, if mortgagor is a trustee.

19. Full copy of building restrictions affecting the mortgaged premises, particularly if loan is a construction loan.

20. Leases to key tenants and assignments thereof to mortgagee.

21. Where a franchised chain is involved, e.g., a Holiday Inn, the mortgage should give the lender the right to declare the mortgage debt due if the franchise is revoked. It should also provide that the mortgagee can expend any sums needed to retain or revive the franchise and add these sums to the mortgage debt. Likewise, the mortgagee should have a side agreement with the chain that in case of foreclosure the chain will franchise the mortgagee as an operator and will render technical aid to bring the operation up to chain standards.[3]

---

[3] Kratovil, *Real Estate Law*, 5th ed. (Englewood Cliffs, N.J.: Prentice-Hall, Inc., 1969), pp. 249–250, © 1969.

10

The Mortgage Debt

§ 102. In general. In order for a mortgage to exist, there must be a debt for the mortgage to secure. A mortgage without any debt has no effect. Any contractual obligation reducible to a money value may be secured by a mortgage. The obligation secured is ordinarily one for the payment of money, such as a promissory note or bond. A bond is nothing more than a promise to pay money. The obligation secured may or may not be negotiable.

§ 103. Necessity for promissory note, bond, or other obligation. A mortgage is quite valid even though it does not secure a promissory note, bond, or other separate obligation. *M. De Matteo Const. Co. v. Daggett,* 341 Mass. 252, 168 NE2d 276. Indeed, for the first few hundred years of mortgage law, the separate obligation was undreamed of. The only description of the debt was found in the mortgage defeasance clause.

§ 104. Necessity for personal liability—nature of mortgage debt. There is no necessity that the mortgagor have personal liability for repayment of the mortgage debt. It is competent for the parties to make such bargain upon this subject as they please. They may agree that the mortgagee will rely solely on the land as security for repayment of the mortgage debt. *Bacon v. Brown,* 19 Conn. 29; *Boyd v. Goldstein,* 223 Md. 164 A2d 336; *R.M. McArthur v. Louis Merwitzer,* (Fla.) 180 So2d 164. It is difficult to understand why some lawyers continue to argue for the necessity of a personal liability. This claim is baseless. Virtually every mortgage made by a trustee contains an exculpatory clause absolutely negating personal liability. In many deed absolute situations no personal liability exists. *See* § 20.

In the case of the usual mortgage transaction, there is a borrowing of

71

money, so that there is no doubt that a debt exists. However, since there has been so much discussion of the nature of the debt or obligation required for a mortgage to exist, a very brief excursion into this territory seems necessary. In deed absolute cases the statement has often been made that a debt is essential. Osborne, *Mortgages* § 103. Yet it is precisely in this situation that homespun documentation is commonplace and the creation of a formal debt relatively rare. But the need to protect the needy and unsophisticated is greatest here, for if there is no mortgage, the protection of foreclosure and redemption is out the window. This, few if any courts will endure. Indeed, the lack of sophistication on the landowner's part is a factor typically taken into consideration in determining whether a deed is in truth a mortgage. *See* § 20. And in the conditional sale cases framed in terms of a deed with option to repurchase, there is no obligation on the grantor to exercise the option. *Doovy v. Babcock,* 438 P2d 1008; 21 Mo.L.Rev. 257; 32 Tex.L.Rev. 839; 8 CJS 329. *See* § 26. Yet in these situations all doubtful cases are resolved in favor of holding the transaction to be a mortgage. Osborne, *Mortgages* § 88. If presence of an obligation is indispensably necessary for the existence of a mortgage, necessitous borrowers in the conditional sale cases would have no protection against usurers. Fortunately, courts, recognizing that much of mortgage law is concerned with protecting the necessitous borrower, are not bemused with technicalities of this sort. *See* § 181. In the deed absolute situations, the function of parol evidence is to reveal the true nature of the transaction. If the circumstances reveal that a true sale was not intended, as where the amount received by the grantor is substantially less than the value of the property and the grantor remains in possession, the courts conclude that a sale was not intended. Sale being eliminated, the transaction must be a mortgage, it is reasoned. The absence of a note or other obligation makes the task harder for a grantor who seeks to establish that his deed was intended as a mortgage. His task is especially difficult where a deed given by a mortgagor to his mortgagee in lieu of foreclosure of the mortgage debt was accompanied by cancellation of the mortgage debt. Osborne, *Mortgages* § 76. But the task is never impossible and where disparities are great courts have often held a deed to be a mortgage even though an "obligation" was lacking. In this age of "consumerism," it seems clear, technicalities are likely to receive short shrift.

Nevertheless, in doubtful cases, especially those involving sophisticated borrowers, the court may choose to hold that no mortgage was intended and may rest its decision on the innumerable decisions requiring the presence of a mortgage debt. *See,* e.g., § 380.

§ 105. Debt of a third party. A mortgage may be given to secure a debt of a third party. 59 CJS *Mortgages* § 90.

§ 106. The promissory note. Whenever possible the obligation secured by the mortgage should be a negotiable note. Where the mortgage secures a negotiable note, the great weight of authority is that a negotiation of the note to a holder who takes it in good faith, for value, and without notice before maturity, i.e., a holder in due course, to whom the mortgage is then formally assigned, will take the mortgage as he takes the note, free from defenses that would have been available to the mortgagor against the mortgagee. Kratovil, *Real Estate Law,* 233 (5th ed. 1969); 59 CJS *Mortgages* § 369. The advantages offered by this rule are so important that it is difficult to understand why so many mortgage lenders persist in using non-negotiable obligations. The need for preparing a negotiable note requires study of the Uniform Commercial Code, where the modern rules of negotiability are set forth. The Code provides that the statement (commonly occurring in mortgage notes) that the note is secured by a mortgage does not render the note non-negotiable. UCC § 3-105(1)(e). Where the note is executed by a partnership or a trustee, the note is negotiable even though payment is limited to the assets of the partnership or trust. UCC § 3-105(1)(h). But to make the note payable only out of the land mortgaged and not out of the entire assets of the partnership or trust leaves the note non-negotiable. *Ibid.* While the Code requires the note to be payable at a definite time, a note that is "subject to any acceleration" complies with that requirement. UCC § 3-109(1)(c). This is liberal language. One would think that the note could list events of default that would subject the note to acceleration in a form as comprehensive as the events of default spelled out in the mortgage. The note may refer to the mortgage for the events of default. UCC § 3-105(c).

At times the note is signed not only by the mortgagor but by some third party as surety and co-maker. This practice is preferred by some lawyers to the practice of having the third parties sign guarantees of payment. There is a bankruptcy problem with respect to guarantees. *See* § 410. Likewise there is a procedural problem. In some states deficiency judgments cannot be procured against guarantors. *City of Chicago v. Chatham Bank,* 54 Ill.App.2d 405, 203 NE2d 788.

§ 107. **Consideration.** In a number of cases the statement is made that a mortgage must be supported by consideration. This is an inaccurate statement. What the court means to say, of course, is that since a mortgage is a conveyance given to secure a debt, a mortgage cannot exist without a debt. That consideration is not necessary is quite evident from the fact that mortgages existed for hundreds of years before the doctrine of consideration sprang into being. 5 Tiffany, *Real Property,* 276. It must also be kept in mind that a mortgage can be given as security for a pre-existing debt. This universally recognized rule makes it perfectly clear that the doctrine of consideration does not enter into mortgage transactions.

§ 108. **Anaconda mortgage.** Occasionally a mortgage contains a clause stating that it secures all items of indebtedness of mortgagor that shall at any time be due and owing to the mortgagee. Under such a clause the mortgagee could go out and acquire all debts of the mortgagor to others, often at substantial discounts, and enforce them at 100 cents on the dollar by foreclosure of the mortgage. This tendency of such a mortgage to enwrap the unsuspecting debtor in the folds of indebtedness embraced in the mortgage has led the courts to characterize this as an *anaconda mortgage. Caporasa v. First Nat. Bank,* 36 Wis.2d 714, 154 NW2d 271. These dragnet clauses are regarded with disfavor.

EXAMPLE: A mortgage executed by R and S contained a dragnet clause. E, the mortgagee, bought up other debts owing by R to various creditors. It was held that these created a lien only on R's interest in the land. *First v. Byrne,* 238 Ia. 712, 28 NW2d 509, 172 ALR 1072.

§ 109. Balloon notes. Most mortgages are payable in monthly installments. However, in some cases the monthly installments are too small to amortize the mortgage, so that the mortgage has a *balloon* at the end; that is, the last payment picks up the entire balance due. This, if substantial, may catch the mortgagor by surprise and force him to refinance with the mortgagee on terms advantageous to the latter. Some states have legislation forcing the mortgagee to extend payment of the balloon. Fla. Stat. Annot. § 697.05. More legislation of this type is likely. Regulations regarding federal savings and loans forbid balloon notes. Reg. 541. 14.

§ 110. Indemnity mortgages. There has never been any doubt that an indemnity mortgage is valid. 36 Am.Jur., *Mortgages* § 63; 4 American Law of Property 125 (§ 16.66); 59 CJS *Mortgages* § 171; 1 Glenn, *Mortgages* § 5.6; 1 Jones, *Mortgages* § 428; Osborne, *Mortgages* §§ 105, 116.

EXAMPLE: R mortgages his land to E to indemnify E against loss E may sustain from embezzlements by X, whom E employed as a cashier at the request of R. The mortgage is a valid mortgage. If X embezzles funds, E may foreclose the mortgage.

The only problem worth arguing is whether this is to be treated as an obligatory advance mortgage, good against the whole world from the date of its recording. *See* § 115. The only possible answer is in the affirmative, although there is a dearth of case law on the question. Even though *E* makes no contract to hire *X* for any length of time in the example given, obviously the mortgage is of no value to *E* if it becomes a lien only from the moment that *X* embezzles some money. By that time a dozen liens may be ahead of *E's* mortgage. The only sensible answer is the answer that it creates a lien from the moment the mortgage is recorded. *Krutsinger v. Brown,* 72 Ind. 466; *Watson v. Dickens,* 20 Miss. 608; 1 Jones, *Mortgages* § 467.

§ 111. Description of debt. A mortgage must in some way describe and identify the debt that it is intended to secure. The character and amount of the debt must be defined with reasonable certainty in order to preclude the parties from substituting debts other than those described. *Bowen v. Ratcliff*, 140 Ind. 393, 39 NE 860. Otherwise, in some states, subsequent mortgagees, purchasers, or judgment creditors will acquire rights superior to those of the mortgagee.

EXAMPLE: *R* borrows $10,000 from *E* and gives *E* his note therefor. To secure the loan, *R* gives *E* a mortgage, but the mortgage does not recite the amount of the loan. The mortgage is recorded. Thereafter, *X* obtains a judgment against *R*. *X's* judgment is a prior lien, coming in ahead of *E's* mortgage. *Bullock v. Battenhousen,* 108 Ill. 28.

If the debt described in the mortgage is different from the debt that actually exists, subsequent mortgagees, purchasers, and judgment creditors may acquire rights superior to those of the mortgagee.

EXAMPLE: A mortgage, as drawn, recited that it secured a certain note for a certain sum of money. Actually, the mortgagor owed the mortgagee money, but no note had been executed. It was held that subsequent judgment creditors thereby obtained a lien prior and superior to the mortgage lien. The rule requiring that the mortgage accurately describe the debt is for the benefit of persons subsequently acquiring an interest in the land, and if the mortgage is deficient in this regard, such persons will prevail over the mortgagee. *Ogden v. Ogden,* 180 Ill. 543, 54 NE 750.

In many states, however, it is not required that the mortgage state the amount of the mortgage debt. *Henricks v. Brady,* 20 S.D. 599, 108 NW 332; *Nazro v. Ware,* 38 Minn. 443, 38 NW 359; Osborne, *Mortgages* § 108.

North Dakota requires the mortgage to recite the interest rate. Elsewhere this is unnecessary. *Henricks v. Brady,* 20 S.D. 599, 108 NW 332.

Perhaps a distinction should be made at this point. Like other instruments creating an interest in land, mortgages come under the Statute of Frauds and a memorandum or memoranda must exist to satisfy the statute. Thus, either in the mortgage or the obligation it secures the terms of the transaction should be set forth, e.g., rate of interest and maturity of the debt. *Sullivan v. Ladden,* 101 Conn. 166, 125 A 250. However, to satisfy the recording laws, the requirements as to the recorded mortgage are much less rigorous. Quite commonly the rate of interest is omitted from the recorded mortgage (but not from the obligation it secures) to prevent "portfolio raiding." This last is the solicitation of mortgagors by other lenders who offer to refinance the recorded mortgage at lower rates of interest.

There are cross currents at work in this area. With respect to future advances, the trend is definitely toward requiring greater precision of description. As to the *anaconda mortgage,* exact precision is required. With respect to construction loans, statutes now in contemplation will require them to be so labeled, and the better practice today is to state in the mortgage that it also secures the construction loan agreement. This is necessary because the construction loan agreement calls for various expenditures not described in the mortgage or note and arguably these are not secured by the mortgage unless it mentions them in some way. It is unlikely that cases as strict as *Ogden v. Ogden* would be followed today.

§ **112. Maturity of debt.** Failure of the mortgage to state the maturity of the debt does not invalidate the mortgage. However, there are many state laws outlawing mortgages after a stated period of time. Often this time period begins to run from the maturity of the debt, but if the recorded mortgage fails to express a maturity date, then, for the purpose of the statute, the debt will be treated as a debt payable on demand. This is of little concern to institutional lenders, who are quite unlikely to extend indulgence to borrowers for any protracted period of time.

§ **113. Mortgage debt as the measure of the mortgage lien.** The mortgage lien is measured by the amount of the mortgage debt. Thus if a mortgage recites a debt of $10,000, but actually only $5,000 is loaned, the mortgage stands as security for only $5,000. Likewise, the mortgage lien diminishes as the mortgage debt is reduced by payment. Thus if a mortgage of $10,000 is paid down to $5,000, the mortgage lien is reduced accordingly, and if the mortgagee thereafter loans the mortgagor additional funds, these additional funds are not secured by the mortgage unless the mortgage contains a clause covering future advances.

§ **114. Future advances—in general.** Except in the case of a purchase money mortgage, a mortgage debt is rarely created at the same instant that the mortgage is signed. Normally the mortgagor will receive his money sometime after the recording of the mortgage. The question that arises is whether the mortgage has priority over junior mortgages, judgments, and other liens that may attach to the land before the money is paid out on the first mortgage. The problem usually arises in three situations:

1. An ordinary mortgage loan is applied for. The mortgage is executed and recorded. Payment of the mortgage money to the mortgagor is delayed pending the completion of a title search. A judgment or other lien attaches to the land after the recording of the mortgage. Thereafter the mortgagee's title search is completed, but since the search covers only the date of the recording of the mortgage, the mortgagee is unaware of the judgment. Thereafter the mortgagee pays out the mortgage money to the mortgagor.

2. An ordinary mortgage loan is made, and the mortgage money is properly paid out to the mortgagor. The mortgage contains a provision to the effect that it also secures future advances to the mortgagor not in excess of $2,000, or some other sum. This is called an *open-end mortgage*. A year or so after the mortgage has been made, the mortgagor applies to the mortgagee for addi-

tional funds and receives an additional loan of $2,000. Before he receives his money, a judgment or other lien attaches to the land. The mortgagee pays out the $2,000 in ignorance of the existence of the judgment lien.

3. A construction loan is involved. The mortgagee doles out the mortgage money as the building goes up, and before construction is completed other liens attach to the land.

§ 115. Future advances—obligatory advances. Where a mortgagee is obligated, by contract with the mortgagor, to advance funds to be secured by the mortgage, such mortgage will be a valid lien from the time of its recording, as against all subsequent encumbrances, even though the mortgage money is paid to the mortgagor after such subsequent encumbrances have attached to the mortgaged land. This holds true even though the mortgagee is actually aware of the existence of the subsequent encumbrances at the time he pays out the mortgage money. 80 ALR2d 191, 196, 217, 219. Because of the mortgagee's obligation to pay out the money, the mortgage debt is regarded as being in existence from the very beginning. The obligation is usually created in one of two ways: (1) Where the mortgagor has made written application for a mortgage loan and the mortgagee has given his commitment to make the loan, the mortgagee is contractually obligated to go through with the transaction. (2) Where a construction loan is involved, the obligation is usually created by a construction loan agreement. *See* Chapter 17. It obligates the mortgagee to make the loan but authorizes him to disburse the funds as the building goes up.

Let us return to consideration of the application and commitment. It is not always easy for mortgage men to think of these documents as creating a contract for a loan so that the money subsequently advanced is an obligatory advance, and yet a simple illustration will prove that is the case.

EXAMPLE: *A applies to ABD Corporation for a $1,000,000 mortgage loan at 8% interest on his hotel building. The corporation gives a commitment to make this loan. Therafter ABC Corporation refuses to honor its commitment. A goes to XYZ Corporation, which gives him a loan on the same property at 9% interest. Without the slightest doubt, ABC Corporation is liable to A for the difference between 8% and 9% interest over the life of the loan.*

Of course in all states, expenditures made by the mortgagee to preserve the lien of his mortgage, such as payments made by the mortgagee on delinquent real estate taxes that the mortgagor has failed to pay, are considered essentially obligatory expenses, and the mortgagee has the same lien for such advances as he has for his original debt.

The philosophy underlying the obligatory advance doctrine is that the lien of the mortgage does not arise from advances, as they are made. Where the mortgagee is contractually obligated to advance the money, there is an obligation *now*. The fact that money does not change hands until later is of no importance. It is this obligation existing *now* that is at the heart of the obligatory advance doctrine. Osborne, *Mortgages,* 194, 195. If this is understood, it does no great harm to say, as some authorities do, that advances made in such a situation *relate back* to the recording of the mortgage. 59 CJS. 298; 41 CJS 526; 36 Am.Jur. 721; *American Law Property* § 16.71.

Occasionally it has been held that mere delivery of the mortgage and note to the mortgagee obligates the mortgagee to disburse. *Theilen v. Chandler,* 9 Tenn. App. 545; *Utah S. & L. Assn. v. Mechan,* 12 Utah 2d 335, 366 P2d 598.

§ 116. **Future advances—optional advances.** Suppose that the mortgagee has not entered into a binding contract to make the mortgage loan. Despite the fact that the mortgage is duly recorded, it is by no means certain that it will operate as a lien from the date of its recording as against all other liens attaching after that date. The argument that can be made against the mortgage is that a mortgage is a conveyance to secure a debt and that without a debt there is no mortgage. It must therefore follow that *until* the money has actually been advanced to the mortgagor no legal mortgage exists, for until that time the mortgagor owes no money to the mortgagee and therefore no debt exists. In the case of *obligatory advances,* the courts dispose of the argument by saying that since the mortgagee must at all events loan the money, as he has contracted to do, for all practical purposes the debt exists as soon as the obligation to make the loan is created. Since this obligation is normally created, either by application and commitment or by construction loan agreement, before the recording of the mortgage, an obligatory advance mortgage is good against the whole world, including subsequent lienors, from the date the mortgage is recorded. As to mortgages where the mortgagee has not entered into a binding contract to advance the funds, the problem is far more complex, as the ensuing discussion of the open-end mortgage reveals.

The *open-end mortgage* provides that the mortgage secures not only the original note and debt, but also any additional advance that the mortgagee may choose to make to the mortgagor in the future. This means that if in the future the mortgagor wishes to borrow additional funds for the addition of a room or garage or for some other purpose, he can borrow this money from the mortgagee if the latter sees fit to lend it. The advantages are obvious. The expense of executing a new mortgage is obviated. The mortgagee's security is enhanced by the additions or repairs. Recourse to short-term, high-rate consumer financing is eliminated.

It is obvious that the open-end mortgage is an optional advance mortgage. That is, the mortgagee is under no legal obligation to loan the additional funds. The problem here is one of *intervening liens.*

EXAMPLE: *A* borrows $10,000 from *B* on January 31 and gives *B* a future, advance type (open-end) mortgage on *A*'s land, which is duly recorded. On July 1, *A* borrows $1,000 from *C* and gives him a junior mortgage on the land, which he records. On December 1, *A* comes to *B* and borrows an additional $1,000 under the future advance clause of the mortgage. Will this new advance be part of the original first mortgage so that it will enjoy priority over the junior mortgage of July 1, or will the said junior mortgage enjoy priority over the new advance so that the new advance will be, in effect, a third mortgage on the property? In a majority of the states, the additional advance will enjoy priority over the intervening lien, the junior mortgage of July 1, unless *B* had *actual knowledge* of the second mortgage when he gave *A* the advance. In Illinois, Michigan, Ohio, and Pennsylvania, a mortgagee must, before making an optional future advance, search the records for intervening liens. *Record notice* of intervening liens is enough to give the intervening lien priority over the additional advance. 138 ALR 566. In these states, title companies make special, inexpensive title searches to cover mortgagees who propose making additional advances.

A mortgage secures only the debt described therein. Hence a mortgage designed to secure optional future advances should draw attention to that fact. *West Penn. Bank v. Peoples Tr. Co.,* 439 Pa. 304, 266 A2d 773. The older decisions are somewhat liberal in this regard. *5 DePaul L. Rev.* 80; 81 ALR 631. However, since the open-end mortgage has become popular, the notion that such mortgages should describe such future advances seems to be winning acceptance.[1]

It has been said that the distinction between *optional* and *obligatory* advances is one lacking genuine substance, and that the distinction has been preserved so that judges can decide mortgage cases in this area according to their view of the equities of the case. Gilmore, *Security Interests in Personal Property* § 35.4.

§ 117. Future advances—description of future advances in mortgage. It is necessary, also, that the future advances fall within the description thereof given in the mortgage.

EXAMPLE: If the mortage, by its terms, secures future advances made to the *mortgagors*, an advance made to *one of the mortgagors* probably is not secured by the mortgage. *Capocasa v. First Nat. Bank,* 154 NW2d 271 (Wis.). Likewise an advance made to a *grantee* of the mortgagors might not be secured by the mortgage. *Walker v. Whitmore,* 165 Ark. 276, 262 SW 678.

§ 118. Reference to mortgage in documents relating to future advances. Finally, the documents evidencing the future advance should refer to the mortgage, so that it is evident that such advances were meant to be advances secured by the mortgage.

---

[1] Kratovil, *Real Estate Law,* 5th ed. (Englewood Cliffs, N.J.: Prentice-Hall, Inc., 1969), pp. 217–218, ©1969.

WARNING: If the mortgage makes no reference to future advances, any later document evidencing future advances must be executed and acknowledged like an original mortgage, recorded, and the title searches brought down to cover recording, for it is, in legal effect, a new mortgage on the property.

The presently contemplated amendments to the Uniform Commercial Code require every construction loan to be so labeled. This is in keeping with the trend to force the mortgage to describe the debt more specifically. Obviously a mortgage that simply describes the debt as a note for $1,000,000 gives no clue to the tremendously complex nature of the disbursement procedure contemplated, and the staged increase of debt.

§ 119. **Future advances—statutory trends.** The case law that has evolved with respect to future advances has not seemed satisfactory to the legislatures. In time, it seems likely, all states will legislate with respect to future advances. One trend that seems well established is toward statutory limitation of the amount of future advances that may be made under the mortgage. Even the decisional law recognizes this trend. As one court observed, the position of the mortgagee is strengthened if the mortgage places an upper limit on the amount of the future advances. *Kimmel v. Bathy*, (Colo.) 451 P2d 751. The reason for this is the recognized need for the public records to reveal, as accurately as possible, the amount of all liens against the property, so that others can deal intelligently with record owner.

EXAMPLE: *R* gives *E* a mortgage on his home for $20,000 "and all future advances that may be made by *E* to *R* not exceeding $100,000." Here it is evident that no one examining the records can get any idea of how much *E* holds against the property. Newer statutes will hold *E* down to some reasonable amount such as $3,500. But, in return, these statutes may give this reasonable future advance the same priority as the $20,000 originally loaned.

Solely by way of illustration, the following is given as a brief summary of the status of the law in a few states:

North Carolina. This state requires the mortgage or deed of trust to state that it secures future advances, the maximum amount thereof, and the period within which the advances will be made, which shall not extend more than ten years. When so made the advances relate back to recording of the mortgage, as in the case of obligatory advances. N.C. Rev. Stat. § 45–67 *et. seq.*

Ohio. As to optional open-end advances, Ohio has complex legislation. The mortgage must recite that future advances are contemplated and the maximum amount thereof. The mortgage must bear the legend "Open-End Mortgage." If the mortgagee receives actual notice of any subordinate lien or any work or material furnished, subsequent advances will be junior to such intervening liens.

Ohio Code 35301.232, discussed 17 W. Res. L. Rev. 1429. Probably this statute does not apply to obligatory advances. *Wayne B. & L. Co. v. Yarborough,* 11 Ohio St. 195, 228 NE2d 841.

Rhode Island. Here the statute provides that the maximum amount of the advances must be set forth and gives optional advances up to $3,000 the same priority as obligatory advances. *Peoples Bank v. Champlin Lumber Co.,* 258 A2d 82.

California. This state has a decision that in a construction loan all advances are optional if made after the mortgagor's default has relieved the mortgagee of proceeding with construction funds. *Yost-Linn Lumber Co. v. Williams,* 121 Cal.App. 571, 9 P2d 324. By later statute, however, optional advances made to pay mechanics lien claims give the mortgage priority to that extent as of its recording. *Turner v. Lytton S & L Assn.,* 51 Cal.Rptr. 552. However, the *Yost-Linn* rule is left in effect as to situations not covered by this statute. Probably it would not be followed today.

Florida. This state has a law giving priority to all obligatory or optional advances made under the mortgage, regardless of the mortgagee's knowledge of intervening liens or the fact that they appear of record as long as the advances were made within 20 years of the date of the mortgage. This is perhaps the most liberal treatment of future advances one will encounter. Fla. Stat. § 697.04(1). The mortgage is a valid and prior lien as of the date of its recording. One must be certain, however, to comply with other requirements of the statute. 15 U. Fla. L. Rev. 565.

Maryland. Maryland has a statute relative to mortgage to secure future advances. Article 66 § 2. The amounts of intended future advances must be stated and optional advances must not exceed $3,500. The statute states it does not apply to a mortgage deed of trust.

Mississippi. This state once followed the rule that optional advances enjoy priority even though the mortgagee had actual knowledge of intervening liens. *Witczinski v. Everman,* 51 Miss. 841. This case has been overruled and Mississippi now follows the majority rule. *North v. J.W. McClintock Inc.,* 208 Miss. 289, 44 So2d 412.

Texas. This is a difficult state with reference to this problem. Texas has decisions that follow the original liberal Mississippi rule announced in the *Witczinski* Case. *Freiberg v. Magale,* 70 Tex. 116, 7 SW 684. The question remains whether Texas will overrule these off-beat decisions, as took place in Mississippi. And Texas has a statute that gives mechanics liens priority over optional advances if the mechanics lien claimants give notice of their claims to the construction lender. *Regold Mfg. Co. v. Maccafees,* 348 SW2d 864.

§ 120. Future advances—additional advances made though not described in the mortgage. Suppose a mortgage is executed to secure a debt of a stated amount, which, in fact, is loaned to the mortgagor. Later, by oral agreement, the mortgagee loans additional sums to the mortgagor, both intending that they be secured by the mortgage, although the mortgage makes no mention of future advances and none were contemplated at the time. Such advances are not a valid lien as to third parties, such as innocent purchasers. 36 Am.Jur. *Mortgages* § 68. This rule does not apply to necessary expenditures, such as those for taxes.

ADDITIONAL REFERENCES ON OPEN-END MORTGAGES AND FUTURE ADVANCES IN GENERAL: 15 Ala. Law. 115; 14 Ala. L. Rev. 188; 9 Ark. L. Rev. 45; 36 Conn. B. J. 463; 31 id. 173; 5 De Paul L. Rev. 76; 13 Dicta 203; 47 Ia. L. Rev. 432; 16 id. 445; XIX Legal Bulletin (U.S. S & Loan League) 73; 21 Mo. L. Rev. 209; 38 Neb. L. Rev. 172; 31 N.C.L. Rev. 504; 21 Okla. L. Rev. 79; 30 Ohio St. L. J. 458; 28 Penn. B.A. Q. 352; 21 S.W.L. J. 15; 28 Tenn. L. Rev. 354; 23 id. 195; 8 Tex. L. Rev. 371; 34 Tulane L. Rev. 800; 15 U. Fla. L. Rev. 565; 6 Va. L. Rev. 280; 1 Washburn L. J. 453; 56 W. Va. L. Rev. 107; 17 Western Reserve L. Rev. 1429; 1965 Wisc. L. Rev. 175.

11

Acceleration

§ 121. **In general.** The acceleration clause came into general use in the middle of the eighteenth century. It is the most important clause in the mortgage and mortgage note. Because of its importance the acceleration clause is found in virtually all printed forms of mortgages and mortgage notes. Occasionally you will find a homespun equitable mortgage which lacks an acceleration clause. The consequences are likely to be tragic for the mortgagee.

EXAMPLE: *R* borrowed some money from *E*, his father, and his father wrote out an informal, installment mortgage which *R* signed. *R* defaulted. *E* foreclosed for the unpaid installments. Since the mortgage contained no acceleration clause, *E* could not foreclose for the installments not yet due. *P* bid at the foreclosure sale for the amount of the delinquent installments and *R* later redeemed. The land is now free and clear of the lien of the mortgage. The installments not yet due are not a lien on the land. This, at least, is the view taken in some states. In other states the mortgagee will be allowed to have a foreclosure sale subject to the continuing lien of the mortgage for the unpaid balance of the debt. Osborne, *Mortgages*, 680.

§ 122. **Conflict between note and mortgage.** The acceleration clause in the note should not conflict with the acceleration clause in the mortgage. For example, if the note says that acceleration may be declared if a default continues for 30 days, the mortgage should also specify 30 days.

You will see many negotiable mortgage notes that permit acceleration only for default in payment of principal or interest. The clause in the mortgage is much broader, permitting acceleration for breach of any of the mortgage covenants, which include matters such a payment of real estate taxes, maintenance of hazard insurance, and the like. This introduces a problem. To understand the problem, let us first state an obvious proposition of law, namely: the function of the mortgage note is to create a personal liability for payment on the part of the mortgagor, while the function of the mortgage is to create a lien on the mortgage land. Obviously these are two distinct matters.

Nevertheless, it is traditional with mortgagees in many jurisdictions to seek in one action, i.e., the foreclosure suit, foreclosure of the lien of the mortgage and also a deficiency decree or judgment against the mortgagor for any unpaid balance remaining after the foreclosure sale has resulted in the customary pro tanto satisfaction of the mortgage debt. If an acceleration is declared for breach of a mortgage covenant, for example a breach of the covenant to pay real estate taxes, and a comparable event of default permitting acceleration of the mortgage note is not set forth in such note, in many states the mortgagee can foreclose his mortgage but he cannot obtain a deficiency judgment. Likewise, there is a problem if the mortgage contains an acceleration clause but the note does not. All courts hold that in case of default the acceleration clause in the mortgage can be invoked and the mortgage may be foreclosed for the full amount of the mortgage debt. However, some courts hold that the mortgagee cannot obtain a deficiency judgment because by its terms the note is not yet due. *Connerty v. Richsteig,* 379 Ill. 360, 41 NE2d 476. Other courts will permit the entry of a deficiency judgment in such case. *Bollenbach v. Ludlum,* 84 Okla. 14, 201 P 982; 34 ALR 848. These courts regard the mortgage and note as part of one contract. To meet this situation you can set forth in the mortgage note, as an event authorizing acceleration, a breach of any of the covenants of the mortgage. The Uniform Commercial Code permits this. UCC § 3-105(c).

§ 123. Ipso facto acceleration. There are two types of acceleration clauses. One is *elective*. It states that in case of default the mortgage may, at *his election,* declare the entire debt due. The other type of clause is *automatic*. It states that in case of default the entire mortgage debt incomes due. This automatic clause is said to provide for *ipso facto* acceleration 88 U. Pa. L. Rev. 94, 95. Presence of the automatic clause is the result of sloppy draftsmanship. Accidental defaults are so commonplace that it is unlikely that any mortgagee in his right mind would want the debt automatically coming due whenever default occurs. Notice that this would force the mortgagee into foreclosure, for you may be certain the mortgagor who has missed one monthly payment cannot pay off the entire debt. For this reason many courts choose to interpret the clause as elective even though, in phrasing, it seems to be automatic. A few courts read the clause literally, and *acceleration results automatically.* 159 ALR 1077. It is commonplace, of course, for a mortgagee who has accelerated to reinstate the mortgage and cancel the acceleration if the mortgagor cures his defaults.

§ 124. Acceptance of late payments. Under the elective acceleration clause, failure to declare an acceleration for default does not preclude the mortgagee from declaring an acceleration for a later default. *Philmon v. Mid-State Homes, Inc.,* 245 Ark. 680, 434 SW2d 84. In practice most mortgagees accept late payments. The fact that the mortgagee has been accepting late payments does not make it necessary for the mortgagee to warn the mortgagor that he intends to declare an acceleration. *Philmon v. Mid-State Homes, Inc.,* 245 Ark. 680, 434 SW2d 84. This does not mean that a mortgagee may accelerate where he has accepted late payments. Once a late payment has been accepted the mortgagee has lost his right to accelerate as to that payment. He does, however, have the right to accelerate when the next payment falls due and is not paid on its due date. 97 ALR2d 998.

§ 125. **Sale of mortgaged land as creating acceleration.** A mortgage may contain a clause giving the mortgagee the right to accelerate if the mortgagor sells or conveys the land without the written consent of the mortgagee. Such clauses are valid. *Baker v. Leight,* 91 Ariz. 112, 370 P2d 268; *Coast Bank v. Minderhout,* 61 Cal.2d 311, 44 Los Angeles Bar Bulletin 64 (1968); *Jones v. Sacramento Sav. & Loan Ass'n.,* 56 Cal.Rptr. 741; *Jacobson v. McClanahan,* 43 Wash.2d 751, 264 P2d 253. The clause is not an illegal restraint upon alienation. It simply allows the lender to accelerate maturity if an unauthorized sale takes place. The clause was introduced into mortgages to prevent the mortgaged premises from falling into the hands of persons who might fail to maintain the premises properly. However, as interest rates have risen, a few lenders have used the threat of acceleration to exact from acceptable purchasers interest rates higher than those specified in the mortgage. No final court of review has passed on this aspect of the acceleration clause as yet. Some debate continues as to the propriety of using this clause to accelerate the mortgage debt where a perfectly acceptable purchaser is buying the property but the mortgage lender wishes to use the threat of acceleration as a means of increasing the interest rate. *Baltimore Life Co. v. Harn,* 486 P2d 190. There are arguments pro and con. 45 Los Angeles Bar Bulletin 121; U.S. League Legal Bulletin, (January, 1969), pg. 65.

§ 126. **Negotiability.** Under section 3–105(c) of the Uniform Commercial Code, as amended, the mortgage note may refer to the mortgage for the terms of the acceleration clause and this will not impair the negotiability of the note.

§ 127. **Curing the defaults.** Before acceleration takes place, a mortgagor can cure his defaults and prevent acceleration. 1 Glenn, *Mortgages,* 338. Where the mortgagor has defaulted in payment of principal or interest or both, and the mortgagee has declared an acceleration, the courts are not likely to set the acceleration aside simply because the morgagor makes tender of the amounts due before the foreclosure takes place. After all, one important purpose of the acceleration clause is to protect the mortgagee against the chronic delinquent. However, where the acceleration has been declared because of failure to pay taxes or insurance premiums the courts are more likely to set the acceleration aside if these payments are made before foreclosure takes place. 31 ALR 733.

§ **128. Liberal rule.** By the modern liberal rule, a court of equity may refuse to foreclose a mortgage when an acceleration of the due date of the debt would be an inequitable or unjust result and the circumstances would render the acceleration unconscionable. The decisions disclose that foreclosure on an accelerated basis may be denied where the right to accelerate has been waived or the mortgagee estopped to assert it, because of conduct of the mortgagee from which the mortgagor (or owner holding subject to a mortgage) reasonably could assume that the mortgagee, for or upon a certain default, would not elect to declare the full mortgage indebtedness to be due and payable or foreclose therefor; or where the mortgagee failed to perform some duty upon which the exercise of his right to accelerate was conditioned; or where the mortgagor tenders payment of defaulted items, after the default but before notice of the mortgagee's election to accelerate has been given by actual notice or by filing suit to foreclose for the full amount of the mortgage indebtness; or where there was intent to make timely payment, and it was attempted, or steps taken to accomplish it, but nevertheless the payment was not made due to a misunderstanding or excusable neglect, coupled with some conduct of the mortgagee which in a measure contributed to the failure to pay when due or within the grace period. *Campbell v. Werner,* 232 So2d 252 (Fla.); 70 ALR 993.

§ **129. Statutes.** In some states acceleration is regulated by statute. For example, a grace period may be provided, and if payment is made within such grace period, the mortgage is restored to good standing just as if no acceleration had been declared. Ill. Rev. Stat. Ch. 95, § 57. It is likely that more statutes of this type will be enacted.

§ **130. Holder of less than all mortgage debt.** The problem here arises from the fact that a printed mortgage form designed for use with one note is sometimes used to secure two or more notes.

EXAMPLE: *R* signs a deed of trust to secure two notes, both payable to bearer. One is owned by *X*, the other by *Y*. The deed of trust provides that in case of default, acceleration may be declared by the "holder of the debt." Both *X* and *Y* must join in the acceleration. *Sidel v. Holcomb,* 249 Ill. App. 210. Obviously this is disastrous. The deed of trust should provide that a default in payment of either note constitutes a default as to the other note and either may accelerate and foreclose for the benefit of both. Keep in mind that *R* may see to it that one note is in hands friendly to *R*.

§ **131. Notice of acceleration.** It is the rule that notice of acceleration is not necessary. Filing of the foreclosure complaint is of itself a sufficient acceleration. Wisconsin requires notice of acceleration. *Haase v. Blank,* 177 Wis.17, 187 NW 669.

§ 132. Usury. It has been stated if the charges made by the lender such as commission or points are spread over the life of the loan and thus calculated do not exceed the highest rate charged by law, usury is not present. *See* § 176. Suppose, however, that shortly after the loan is made the borrower defaults and the mortgagee declares an acceleration of the debt. Here the commission and points must be spread over a much shorter period and the result mathematically would be to bring the yield to the lender up over the highest rate allowed by law. Nevertheless, nearly all states regard this as legitimate. The loan is not considered usurious. In Florida, however, usury would be present. There is some feeling that the Florida view may gain additional adherents.

12

Extensions and Renewals

§ 133. **In general.** Where a mortgage is renewed or extended at or before its maturity or the evidence of the debt secured is changed by the substitution of new notes the lien of the mortgage is not affected in any way. Its priority is in no wise disturbed. 59 CJS. *Mortgages* § 212. There is some authority to the effect that the extension agreement may be oral. 37 CJS. *Frauds, Statute of* § 232. However, it is the invariable practice to reduce extension agreements to writing.

§ 134. **Effect of extension on junior liens.** The contention is sometimes advanced by a junior lienor that he has been prejudiced by an extension of time on the first mortgage and that therefore his junior security should move to a prior position. This contention is invariably rejected by the courts. The holder of a junior lien is treated as taking his interest subject to the possibility that an extension of time of the senior mortgage will take place. *Guleserian v. Fields,* 351 Mass. 238, 218 NE2d 397; *Mergener v. Fuhr,* 189 Minn. 571, 208 NW 267. However, where the extension is coupled with an increase in the interest rate on the first mortgage, then that portion of the extension is junior to the existing mortgage. Jones, *Mortgages* § 654.

§ 135. **Release of senior mortgage and execution of new replacement mortgage.** In keeping with the rules expressed above, it has been held that where a senior mortgagee releases his mortgage of record and contemporaneously therewith takes back a new mortgage merely for the purpose of extending the time of the debt, the new mortgage enjoys the same priority as the mortgage that has been released. 33 ALR 149, 98 *id.* 843. Obviously, such a procedure involves the taking of an unnecessary risk. It is far better simply to record an extension of the original first mortgage.

§ 136. Renewals. The rule is established everywhere that where a renewal note is given, this in no wise impairs the validity or priority of the mortgage. The situation is complicated by the practice of some bankers in marking the original note "paid by renewal" and surrendering this note to the mortgagor in return for his renewal note. The reason for this, of course, is that the mortgagor does not want two notes outstanding evidencing the same debt. However, the practice is harmless, though obviously it would be far better to enter into an extension agreement, leaving the original note alive, but marking it "extended as per extension agreement dated _____." The extension agreement should be recorded, for many states have enacted laws outlawing mortgages after a stated period has expired after the maturity date as it appears on the public records.

§ 137. Effect of extension on personal liability. It is best to include in the mortgage a provision that any extension of time granted by the mortgagee to any purchaser of the mortgaged land shall not release the personal liability of the mortgagor. This is because of the rule that an extension of time granted to an assuming grantee may release the personal liability of the mortgagor. 41 ALR 277.

SUGGESTED CLAUSE: This mortgage shall secure any and all renewals, or extensions of the whole or any part of the indebtedness hereby secured however evidenced, with interest at such lawful rate as may be agreed upon and any such renewals or extensions or any change in the terms or rate of interest shall not impair in any manner the validity of or priority of this mortgage, nor release the Mortgagor from personal liability for the indebtedness hereby secured.

13

Interest

§ 138. **Description of interest in mortgage.** While a mortgage should describe the principal amount of the debt, evidently the requirements are less rigorous with respect to the rate of interest. As long as the mortgage recites that the debt bears interest, this suffices. *Richards v. Holmes,* 59 US 145. However, one decision holds that if the mortgage does not state the interest rate, purchasers and subsequent mortgagees may assume that it bears the legal rate which is the rate specified by local law of contracts that create no interest rate. *Whittacre v. Fuller,* 5 Minn. 508. North Dakota requires the mortgage to recite the interest rate.

The fact that the mortgage does not recite the higher interest rate called for by the promissory note after maturity of the debt does not prevent collection of such interest. *Henricks v. Brady,* 20 S.D. 599, 108 NW 332.

§ 139. **Interest upon interest.** The courts are divided as to the validity of charging interest on interest. In *compound interest,* accrued interest is added periodically to the principal and interest is then computed on the new principal thus formed. Thus you can have interest on interest on interest, *ad infinitum.* 45 Am.Jur.2d, *Interest and Usury* § 76. This arrangement rarely occurs in mortgage lending. *Interest upon interest* occurs where interest is charged on *overdue* installments of interest. The courts are divided as to the validity of the latter arrangement. 45 Am.Jur.2d, *Interest and Usury* § 77. The state statutes and decisions should be consulted. At all events, even in states that forbid interest upon interest, violation of the prevailing rule does not make the loan usurious although there are a few cases to the contrary. 45 Am.Jur.2d, *Interest and Usury* § 188. At all events, if the mortgagor agrees, after default in payment of interest, that the accrued interest shall become part of the principal, such an agreement is valid, and since the mortgagor is usually asking for an extension of time, the agreement should not be hard to obtain.

Almost all states, in bond issue mortgages, permit interest coupons to bear interest after maturity.

§ 140. Interest coupons. Prior to the economic depression that began in 1929 it was quite customary for a mortgage note to have interest coupons attached. Typically a mortgage would be due five years after its date and ten interest coupons would. be attached, maturing semi-annually. Such transactions are encountered less frequently today. However, they do occur. Even though not so stated on the interest coupon it will bear interest after maturity at the legal rate. *Harper v. Ely,* 70 Ill. 581. If foreclosure proceedings are brought on the mortgage and the principal note is produced with one or more interest coupons detached and unaccounted for, it is presumed that the missing coupons were paid. *Merrick v. Hulbert,* 17 Ill.App. 90.

§ 141. Interest after maturity. Quite commonly a mortgage will call for a rate of interest after maturity that is higher than the interest before maturity. Of itself, such a provision is unobjectionable. If, however, the rate of interest after maturity exceeds the highest lawful rate, a usury question is present. A number of decisions sustain the practice, usually on the theory that the mortgagor can prevent the accrual of such interest by paying the mortgage debt as it falls due. 28 ALR3d 454. However, this view is somewhat unrealistic, since mortgagors default because default is unavoidable. They cannot help themselves. Hence statutes have been enacted in some states forbidding interest after maturity in excess of the maximum allowed by law. 28 ALR3rd 465.

§ 142. Interest escalation clauses. As a result of the tight money situation, a number of articles have appeared in newspapers and magazines indicating that the mortgage, as we know it today, is obsolete. These articles usually go on to conclude that some flexible provision is needed in the mortgage escalating the interest rate as interest rates move upward. Savings and loan associations, in particular, find their loan portfolios loaded with old mortgages carrying interest rates of 5% or less, so that average return on the entire loan portfolio is quite unattractive according to current standards. This brings up the question, of course, as to the validity of these escalation clauses. Whether or not mortgagors might offer sales resistance is another question altogether.

There seems to be a genuine dearth of authority on this proposition. In quite an old New Jersey case a bond called for "lawful interest at such rate as then was, or thereafter might be fixed upon as the legal rate of interest in this state by the legislature thereof." Thereafter the legislation increased the legal maximum interest rate and a question arose as to the validity of this provision in the bond. The court held this arrangement perfectly valid and proper. *Muchlar v. Cross,* 32 N.J.L. 423. In a later New Jersey case the court used this language:

> "Parties dealing for themselves may enter into contracts by which
> the rate of interest to be paid shall change whenever the legal rate
> changes." *Wyckoff v. Wyckoff,* 44 N.J. Eq. 56, 13 A 662.

Many contracts other than mortgages have contained escalation clauses.
The general principle that an escalation clause is valid seems to have been universally accepted. The only attacks that have been launched upon clauses of
this sort have been attacks based upon the contention that the escalated price
was not set forth with adequate certainty. 63 ALR2d 1337. Where, however,
the escalated price is set forth with adequate certainty, clauses of this sort seem
unobjectionable. Thus, for example, where a contract to furnish and erect structural steel for a building contained a provision for an adjustment of the contract
price in the event of an increase or decrease in the prices for component materials
the contract was sustained. *Bethlehem Steel Co. v. Turner Construction Co.,*
2 N.Y.2d 456, 161 NYS2d 90, 141 NE2d 590, 63 ALR2d 1331.

A number of cases dealing with escalation clauses were decided while price
control was in effect in World War II. In one such case the escalation clause
was as follows:

> "Should the maximum prices as promulgated by the Office of Price
> Administration, which are in effect on the date of the opening of
> these bids, be increased or decreased during the life of the contract,
> payment will be made by the District of Columbia at a rate of
> increase or decrease, not to exceed the same ratio that the prices here-
> in quoted bear to the maximum prices authorized by the Office of
> Price Administration."

The court found this clause unobjectionable. *Simpson Bros. Inc. v. District
of Columbia,* 73 F.Supp. 858, aff'd. 179 F2d 430, *cert. den.* 338 US 911.

To be sure, in many instances the escalation is tied to some factual matter
rather than to a change in the law. For example, in leases and contracts, rent
and price are sometimes tied by way of escalation to the depreciating value of
the dollar, as set forth periodically by the Bureau of Labor Statistics. On the
other hand, there seems to be no valid reason for denying validity to an escalation clause that is tied to a change in the law. Thus in 17 CJS *Contracts* § 209
it is said (p. 1010):

> "A contract for an act prohibited by the existing law, but which is
> shown to have been made with reference to the contemplated procur-
> ing of a special statute making the act valid, the enactment of which
> was actually procured before the contract was performed, is not to be
> regarded as illegal."

Specifically, in the law of usury, decisions friendly to the escalation clause are numerous. The general rule is that a statute affecting the allowance of interest will not apply to contracts entered into prior to its effective date. 4 ALR2d 932, 935. But, an important exception to this general rule is found in those decisions holding that usurious contracts are validated by a subsequent statute authorizing the rate contracted for. 4 ALR2d 932, 944.

At all events when the escalation clause is found in a mortgage that carries an interest rate lawful at the time and when the escalation clause seeks only to move the interest rate up to another lawful rate, such a clause would seem unobjectionable.

There remains, of course, the question of definiteness and certainty. For example, suppose a mortgage calls for an escalation to the highest lawful rate and thereafter the statute altogether abolishes the usury law, permitting the charge of any interest whatever. Here the escalation clause might possibly be held void for uncertainty. Obviously, the escalation clause should carry some maximum beyond which it will not go. Another possibility is to have the mortgage provide that, whenever the interest escalates, the mortgagor has the option of prepaying at the old rate.

Of course, all the foregoing is academic in any state that has legislated on the subject. For example, in Illinois any escalation clause that seeks to increase the interest whenever the statutory maximum is increased is void. Ill. Rev. Stat. Ch. 74, Par. 4.

One final thought: These days contracts deemed "unconscionable" are having tough sledding. 18 ALR3rd 1305. But it hardly seems arguable that an interest rate expressly sanctioned by the legislature could be considered unconscionable.[1]

§ 143. The variable mortgage. The variable mortgage, as distinguished from the mortgage containing an interest escalation clause, is one where the interest rate can move down as well as up. Lenders using this form sometimes use an *inside standard* to determine the interest rate the borrower must pay. An example of an inside standard would be the rate of interest currently being paid by the institution to its depositors, the mortgage rate being pegged at, say, three points above the depositors' rate. Other institutions may use an *outside standard*; for example, the rate being paid on U.S. government securities.

§ 144. Adjusting the term of the mortgage. Where the interest rate escalates upwards, it seems impractical to increase the size of the monthly payment. Many borrowers start out with a monthly payment that is as high as they can afford to pay. Any increase would put them in default. Thus these variable mort-

---

[1] Kratovil, "Interest Escalation Clauses," *American Banker*, May 19, 1970, p. 34, © 1970.

gages tend to leave the monthly payment alone, but simply prolong the life of the loan if interest rates move upward. The only objection to this is the fact that some lenders are fettered by laws that specify a maximum term of the mortgage loan and the possibility is always present that the escalation may take the term of the loan over this limit. At this moment, no solution has been offered to this problem.

Variable mortgages have already encountered state regulation. Calif. Civil Code § 1916.5.

14

Usury

§ 145. **In general.** As a consequence of tight money, usury has become a subject of considerable interest, litigation and legislation. Money, it is clear, is a commodity responsive to the law of supply and demand. When lendable funds are abundant, interest rates tend downward. When such funds are in short supply, interest rates rise.

§ 146. **Definition.** Most states have laws that fix a maximum interest rate that may be charged. Usury is present when the lender charges a greater rate of interest than the maximum rate allowed by law. Because there is rather frequent change in these laws there would no point in including here any table of maximum rates. Prentice-Hall and Commerce Clearing House publish loose-leaf services that will give you up-to-date information on such laws.

§ 147. **Financial pressures that create usury problems.** As lendable funds dwindle in a tight money situation, there will be borrowing by those who cannot postpone their borrowing (for example, an employee transferred to a locality where he must purchase a home because apartments are not available in areas he deems acceptable), and by those who fear that interest rates may go even higher, for example, businessmen who need to expand plants. The population explosion causes increasing demand for housing, hence increased demand for mortgage funds. At the same time, tight money causes interest rates to rise on other types of borrowings, for example, high-grade corporate bonds. If a lender can obtain a yield of, say, 8% on a high-grade corporate bond, he is not going to do much mortgage lending in a state where the maximum interest on home loans is 8%. There is no red tape (credit reports, title reports, surveys, mortgage documents etc.) and virtually no risk in high-grade corporate bonds. Savers withdraw their funds from savings institutions to buy the high-yield bonds. This aggravates the shortage of funds lendable on home loans.

This demand exerted upon a shrinking supply of lendable funds tends to push interest rates above the maximum fixed by law. Lawmakers traditionally lag behind the times. Moreover, especially in states where financial interests are weak and debtor interests (labor unions, farmers) are strong, legislators, being responsive to the wishes of their constituents, tend to try to keep interest rates from rising by refusing to raise the maximum rates, or by raising them in driblets. This is ineffective.

Another reason why usury laws are ineffective in times of tight money is the presence in virtually all states of loans that are exempt from the usury laws, such as corporate loans or business loans. Obviously all lenders in times of tight money will seek to funnel their mortgage money into loans that are exempt from the usury laws.

With all these openings in the usury wall, it is irrational to suppose that lenders will stay within the statutory maximum. Even where funds are loaned in situations where the statutory exemption is applicable, lenders tend to resort to devices that create a yield in excess of the statutory maximum.

EXAMPLE: *A, who is being transferred from State X to State Y, must sell his home. B, who is being transferred to State X, is compelled to buy a home. A sale price of $30,000 is decided upon in the sale from A to B. C, a lender, is willing to give a mortgage of $20,000 to B at 8%, which is the statutory maximum in State X. But C demands "ten points" to make the loan. This means that A must pay X 10% of $20,000 to induce C to make the loan. Thus, in effect, C is loaning only $18,000 ($20,000 minus $2,000) but will collect the entire $20,000. Obviously this gives C a yield substantially in excess of 8%. Is this a legally valid way of circumventing usury laws? This is discussed subsequently. See § 168. Even if it is not, experience reveals that only a negligible percentage of borrowers are aware of or attempt to take advantage of the usury laws. Hence if a lender occasionally takes a loss on a usurious loan, he can absorb it because of the gains in the uncontested remainder of his loan portfolio.*

§ 148. **Geographic factors.** It is difficult for a layman to believe that money does not move freely. Nevertheless that appears to be the case. For example, in the northeast portion of the country where many financial institutions have their homes lendable funds are relatively abundant. Hence, in Massachusetts, for example, which has no usury law at all, interest rates are traditionally lower than the national average.

§ 149. **Devices to evade the usury laws.** Obviously no lender will give a loan that calls for interest in excess of the statutory maximum. There is always some attempt to conceal the presence of usury. Most of the law of usury deals with such devices.

EXAMPLE: In a state where the maximum interest rate is 6%, *R*, a home-owner, seeks a $20,000 loan from *E*. *E* demands that *R* "sell" his house to *E* for $20,000 with an "option to repurchase" the house within a year for $22,000, *R* being permitted to remain in possession. Obviously this is a loan at 10% interest.

EXAMPLE: *E* makes a loan to *R* at the statutory maximum but charges a 3% "commission" to make the loan. The loan is usurious.

EXAMPLE: The "points" example given above is another illustration. See §147.

§ 150. Penalties for usury. The usury penalties provided by law vary from state to state. In some states the entire mortgage is void. In other states all interest is forfeited. In still other states only the interest in excess of the maximum is forfeited. In still other states, the borrower is given the right to sue the lender for some penalty fixed by law, for example, twice the amount of the excessive interest. These penalties are revised from time to time. Historically they have always proved ineffective, except to the extent that in states where the usury penalty is excessively harsh, mortgage money dries up. Lenders make or buy their loans in states where the laws are more lenient. Necessitous borrowers, moreover, have no choice, and there are always some lenders who are willing to take the risks. Indeed, in the financial community when it is evident that the local maximum rate is unrealistic, no opprobrium attaches to the charging of interest in excess of that rate. And, interestingly, in those states that have no usury laws, such as Massachusetts, the average interest rates are usually *under* the national average, indicating that the usury laws serve no useful purpose.

§ 151. Effect of religious and ethical beliefs. Both Christians and Jews have inherited a tradition that frowns upon usury. Indeed, from a religious point of view, usury was originally considered to be the charging of any interest at all. These religious and ethical beliefs were never effective in controlling banking practices. They have, however, left some residue of this philosophy that even today enters into usury litigation.

EXAMPLE: *R* sells his home to *E* and *E* borrows from *X* on a mortgage carrying the maximum rate of interest. *X* insists that *R* pay him a commission of 2% of the amount of the loan, which *R* does in order to consummate the transaction. Viewed in the abstract, one could reason that usury is not present, because the purpose of usury laws is to protect the borrower, and here the borrower has not been injured by the seller's payment of the commission. The borrower has not been forced to *pay* more than the maximum interest. Viewed from an ethical-religious point of view, usury is present because the lender has *received* more than the law allows. Indeed in the states that define usury as *receiving* more than the maximum rate (as distinguished from laws that speak in terms of *charging the borrower* more than the maximum rate), this result seems justified. However, the language of the language of the statute is not conclusive on this question.

EXAMPLE: In Tennessee the usury law speaks of the maximum interest the borrower can be compelled to *pay*. Yet the Tennessee cases make the test of usury turn on whether the lender has *received* more than the maximum interest. *Silver Homes Inc. v. Marx Bettendorf,* 206 Tenn. 361, 333 SW2d 810. Viewed from a practical point of view, the likelihood is that the seller will seek to pass the charge along to the buyer-borrower in the form of an increased price for the house. See § 167. The question is not at all academic.

EXAMPLE: In the wrap-around mortgage (see § 393) the borrower receives $5,000,000 in the illustration given, but pays interest on $10,000,000 because the second mortgagee binds himself to pay off the existing first mortgage of $5,000,000. Moreover, since the borrower pays at the present statutory maximum (say 8%) while the second mortgagee pays only the old stated interest rate on the first mortgage (say 6%) the yield to the second mortgagee is in excess of 8%. One could argue that the borrower is not hurt, for if he refinanced the old first mortgage at this time, the interest would undoubtedly be 8%. Nevertheless the fact remains that what makes the wrap-around attractive is the yield in excess of the statutory maximum. A court disposed to look at the impact on the borrower might sustain the transaction. A court disposed to punish lenders who step over the line established by law might regard the transaction as usurious.

Again, the highly punitive laws seem hopelessly outdated. The notion that usury is sinful goes back to Old Testament times. Today, however, the return that a lender exacts is determined to a great extent by how much the lender must pay depositors, for example, and by the interest rates its competitors are charging. In these circumstances harsh punishment of the lender who steps over the line seem unwarranted.

Some statutes call for imprisonment in a penitentiary of persons convicted of charging high rates of interest, for example 25% in New York. These statutes are aimed at the gangster juice-type loan.

§ 152. Intent. It is often said that for usury to be present there must be an *intent* to charge usury. This, by and large, is a meaningless statement. The lender intends to charge what he charges the borrower, and if this exceeds the statutory maximum, usury is present even if the lender thought the charges he exacted would not create usury. *Terry v. Teachworth* 431 SW2d 918 (Tex.Civ. App.); 53 Va.L.Rev. 341. For example, a lender who charges a lender's commission on top of the maximum rate is guilty of usury even though the lender is unaware that such a charge was unlawful. Likewise, the intent of the borrower to make the unlawful payments, as where the borrower proposes the charges that make the loan usurious, does not take the loan out of the usury law. *Mission Hills v. Western Small Business,* 67 Cal. Rptr. 505. *But see* § 185.

§ 153. Usury law in actual application. The law of usury deals to a considerable extent with: (1) Disguised loans, that is, arrangements designed to disguise a loan transaction as something else, such as a sale. (2) Computational devices designed to create the illusion of compliance with the law. (3) Charges that increase the yield to the lender though not called "interest," such as "points."

We can divide this last group into *permitted charges* (which can be charged in addition to the statutory maximum without making the loan usurious) and *usurious charges,* which will make the loan usurious if they bring the yield up over the statutory maximum. (4) Borrower-controlled situations, in which the yield to the lender exceeds the statutory maximum, but the result is sanctioned because, in theory, the extra charges can be prevented by the borrower. (5) Borrowers exempted from the operation of the usury laws. (6) Lenders exempted from the usury laws. (7) Transactions exempted from the usury laws.

§ **154. Exempt borrowers.** In many states a corporate borrower is not subject to the usury laws. He can agree to pay any rate of interest. 55 Calif.L.Rev. 207. The philosophy here is that usury laws are for the protection of the unsophisticated poor. See e.g., Sec. 3. 605 Uniform Consumer Credit Code. Corporations represent sophisticated venture capital. Therefore corporations in their quest for profits should be permitted to borrow money on any terms. 47 Minn. L.Rev. 267. Moreover, businessmen and their lawyers deal with bankers on equal terms. They do not need the usury law's protection.

The problem arises where an individual applies for a loan and the lender, it is later contended, forced him to incorporate for the purpose of agreeing to pay the higher interest rate, the corporation being merely a sham.

EXAMPLE: *A,* an individual, applies to *B* for a loan. *B* agrees to give *A* the loan, but later discovers that the interest rate is higher than the law allows. *B* directs *A* to form a corporation, and *B* makes the loan to the corporation. The corporation will be allowed to contend that the loan is usurious. *Felier v. Architect's Display Inc.,* 54 N.J. Super. 205, 148 A2d 634.

It is difficult at times to determine whether the corporation is a sham. For example, if a corporation is formed with capital ample to repay the loan, the corporation is not a sham and the loan is not usurious.

In New York and possibly other states the fact that the corporation was formed with the purpose of evading the usury laws does not make the law usurious. *Leader v. Dinkler Mortgage Corp.,* 20 N.Y.2d 393, 230 NE2d 120.

In some states the corporation exemption does not apply in certain cases (e.g. single family dwellings) or some sort of ceiling is placed on the usury rate that can be charged. In states where a corporation borrower is exempt from the usury laws, the defense of usury is not available to individuals who sign written guarantees of the corporate note. *Raby v. Commercial Banking Corporation,* 208 Pa.Super. 52, 220 A2d 659; *Nation Wide Inc., v. Scullin,* 256 F2d 929; 63 ALR2d 954.

Where the note is signed both by the corporation and an individual, and both are primarily liable, that is, the lender can exact payment directly from both of them, the individual is, according to some decisions, entitled to the defense of usury. *Grove v. C.T.&T. Co.,* 25 Ill. App.2d 402, 166 NE2d 630;

Meadow Brook National Bank v. Recile, 302 F Supp. 62, 63 ALR2d 953. But
the better rule is that if the loan is really made to the corporation, and the individual co-maker is, as between himself and the corporation, entitled to require the
corporation to pay the debt, so that the lender looks to the individual only if
the corporation does not pay, the individual is not entitled to the defense of
usury. 63 ALR2d 950. Technically this is a suretyship situation and sureties
should be given the same treatment as guarantors.

But the individual guarantee cannot be used to disguise a loan to a sham
corporation.

EXAMPLE: *A,* a wealthy individual, applies to *B* for a loan, and *B* directs
him to form a corporation, which has a capital of $1,000. *B* loans the corporation
$100,000, and the loan is guaranteed by *A* individually. The loan is usurious, be-
cause it is clear that the loan is really being made to *A,* and the corporation is
nothing but a sham. *Walnut Discount Co. v. Weiss,* 205 Pa. Super. 161, 208 A2d
26.

Where a modern statute exempts borrowers such as partnerships, joint ventures, and trusts from the usury laws, questions will arise as to whether such as
entity was formed to evade the usury laws. *Havens v. Woodfills,* 226 NE2d 221.

There is no statute law to the effect that usury laws have no application to
sophisticated borrowers. Nevertheless, quite a body of case law is growing up
to the effect that the usury laws were designed to protect the necessitous and
the ignorant. There is no true equality of bargaining power between such persons and lenders. But where the borrower is sophisticated, has legal advice, and
can shop various lenders to get the best terms, he ought not to be allowed to
raise the defense of usury. *White v. Satzman,* 41 Cal.Reptr. 359; *Meridian
Bowling Lanes v. Brown,* 30 Ida. 403, 412 P2d 586; *Monmouth v. Holmdel,*
92 NJS 480, 224 A2d 35; *Bowman v. Price,* 143 Tenn. 366, 226 SW 210. This
is not to say that the courts would sustain a loan calling for 15% interest if the
maximum rate is 10%. It simply means that the courts will endeavor to so
construe the transaction that the defense of usury will not be available. For
example, if the transaction is, in form, a sale, but the seller is arguing that it is
a disguised loan, he will probably not get very far if he is a sophisticated person and has had advice of counsel.

§ 155. Exempt lenders—in general. In many states there are lenders who
are exempt from the usury laws; for example, banks and trust companies and
building and loan associations. Here the philosophy is that state-regulated,
responsible financial institutions will not extort unreasonable interest rates from
their borrowers.

§ 156. Exempt lenders—banks and trust companies. A number of states
exempt loans by banks and trust companies from the usury laws. One would
think that this might present a problem of class legislation. For example, in a

state that has a law of this character but denies a usury exemption to building and loan associations, it seems difficult to justify this arbitrary preference for banks and trust companies. Nevertheless, the United States Supreme Court has sustained this law and many states have approved this decision. *Griffith v. Connecticut,* 218 US 565. Some states (Missouri, for example) have constitutions so strict that classifications of this sort might be unconstitutional.

Where a national bank is the lender, the penalty for usury is not that fixed by state law. Instead, the penalty is that fixed by the federal statute. 12 USCA § 85. It has been held that where a national bank makes a mortgage loan outside of the state in which it has its home office, it is governed by the usury laws of that state. *Meadow Brook National Bank v. Recile,* 302 FSupp. 62. This decision probably will not stand. *See* 87 Banking L. Journal 483.

§ 157. **Exempt lenders—building loan associations.** Another fairly common state law exempts building and loan associations from the usury laws. In older days this law made sense. These associations were true cooperatives. The members met periodically, often monthly, and that member-saver who made the highest interest rate bid for the lendable funds was given the loan. In such a situation it would have been folly to attempt to apply the usury laws. Hence state law typically made building and loan association laws exempt from the usury laws. Today, however, the situation is quite different. Savings and loan associations operate in much the same way as banks. Yet the preference in the usury law remains. The question that is presented, then, is whether the savings and loan association is sufficiently different from other lenders to justify this preference. On balance, the answer should be in the affirmative. Savings and loan associations are the traditional lenders in home loans. They make loans more conservative lenders might reject. Clearly, a reasonable basis for classification exists. That is all the law requires.

§ 158. **Exempt transactions—business loans.** In some states all loans for business purposes are exempt from the usury laws, even where the borrower is an individual. The philosophy is the same as in the case of corporate loans. In still other states all loans in excess of a figure stated in the usury law are exempt. Here the philosophy is that the big borrower is sophisticated and does not need protection. These laws are sensible because it seems pointless to require a businessman to form a corporation that will subject him to an income tax disadvantage.

§ 159. **Exempt transactions—FHA loans.** In a number of states laws have been enacted that exempt FHA insured loans from the usury laws. These laws present some problems. The first problem is a technical one. Can a state key its laws to present and future federal legislation so that in effect, the state gives up all control over FHA insured loans, regardless of the interest rate FHA approves? In general the answer to this question seems affirmative. No reason exists why state law should not make such a practical adjustment of its laws to the financial realities. 38 Ia.L.Rev. 705; 133ALR 401. However, in West Virginia, the attorney general has indicated a belief that this type of law might be invalid. The technical defect here is the fact that the state legislature is "delegating" to the federal government its judgment as to what the maximum interest rate should be.

A more difficult question relates to the form of legislation, which, unhappily, raises questions that could have been avoided. For example, in some states the law has provided that banks and trust companies may make FHA loans and will not be subject to the usury laws. This raises the question of whether this is unlawful class legislation. Why, might one ask, should this privilege be accorded to banks and trust companies only? This is a difficult question. *See* § 156.

§ 160. Exempt transactions—time-price rule. It is obvious that one who sells for cash is likely to charge less than where he sells on credit. If he sells for cash, he can immediately invest the money. This is a privilege he gives up when he sells on the installment plan. This is an economic fact of life. It has created the time-price rule. Under this rule no usury is present if the seller charges a higher price on the credit sale.

EXAMPLE: *A* is willing to sell his house for $15,000 cash or for $20,000 if payable in installments over a 20-year period. This is lawful. 71 Harv. L. Rev. 1143; 91 CJS 589; 14 ALR3rd 1065.

In connection with the "time-price" rule it must be remembered that according to a number of decisions a sale of property creates a debt on the part of the purchaser to the seller. If the seller forgoes immediate payment, this is a "forbearance of money" within the meaning of the usury laws. And if the seller makes a charge for the forbearance and such charge goes over the usury limits, usury is present. *State v. J.C. Penny Co.,* 179 NW2d 641 (Wis. 1970). In other decisions, however, the statement is made, usually without explanation, that the usury laws apply to loans, not contracts or sales. *Contract Buyers League v. F & F Investment Co.,* 300 FSupp. 210; *Nelson v. Searritt,* 48 So2d 168 (Fla).

The situation discussed is distinguishable from the true *time-price* rule. Under the time-price rule a seller is permitted to charge a higher price for the land when he sells on credit than when he sells for cash. But if the seller, in addition to the sale price, makes a charge for the credit extended, and this charge exceeds the usury limits, this, according to some cases, creates usury. *State v. J.C. Penney Co.,* 179 NW2d 641 (Wis. 1970). In the true time-price situation the charge made for the credit is not separately stated.

This rule, to be sure, encounters philosophical difficulties. If the time-price rule is followed, the seller should, it is arguable, be able to manipulate either the sale price or the carrying charge, either the principal or the interest. *Mandelino v. Fribourg,* 23 NY2d 145, 295 NYS2d 654, 242 NE2d 823; *Manu-*

facturers Finance Co. v. Stone, 251 Ill.App. 414 (citing 27R.C.L.214); 45 Am. Jur.2d *Interest and Usury* § 123. Certainly the consequences are identical so far as the buyer is concerned. This argument is met, in part, by the counter-argument accepted by some courts that for a true time-price transaction, it is necessary that the seller explicitly reveal the two prices (cash price and credit price). 14 ALR3rd 1128. Of more relevance is the obvious fact that in this age of "consumerism" the time-price rule is under attack and its scope is being narrowed.

§ **161. Exempt transactions—purchase money mortgage.** Somewhat similar to the time-price sale is the purchase money mortgage situation.

EXAMPLE: In a state where 6% is the maximum rate, A offers to sell the land to B, at B's request, with the price payable over a ten-year period. He could offer a cash contract or an installment contract, and offer the option mentioned in the example above. Or he could offer a purchase money mortgage with a sale at $15,000, with the time-price differential represented by charging 10% instead of 6% on the purchase money mortgage. In other words, so far as the economics of the situation are concerned, the seller can raise his *price* for an installment sale, or leave the price alone and raise the *interest rate.* As usual, the courts struggle with this idea. The notion that a lender can go over the maximum rate simply because a sale is involved seems to trouble some courts. Economically it makes no difference whatever to the debtor whether you raise the *price* or the interest. At all events many decisions sustain the purchase money mortgage with the interest rate in excess of the statutory maximum. *Mandelino v. Fribourg,* 23 NY2d 145, 242 NE2d 828, 20 Syracuse L. Rev. 762; 91 CJS 591; 55 Am. Jur. 340; 45 Am. Jur. 2d 108.

§ **162. Charges—costs incurred by mortgagee—services actually rendered.** It may be stated as a general rule that additional charges by a lender for necessary expenditures incidental to making the loan or which constitute reasonable fees for services actually rendered by the lender to the borrower will not render the transaction usurious. Charges for appraisals, credit reports, surveys, costs of title search and title insurance, attorneys' fees for title work and the preparation of loan documents, hazard insurance premiums, and recording fees have been held acceptable because they are not payments made to the lender for the use of money and therefore are unrelated to the question of usury. *Union Central Life Insurance Co. v. Edwards,* 219 Ky. 748, 294 SW 502; Hershman, *Usury in the Tight Mortgage Market,* 22 Bus. Law, 333. The mere labeling of certain payments as service charges, however, will not alone insure the validity of such charges. The charges must be made for services actually rendered to the borrower and not intended merely to provide a vehicle for avoiding the usury laws. *New England Factors, Inc. v. Genstil,* 322 Mass. 36, 76 NE2d 151.

§ **163. Charges—commissions to lender.** Brokers, in negotiating loans of other people's money, may charge the borrower a commission, even though the loan bears the highest rate of interest allowed by law. Such a commission is compensation to the broker for his services in obtaining the loan.

EXAMPLE: *R*, who wishes to borrow $500,000 to erect an apartment building on his land, seeks out *B*, a broker. *B* arranges a loan for *R* with *E*, an insurance company with whom *B* has done business, at the statutory maximum of 8%. *B* charges a 2% commission for this service. This is perfectly legal. *R* pays more than 8% for this loan, but the excess is represented by genuine services and value.

A closer question is represented where the broker advances his own funds to the borrower, and later receives reimbursement by the lender. Some decisions appear to sustain the transaction. *Webb v. Southern Tr. Co.*, 227 Ky. 79, 11 SW2d 988; *Oliver v. United Mortgage Co.*, 230 A2d 722. *Contra*: *U.S. v. Desert Gold Mining Co.*, 282 FSupp. 614. But a commission charged directly or indirectly *by the lender himself* in addition to the highest rate of interest renders the loan usurious. It is perfectly obvious that such a commission is merely a device employed to disguise a usurious transaction.

EXAMPLE: *R* gave *E* a maximum rate mortgage of $65,000 but received only $50,000. The other $15,000 was divided between *E* and his broker. The loan was usurious. *National-Am. Life. Ins. Co. v. Bayou Country Club*, 16 Utah 2d 417, 403 P2d 26.

EXAMPLE: The loan is usurious where *R* hires *B*, a broker, *B* being a corporation whose stock is 50% owned by *E*, the mortgagee. *Modern Pioneers Ins. Co. v. Nandin*, Ariz. 437 P2d 658; *Roanoke Mtg. Co. v. Henritze*, 151 Va. 220, 144 SE 430.

There are some decisions, mostly older ones, in which, under various circumstances, courts have sanctioned payment of lender's commissions even though they took the interest over the usury rate. 52 ALR2d 729.

§ 164. Charges—standby commitments. At times a borrower arranges for a construction loan but has no commitment for permanent financing. In such situations, knowing that the construction lender will want to be paid off as soon as the construction is completed, the borrower may arrange for a *stand-by* commitment. This is a commitment by some lender to make the permanent loan upon the borrower's demand. Because this ties up the lender's funds with no real assurance that the loan will actually materialize, such a lender will charge a commitment fee that, if figured as interest, would make the loan usurious. Obviously these loans are not usurious. The commitment fee is not for interest. It is a charge made for a legitimate service, for the privilege of borrowing money later. *D & M Development Co. v. Sherwood & Roberts Inc.*, 93 Ida 200, 457 P2d 439; *United American Life Ins. Co. v. Willey*, 21 Utah 2d 279, 444 P2d 755; *Paley v. Barton S & L Assn.*, 82 NJS 75, 196 A2d 682; *Pivot City Realty Co. v. State Savings & Trust Co.*, 88 Ind. App. 222, 162 NE 27; *Regional Enterprises v. Teachers Assn.*, 352 F2d 768.

§ 165. Charges—late charges. Some mortgages provide that if the mortgagor defaults, the mortgagor must pay a sum, called a late charge, for the mortgagee's expenses, time, and trouble in sending out a notice of delinquency, computing additional interest, and so on. It is a definite nuisance for the lender to have this additional paper work. Most courts sustain reasonable late charges. *Brown v. Quality Finance Co.,* 112 Ga. 369, 145 SE2d 99; 91 CJS 609 Some state laws now limit the amount of late charges.

§ 166. Charges—FHA fees. There is additional paper work involved in FHA loans. Likewise, the lender must pay the premium for FHA insurance. Both these items can be charged to the borrower without making the loan usurious. *Silver Homes v. Marx,* 206 Tenn. 361, 333 SW2d 810; *Altherr v. Wilshire Mortgage Corp.,* 104 Ariz. 59, 448 P2d 859.

§ 167. Charges—commission to seller or his broker. There are two conflicting lines of decisions dealing with commissions paid to the seller or his broker.

EXAMPLE: *V* agrees to pay *E* $500 if he will make a loan of $20,000 to *P*, the purchaser at the maximum interest rate. The court held the charge legal. Usury was not present. *MacArthur v. Scheack,* 31 Wisc. 673. The philosophy here is that the usury law is for the protection of the borrower, and he is paying no more than the law allows.

Courts that hold such a charge usurious tend to emphasize that the lender is *receiving* more than the law allows, and this makes the loan usurious. *Pottle v. Lowe,* 99 Ga. 576, 27 SE 145.

Able lawyers argue that the loan should be held usurious on a different ground. The charge to the seller is usually passed along to the borrower in the form of a higher price for the house.

§ 168. Charges—points, service charges, origination charges overhead. In an effort to cloak usury, lenders make various charges, called "points," "service charge," "loan origination charge," and the like. If the charge is intended to cover general overhead costs of the lender (rental of space, payroll etc.), it is not legitimate. The lender cannot charge his overhead to the borrower in addition to the maximum rate of interest. *Winston v. Personal Finance,* 249 SW2d 315; *Strickler v. State Auto Finance Co.,* 220 Ark. 565, 249 SW2d 307. *Grady v. Price,* 94 Ariz. 252, 383 P2d 173. The philosophy here is that the law does not guarantee the lender that he will receive a net of 8%, if 8% is the statutory maximum. Every businessman has an overhead. Moreover, if the law limits the lender to charging items he pays to third parties, as for credit reports, there is some way of keeping a check on the matter. But how much could you reasonably allocate to overhead?

In addition to the highest rate allowed by law, a mortgage lender may seek to collect some additional charge. This may be in the form of a flat charge which is some percentage of the amount of the loan. If the charge is absorbed by the mortgagor, usury is present.

EXAMPLE: *A, a builder, is selling a home to B and XYZ is giving B a mortgage of $10,000 for 20 years at 6%. XYZ demands five "points." This means he will advance only $10,000 minus 5% thereof or $9,500, though he will expect to be repaid the full $10,000,00. That gives the lender a yield of 6.65%. If B absorbs the $500, the loan is usurious in states where 6% is the maximum interest that can be charged.*

If the charge is against the seller and the seller does not increase the price of his house to the buyer by reason of this charge, the problem becomes more difficult. In some states it will be considered that usury is present. *Bankers Gty. Title Co. v. Fischer,* 2 Ohio Misc. 18, 204 NE2d 103; *B.F. Saul Co. v. West End Park Co.,* 250 Md. 707, 246 A2d 591. In other states the contrary is true. In the philosophy of usury in some states, the attitude is that usury is intended as a protection to the borrower. If he pays no more than the highest rate allowed by law, usury is not present. In other states the view is that the lender should not be allowed to receive more than the highest rate regardless of who pays the excess.

In a number of states this practice is now regulated by law. In general the current attitude is that points provide a means of evading the usury laws and it seems likely that this practice will disappear in time.

§ 169. Charges—Construction loans. Where a lender disburses construction loan funds, obviously this involves more work than in the ordinary loan. Construction money is disbursed as the building goes up. As each payment is made, some inspection of the building is made by the lender to determine that work is in place warranting that particular disbursement. Also papers must be prepared whereby contractor and subcontractors relinquish mechanics liens against the property. Even though the mortgage carries the highest rate of interest allowed by law, the mortgage lender may charge an additional amount, if reasonable, for the burden of disbursing the construction loan. *Altherr v. Wilshire Mortgage Corp.,* 104 Ariz. 59, 448 P2d 859; *T & CO. v. Jensen,* 271 Ill.App. 419.

There is some danger in making a flat charge, say 1% of the face amount of the loan. Thus, 1% of a loan of $1,000,000 is much more than 1% of a loan of $100,000, and yet the paper work is much the same.

Moreover, the lender must charge interest only on money actually disbursed. He cannot charge interest, from the beginning, on the face amount of the loan. *Williamson v. Clark,* (Fla.), 120 So2d 637.

§ 170. Charges—Life insurance. A reasonable requirement of many lenders is that the mortgagor take out life insurance payable to the mortgagee, so that in case of his death funds will be available to retire the mortgage debt.

Most courts would sustain a provision of this sort. *Equitable Life Assur. Soc. v. Scali,* 38 Ill.2d 544, 232 NE2d 712. If the mortgagee is a life insurance company, the clause has a better chance of being sustained if the mortgagor is given the option of procuring the insurance in any acceptable life company. Statutes and court decisions tend to frown on *insurance coercion,* that is, forcing the mortgagor to buy insurance from the mortgagee.

§ 171. **Charges—interest paid by mortgagee to borrow funds from third party to lend to mortgagor.** If the mortgagee borrows from his own banker in order to raise funds to lend to the mortgagor, the decisions are in conflict as to the propriety of charging against the mortgagor the interest thus paid by the mortgagee. If so doing results in bringing the mortgagor's interest over the maximum, some courts find usury to be present. Other courts sanction the practice if the mortgagor is informed as to the source of the loan funds and consents that they be obtained in this fashion. 91 ALR2d 1389.

§ 172. **Charges—prepayment penalties—statutes.** It is obvious that prepayment penalties may operate harshly against the mortgagor, especially if prepayment is made in the early part of the loan. Like other charges, if these are spread over the actual life of the mortgage, they run up the cost of the loan to the borrower. For this reason, there is some tendency to limit these charges. *See* local statutes, as in Rhode Island.

§ 173. **Computational devices—discounts and add-on.** *Discount* and *add-on* loans are treated very briefly here for they are not common in real estate mortgaging.

EXAMPLE: In an *add-on* loan a borrower who borrows $100 has the interest (say 6%) added on immediately, so that his monthly or weekly payments include payments on a principle of $106 rather than one of $100. Obviously the yield to the lender is in excess of 6%. Indeed, it is in the neighborhood of 11%.

EXAMPLE: In a *discount* loan the borrower who borrows $100 at say 6% is given only $100 minus 6% of $100 or $94, though he pays interest on $100. The result is that the yield to the lender is increased to the neighborhood of 11 1/2 percent.

To the extent that devices of this sort are sustained they are sustained in the case of short-term loans, usually one-year or less and on the basis of custom.

As you can see, if either method were used in the typical long-term real estate mortgage loan the results would be fantastic. What would the borrower receive in a 20-year loan if all the interest were deducted in advance as in the discount method?

EXAMPLE: On 20-year loan of $20,000 at 6% figured in the normal way, that is, with a monthly payment first applied to interest, balance in principal, the total payments at the end of 20 years amount to roughly $34,400. Thus the borrower has paid, over the life of the loan, interest amounting to $34,400 minus

$20,000 or $14,400. If this amount were deducted at the inception of the loan the borrower would receive only $5,600. This illustrates why this method is not permitted in long-term financing.

§ 174. Computational devices—declining balances. Since most mortgage loans are amortized, that is, periodic, usually monthly, payments are made to retire the loan, it is necessary that the interest be computed on the declining balance. The correct rule is that the mortgagee must calculate the interest whenever a payment is made. The payments are applied in payment of the interest. The balance is applied in reduction of the principal. Subsequent interest calculations are on the principal. This is the *United States Rule, Story v. Livingston,* 38 U.S. 359; 47 CJS *Interest* § 66. If the lender continues to compute interest on the original amount of the loan, this results in usury if the amount of interest thus exacted brings the interest over the statutory maximum. 18 So. Cal.L.Rev. 275.

§ 175. Computational devices—compensating balances. A commercial bank often will require its borrower to keep a portion of the loan funds on deposit with the bank. Theoretically this is to be applied in payment of the loan.

EXAMPLE: *E* loans $100,000 to *R* but requires *R* to leave $15,000 of the loan proceeds with *E* for one year, the life of the loan. This is the same as loaning *R* $85,000 but charging interest on $100,000. The yield to *E* obviously exceeds the maximum. Yet the courts permit this. 45 Am. Jur. 2d 100. *Contra:* 12 ALR 1422.

§ 176. Computational devices—spreading theory. In general, when the loan calls for interest close to the statutory maximum, and the lender makes charges that legally must be considered to be part of the interest (lender's commission, for example, or lender's service charges for his overhead), these charges are spread over the life of the loan. For example, if the loan is a 20-year loan, payable monthly, you divide these charges into parts, allocable equally to each monthly payment. If they do not bring the monthly payment over the usury level, usury is not present. 91 CJS 603; 16 Bus. Law. 181.

In actual practice, courts use somewhat varying methods in making the computations under the spreading theory.

The following are helpful decisions discussing methods of computation: *Wilson v. Connor,* 106 Fla. 6, 142 So 606; *Smith v. Persons,* 55 Minn. 520, 57 NW 311; *Garland v. Union Trust Co.,* 63 Okla.243, 165 P 197.

§ 177. Computational problems—prepayment. Many mortgages bearing the maximum interest rate contain provisions for the payment of an additional sum, sometimes called a *prepayment penalty* or *prepayment premium,* if the borrower chooses to prepay the mortgage debt. In the past this has been considered unobjectionable. The theoretical justification is that this is wholly optional with the borrower. If he lets the loan run its full course, he incurs no prepayment penalty. Hence he should not be able to charge the lender with usury simply because he chooses to prepay the loan. *Shalet v. Investors S. & L. Assn.,* 101 N.JSupp 283, 244 A2d 151; 130 ALR 73; 75 ALR2d 1265. But this reasoning is specious. People prepay out of necessity, as where an employee is transferred to another area. This economic compulsion to prepay the loan makes it unfair, it is thought by some, to saddle the mortgagor with these additional payments. Moreover, if the borrower has paid a lender's commission, it is unfair, some argue, to stick the borrower with the entire commission if he is compelled to prepay the loan in its early stages. There is some trend, therefore, toward compelling the lender to forego that part of the prepayment penalty that causes yield to exceed the usury rate. Both statutes and court decisions are likely to go in this direction.

§ 178. **Computational problems—acceleration.** The general rule is that acceleration does not cause usury. An explanation is needed. Suppose in an 8% state R borrows $20,000 from E at $7\frac{7}{8}$% on a mortgage loan for 20 years with a two-point lender's commission, that is, a commission of 2% of $20,000 or $400. Spread this $400 over the life of the loan under the spreading theory and the interest is still under 8%. But if R defaults on his first payment and E accelerates, it is obvious that the $400 spread over the one-month life of the loan brings the yield up over 8%. Nevertheless the loan is not deemed usurious, because R theoretically has control of the situation. All he has to do is make his payments in time and the yield is kept under 8%. This is unrealistic. Borrowers rarely default voluntarily. Necessity causes defaults, mostly illness, unemployment, and family trouble. In recognition of this fact statutes are being enacted making the excess interest uncollectible. Florida arrives at this result by case law.

§ 179. **Equity participation.** There is a growing feeling on the part of the big lenders that since they are taking a substantial risk in lending money on new ventures, they should receive a share of the profits. This concept is variously referred to as "equity participation," "a piece of the action," or the "kicker." The question of usury has arisen. Unfortunately, there is little reliable law in this area.

If the transaction is one that is exempt from the usury laws, no problem is presented.

EXAMPLE: The borrower is a corporation in a state where corporations are not subject to the usury laws.

EXAMPLE: The lender is a bank in a state where bank lenders are exempt from the usury laws.

EXAMPLE: The loan is a business loan in a state in which business loans are exempt from the usury laws.

But if the transaction is not exempt from the usury laws, the loan calls for the maximum interest rate, and also for a share of the earnings of the venture, then there is some law to the effect that usury is present. 16 ALR3rd 482.

If the loan is not unconditionally repayable, and repayment of the principal is dependent upon the success of the venture, so that the lender is running an actual risk of loss of his investment, the loan is not subject to the usury laws. *Marsch v. Smith,* 262 Wis. 75, 53 NW2d 769; *Owens v. Connelly,* 77 Ariz. 349, 272 P2d 345, 16 ALR3rd 486; 42 Cal.L.Rev. 198.

If, for example, the business of the borrower is such that profits are highly conjectural, the courts incline toward holding the situation to be free from usury. *Beavers v. Taylor,* 434 SW2d 230 (Tex. Civ. App.).

And if the lender is to share in the profits only in the case some event occurs that is theoretically under the borrower's control, there is authority for the view that usury is not present. *United Am. Ins. Co. v. Willey,* 21 Utah 2d 279, 444 P2d 755.

EXAMPLE: *R*'s mortgage to *E* provides that if *R* is in default for six consecutive months, then, when business goes back to a profitable basis, *R* must pay *E* one-third of the net profits. Some courts would hold this non-usurious.

And if the lender is to receive no interest, but only a share of the profits, again there is authority for the view that usury is not present. *Dublin v. Veal* (Ky.) 341 SW2d 776. The lender is running the risk that he will receive no return at all. The problem here of course, relates to the situation of a loan to a business that has been highly profitable over a long period of time. Here the prospect of loss may be small. Nevertheless even such businesses have lean times. The fact that they continue to pay dividends is immaterial. Dividends may be paid out of corporate surplus even when the corporation is losing money. But in the situation discussed here the lender gets no return at all if the business has a losing streak.

But if the event that will cause the lender to lose his principal is remote and unlikely to occur, or the loss to be suffered is slight compared with the anticipated profit, usury may be present. *American Ins. Life v. Regenold,* 243 Ark. 906, 423 SW2d 551. Risk of loss that will take the loan out of the usury law must be a risk substantially greater than that involved in the typical mortgage situation.

If the loan calls for interest less than the statutory maximum, with a share of the profits, but in no case is the annual return to exceed the maximum interest rate, most lawyers feel that the usury law is not violated. 103 ALR. 86.

At times a transaction is cast in the form of a sale and leaseback on the theory that "kickers" in the form of additional *rent* are not *interest*. But if this is combined with some other feature, such as a contract by the lessee to buy the property back, there is the chance that the transaction might be viewed as a disguised loan and therefore subject to the usury laws. *See* Chapter 32.

§ 180. **Equity participation—joint ventures.** Where the lender in addition to making the loan insists on becoming a joint venturer with the borrower there is a definite possibility that the return to the lender may exceed the statutory maximum. Since this is a commonplace situation today it becomes necessary to give a brief description of a joint venture. A partnership is a business association so well-known that it requires no description here. A joint venture is like a partnership except that it is formed for one venture only. A partnership is a continuing relationship and contemplates a succession of transactions. A joint venture is limited to one transaction such as the erection and operation of one office building. Where the lender joins his borrower in a joint venture a usury problem is presented.

EXAMPLE: R goes to E for a loan of $10,000,000 to erect an office building. E agrees to make the loan and the mortgage is signed by R. Immediately the property is conveyed to a joint venture consisting of R and E. The total return to E may exceed the statutory maximum. Nevertheless, as in any business transaction, there may be no profit. Indeed, there may be a loss. This has prompted some courts to hold that usury is not present. *Salver v. Havivi*, 215 NYS2d 913. Even if R gives his guarantee to E that E would suffer no loss, some courts feel usury is not present. *Leibovici v. Rawicki*, 290 NYS2d 997. After all, this promise is not binding on the creditors of the joint venture, who may well decide to pursue E. *See also* Chapter 33.

Nevertheless, questions remain, and some life companies that go into joint ventures because they seek equity positions that provide a hedge against inflation refuse to make the mortgage loan. They insist that the joint venture borrow from some other lender.

In equity participation situations, if the granting of a mortgage loan is conditioned on acquisition by the lender of a joint venture interest for less than its value, it has been argued that there is present in essence the same problem involved where a lender contemporaneously buys another asset from the borrower for less than its value. *See* § 182.

§ 181. **Disguised loans—purchase and resale.** There is a class of cases that lends itself to the charge that a disguised mortgage exists. Nevertheless the transactions are not mortgage transactions.

EXAMPLE: A finds a tract of land for sale that he believes offers a good business opportunity. He persuades B to put up the sale price for the property. B buys the property and becomes the owner. He immediately enters into an installment contract to sell the land to A. Usually the price is higher than the sale price to B. This is a true purchase and resale. It is not a mortgage transaction. Notice that A never had any interest in the property until he got it through B. This is the distinguishing characteristic. *Stark v. Bauer Cooperage Co.*, 3 F2d 214. See Chapter 27.

Suppose that *A* owns some real estate worth $20,000 and is in need of funds. He goes to *B*. *B* arranges to have *A* make a deed to *B*. *B* pays *A* $10,000 for the deed. *B* now enters into an installment contract to sell the land back to *A* for $12,000, the installments bearing the highest legal rate of interest permitted in the state. It is evident that this is a disguised mortgage transaction. The purpose is to give *B* a bonus of $2,000 dollars over and above the highest legal rate of interest. *Hausler v. Nuccio,* 39 So2d 734.

EXAMPLE: *A,* being in need of funds, goes to *B*. *B* takes a deed from *A*, giving *A* $10,000. *B* also gives *A* an option to buy the property back for $12,000. The property is worth $20,000. It is perfectly clear that this is nothing but a loan transaction. Corbin, *Contracts* § 1501.

Obviously here we have two problems, namely: (1) Is the deed really a deed absolute in the nature of a mortgage? (2) If it is, is usury present?

The question intrudes itself into the sale and leaseback situation and the sale and buy-back. *See* Chapters 31 and 32.

§ 182. Disguised loans—sale for more or less than true value. This problem can best be explained by illustrations.

EXAMPLE: *R* borrows from *E* on a mortgage on Lot 1 and contemporaneously sells Lot 2 to *E* at a price far less than its value. Usury may be present. 91 CJS 589-592.

EXAMPLE: *R* borrows from *E* on a mortgage on Lot 1 and contemporaneously buys Lot 2 from *E* at a price greater than its value. Usury may be present.

§ 183. Brundage clause. If the mortgage contains a clause requiring the borrower to pay any tax that may be imposed on the mortgagee's mortgage, this, in some states, makes the loan usurious if the tax thus imposed, plus interest, carries the borrower's rate of payment over the statutory maximum. 22 Bus. Law. 343; 21 ALR 883; 91 CJS 635. If, however, the clause simply provides that the mortgagee may accelerate if such law is passed, it is valid.

§ 184. Negotiable instruments. If the note is a negotiable note, a holder in due course will be able to enforce it free from any claim of usury practised by the original lender. 91 CJS 736. There are a few states (Illinois and Minnesota, for example) that do not treat the mortgage as negotiable simply because it secures a negotiable note. *See* § 192. In those states usury would be a good defense even as against a holder in due course.

§ 185. Waiver of defenses—estoppel. While a waiver of defenses is quite effective in protecting an assignee of a mortgage against defenses available to the mortgagor (*see* § 193), there is a conflict of authority as to the defenses to protect an assignee of the mortgage against the mortgagor's claim of usury. Under one view a waiver of defenses signed contemporaneously with the usurious mortgage is ineffective. *Hall v. Mortgage Security Corp.,* 119 W. Va. 140, 192

SE 145; *Trinity Fire Ins. Co. v. Kerrville Hotel Co.,* (Tex. Civ. App.) 103 SW2d 121, 110 ALR 442; *Marks v. Pope,* 289 Ill.App. 558; 31 CJS *Estoppel* § 81. In other states the waiver of defenses seems effective in this situation. *Weyh v. Boylan,* 85 N.Y. 394, 39 ALR 669. See § 193.

There are a few decisions holding that if a borrower initiates the loan transaction, including its usurious aspects, he will not be permitted to take advantage of his own wrong, and will not be permitted to raise the defense of usury. 16 ALR3rd 510, 513. This rule should be applied only when other circumstances are present, as where a lawyer-borrower entraps a lender-client.

§ 186. Right of junior mortgagee to attack usurious first mortgage. Some cases hold that a junior mortgagee cannot attack a first mortgage on the ground of usury. 121 ALR 879. Other courts permit such an attack. In those jurisdictions in which a junior mortgagee has the right to set up usury in a senior mortgage, it has been held that it is a condition precedent to his exercise of such right, in order to obtain affirmative relief, that he do equity by tendering or paying the amount actually advanced by the senior mortgagee. To this effect are *Carter v. Dennison,* 7 Gill (Md.) 157, and *Stuart Court Realty Corp. v. Gillespie,* 150 Va. 515, 143 SE 741, 59 ALR 334.

§ 187. Right of assuming grantee to attack mortgage on grounds of usury. Many decisions refuse to permit an assuming grantee (*see* § 273) to attack the mortgage he has assumed on the ground that it is usurious. 82 ALR 1153. The philosophy here is that whatever commissions, points or other charges were exacted of the mortgagor that brought the yield to the mortgagee over the usury rate caused damage to the mortgagor but certainly did not enter into the purchase price willingly paid by the grantee. Since the grantee has not been harmed, he cannot take advantage of usury that harmed only the mortgagor. 2 Glenn, *Mortgages,* 1213. A like rule applies where the grantee takes subject to the mortgage but does not assume. To this general rule there is at least one exception. A number of cases recognize the proposition that the purchaser of property charged with a usurious mortgage debt may plead the usury as a defense or as a ground of relief when he is so joined in the defense by the mortgagor, although he purchased subject to the mortgage, or expressly assumed the mortgage debt.

§ 188. Conflicts. There will be instances where the laws of several states have some bearing on the mortgage transaction, and the usury rates and laws of these states may differ. This brings up a problem of *conflicts of law.*

EXAMPLE: R, who lives in *State A,* executes a mortgage in *State B,* where E, the mortgagee, resides and where the debt is payable. The debt is payable in *State B.* The mortgaged land is located in *State C.* Here the mortgage foreclosure must be filed in *State C,* where the land lies, but the question that arises in that state is, by what state laws should the validity of the transaction be judged? Suppose the mortgage calls for a rate of interest that would be permitted only in *State B*. The great majority of the courts in this country would apply the law of *State B*. The validity of a mortgage will be sustained against the charge of usury if it provides for a rate of interest that is permitted by the general usury law of any state with which the mortgage contract has a substantial relationship. This is in obedience to the principle that the courts will usually select the laws of that state whose laws sustain the validity of the contract. *Trinidad Indust. Bank v. Romero*, (N.M.) 466 P2d 568; 45 Am. Jur. 2d *Interest and Usury* § 20. This is subject to an exception that the mortgage will not be sustained if it is a particularly raw one; that is, a mortgage that calls for a rate of interest substantially in excess of that permitted by the state where the foreclosure suit is filed. *Bridgemen v. Gateway Ford Truck Sales*, 296 FSupp. 233.

A mortgagee would be best advised by resorting to a companion principle, namely, that if there are several states that have some substantial connection with the mortgage loan, as in the example given above, the parties, as long as they are acting in good faith and not for the purpose of evading the usury laws, are at liberty to stipulate in the mortgage and note that it will be governed by the laws of some one of these states, and the courts will be guided by that stipulation, except, again, that the foreclosing court will not enforce a mortgage that it finds offensive, such as one calling for an interest rate far in excess of that permitted under local law. But the great majority of the cases will follow the rule that the parties can agree on the state whose law will govern the transaction. 125 ALR 483.

While conflicts law involving real estate often defers to the law of the situs of the land, this is not true of conflicts law relating to mortgages. Often the courts apply the law of a state other than the state where the land is located. 125 ALR 497.

Where we are concerned with a usury exception relating to the *mortgagee*, generally the rule is that the state law granting this exception will be honored only in that state.

EXAMPLE: In *State A* banks making loans are exempted from the operation of the usury laws. *E*, a bank incorporated in that state, makes a mortgage loan on land in *State B*. *State B* does not have such an exemption in favor of state banks. *State B* will not allow *E* to exceed the interest maximum permitted in *State B*. If it did not follow this rule, banks formed outside of *State B* would enjoy a competitive advantage over local banks. This, obviously, *State B* cannot permit. *Continental Adjustment Corp. v. Klause*, 12 N.J. Misc. 703, 705 (Dist. Ct. 1934); *E.C. Warner Co. v. W.B. Foshay Co.*, 57 F2d 656, 661 (8th Cir. 1932); *Falls v. United States Sav. Loan & Bldg. Co.*, 97 Ala. 417, 422, 13 So 25, 27 (1892); *Rhodes v. Missouri Sav. & Loan Co.*, 173 Ill. 621, 628, 50 NE 998, 1000 (1898); *Meroney v. Altanta Bldg. & Loan Ass'n*, 116 N.C. 882, 889, 21 SE 924, 926 (1895); *Washington Nat'l Bldg. Loan & Inv. Ass'n v. Stanley*, 38 Ore. 319, 341, 63 P. 489, 495 (1901).

On the other hand, where the exemption relates to the *mortgagor*, such as one exempting corporations from the usury laws, a corporation formed in such a state will be allowed to contract for any rate of interest in any other state in which it borrows money. Its exemption from the usury laws, in most states, follows it from state to state. *Cooper v. Cherokee Village Development Co.,* 236 Ark. 37, 364 SW2d 158; 63 ALR2d 960; 24 Bus.Law. 1121; 68 Colum.L.Rev. 1390.

Increasingly, states seem inclined to enact statutes setting forth their conflict of law policies.

ADDITIONAL LOCAL REFERENCES: 18 Stanf. L Rev. 381; 8 U.C.L.A. L. Rev. 555; 34 Conn. B. J. 296; 32 *id.* 220; 24 U. Miami L. Rev. 642; 14 Loyola L. Rev. 301 (La.); 27 Md. L. Rev. 252; 21 Minn. L. Rev. 585; 38 Miss. L. J. 347; 8 Ala. L. Rev. 431 (Miss.); 24 Mo. L. Rev. 225; 26 *id.* 217; 40 Neb. L. Rev. 433; 6 Rutgers L. Rev. 568 (N.J.); 38 Banking L. J. 409 (N.Y.); 24 Fordham L. Rev. 715 (N.Y.); 47 N.C. L. Rev. 761; 21 S.C. L. Rev. 206; 27 Tenn. L. Rev. 403; 22 S.W.L.J. 223 (Tex.); 71 W. Va. L. Rev. 326; 1963 Wisc. L. Rev. 515.

ADDITIONAL GENERAL REFERENCES: Anderson, *Tight Money Real Estate Financing,* 24 U. of Miami L. Rev. 642; Altman, *Lender Participation in Borrower's Venture,* 8 Houston L. Rev. 546.

15

Assignment of Mortgage

§ 189. In general. A mortgage is assignable. The mortgage cannot be assigned except in connection with a sale of the mortgage debt. The reason is that the mortgage exists only for the purpose of securing payment of the mortgage debt, and a person who does not own the mortgage debt can have no reason for obtaining the ownership of mortgage.

Whatever is sufficient to transfer the mortgage debt will transfer a mortgage given to secure it. The reason is that the debt secured by the mortgage is the principal thing and the mortgage is a mere security for its payment. Osborne, *Mortgages* § 231. Thus, if a regular mortgage secures a promissory note, a transfer of the note, for example by mere delivery of a bearer note, without any assignment of the mortgage, will give the purchaser of the note a right to foreclose the mortgage on default.

§ 190. Recording of assignment. The rule just stated is of little practical importance. In connection with any regular mortgage that is being assigned, an assignment of the mortgage must be executed and recorded because of the *release rule.*

EXAMPLE: *R* gives a mortgage to *E. E* assigns the note and mortgage to *A*, but no assignment is recorded. Conspiring to defraud *A*, *R* and *E* now work up a deal under which *E* executes and records a release of the mortgage. Because there is no recorded assignment, this looks, upon the records, like a perfectly good release of the mortgage. *R* sells and conveys the land to *P*, who is an innocent purchaser having no knowledge of the unrecorded assignment. The mortgage is extinguished. 2 Jones, *Mortgages*, 393, 430; 89 ALR 184. This rule is often called the *release rule.* It is an important rule. An assignment of mortgage must be recorded. Glenn, *Mortgages* § 338; Osborne, *Mortgages*, 477.

116

EXAMPLE: The facts are as in the preceding example, except that instead of a *deed* to P, we find R giving a mortgage to P, who is an innocent mortgagee. P will have a first lien on the land, paramount to E's lien.

In most states the rule that a recorded release deed protects an innocent purchaser gives no protection to one *making payment* of a mortgage debt. *See* § 439.

In connection with apparent merger, a problem arises that is akin to the wrongful release rule.

EXAMPLE: *R* makes a mortgage to E. E assigns the mortgage to A, but the assignment is not recorded. E concocts a fraudulent scheme. He buys the land from R and receives a deed from R. Now the public records show both the land and mortgage as being owned by E and to all appearances a merger has taken place. E now sells and conveys the land to P, an innocent purchaser. Some courts will protect P, and hold that the mortgage has been extinguished. *McCormick v. Bauer,* 122 Ill. 573, 13 NE 852; *Landis v. Robacker,* 313 Pa. 271, 169 A 891; 89 ALR 171, 104 ALR 1304; 29 Ill. L. Rev. 121; 82 U. Pa. L. Rev. 547.

Some courts, however, say that a recorded release deed is necessary for the release rule to operate, and will not protect the innocent purchaser who relies merely on an apparent merger of the mortgage in the title to the land. *Zorn v. Van Buskirk,* 111 Okla. 211, 239 P 151; 2 Glenn, *Mortgages,* 1422; Osborne, *Mortgages* § 276.

The same sort of problem may arise in connection with a foreclosure of the mortgage.

EXAMPLE: *R* makes a mortgage to E. E assigns the mortgage to A, but the assignment is not recorded. E goes through a foreclosure of the mortgage. At the foreclosure sale, the land is sold to P, an innocent purchaser. P is protected. He becomes the owner of the land and the mortgage is extinguished even though A receives nothing. *Huitink v. Thompson,* 95 Minn. 392, 104 NW 237.

The same problem may arise in connection with other types of court proceedings:

EXAMPLE: *R* makes a mortgage to E. E assigns to A but the assignment is not recorded. The city of X files a condemnation suit against the mortgaged land. R and E are made parties to the condemnation suit. A is not made a party, because the assignment to him has not been recorded. The mortgagee's share of the condemnation award is paid to E. The city has good title to the land and the mortgage is extinguished. *First National Bank v. Paris,* 358 Ill. 378, 193 NE 207; 1 Jones, *Mortgages,* 817; 89 ALR 182.

§ 191. Notice of assignment. Because of the various rules involved in connection with payment of the mortgage debt, it is also a practical necessity for the assignee of a mortgage to give the mortgagor personal notice of the assignment.

EXAMPLE: *E*, mortgagee, assigns a mortgage securing a non-negotiable note to *A*, who fails to record his assignment. The mortgage and note are delivered to *A*. *R* makes full payment to *E*. Is this payment good against *A*? It can be argued that *A* was negligent in not recording his assignment and in failing to serve personal notice on *R*. As against this, it can be argued that *R* paid without requiring production of the mortgage paper. Probably most courts would hold for *R*, on the ground that the assignment of a mortgage is not complete until notice of the assignment has been given the debtor. 5 Tiffany, *Real Property*, 495; 496; 29 Colum. Law Rev. 61, 62. It is the general rule that where a mortgage is given to secure a non-negotiable instrument, the mortgagor, until notice of the assignment, is entitled to deal with the mortgagee or his personal representative on the supposition that no transfer has been made. 89 ALR 191. The mortgagor's neglect to call for production of the mortgage paper can be excused on the ground that such paper is not always readily available. *Buehler v. McCormick*, 169 Ill. 269, 48 NE 287. Also, it is easy for the assignee to serve notice on the mortgagor, and thus protect himself. A contrary result has been reached in a few cases on the ground that a party making a *final* payment is negligent in not requiring production of the document paid. This rule has been criticized. 5 Tiffany, *Real Property*, 495, 496.

This and kindred problems will be more fully developed in the chapter on payment. *See* Chapter 37.

§ 192. Mortgage securing negotiable note. Shortly before the Civil War, in an effort to give the purchaser of a mortgage better protection than he had enjoyed in the past, American mortgage bankers began the experiment of having the mortgage secure a negotiable note. The experiment proved highly successful. In all states except Illinois, Minnesota, and Ohio, it is now the rule that a holder in due course of a negotiable note secured by a mortgage, that is, one who buys the note and mortgage in good faith before the debt is overdue and without knowledge of any infirmities, takes the mortgage as well as the note, free from defenses that would have been available to the mortgagor against the original mortgagee. The theory is that negotiable notes, like money, should pass freely from hand to hand, without the necessity of an inquiry by purchasers thereof as to the possible invalidity of the paper. And since the mortgage is a mere security for the note, it should enjoy the same protection that the law accords to the note. 127 ALR 190.

EXAMPLE: *R* gave *E* a mortgage securing a negotiable note for $50,000, but never received any money from *E*. *E* sold the note and mortgage to *A* before the due date of the note. *A* can foreclose the mortgage even though *R* never received the mortgage money. As an innocent purchaser of a negotiable note, *A* is protected against any defenses that exist between *R* and *E*.

In some states (Illinois, Minnesota, and Ohio, for example) the fact that the mortgage secures a negotiable note does not impart the quality of negotiability to the mortgage. 127 ALR 206.

Many unsophisticated persons have suffered at the hands of unscrupulous merchandisers or home improvement companies. These enterprises have the consumer or homeowner sign a negotiable note which is immediately transferred to a finance company as a holder in due course. If the consumer complains about defective merchandise or shoddy workmanship, the finance company claims it is a holder in due course with no knowledge of this defense. Often all the forms signed by the consumer or homeowner are those furnished by the finance company. The finance company often is quite familiar with the operations of the merchandiser or home improvement company. There is slowly building up a body of law that refuses to protect the finance company against the defense of shoddy merchandise or defective home improvements. 11 Boston College Ind. and Comm. L. Rev. 90; *Fin. Credit Corp. v. Williams,* 246 Md. 575, 229 A2 712. This trend is likely to continue.

§ 193. **Waiver of defenses.** In a minority of the states the rule that a negotiable note imparts the quality of negotiability to the mortgage is not followed. 138 ALR 566, 576. Even in states that follow the majority rule, events may occur that may deprive the assignee of the benefits of negotiability. For example, installment notes are commonplace today. In some states the fact that at the time of the purchase of the note some prior installment was unpaid may prevent the purchaser from being a holder in due course. 170 ALR 1029. For these reasons the mortgagee's attorney will probably require the mortgagor to sign a *waiver of defenses,* also sometimes called a *declaration of no set-off* or an *estoppel certificate.* This document is commonly addressed *To All Whom It May Concern,* and recites that the mortgagor has no defenses to the enforcement of the mortgage or mortgage note. This constitutes a representation made to any subsequent purchaser of the note, is intended to be relied upon by the purchaser, and when so relied upon creates an estoppel. 2 Jones, *Mortgages* § 792; 59 CJS *Mortgages* § 369; 31 CJS *Estoppel* § 81; 51 ALR2d 886, 894. Thus, through the operation of estoppel, defenses good between the mortgagor and mortgagee, such as the defense of absence of consideration, are unavailing as to the assignee.

The purpose of a waiver of defenses is to dispense with personal inquiry by a purchaser of the mortgage as to whether there is any equity or defense. Thus the party giving such declaration will ordinarily be estopped to assert any defense or equity against an assignee who purchases the mortgage on the faith of it, but such declaration will not operate as an estoppel where the assignee had actual notice of the defense or equity or where the circumstances under which he became assignee were such as to put him on inquiry. *Quigley v. Breyer Corporation,* 362 Pa. 139, 66 A2d 286.

The practical effect of a waiver of defenses is to give the assignee a legally enforceable mortgage even though the mortgage does not secure a negotiable note and the mortgagee could not have foreclosed. For example, if the mortgagee had paid out no money or had received payment in full, he could not foreclose. But an assignee who receives a waiver of defenses can foreclose, since he received the mortgagor's written assurance that the mortgage is valid and enforceable. 59 CJS 531; 110 ALR 457.

EXAMPLE: *R* gave *E* a mortgage securing a note for $50,000. *R* also signed at this time a waiver of defenses reciting that he had received all the mortgage money and had no defenses to the enforcement of the mortgage. This is commonplace. Mortgagors sign all papers that mortgagees place before them. *R* never receives any money from *E*. *E* sold and assigned the note and mortgage to *A* before the due date of the note. *E* also delivered to *A* the waiver of defenses signed by *R*. *A* can foreclose the mortgage even though *R* never received the mortgage money. As an innocent purchaser relying on a waiver of defenses, *A* is protected against any defenses that exist between *R* and *E*.

The waiver of defenses is quite effective in protecting the assignee against most defenses the mortgagor may assert, such as lack of consideration for the mortgage. With respect to *usury,* the situation is somewhat more complex. It has been said that an assignee of a mortgage taking it in good faith with no knowledge of usury is protected against the defenses of usury by a waiver of defenses executed at the time of the mortgage. 91 CJS 739; 110 ALR 457. However, there are other authorities indicating that where the defense of usury is involved the waiver of defenses must be executed at the time of assignment. 31 CJS 293, *Estoppel* § 81; 21 CJ 1144. The philosophy underlying this last statement is that the mortgagor, having already received the mortgage funds, is under no compulsion to execute the waiver of defenses at the time of the assignment and therefore does so voluntarily, whereas his necessities may compel him to execute almost any document when he first applies for the mortgage loan. *Marks v. Pope,* 289 Ill.App. 558. *See also* § 185.

§ **194. Mechanics of assignment.** In the case of a regular mortgage, it is necessary to execute an assignment, which is a brief form providing that the mortgagee, the assignor, transfers and assigns the mortgage and mortgage note to the purchaser thereof, the assignee. The mortgage is identified by a recital of the names of the parties thereto, its date, the recording date, the book and page of the record where the mortgage is recorded, and so on. The assignment should be signed by the mortgagee, acknowledged, delivered to the assignee, and recorded. The mortgage note, too, should be endorsed or delivered to the assignee. The assignee should also receive the original mortgage.

The mortgage cannot be assigned except in connection with a sale of the mortgage debt. The reason for this is that the mortgage exists only for the purpose of securing payment of the mortgage debt, and a person who does not own the mortgage debt can have no reason for obtaining the mortgage. Thus the assignee of the mortgage must insist on receiving the mortgage note, since if the mortgagee has already transferred the mortgage note to someone else, he can no longer make a valid assignment of the mortgage.

For reasons stated elsewhere in this chapter, the intending assignee should make a check of the public records to make sure that no prior assignment has been recorded. *See* § 198.

There is a special problem with respect to federal liens. A mortgage is personal property. As to a mortgage, therefore, a federal lien for taxes owing by its owner is valid if filed in the county of the owner's domicile. *Badway v. U.S.,* 367 F2d 22. Hence an intending assignee of a mortgage must search the records of federal liens in this county. This is not necessary where the mortgagee secures a negotiable note and the assignee becomes a holder in due course.

The assignee should also give personal notice to the mortgagor of the assignment.

Other documents, such as the fire insurance, assignment of leases and rents, and the like should also be assigned to the assignee.

§ 195. **Defective assignments.** Since an assignment of a mortgage strikes the average layman as a rather informal transaction, countless defects and informalities occur in these documents, notably lack of acknowledgments and witnesses. Many states have enacted laws curing these defects. Basye, *Clearing Land Titles* § 353.

§ 196. **Equities—latent equities.** In contrast to the well-settled rule that an assignee of a debt secured by a mortgage takes subject to the equities of the *obligor,* it is a matter of dispute as to how far an assignee is subject to equities of *third persons. Latent equities* embrace those equities which are secret and undisclosed at the time of the assignment of the mortgage residing either in some prior assignor or in some third party, a stranger to the assignment. Put more briefly, a latent equity is one that cannot be discovered by inquiry of the mortgagor. The question whether the transferee of a debt secured by a mortgage, takes it, with the benefit of the mortgage security, free from equities in favor of persons other than the mortgage debtor, is determined by the general rule prevailing in that jurisdiction as to the rights of assignees of choses in action. The majority view is that a bona fide assignee for value and without notice of such latent equities takes free of them. 59 CJS 288.

There is some disagreement, it is true, among the authorities as to the extent to which a bona fide assignee is protected against latent equities of third persons. 20 U. Chi.L.Rev. 699. However, the authorities appear to be in agreement that where a chose in action is represented by a document, the surrender of which is required for the enforcement of the right representative by the document, then a bona fide assignee is protected against the latent equities of third persons. *Ibid.* It is currently arguable that a mortgage and mortgage note fall in this category. Therefore it is important that persons seeking to enforce equities against the mortgage and mortgage note protect themselves against applications of this rule.

EXAMPLE: A first mortgage is being subordinated to a new mortgage now being placed on the property. The two mortgagees enter into a subordination agreement which is recorded in the recorder's office. Suppose, however, that the subordinated mortgage is later assigned to a bona fide purchaser who purchases the same in reliance upon the evidence of title brought down only to the date of the recording of that particular mortgage. Such purchaser would not be aware of the subordination agreement. Under the rule given above, this purchaser might very well take free and clear of the subordination. *Chatten v. Knoxville Tr. Co.*, 154 Tenn. 345, 289 SW 536; 56ALR 537. It is therefore advisable that the subordination be noted as a legend on the promissory note and on the mortgage so that anyone purchasing the same can see from the face of the instruments that a subordination has taken place.

§ 197. Assignment of deed of trust. One purpose served by the deed of trust is that of facilitating transfer of the mortgage. Quite often the deed of trust secures a negotiable note payable to bearer. Here the common understanding is that sale and physical delivery of the deed of trust and note to the purchaser is all that is needed to effect a transfer of the mortgage to the purchaser. Under the *incident theory,* the debt is the chief thing, and the mortgage but an incident, so that the purchaser of the note acquires the mortgage and the right to enforce it. This, indeed, is the law in most states. *LeBurn v. Prosise,* 197 Md. 466, 79 A2d 543; Osborne, *Mortgages* § 239.

Additional reasons for this rule can be marshalled. In the case of a mortgage, a release thereof will be executed by the mortgagee and will protect an innocent purchaser of the land unless an assignment of the mortgage, if one was executed, has been recorded. *See* § 190. But in the case of a deed of trust the release deed will, in nearly all states, be executed by the trustee, so that recording of the assignment serves no useful purpose so far as the release rule is concerned. *Foster v. Augustana College,* 92 Okla. 96, 218 P 335, 37 ALR 854.

Moreover, so far as payment problems are concerned, it would be folly for anyone to make payment of a negotiable note without demanding its production. Again, recording an assignment serves no purpose.

However, in some states (Virginia, for example), by law it is the assignee of the note, not the trustee, who executes the release. In these states recording of the assignment of note secured by the deed of trust is necessary.

In other states (California, Delaware, Kansas, Kentucky, Massachusetts and Utah for example), while recording of the assignment is not legally necessary, it does impart constructive notice of the sale of the mortgage debt, and thus serves a useful function.

EXAMPLE: *R* executes a deed of trust deed to *T* to secure a note payable to the order of *E. E* records an assignment of the note and deed of trust to *X.*

The city of *Y* files a condemnation suit against the property. *X* is a necessary party to the suit because the assignment to him has been recorded. *Domarad v. Fisher & Burke Inc.*, 76 Cal. Rptr. 529.

Were the assignment not recorded, he might find his deed of trust extinguished by a condemnation suit of which he received no notice.

§ 198. **Competing assignments.** Cases involving competing assignments of the same mortgage present problems of great complexity. The rules regarding competing assignments of a chose in action are inapplicable because of the recording laws. 5 Tiffany, *Real Property*, 447–448.

a. *Where the mortgage secures a non-negotiable note*:

EXAMPLE: *E*, the mortgagee, assigns to *A-1*. The assignment is not recorded and *E* retains the mortgage and note. *E* thereafter assigns to *A-2*, a bona fida assignee, who receives the mortgage and note and who records his assignment. *A-2* prevails, since he has no notice, actual or constructive, of the earlier assignment. 1 Jones, *Mortgages*, 829; 2 *id* 483; 5 Tiffany, *Real Property*, 448; 89 ALR 171; 104 ALR 1301; *Price v. Northern Bond & Mfg. Co.*, 161 Wash. 690, 297 P. 786. The later assignee is protected by the recording law against the earlier unrecorded assignment.

b. *Mortgage secures non-negotiable note and first assignee receives note and mortgage*:

EXAMPLE: *E*, a mortgagee, assigns to *A-1* and delivers note and mortgage to him. No assignment is recorded. *E* thereafter assigns to *A-2*, whose assignment is recorded. *A-1* prevails. The fact that *A-2* did not receive the note and mortgage puts him on inquiry. 5 Tiffany, *Real Property*, 447-448; 2 Jones, *Mortgages*, 411. Rule is same if *A-1* receives the note and *A-2* receives the mortgage. *Syracuse Bank v. Merrick*, 182 N.Y. 387, 75 NE 232. Of course same rule applies to negotiable notes, since a transferee who does not receive the note cannot be a holder in due course.

c. *Mortgage secures non-negotiable note*:

EXAMPLE: *E*, mortgagee, assigns to *A-1* and assignment is recorded. *E* retains mortgage and note. Thereafter *E* assigns to *A-2*, who receives note and mortgage and records his assignment. The few existing cases tend to protect *A-1*. 5 Tiffany, *Real Property*, 447-448.

d. *Mortgage secures negotiable note*:

EXAMPLE: *E*, a mortgagee, assigns to *A-1*, who records his assignment. Mortgage and note remain in *E*'s possession (as might be the case where original mortgagee acts as collection agent). *E* thereafter assigns to *A-2*, a holder in due course. Here the issue is between the assignee under the first recorded assignment and a holder in due course of the note. Some cases protect the holder in due course. *Foster v. Augustana College*, 92 Okla. 96, 218 P 335; 37 ALR 854. Other courts protect the first assignee on the ground that the reference in the note to the fact that it is secured by a mortgage charges any assignee with notice of earlier recorded assignments. *Strong v. Jackson*, 123 Mass. 60; 16 Minn.

L. Rev. 112, 130. Clearly the rule of the *Augustana Case* is the better rule. It has been suggested that if the negotiable note does not bear any reference to the mortgage securing it, a holder in due course who lacks actual knowledge of the existence of the mortgage security should be protected. 5 Tiffany, *Real Property*, 448. This distinction is inadmissible. The cases are to the effect that mere reference in the note to the existence of a mortgage security does not render the note non-negotiable. 127 ALR 190, 198. Yet the result of the Massachusetts decisions is, in effect, a destruction of the negotiability of the note.

    e. Of course, where the second assignee has actual knowledge of the earlier assignment, the first assignee will prevail.

§ 199. Warehousing. In construction lending, the construction lender usually anticipates a "takeout" by the permanent lender. *See* § 209. Often, the construction loan is made by a mortgage banker with relatively limited resources. Such corporations need to borrow money during the interim period before the takeout occurs.

EXAMPLE: *R* makes 100 construction loan mortgages to *E*, a mortgage banker. Each is for $25,000. There is a permanent loan takeout by *I*, an insurance company, for mortgages of $27,500. During the period of construction *E* will need financial help, since it has a number of such projects going, as well as shopping centers and other large commercial loans. In some fashion, *E* will borrow from *B*, a commercial bank, on the strength of the advances made by *E* and the takeout commitment by *I*. Some sort of pledge or security transaction takes place. For example.

    1. *B* may appoint an employee of *E* to act as "custodian" of the construction mortgages.

OR

    2. *E* may deliver assignments of the mortgages to *B*, which probably will not be recorded.

Some other arrangement may be made. The commitment by *I* to make the permanent loans will be assigned and pledged as security for *B*. Quite possibly *I* will not be notified of this pledge. The whole idea is to arrange this short-term credit with a minimum of expenses.

The arrangements outlined seem quite logical and practical. Nevertheless, there are some risks involved.

EXAMPLE: *R* and *E*, being in financial difficulties, arrange to release the mortgages so that *R* can sell out the whole project to *X*, an innocent purchaser. If no assignments to *B* have been recorded, *X* may wind up with good title free and clear of the mortgages pledged to *B*. See § 190.

EXAMPLE: *E*, being in financial difficulties, sells and assigns these mortgages to *E-1*, who has no knowledge of *B*'s interest. Here we have a question of successive and competing assignments of the mortgage. If *B* does not obtain possession of the mortgages and if the assignment-pledge to *B* has not been recorded, *E-1* will prevail. *Guaranty Mtg. & Ins. Co. v. Harris*, 193 So 2d 1.

As long as these transactions are handled on this informal basis, risk to *B* is difficult to eliminate. 104 U. Pa. L. Rev. 494.

§ 200. **Express warranties.** It is quite common for one who sells and assigns a mortgage to give certain warranties to the investor-purchaser. Usually such warranties are given by a mortgage banker who originates mortgages for the express purpose of selling them to the investors whom he represents. With each such investor the mortgage banker has a *servicing agreement.* This is an agreement under which the mortgage banker will continue to collect the mortgage payments and remit them to the investor after the mortgage has been sold to the investor. Such agreements routinely provide that in the case of each such mortgage the mortgage banker warrants: (1) that the mortgage is a valid and first lien on the land; (2) that the mortgage is free of any pledges to other lenders; (3) that the full principal amount of the mortgage was advanced to the mortgagor; (4) that no part of the land has been released from the lien of the mortgage; (5) in the case of an FHA mortgage that the FHA insurance is in full force and effect; (6) in the case of a VA mortgage that the VA guarantee is in effect; (7) that a valid title insurance policy has issued on the mortgage; (8) that proper hazard insurance is in effect covering the mortgagee's interest; and (9) that all the loan documents are genuine.

As a rule, investors rely on such warranties. They are not too concerned, therefore, whether the mortgage note is negotiable and travels free from defenses of the mortgagor. The investor feels that the mortgage banker has taken all precautions to see that the investor is buying a valid mortgage and note.

§ 201. **Implied warranties.** Even though an assignment is made "without recourse," there is an implied warranty that the mortgage and note are genuine and valid, that there are no defenses not apparent at the time of the assignment (*e.g.,* usury), and that the amount purporting to be due at the time of the assignment was actually then due and owing. 6 Am.Jur.2d *Assignments* § 107.

§ 202. **Pledges of mortgages.** Pledges of mortgages are common, especially in short-term loans.

EXAMPLE: *R* makes a mortgage in the sum of $100,000.00 to *E. E,* being in need of funds, goes to his banker, *E-2,* who makes *E* a loan of $60,000. *E* signs a collateral note. This note contains a number of fine-print paragraphs, among them: (1) a provision that if *E-2* deems himself insecure he may call upon *E* for additional collateral, and if this is not forthcoming, *E-2* may accelerate maturity, this clause being imported from loans on corporate stock; (2) an acceleration clause in usual form covering default in payment of interest or principal; (3) provision that in case of default and acceleration *E-2* may hold a private or public collateral sale, with or without notice; (4) at such sale *E-2* is authorized to bid and acquire the collateral. The mortgage and mortgage note are assigned to the pledgee.

Note that provision is made for a collateral sale of the note and mortgage. This is necessary. A provision in the collateral note that the note and mortgage automatically become *E-2*'s property on default is void. Like mortgages, pledges must be foreclosed. As a rule, *E-2* will hold the sale in his office. The provision in the collateral note that *E-2* need not notify *E* of the sale should not be relied on. If this notice is not given, courts are prone to set the sale aside for unfairness to *E*. The provision that *E-2* may purchase at the sale is valid.

If a bitter controversy exists between *E* and *E-2*, *E-2* may go into court to foreclose his pledge. Judicial foreclosure of a pledge is universally recognized, though rather uncommon.

Some careful lawyers have the pledgor's assignment of the note and mortgage to the pledgee recorded. Generally, however, the pledgee relies on his possession of the paper to give notice of his rights. 79 Harv.L.Rev. 272.

It is unclear at the moment whether a pledge of a mortgage and note should be perfected under the Uniform Commercial Code by filing a financing statement on the theory that a general intangible is involved. Most lawyers seem to think this unnecessary. The pledgee's possession gives notice of his rights. 79 Harv.L. Rev. 271.

In the states that hold that a mortgage becomes negotiable when it secures a negotiable note, a pledgee who is a holder in due course should expect to be protected against defenses, such as payment before maturity. 3 Houston L. Rev. 327. The situation with respect to latent equities seems shrouded in some doubt. *Ibid.*

In the certificated trust indenture (CTI), a mortgage banker or his subsidiary borrows money from a large investor and pledges a number of mortgages as security. The pledge runs to a trustee. The mortgage banker continues to service the loans. If a loan gives into default, the mortgage banker takes it back and substitutes another mortgage. This pledge device eliminates the "doing business" problem the investor would encounter if it were making loans on land. Also the investor pays no servicing charge. Finally, the borrower is invariably a corporation, and in most states this eliminates all usury problems.

ADDITIONAL REFERENCES: 7 Houston L. Rev. 70 covering warehousing of mortgages; whether payments made by mortgagor to correspondent mortgagee are good against the permanent lender; whether payments made to mortgagee are good against warehousing bank; rights of permanent lender or mortgagor as to escrows set up by mortgagee for taxes and insurance; allocation of loss (where mortgagee is bankrupt) as between mortgagor, warehousing bank and trustee in bankruptcy; transfer to warehousing bank as a bankruptcy preference.

ADDITIONAL LOCAL REFERENCES: 7 U. Fla. L. Rev. 93; 17 Ore. L. Rev. 83; 8 Utah L. Rev. 128; 3 Powell, *Real Property*, §455 (discussing various state statutes).

16

Participations

§ 203. In general. Quite commonly today lending institutions seeking out-lets for their loanable funds will buy participations in another lender's mort-gages. A participation is a shared loan whereby one lender, usually called the *lead company,* divides into shares a large loan which it has or will make, a share or shares then being offered for sale to a participant lending institution.

EXAMPLE: R mortgages his land to E for $100,000. The mortgage is re-corded. E sells a participation of 50% to E-2. A participation agreement is signed by them outlining their rights and duties. E remains as the owner of the mortgage according to the public records. R is not notified of the transaction. He continues to make his payments to E. E will transmit to E-2 the share of principal and interest to which E-2 is entitled. If foreclosure becomes necessary, E will attend to it in his name. So far as all third persons are concerned, E remains the owner of the mort-gage. However, as between E and E-2, E-2 owns half the note and mortgage and *half* of any other collateral.

Because E remains as the owner of the mortgage according to the public records, obviously he is in a position to defraud E-2 much as in the case of an unrecorded assignment of mortgage.

EXAMPLE: In the above example, by agreement between R and E, R pays E $60,000 and E records a release of the mortgage. R sells the land to X, a bona fide purchaser. X owns the land free of the mortgage. All E-2 has is a right to sue E.

Since the participation agreement so provides, obviously the lead company has full authority to receive payments of principal and interest. All documents remain in the lead company's possession. The participant holds only his duplicate copy of the participation agreement.

127

Probably the mortgagee would have the power to extend the time of payment of the mortgage debt, even if the participation agreement forbids this, since the mortgagor has no *knowledge* of the participation agreement or its terms.

There is a certain amount of case law discussing the question of priority of a lien as between the lead company and the participant where the participation agreement is silent on this score. 26 Va.L.Rev. 825. For example, if a mortgagee selling a participation guarantees payment of the debt, this automatically subordinates his interest to that of the participant. It seems rather pointless to go into this in any great detail because modern participation agreements always cover this point. Usually they provide for equality of lien as between lead company and participant.

It seems that a participation is a sale of a security within the scope of the anti-fraud provisions of the Securities and Exchange Act of 1934, and particularly Rule 10b-5, and consequently that a lead company will be liable to a participant for all losses sustained by the participant if the lead company failed to disclose a material fact relating to the credit of the mortgagor. *Lehigh Valley Tr. Co. v. Central Bank,* 409 F2d 989, 87 Banking L. J. 99. State security laws should also be consulted.

Formerly it was not unusual for a lead company to subordinate its share of the loan to the participant's share. This, of course, made the participation quite attractive. Such transactions are rare today.

§ 204. Piggy-back mortgages. An exception to the statement last made occurs where a large corporation wishes to procure a loan for a valued customer. Here the large corporation may procure a large loan from an investor for this customer. The corporation enters into a participation with the investor but subordinates its share of the participation to the investor's share. This enables the investor to make the loan, for in the absence of the subordination the loan might well exceed the loan-to-value percentage prescribed by the investment laws under which the investor operates.

Also, according to an opinion of the General Counsel of FHLBB issued on July 3, 1969, savings and loan associations may engage in participation lending where there are two notes, one subordinated to the note held by the association.

EXAMPLE: Under a typical situation involving the type of financing described in the above opinion a home buyer might be earning $25,000 a year and be capable of carrying a home worth $50,000 but has only $5,000 with which to make a 10% down payment. The financial institution would make an 80% loan of $40,000. The buyer, arranging through the lending institution for supplemental financing, borrows the remaining $5,000 from a corporation which is not subject to loan-to-value or first lien restrictions. Notes are issued for both loans with the supplemental loan note being subordinated to the note held by the lending institution. The arrangement between the two lenders is evidenced by an investing and servicing agreement with the lending institution having all of the rights of a first mortgage. The 90% financing package then is secured by a first mortgage running to the lending institution. All payments are made to the lending institution with the appropriate share being sent on to the supplemental lender. In some states the usury ceilings may provide a practical barrier to such lending operations.

In such case for reasons stated elsewhere (*see* § 130) a special form of acceleration clause is needed.

FORM: Default in the payment of any installment of principal or interest on either note secured by this mortgage shall, at the option of the holder of the other note, constitute a default of said other note, entitling the holder to accelerate.

§ 205. **Loan decisions.** Obviously the participation agreement should spell out the authority, as between the parties, to make loan decisions, such as recasting the loan when the borrower gets in trouble, deciding to foreclose, rent or sell property acquired by foreclosure, and the like. Where the loan is made in *State A* and the lead company is a local lender, many decisions may well be left to the judgment of the lead company. As the loans grow in size, it becomes more likely that the participant will wish to share in the decisions and, of course, a participant who has acquired, say, 90% of the loan will want to participate in all decisions. To repeat, however, as long as the records show the lead company as the mortgagee and the mortgagor is unaware of the participation, the lead company is legally in a position to affect or even extinguish the participant's rights.

§ 206. **Agreements to repurchase.** A provision occasionally encountered in continuing participation arrangements is to the effect that if the loan-to-value ratio exceeds a specified percentage the lead company will repurchase the mortgage in case of default, this obligation to repurchase to cease when the specified loan to value has been reached.

17

Construction Loans

§ 207. **In general.** Construction lending encounters some rather technical rules of law and involves some rather complicated paper work.

§ 208. **Building operations as dependent on mortgage credit.** Before sub-contractors (electrical contractors, plumbing contractors, and so forth) and building materials suppliers put their labor and materials into a building they want to know where their money is coming from. Since the builder lacks the capital to pay these people from his own funds, he must be able to show them that he has a dependable source of mortgage money. Even if a dependable source of mortgage money exists, subcontractors and materialmen want their money rather promptly. On big jobs the custom is to pay on a monthly basis for work and material furnished.

§ 209. **Interim and permanent loans—takeout commitments.** A construction loan requires considerable supervision on the part of the interim lender and a staff capable of providing this supervision. Supervision is necessary because the mortgage lender must see that construction of the building is completed; that the construction is according to the construction plans and specifications approved by the lender; and that no mechanic's liens arise in the process of construction. Not all mortgage lenders are willing to engage in construction lending. Some want long-term permanent mortgages on completed buildings. On the other hand, mortgage lenders who do engage in construction lending (*interim lenders*) do not want their funds tied up over the long period of time, often fifteen years or longer, that it takes to pay off a mortgage. They want to turn their capital over constantly. Their income is derived not mainly from interest on mortgage loans, but from commissions which the borrower pays in order to receive the mortgage loan and from *service charges*. This latter item requires a word of explanation. In order to keep its capital turning over, the interim lender must sell the mortgage loan, after completion of construction, to an investor that is willing to take the mortgage as a permanent investment. The sale may be to a *permanent lender* with whom the construction lender has some permanent working arrangement; that is, the construction lender may be a *loan correspondent* for the permanent lender. After completion of the building, the mortgage is sold and assigned to the permanent lender, and, after sale of the mortgage to the permanent lender, the loan correspondent looks after the payment of taxes and insurance renewals, collects the mortgage payments, remits the payments to the permanent lender, making a charge, the service charge, for this service, and makes inspections from time to time to determine whether the mortgagor is maintaining the building properly. Before he agrees to finance construction of the building, the interim lender insists on the issuance of a *takeout commitment* by the permanent lender; that is, an agreement by the permanent lender to buy the construction mortgage after the building has been completed free from mechanic's liens and after all risks of construction are over.

SUGGESTION TO CONSTRUCTION LENDER: Make the construction loan commitment subject to the same conditions as those contained in the takeout commitment. That is, if the permanent lender is making requirements, for example, as to key leases that he wants signed, the construction loan commitment should be subject to the same requirements, so that all these are met before disbursement is to begin. A key lease can be signed by the mortgagor and his tenant (subject of course, to completion of the building before it becomes effective), and this lease can be approved by the permanent lender before disbursement of the construction loan begins. It is a good idea to have all documents required by the permanent lender approved by him to the greatest extent possible. This will avoid the pitfall of running into an insoluble difference with the permanent lender, thus forcing you to look elsewhere for a permanent lender. Some permanent lenders will furnish their mortgage, note and other forms to the interim lender. The interim loan documents are on forms, in consequence, that the permanent lender has prepared and is willing to accept. Of course, the promissory note then has a double aspect. It will call for payments (usually interest only) during the course of construction "according to the tenor of the construction loan agreement," and thereafter in installments as set forth in the commitment for the permanent loan. Incidentally, this will reduce mortgage tax fees and recording fees involved in the use of different documents for the interim and permanent loans. It is customary to provide in the mortgage and note that default by the mortgagor in performance of his construction loan agreement covenants is a default giving rise to a right of acceleration under the mortgage. The permanent loan commitment should be checked with care. For example, if it expires in one year, and the building will take two years to complete, the interim lender cannot commit. The interim lender needs a margin of at least 30 days after construction ends to get the papers ready for delivery to the permanent lender. Since construction completion dates are rarely met, it is also wise to provide for extensions of the permanent loan commitment on payment of agreed fees. It probably is a sensible precaution for the construction lender to make certain that the building plans he is checking are the same as those furnished the permanent lender. The permanent lender will turn down the loan if the building is not completed according to plans he has been given, and this means that the construction lender must determine that they are identical with his plans.

SUGGESTIONS TO THE PERMANENT LENDER: The permanent lender obviously will, before he makes the takeout commitment, develop all the conditions that ensure payment of the permanent loan, such as occupancy by key tenants under leases approved by the permanent lender and proof of compliance with all ordinances. At takeout time the permanent lender determines that all of these conditions have been complied with. A key document at this point is the architect's certificate that the building has been completed as per plans and specifications and that the city authorities have issued the certificate of occupancy required by local ordinances. This certificate also certifies that the building complies with local ordinances. The permanent lender may charge the borrower a stand-by commitment fee, returnable only if and when the loan is delivered to the permanent lender. The permanent lender should take a careful look at the construction lender if he intends to buy the construction loan. The takeout lender, on buying the loan, is concerned with the validity and enforceability of the construction mortgage. Necessarily this plunges the permanent lender into the midst of "doing business problems." If the construction lender is an unqualified foreign corporation, the mortgage may not be enforceable, since most doing business loans deny the foreign corporation access to the local courts, and such denial of access extends to an assignee other than a holder in due course.

BUY-SELL AGREEMENT.   The interim lender and permanent lender enter into an agreement for sale and assignment of the mortgage to the permanent lender when the building has been completed. Often the mortgagor is a party to this agreement on the theory that he should have a contractual right to insist that the permanent lender buy the mortgage.

As an alternative to the takeout commitment that calls for the interim lender to assign the mortgage to the permanent lender, the construction lender may be willing to finance construction if the builder can procure from some permanent lender a commitment to make a new mortgage loan when the building has been completed, the proceeds of the new mortgage loan to be used to pay off the construction mortgage. This is also called a *takeout commitment.*

You will also find a takeout commitment in the form of a commitment to buy the land, give back a lease, and lend money to the tenant on a leasehold mortgage.

When the loan arrangements contemplate that the construction mortgage will be released at the conclusion of construction and a new mortgage given to a permanent lender, usually the first step is for the prospective mortgagor to apply to the permanent lender for the permanent mortgage loan. The permanent lender then gives its commitment to this mortgagor, who then gives an assignment of the commitment to the construction lender. After the assignment has been given, the construction lender notifies the permanent lender of the assignment, so that no modifications or cancellations between the mortgagor and the permanent lender will be binding upon the construction lender. In other words, the assignment of commitment and notice thereof give the construction lender the legal right to enforce the commitment against the permanent lender. The interim lender will then, and only then, finalize his construction loan commitment.

Takeout commitments are bankable. That is, an interim lender can pledge such a commitment to his own bank and thus obtain funds to make other loans.

§ 210. **Provisions of construction loan commitment.** Even where a later construction loan agreement is contemplated, the commitment on a construction loan will contain considerable matter relating to the construction loan, for example:

1. Provisions for compensating the lender for various expenses if the loan transaction is not consummated.
2. Listing of all charges or types of charges the borrower will pay if loan does go through.
3. Description of all documents the borrower must furnish or execute, including construction loan agreement.
4. Title insurance requirements, including title insurance to cover each loan disbursement if that is to be done.
5. Hazard insurance requirements during period of construction.
6. Lender's requirements concerning contractor's bonds.
7. How interest will be computed during construction period.
8. Any restrictions lender requires on assignment of loan commitment.
9. Restrictions on junior financing, if lender insists on this.
10. Whether disbursement will be made to general contractor, or to general contractor and subcontractors. *See also* § 47.
11. Specification of the lender's requirements with respect to the architect's certificate to be furnished at the time of each disbursement. In addition to certifying that work is in place according to plans and specifications, this certificate will be required to state that (a) the amount of the draw does not exceed 90% of the value of work in place (this being in accordance with the terms of the construction contract), and (b) that the work complies with building restrictions and building codes.
12. Requirements of lender as to guarantees of third parties.
13. It will require that licenses or permits to operate, such as those required in connection with operation of a convalescent home, be furnished before disbursement begins.

14. Provision for handling extras, usually by deposit of fund by borrower to cover same when they come to light, plus a reserve for possible extras to be deposited before disbursement begins.

15. Deposit of reserves to cover interior finishing to be done as tenants are found for space in the building.

16. Requirement for chattel lien to be given on chattels required for operation, e.g., furniture, linens, etc., in a hotel.

17. Provision for reserves to assure installation of chattels needed for operation, coupled with an assurance by some reliable dealer in such chattels that he has committed to complete the furnishing of such chattels at a figure within the construction loan.

§ 211. **Construction loan agreement.** A construction loan is paid out in installments as construction goes forward. During the construction period, which may extend over a year on big jobs, other liens may come into being. It is important to preserve the priority of the construction mortgage over such liens.

EXAMPLE: *A* records a construction mortgage to *B* on February 1, 1968. On March 1, 1968, construction begins. On April 1, 1968, *B* makes his first disbursement of construction funds to the general contractor and subcontractors. On May 1, 1968, *A* records another mortgage to *C* to obtain funds for final completion of a building on another tract of land and receives this money on May 15, 1968. On June 1, 1968, *B* makes another disbursement on the construction mortgage. *B* will wish to be certain that this disbursement and all subsequent disbursements have priority over *C*'s mortgage. *C* will argue that he comes ahead of all disbursements made after the recording of his mortgage. Hence it is important that *B* come under the protection of the *obligatory advances rule. See* § 115. This means that before disbursement begins on the construction loan *A* and *B* should sign a construction loan agreement which obligates *B* to pay out the money as construction goes forward. Two problems arise in this connection:

1. It may be contended that the advances are, in fact, optional (rather than obligatory) if the construction loan agreement authorizes the mortgagee to stop making loan advances under certain circumstances; for example, when the construction fails to go forward according to the agreement. 80 ALR2d 201.

Virtually every construction loan agreement or loan commitment authorizes the lender to discontinue disbursing if the mortgagor is guilty of a default. Usually the "events of default" are set forth in some detail. Even if no such clause is present, the rule is that where one party to a contract is guilty of a substantial default, the other may discontinue performance. The question, therefore, is whether the presence on the part of the mortgagor of a substantial default such as failure to contribute his share of the construction funds, releases the mortgagee of any duty to continue disbursing construction funds, resulting in all future disbursement being considered optional on the part of the mortgagee. The dilemma is obvious. Many mortgagees will wish to continue disbursing so that the building can be completed. But if mechanics' liens or other liens are filed meanwhile, these disbursements may be junior to such intervening liens.

EXAMPLE: *R* executed construction mortgage to *E.* The construction loan agreement gave *E* the right to discontinue disbursing if work was abandoned for 30 days. Such an abandonment occurred. *M* filed a mechanic's lien claim. *E* continued disbursing if work was abandoned for 30 days. Such an abandonment occurred. *M* filed a mechanic's lien claim. *E* continued disbursing. The court held that all disbursements made by *E* after *M*'s lien was filed were junior to *M*'s lien. *Yost Linn Lumber Co. v. Williams,* 121 Cal. App. 571, 9 P2d 324; *Housing Mortgage Corp. v. Allied Const. Co.,* 374 Pa. 321, 97 A2d 802.

This is bad law. No party to a contract should be forced to declare the other party in default. The courts should encourage, not discourage, performance of contracts. Moreover *E* has no real choice. He is under an economic compulsion to complete the building, just as he is under an economic compulsion to pay real estate taxes if the mortgagor fails to pay them. Such payments made on taxes are part of the mortgagee's first lien on the land. Construction funds should receive a similar treatment. The better cases hold for the mortgagee. *Landers-Morrison-Christenson Co. v. Ambassador H. Co.,* 171 Minn. 445, 214 NW 503, 57 ALR 573; *Hyman v. Hauff,* 138 N.Y. 48, 33 NE 735.

In a few decisions courts have treated as a full and immediate disbursement, creating an immediate lien, the issuance by the mortgagee of a check to the mortgagor which the mortgagor immediately endorsed to the mortgagee's special construction loan account. *Western Nat. Bank v. Jenkins,* 131 Md. 239, 101 A 667; *Tony Schloos Properties Corp. v. Union Fed. S. & L. Assn.,* 233 Md. 224, 196 A2d 458. Of course if the result of this arrangement is to create a situation where the mortgagee is legally obligated to disburse the funds as paid bills are produced, then the disbursements can be treated as obligatory disbursements, and you get the same result though under a different theory. *Hance Hardware Co. v. Denbigh Hall Inc.,* 17 Del.Ch. 234, 152 A 130; *Smith v. Anglo. Calif. Tr. Co.,* 205 Cal. 496, 217 P 898.

2. The provisions of the construction loan agreement tend to be rather general and vague, such as the requirement that insurance policies be "satisfactory to the lender." It may be argued that the agreement is void for uncertainty. What kind of insurance was meant? Fire? Builder's risk? Liability? If the contract is void for uncertainty, all advances by the lender would be optional, and the lender's various advances might be subordinated to other liens, such as judgment, attachment, or sales tax liens attaching during the course of instruction. As a matter of law, it is not necessary that all details be settled with minute precision. Reasonable satisfaction and reasonable certainty are adequate guidelines for judges and businessmen. *Collins v. Vickter Manor,* 47 Cal2d 875, 306 P2d 783. Nevertheless it is best to guard in advance against this danger.

It is advisable to draft the construction loan agreement in such a way that if the borrower defaults, the lender may continue the agreement by completing the building himself. Additional safeguard clauses are useful.

SUGGESTED CLAUSE: In the event of a material failure of performance by the borrower, the lender may perform its obligations hereunder by taking possession of the premises together with all materials, equipment, and improvements thereon, whether affixed to the realty or not, and performing any and all work and labor necessary to complete the improvements substantially according to the plans and specifications.

To implement the rights of the lender under this paragraph, the borrower hereby constitutes and appoints the lender its true and lawful attorney in fact with full power of substitution in the premises to complete the improvements in the name of the borrower and to pay all bills and expenses incurred thereby and hereby empowers the lender as his attorney as follows: to use any funds of the borrower, including any balance which may not have been advanced, for the purposes of completing the improvements; to make such additions, changes, and corrections in the plans and specifications as may be necessary or desirable to complete the improvements in substantially the manner contemplated in the plans and specifications; to employ such contractor's agents, architects, and inspectors as shall be required; to pay, settle, or compromise all existing bills and claims which may be or become liens against the premises or as may be necessary or desirable for completion of the improvements or for the clearance of title; to execute all applications, certificates, or instruments in the name of the borrower which may be required by any governmental authority or contract; and to do any and every act which the borrower might do in its own behalf. It is further understood and agreed that this power of attorney shall be deemed to be a power coupled with an interest and cannot be revoked. The abovementioned attorney shall also have power to prosecute and defend all actions and proceeding in connection with the construction of the improvements on the premises and to toke such action and require such performance under any surety bond or other obligation or to execute in the name of the borrower such further bonds or obligations as may be reasonably required in connection with the work.

Anything herein to the contrary notwithstanding, it is specifically understood and agreed that all funds furnished by the lender and employed in performance of the obligations of the borrower under this agreement shall be deemed advanced by the lender under an obligation to do so regardless of the identity of the person or persons to whom such funds are furnished. Funds advanced by the lender in the reasonable exercise of his judgment that the same are needed to complete the improvement or to protect his security are to be deemed obligatory advances hereunder and are to be added to the total indebtedness secured by the note and mortgage and said indebtedness shall be increased accordingly.

Any requirement of this contract not otherwise specifically set forth in detail shall be deemed to call for performance that is reasonable under the circumstances. In the event that a requirement of reasonable performance shall nevertheless be deemed too vague or uncertain as to admit of legel enforcement, such requirement shall be deemed null and void, but without other effect on the enforceability of this contract.

The provisions of this paragraph shall prevail over inconsistent provisions of this agreement.

A good part of the construction lender's requirements can be incorporated in the lender's *printed form construction loan agreement*. Any deviation from the form should be covered in advance in the loan commitment, for legally a lender cannot demand provisions in the construction loan agreement that are not in the loan commitment. The loan commitment should, of course, call for the borrower to sign the lender's standard form construction loan agreement as modified by the loan commitment. This enables the lender to omit from the commitment a mass of detail that might frighten away a timid borrower. All the precautions mentioned in this chapter are covered in the construction loan agreement.

In some states statutes exist regarding the construction loan agreement.

EXAMPLE: New York requires the construction loan agreement to be filed for record before the recording of the construction mortgage. The statute sets forth certain matters the contract must set forth. New York requires such a mortgage to contain the trust fund clause required by § 13 of the Lien Law to the effect that the proceeds of the loan are held in trust for those furnishing labor and material. Harvey, *Real Property Law* § 845. Ohio also has some statutory law on this type of loan. Ohio Code § 1211-14. Proposed amendments to the Uniform Commercial Code would require every construction loan to bear a legend indicating it is a construction loan. This seems part of the current trend toward requiring the records to contain a more specific description of the mortgage debt.

§ 212. Precautions in construction lending. Given the fact that many construction lenders would regard as a major disaster their inability to turn their construction loan situation over to a permanent lender on a takeout, certain facts are obvious. The prudent construction lender must be certain that the building will be completed, as per contract, and free of mechanics' liens, for these are basic conditions the takeout lender insists upon. This means that the construction lender will check the loan out carefully. The general contractor must measure up to the job. The lender may insist upon a performance and payment bond, with the lender as co-obligee. The lender may insist that loan disbursements be checked out by a title company that is willing to insure each disbursement against mechanic's lien claims. The lender may keep his loan down to a lower percentage of construction cost than was common formerly. In other words, in periods of tight money, when permanent loans are hard to come by, the construction lender who has a takeout lined up will struggle to be certain that nothing occurs to prevent him from delivering a properly constructed lien-free building on time.

In making a construction loan, the lender asks himself some questions the owner would ask, such as:

1. Will the building violate zoning laws either as to type of building or setback lines?
2. Will it violate recorded building restrictions or easements?
3. Does the building have the legal right to connect to sewer and water?
4. Will the building interfere with existing drainage or utility lines?
5. What does the survey show as to the true boundaries and area of the property and encroachments by the building or by adjoining owners?
6. Is a reliable general contractor involved?

7. Are firm subcontracts let, so that the true cost of construction can be determined?

Also the lender is certain to demand that the owner deposit with him the difference between the construction loan funds and the cost of construction.

Likewise, if the project is part of a larger project, for example, a department store in a shopping center, a lengthy declaration of easements will be needed. *See* §§ 263, 265. Probably the lender will require title insurance insuring the validity of all easements required to service the property.

§ 213. Construction loan disbursement. Before any disbursement is made on bigger jobs, the lender will obtain a certificate from the architect that work is in place (according to the building contract, plans, and specifications in the lender's files) warranting the disbursement requested; he will make his own inspection to see that the work is in place, and, indeed, may make unannounced inspections to make sure that the work is being done properly; he will have the owner's signed direction to make the disbursement, since the borrowed money belongs to the owner and the owner may otherwise complain about defects in construction; he will seek mechanic's lien protection; he will have the architect certify that the balance of loan proceeds will suffice to complete the building; the lender will stop disbursement if unauthorized extras appear or liens appear or if loan proceeds appear inadequate to complete construction; at each disbursement, a date-down survey will be furnished showing that new construction is within lot lines and does not violate building lines or other regulations established by zoning ordinances, building codes, or private building restrictions.

As a rule, construction lenders will advance construction disbursements only on work and materials actually incorporated in the building. Materials delivered to the site but not so incorporated may never find their way into the building. Theft may occur. Or the materials may be diverted to other jobs.

§ 214. Mechanic's lien protection in general. A mortgagee paying out a construction loan must protect both itself and the mortgagor against mechanics' liens. This is no easy task.

It is necessary, first of all, for the construction lender to be aware of the different rules followed throughout the country as to the priority of mechanics' liens over construction mortgages. There are a number of such rules:

1. In a few states (Washington, for example), the lien of any particular mechanic attaches when he commences *his* particular work. In such states, the mechanic's lien is not prior to any mortgage that was recorded prior to the commencement of the very work for which the lien is filed.

EXAMPLE: *A* and *B* commence work on a building and afterward the owner mortgages the land to *C*. Thereafter, *D* and *E* begin work on the same construction job. *A* and *B* have priority over *C*, and *C* has priority over *D* and *E*.

2. In many states (Arkansas, California, District of Columbia, Georgia, Louisiana, Michigan, Minnesota, Nevada, New Mexico, Ohio, Oklahoma, Tennessee, Utah, and Wisconsin, for example), all mechanics' liens growing out of a particular construction job date back to the beginning of the job.

EXAMPLE: *A*, a landowner, hires *B* to erect a building, and *B* hires *C* to dig the foundation. *C* begins work in January, 1968. In February, 1968, *A* records a mortgage to *X*, which mortgage is intended to provide funds for construction. The carpenter, mason, electrician and so on come on the job in March, 1968. All mechanics' liens date back to January and all liens therefore have priority over *X's* mortgage.

3. In a few states (Illinois and Maine, for example), a mechanic's lien attaches to the land as of the date of the contract for the improvement; that is, as of the date on which the owner ordered the work done.

EXAMPLE: *A*, a landowner, hires *B* on January 8, 1968, to build a building in Chicago. As is true of most contracts for construction, the contract is not recorded. On January 10, 1968, *A* records a mortgage to *X*, which mortgage is intended to provide funds for construction. Work on the construction site begins on January 17, 1968. All mechanics' liens date back to January 8, 1968, and therefore all enjoy priority over *X's* mortgage.

4. In a few states (New York and South Carolina, for example), a mechanic's lien does not arise as against the mortgagee until notice thereof is filed in the proper public office.

EXAMPLE: *A*, a landowner, on January 8, 1968, hires *B* to erect a building. *B* commences work on January 12th. On January 19, 1968, *A* records a construction mortgage to *X*, and *X* disburses funds under this mortgage for such construction until February 28th, when a mechanics' lien claim is filed by a subcontractor. *X* discontinues disbursement and files a foreclosure suit. *X* has complete priority over the mechanics' liens, because all his disbursements were made prior to the filing of any mechanics' liens.

5. In some states (Colorado, Illinois, Missouri, North Dakota, Oregon, South Dakota, Virginia, and Wyoming, for example), the law declares that a mechanic's lien for work or materials furnished after a mortgage lien has attached to the land shall have priority over the mortgage *as to the building but not as to the land*. In a number of these states the matter of priority of lien as between the construction mortgage and the mechanic's lien claimants is decided in a way that is quite disadvantageous to the mortgagee.

EXAMPLE: *A*, an owner of vacant land, procures a construction loan mortgage from *X*, which is recorded on January 10, 1968. On January 17th *A* hires *B* to build the building. Construction begins on January 24th. Mechanics' liens are filed. Both *X* and the mechanic's lien claimants file suits to foreclose. The court will hold that the mechanics' liens are a prior and superior lien as to the *buildings*, so that, in practical effect, the mechanics' liens will be a prior lien as to most of the value of the property and the mortgagee will have no choice but to pay off the mechanic's lien claimants. 107 ALR 1012.

6. In Indiana the mechanics' liens enjoy equality of lien with the construction mortgage. *Ward v. Yarnelle*, 172 Ind. 535, 91 NE 7, 80 ALR2d 187.

7. In Missouri a curious rule is followed. The construction lender is considered, from the very fact that he has made a construction loan, to have subordinated his mortgage to the mechanics' liens. *H.B. Deal Const. Co. v. Labour Discount Center*, 418 SW2d 940.

Reference: *See* 4 Am.Law Property § 16.106F (articles on state law of mechanics' liens).

It is also necessary for the construction lender to be familiar with the distinction between *partial waivers* and *final waivers*. As construction or repair work goes forward, liens of the general contractor and subcontractors attach to the land. Both the landowner and any mortgagee involved naturally want to get rid of these liens, which can be accomplished by procuring waivers of their liens from the parties furnishing labor or material. There are *partial waivers* and *final waivers*. Suppose that a subcontractor, such as a plumbing, electrical, or plastering subcontractor, has finished half his job and wants to be paid for that half. When the mortgagee pays him, he demands from the subcontractor a waiver of his lien for the work and materials furnished. This waiver recites that it waives all lien for *work and materials furnished*. This means, of course, for work and materials furnished *up to the date of the waiver*. No lien is waived as to the work still to be done. When final payment is made to that particular party, the mortgagee demands a final waiver, which waives all lien *for work and materials furnished or to be furnished,* meaning that the subcontractor has no lien at all on the land or buildings. Even if he must come back to repair or replace defective work or material, he can claim no lien on the property, which is important. The objective is always to get the house built at the price and at the bids submitted by the various mechanics. There is trouble ahead if any of the mechanics is legally able to assert a lien for a sum greater than the amount he agreed to work for.

In *priority states,* that is, the states following rule No. 2 above, if a mortgage is recorded and becomes a lien on the property before any construction begins, the mortgage will enjoy priority over any mechanic's lien arising out of such construction.

It is obvious that if visible construction actually begins before the mortgage is recorded or becomes a lien, some or probably all of the mechanics' liens will be prior and superior to the mortgage. It is therefore necessary for any construction mortgagee to know exactly when construction begins. 1 ALR3rd 822.

SUGGESTION: Immediately after recording of the mortgage, let the lender take affidavits from the builder and homeowner that construction has not begun or material been delivered to the site, and let him verify this by an actual inspection of the premises. The inspector should make a written report, with a photograph of the property, which report should be signed and dated and held in the mortgage file against the possibility of litigation. In this connection, it is to be observed that staking off lots, cutting trees, and removing brush do not constitute the commencement of construction. They are merely preparatory to the commencement of construction. *Clark v. General Electric Co.*, 243 Ark. 399, 420 SW2d 830; *Reuben E. Johnson Co. v. Phelps*, 156 NW2d 247 (Minn.). For work to constitute the commencement of construction, within the meaning of the rule, it must be of such a substantial and conspicuous character as to make it reasonably apparent that building has actually begun.

In any state where prior recording of the mortgage does not give the mortgage protection, and in all big loans in general, the mortgagee usually has no choice but to see that no mechanic's lien claims are filed. Keep in mind, also, that increasingly today courts require the construction lender to protect the *mortgagor* against mechanics' liens.

The construction lender should procure from the general constractor a sworn list of all the subcontractors he has hired, and as each disbursement is made, he procures a supplementary affidavit reflecting any changes. Each such affidavit shows how much work or materials each subcontractor has put in, and each subcontractor, on receiving payment of that amount, gives a partial lien waiver for all work and materials furnished to the date of the affidavit. The general contractor also gives such waivers. Dollar amounts recited in the affidavits are checked against dollar amounts recited in the lien waivers. Any discrepancy is questioned for it may reveal an unauthorized extra. As each subcontractor receives final payment for his work, he gives a final waiver for all work and materials furnished or to be furnished so that he can claim no lien for work needed to correct defective construction that shows up.

Special state statutes should be followed. In Florida, the mortgagee should record the construction mortgage at least one day before notice of commencement of construction is recorded. In California, the mortgagee should record a notice of completion as soon as construction has been completed, for this starts the running of the period for the filing of mechanics' liens. And in California, if a lien claimant serves a "stop notice" on the mortgagee, this, in effect, gives the lien claimant a lien on the construction loan proceeds.

The landowner also gives the mortgagee an affidavit listing all persons furnishing work or materials *on his order*, for some owners let work out to parties other than the main contractor.

The mortgagee makes payouts as the building goes up, according to a schedule included in the construction loan agreement. He makes payouts directly to the subcontractors on the basis of vouchers or orders signed by the general contractor and approved in writing by the supervising architect, if there is one. If there is no architect, the mortgagee himself checks at the time of each disbursement to determine that there is "work in place" warranting such disbursement. The general contractor often brings in waivers signed by subcontractors, states that he has paid them in full, and asks that he be paid the amount represented by these waivers. To comply is risky. A dishonest builder will forge lien waivers. Such waivers are void. And even if the lien waivers are genuine, the builder may have paid the subcontractors with "rubber" checks, and when the checks "bounce," the subcontractors may file foreclosure suits despite the lien waivers. Probably they will not prevail in such suits, for the landowner or mortgagee relied on the lien waivers in paying out, and the courts would say that the subcontractors are therefore barred or estopped from repudiating their lien waivers. *P. A. Lord Lumber Co. v. Callahan,* 181 Ill.App. 323; *McClelland v. Hamernick,* 264 Minn., 345, 118 NW2d 791. Check each lien waiver carefully. Most of them come from corporations, and if the corporate seal is attached and a certificate of acknowledgment appears thereon, you can depend on its regularity. Trouble arises with respect to the thousands of unincorporated enterprises. You may get a lien waiver by "Triangle Plumbers," whoever they are, signed by "Joseph Doakes," whoever he is. He might be the office boy, of course, and wholly unauthorized to sign anything. Verify these the best way you can. Often a phone call will suffice.

Before making payment to any subcontractor, the prudent lender should require him to sign a verified statement as to all material put into the job and any sub-contractors he has hired. Just as in many states the law requires you to see that all the general contractor's subcontractors are fully paid, so it is required in many states that you see that each subcontractor's sub-subcontractors are fully paid. If any material used was procured on credit, you must make payment to, and get a waiver from, the materialman, for he is also entitled to a lien.

§ 215. Mechanic's lien protection—"no lien contracts." Same mortgagees insist that the building contract contain a waiver of all mechanics' liens and be recorded in the recorder's office. In some states (Illinois and Indiana, for example), this wipes out all mechanics' liens and is even binding on subcontractors if recorded or if some other notice thereof is given to subcontractors. 76 ALR2d 1097.

Lenders are reluctant to rely on these "no lien" contracts. Among the reasons for this reluctance they give the following:

1. If the general contractor goes broke and a new contractor is hired to complete the job, he is not bound by the original "no lien" contract and may refuse to sign such a contract covering his work.

2. The contract does not cover work ordered by tenants, which is often substantial. Yet this work may result in mechanics' liens covering the whole building and land, on the theory that where the owner signs a general contract that obviously requires certain tenants to complete their own quarters, he agrees that such work will create a lien on his land and building.

3. If a general contract is signed, and later the general contractor, without receiving additional consideration, signs a "no lien" contract, it is arguable that such a contract is invalid for lack of consideration.

4. Such a contract signed by the general contractor would have no application to later contracts let by the owner for part of the work not covered by the general contract. This is a new general contract. 76 ALR2d 1101.

5. If the landowner and general contractor are corporations with identical shareholders, there is doubt concerning the validity of such contracts.

§ 216. Mechanic's lien protection—interim certification, completion guarantees and builder's control. In some areas, title companies offer a service known as *interim certification.* The title company checks the lien waivers on each construction disbursement, receives assurance that work is in place for the amount of the waivers, and up-dates its mortgage title policy with an endorsement insuring the building to be lien-free for the work completed.

In some areas of the country, the title company will offer the lender *completion guarantee service,* under which the construction funds are disbursed by the lender to the title company, which insures the mortgagee that the building will be completed at the agreed figure and will be free of liens.

Other areas offer *construction escrows,* under which the lender disburses to the title company, which insures the lender that the money disbursed by the title company is lien free.

In California there are *builder's control companies* which offer part or all of the foregoing services.

A lender that has adequate sophistication to pay out construction loans on single-family dwellings is prone to use one of these services when embarking upon some unfamiliar type of project.

Especially on smaller loans, and in the so-called priority states, the lender gets protection against mechanics' liens by receiving the ALTA loan policy, which insures against mechanics' liens which arise out of work the lender has committed to the project. This policy does *not* insure completion of the project, nor does it insure quality of workmanship.

§ 217. Mechanic's lien protection—tenant work. In big projects, an office building, for example, as much as 20% of the cost of construction may go into tenant work. Big tenants cannot be fitted into standard space, for they have their own requirements as to divisions of the area, decorating, etc. This means that a new general contract is entered into between the tenant and the general contractor. This raises thorny problems.

1. It is possible that in some states mechanics' liens for this work may relate back to the date of the commencement of the office building project. 40 C.J. 200. There are, of course, many decisions to the contrary. *Planters Cotlon Oil Co. v. Galloway,* 170 Ark. 712, 280 SW 999; *Streuli v. Wallen-Dickey Co.,* 227 Ark. 885, 302 SW2d 522; *American First Title & Trust Co. v. Ewing,* (Okla.), 403 P2d 488; *New Prague Lumber Co. v. Bastyr,* 263 Minn. 249,

117 NW2d 7; *Fryman v. McGhee,* 108 OA 501, 163 NE2d 63; *Palm Beach Bank & Tr. Co. v. Lainhart,* 184 Fla. 662, 95 So 123. Likewise, the rule seems to be that the new work does not prolong the time for filing mechanics' liens on the main job. 57 CJS *Mechanics' Liens* § 144c (2).

2. Any "no lien" contract with the original general contractor does not cover this work.

3. The same is true of the contractor's bonds on the main job.

4. Likewise the lien coverage of the ALTA loan policy is confined to the work committed for by the construction lender at the time the construction loan was made.

§ 218. **Contractor's bonds.** Among the risks in construction are: (1) Unforeseen delays owing to weather, strikes, soil conditions not revealed by soil tests, misapplication of newly evolved construction procedure. Any of these can halt foundation work, for example, while materials are already on their way to a building site where there is no storage space. (2) Insolvency of the general contractor or key subcontractors owing to underbidding of jobs, unforeseen construction problems, etc, unforeseen cost increases, overexpansion whether on this or other jobs. (3) Death of key contractors. To protect against these risks contractor's bonds can be obtained.

Since this area of law is extremely technical, some over-simplification becomes necessary. It is customary to receive two bonds from the surety company, often on forms approved by the American Institute of Architects (AIA). One bond, the *performance bond,* provides assurance to the landowner that the building will be completed as per contract. If the general contractor fails to do so, the bonding company takes over and completes the job. The bonding company also gives the owner an AIA *payment bond* which assures that material and labor furnished in construction of the building will be fully paid for, so that no mechanics' liens will be filed.

The *payment bond* protects the subcontractors and materialmen. Thus, if a subcontractor is not paid, he can take his claim directly to the bonding company.

For the best available protection, a landowner should demand both the performance and the payment bond, especially since one premium pays for both bonds. The performance bond alone may be inadequate. True, where the construction contract expressly requires the contractor to satisfy all legitimate claims for mechanics' liens, a bond guaranteeing performance of the contract may be interpreted to require the bonding company to complete the building and pay mechanics' liens. 77 ALR 62, 118 ALR 66. Indeed, some courts will read into every construction contract an agreement to deliver the building free of mechanics' liens, and such courts will go on to hold that a bond to complete the building is a bond to complete it free of liens, for any other rule would subject the landowner to crushing liabilities over and above the contract price and would "keep the word of the promise to the ear but break it to the hope." *Wolverine Ins. Co. v. Phillips,* 165 FSupp. 335; *Stoddard v. Hibbler,* 156 Mich. 335, 120 NW 787. But not all courts have so held. If the construction contract does not expressly require the contractor to pay mechanics' liens, or where the bond simply reads that the bonding company guarantees that the contractor shall faithfully perform the work, bonding companies have denied liability for mechanics' liens and some courts have sustained the bonding company. 24 L.R.A.N.S. 1075; 118 ALR 67.

In modern times it seems safe to agree with the author of a recent article that the duty of the contractor, owed to the owner, to pay laborers and materialmen may be implied under construction contracts from the fact that, if he does not pay them, the laborers and materialmen will be entitled, under the law of most states, to a lien on the owner's property superior to all other claim. And, at all events, under most contracts the duty need not be implied since, by the terms of the contract or the bond, the contractor expressly promises the owner that he will pay all laborers and materialmen. Until he does so, the contract is not complete and the owner is not obligated to pay the balance of the contract price. 41 Ore.L.Rev. 11. Retentions are discussed later in this section.

Many surety companies have their own bond forms. Obviously these must be carefully studied by the lender.

The AIA form we have been discussing extends protection to the *landowner.* The *mortgage lender* who is advancing the construction funds also wishes to be protected by the surety bonds. Bonding companies are usually willing to add the name of the mortgagee as a party protected by the surety bonds. However, the bonding company will then add a clause to the bonds that is commonly called the *Los Angeles Clause.* In practical effect, this clause makes the mortgage lender's protection contingent upon the owner's performing his part of the bargain under the construction contract. The philosophy here is that the bonding company carefully checks the general contractor and is willing to guarantee that *he* will do his job, but is unwilling to insure that *the owner* will do his job. Thus, for example, if a construction job will cost $10,000,000 of which $8,000,000 will be supplied by the mortgage lender and $2,000,000 will be supplied by the owner, the mortgage lender is not protected if the owner fails to come up with his $2,000,000. Such a bond, with the Los Angeles Clause, is sometimes called a *dual obligee bond.* The language added may be as follows:

Any default by either or both of the obligees will automatically relieve the principal and the surety from the performance of the contract.

Another example of language used to perform a similar function is as follows:

> The surety shall not be liable under this bond to the obligees, or either of them unless the obligees, or either of them, shall make payments to the principal, strictly in accordance with the terms of said contract as to payments and shall perform all the other obligations to be performed under said contract at the time and in the manner therein set forth. This agreement is hereby attached to and becomes a part of the bond.

To preserve this performance bond protection (and incidentally to preserve the mortgagee's protection as a dual obligee) the owner must not deviate from the construction contract.

EXAMPLE: The owner must not pay progress payments in advance of the contract date and he must deduct and retain the retentions specified in the contract. *Sandusky Grain Co. v. Borden's Condensed Milk Co.,* 214 Mich. 306, 183 NW 218, 127 ALR 10; 41 Ore.L.Rev. 16; 17 Am. Jur. 2d 213.

Whether the owner must go further and comply with all the statutory requirements set forth in the mechanic's lien laws in order to retain his completion bond coverage is a matter on which there appears to be a dearth of authority.

EXAMPLE: O, the landowner, is required by the local law to obtain a verified list of subcontractors from the general contractor and hold back enough money to pay them. It has been held that O will lose his performance bond coverage if he fails to do this. 127 ALR 42.

The result of all this is to render precarious the protection of the mortgagee as a dual obligee, since whatever destroys or diminishes the protection afforded the landowner destroys or diminishes the protection afforded the mortgagee as dual obligee. There is very little law on this subject. One court has held that the lender has rights under the dual obligee bond that are superior to those of the landowner. *New Amsterdam Casualty Co. v. Bettes,* 407 SW2d 307 (Tex. Civ.App.). This case appears to stand alone. The moral seems to be that the mortgagee must have complete control of disbursement.

At all events the derelictions of the owner can affect only his performance bond coverage. They will not affect the separate and independent coverage afforded subcontractors by the payment bond. 77 ALR 21, 62, 118 ALR 57, 66. Where the bond is a combined performance and payment bond, the result is the same. *Ibid.*

It now becomes necessary to explore a further aspect of the mortgagee's bond protection. Originally the AIA performance and payment bond were combined in one instrument. Later the coverage was divided into the present two bond forms in order to eliminate the conflict of interest between the landowner and the subcontractors. AIA Handbook of Architectural Practice (8th ed. 1958) § 8.06. This being the case it seems that the protection of the landowner (and incidentally that of his mortgagee as dual obligee) is provided by the performance bond only, a conclusion fortified by the fact that in the payment bond he is named as obligee "for the use and benefit of claimants."

However, if the landowner (and his dual obligee mortgagee) have lost protection under the performance bond, a problem arises if the surety pays the mechanics' liens under the terms of the payment bond. The surety may seek to be subrogated to the mechanics' liens. *Am.Surety Co. v. Sampsell,* 327 US 269, 30 Minn.L.Rev. 542; 41 Ore.L.Rev. 24. This could complicate the mortgagee's situation.

In certain situations the bonding company will be willing to give the construction lender a *completion bond.* This is a bond that assures the lender that the building will be completed according to contract and free and clear of mechanics' liens. Here the bonding company is assuring that both the contractor and the owner will perform properly. This would be in a situation, for example, where a bank is constructing a new bank building and is borrowing part of the construction money from an insurance company. The bonding company is willing to assure the insurance company that a top-notch contractor and a reliable bank working together will complete the building properly and free of all liens.

On big jobs there may be more than one general contract. One contractor, to be sure, is likely to be hired to do the bulk of the construction, but the owner may contract separately with *Contractor X* to put in the foundations, *Contractor Y* to do the heating and air conditioning, and so on. Obviously, if you are seeking surety bond protection you will need separate surety bonds on each of these contractors. Moreover, on big jobs where there is only one general contract, the prudent general contractor may insist on contractor's bonds covering the big subcontractors, for if they fail to do work properly or fail to pay for work or material they order, the loss will fall on the general contractor.

Again, many large projects are so planned that key tenants finish the interior of the leased quarter, installing interior walls, plumbing fixtures, lighting, and so on. Since these jobs are done under separate general contracts, they are not covered by bonds issued on the main construction job.

In some states one wishing to free his land from filed mechanics' liens may procure and file in some public office a surety company bond protecting against such liens. *Jungbert v. Marrett,* 313 Ky. 338, 231 SW2d 84. Of course if such a bond is requested, the surety company will probably ask to have collateral put up, but the bond wipes out the liens and insures litigation at leisure with the mechanic's lien claimants if there is any contention that their work was done improperly. Almost everywhere, purchasers, mortgagees, and title companies will accept such surety bonds, even though there is no law that the bond wipes out the lien.

In virtually every construction situation, the contract calls for a retention or hold-back of part of each construction disbursement. This retention insures that the job will be done right and free of liens. If any kind of trouble develops, the retention is not paid, and the contractor is thereby compelled to take care of the situation. On big jobs there will be retentions on the bigger subcontracts as well as on the general contract. In quite a number of states this retention is considered as being held back for the benefit of the surety on the contractor's bond as well as for the benefit of the owner or his mortgage; *National Surety Corp. v. State National Bank,* (Ky.) 454 SW2d 354; 107 ALR 960. The documents in a contractor's bond deal today always call for an assignment of the retention to the surety company. This, of course, means that both owner and mortgagee must protect the surety company's rights in their dealings with the retention. Obviously if the contractor is not paying his subcontractors, and this is known to the owner and his mortgagee, if they consent to payment of the retentions to the contractor, they will be unable to collect from the surety company to the extent that this action has prejudiced the surety.

It is unclear whether the surety's rights to the retentions is a security interest coming under the Uniform Commercial Code.

EXAMPLE: *B* contracts to build a building for *O* and provides *O* with a performance and payment bond by *XYZ Co. B* assigns his retentions to *XYZ Co.* as security for his faithful performance of the work. *B* later pledges the same retentions to *ABC Bank* and the Bank makes a code filing of this security transaction. The question is whether this gives the Bank priority over *XYZ Co's* rights as assignee and as a surety entitled to subrogation. This is an unanswered question. 5 Boston College Ind. and Comm. Rev. 250.

§ 219. Builders risk insurance. Builders risk insurance is a type of fire and extended coverage insurance that extends protection to a building under construction. In addition to the landowner, the contractor doing the construction is also covered under this type of policy, since the risk of loss during construction is a risk he legally bears.

EXAMPLE: A building that is 50% completed is destroyed by fire without any fault on the contractor's part. The contractor must rebuild this portion at his expense. 22 ALR2d 1345.

Of course this could bankrupt a contractor, so insurance coverage is needed. And because the construction lender wants control over the proceeds of the insurance, the standard mortgage loss is attached.

Unlike fire policies, which are written for a stated amount, builders risk insurance increases its coverage automatically as the building goes up.

The builder's risk policy today quite often covers a number of risks other than fire. A variety of such policies are offered under the name "all-risk" coverage. Unfortunately, many of such policies contain numerous exclusions, listing many types of hazards not covered so that they, in fact, are not true "all-risk" policies. Exclusions from coverage may include damage caused by earthquake, flood, glass damage, and many other hazards that really should be covered. However, truly comprehensive policies are offered by various insurance companies. The moral, of course, is that the advice of a competent insurance broker should be sought. Of course, even the best policy will contain some exclusions. Cost of replacing defective construction is excluded, for example, but that is covered by a surety company's performance bond.

The amount of the deductible must be decided on a case-by-case basis. Obviously, it should be kept to a figure one would reasonably expect the contractor to absorb financially.

This type of policy does not cover damage occurring after completion. This damage is picked up by the regular policies, which, of course, must also be carefully analyzed as to scope of coverage.

§ 220. Liability coverage during construction. Liability during construction is offered by the *comprehensive general liability policy*. These policies contain exclusions from coverage that must be carefully studied. Again, an expert insurance broker should be consulted, so that a truly comprehensive policy is selected.

§ 221. Architect's insurance. A mistake by an architect can obviously hurt a building project substantially. Of course, the architect will be liable. 25 ALR2d 108, 51; 43 ALR2d 1229. But he probably will lack the financial resources to make good. If *errors* and *omissions* insurance on the architect is required, this may prevent financial collapse of the project.

§ 222. Certificate of insurance. At times an insurance company will issue a policy to *A* and will issue to *B* a brief certificate that such a policy has issued. Obviously an attorney for an owner, lender, or contractor must insist on examining the policy itself.

§ 223. Construction loans by national banks. Construction loans by national banks are governed by the following statute and ruling:

(a) Law—12 U.S.C. 371 [third paragraph]

"Loans made to finance the construction of industrial or commercial buildings and having maturities of not to exceed thirty-six months where there is a valid and binding agreement entered into by a financially responsible lender to advance the full amount of the bank's loans upon completion of the buildings and loans made to finance the construction of residential or farm buildings and having maturities not to exceed thirty-six months, shall not be considered as loans secured by real estate within the meaning of this section but shall be classed as ordinary commercial loans whether or not secured by a mortgage or similar lien on the real estate upon which the building or buildings are being constructed: *Provided,* That no national banking association shall invest in, or be liable on, any such loans in an aggregate amount in excess of 100 per centum of its actually paid-in and unimpaired capital plus 100 per centum of its unimpaired surplus fund. Notes representing loans made under this section to finance the construction of residential or farm buildings and having maturities not to exceed nine months shall be eligible for discount as commercial paper within the terms of [12 U.S.C. 343] if accompanied by a valid and binding agreement to advance the full amount of the loan upon the completion of the building entered into by an individual, partnership, association, or corporation acceptable to the discounting bank."

(b) Application

The third paragraph of section 371 is intended to enable a national bank to finance the construction of industrial or commercial buildings, or residential or farm buildings, to a limited extent, without such credits having to conform to the provisions of the first paragraph of section 371.

The construction loan requirement contained in the third paragraph of section 371, that there be a "valid and binding agreement entered into by a financially responsible lender to advance the full amount of the bank's loans upon the completion of the buildings," may be met by any form of takeout provision which includes a valid and binding agreement by a financially responsible party and which will result in the full repayment of the bank's loan upon completion of the buildings. The purpose of the statute is that there be adequate provision for the repayment of the full amount of the bank's loan within the time prescribed. This may be provided by a financially responsible buyer as well as by such a lender. The words "lender" and "advance" should be regarded as illustrating rather than requiring a particular form of take-out provision.

§ 224. Garnishment of construction funds. There is little law on the subject of garnishment of construction loan funds by creditors of the mortgagor. It seems probable that such garnishment is illegal. The mortgagee has a vital interest in having the funds applied to the construction of the building. Likewise, contractors working on the building have an interest in the funds. This suffices to protect the funds from garnishment. *Ralph C. Sutro Co. v. Paramount Plastering Inc.,* 31 Cal.Rptr. 174. To some extent the rights of creditors will depend on the language of the construction loan agreement. *Demharter v. First Fed. S & L Assn.,* 412 Pa. 242, 194 A2d 214.

Likewise the courts have held that if the status of construction is such that the contractor is not entitled to receive payment, his crediors cannot garnishee the construction loan funds. *Harris v. Valen Const. Co.,* 49 Ill.App2d 265, 200 NE2d 70.

§ 225. Garnishment of mortgage escrow funds. Quite commonly mortgages today require that each monthly payment contain a sum that at the end of the year will be adequate to defray taxes and insurance. These are spoken of, inaccurately, as "mortgage escrow deposits." Creditors of the mortgagor cannot garnishee or attach such funds because the mortgagor has parted with all control over them. *Valerio v. College Point Bank*, 264 NYS2d 343; *Central Suffolk Hosp. Assn. v. Downs*, 213 NYS2d 192. The relation of debtor and creditor does not exist as to the escrow funds. This also insulates the funds from seizure by the mortgagor's trustee in bankruptcy. *In re Simon*, 167 FSupp. 214.

§ 226. Liability of construction lender for construction defects—negligence liability. In a recent landmark decision the principle was announced that where a construction lender finances the construction of moderately priced homes, and where the builders are relatively inexperienced and undercapitalized, the construction lender becomes liable to the homebuyers for defects in construction. *Connor v. Great Western S & L Assn.*, 73 Cal. Rptr. 369, 447 P2d 609, 73 Dick. L.Rev. 730; 10 Boston College Ind. & Comm.L.Rev. 932. The decision has been viewed with disfavor and the rule has been abolished in California by statute. It seems unlikely that this decision will command substantial support. 47 N.C.L. Rev. 989; 25 Bus. Law. 1309.

The mortgagee must exercise care in disbursing the loan proceeds for he may become personally liable to the mortgagor for any loss suffered by the mortgagor owing to the mortgagee's negligence.

EXAMPLE: (1) The mortgagee paid all construction funds to general contractor when the building was only one-third completed. *Robinson v. Keaton*, 239 Ark. 587, 393 SW2d 231. (2) The mortgagee disbursed construction funds without checking to see if construction work was in place to warrant such disbursement. *Equitable S. & L. Ass'n. v. Hewitt*, 67 Ore. 280, 135 P 864. (3) The mortgagee paid out construction funds without demanding lien waivers or paid bills. In all such cases the mortgagee was held liable for loss resulting to the mortgagor. In other words, in recent times the courts have felt that the mortgagee must protect the mortgagor as well as his own interests. *Speights v. Arkansas A. & L. Assn.*, 239 Ark. 587, 393 SW2d 228; *Home Electric Corp. v. Russell*, 17 Utah2d 276, 409 P2d 388,; *Hummell v. Wichita F. S. & L. Assn.*, 190 Kan. 43, 372 P2d 67.

The first mortgage construction lender owes no duty to junior lienors to see that the construction funds find their way into the building. 59 CJS 339. If he wishes to trust the mortgagor, he may turn over the construction funds to him, and if he diverts the money to other projects the junior lienors have no rights as to the construction lender.

18

Priorities—Recording—Marshalling of Assets—Circuity of Lien

§ 227. **In general.** The most important problem in mortgage law is that of *priority of lien.* If a mortgagor remains solvent, he pays the mortgage debt. No problem exists. Where the mortgagor becomes insolvent, he often owes a number of creditors, and of this group some will have liens on the land. Since the land will be inadequate to pay all creditors, each creditor will struggle to establish his lien as one having priority over other liens. The rules of priority derive from several sources; for example, statutes (*e.g.,* recording laws), case law (*e.g.,* the purchase money mortgage rule), and provisions of the mortgage or other documents (*e.g.,* subordination clauses and agreements).

§ 228. **Recording.** The problems of recording law are of utmost importance in mortgage law. However, excellent discussions of this aspect of the law will be found in other treatises and need not be elaborated here to any great extent. Osborne, *Mortgages* § 194.

§ 229. **Chain of title.** Except in a few states a title searcher tracing title by means of the public records employs an official index of names, called the Grantor-Grantee Index. Suppose, for example, that the United States Government records show that the United States sold a particular tract of land to John Jones on March 15, 1840. The title searcher will turn to the Grantor Index, which is arranged alphabetically, and, beginning with the date March 15, 1840, he will look under the letter "J" for any deeds or mortgages made since March 15, 1840, by John Jones. Naturally he would not expect to find any deeds or mortgages of that land made by Jones prior to March 15, 1840, because Jones did not become the owner until that date. Therefore the law does not require him to look for any such deeds or mortgages prior to that date. Suppose he finds that John Jones conveyed the land to Joseph Smith by deed dated September 10, 1860, and recorded November 1, 1860. He will now look under the letter "S" for any deeds or mortgages made by Smith on or after September 10, 1860, the date when Smith acquired title. This process is repeated until he has brought the title down to the present. This process is called *running the chain of title.*

To be considered properly recorded, a deed or mortgage must be in the *chain of title,* that is, it must be dated in the proper chronological order.

EXAMPLES: At a time when his negotiations for the purchase were virtually concluded, Joseph Smith made a mortgage on the land dated September 5, 1860, and recorded September 6, 1860. Both of these dates were prior to the date of the deed by which Smith later acquired ownership, namely, September 10, 1860. A title searcher would not find this mortgage, since he would not look under the name "Smith" for any deed or mortgage prior to September 10, 1860. Such a mortgage is not in the line of title. It is also said that the mortgage is not in the *chain of title. The legal result is the same as though the mortgage had not been recorded at all.* A person buying the land not knowing of the existence of this mortgage would get good title free and clear of the mortgage.

In other words, the records show the ownership of land passing from one person to another, and the name of each successive owner as that name appears on the public records must be searched only during the period of his ownership as such period is revealed by the public records to see what recorded deeds and mortgages he has signed.

Because of the *chain of title theory,* it is important that names be spelled correctly in deeds and mortgages.

EXAMPLE: A deed runs to *John O. Malley* and a mortgage is thereafter made by *John O'Malley.* The mortgage is not in the chain of title and is treated as an unrecorded mortgage. The deed is indexed under M, the mortgage under O.

§ 230. **Tract indexes.** In a few states (Iowa, Louisiana, Nebraska, North Dakota, Oklahoma, South Dakota, Utah, Wisconsin, and Wyoming, for example), the name index (Grantor-Grantee Index) has been supplemented or replaced by a Tract Index. This index allocates a separate page in the index to each piece of property in the county, and if you are interested in a particular piece of property, you simply locate the proper page in the index, where you will find listed all recorded deeds and other documents relating to this piece of property.[1]

§ 231. **Instruments recorded or liens or interests attaching on the same day.** This problem can be illustrated by an example.

---

[1] Kratovil, *Real Estate Law,* 5th ed. (Englewood Cliffs, N.J.: Prentice-Hall, Inc., 1969), pp. 64–65, © 1969.

EXAMPLE: *R* gives a mortgage to *E* which *E* records on July 30, 1970, at 10:00 A.M. *R* gives another mortgage to *E-2* which *E-2* records on the same day at 3:00 P.M. Other things being equal, *E* has the prior and superior lien. The law will inquire into fractions of a day for this purpose, even though the general rule in other fields is that fractions of the day may be disregarded. 52 Am. Jur. 341.

The same is true when a judgment becomes a lien on the land the same day the mortgage is recorded. 1 Black, *Judgments,* 555; 2 Freeman, *Judgments,* (5th ed.) 2060–2064; *Winchester v. Parm,* 16 Del. Ch. 84, 141 A 271; *Cleason's Appeal,* 22 Pa. 359; *Murfree's Heirs v. Carmack,* 4 Yerg (Tenn.) 270. The cases adjudicating this proposition are numerous.

On the other hand when two mortgages are recorded simultaneously, the fact that one was given a lower document number by the recorder is of no significance. This does not give that mortgage priority. 59 CJS 317. In such cases priority must be determined in some other fashion. It is the invariable practice of a mortgagee who is to receive a first mortgage and who knows another mortgage is to be filed simultaneously to insist that the other mortgage be marked with a legend indicating it is *subject to* the intended first mortgage.

§ 232. Priority of notes secured by same mortgage. Where one mortgage secures several notes, and the notes are sold to different persons, the various states have different rules governing the relative priority of such notes:

1. In a number of states, Iowa, Indiana, New Hampshire, Ohio, Missouri, Kansas, Florida, Illinois, and Wisconsin, for example, there are court decisions to the effect that a mortgage given to secure two or more notes maturing at different dates must be considered as if there were as many different successive mortgages as there are notes. In other words, the various notes enjoy priority of lien in the order of their maturity. If the mortgage secures five notes, one due each year after the date of the mortgage, there would be, in legal effect, not one but five mortgages. The first note falling due would be a first mortgage on the land; the second note due, a second mortgage; and so on. *In re Lalla,* 362 Ill. 621, 1 NE2d 50. The operation of this rule is not affected by the fact that the original mortgagee sold the various notes at different times to different people. Thus, if the mortgage secures five notes, one due each year after date, and the original mortgagee sells note number 5, and retains the earlier maturing notes, he still has priority over note number 5. *Domeyer v. O'Connell,* 364 Ill. 467, 4 NE2d 830, 108 ALR 476.

2. An entirely different rule is followed in a number of states. These states, Georgia, Alabama, Virginia, West Virginia, and Oklahoma, for example, follow the rule that when a mortgage secures a number of notes, and the mortgagee originally holds all the notes, and he thereafter sells and assigns one or more of the notes, but retains the remainder of the notes, the mortgagee thereby auto-

matically makes the notes that he retains subject and subordinate to the notes he has sold. And this rule operates regardless of the maturity dates of the notes. Thus, if a mortgage secures five notes due one each year after date, and the mortgagee originally owns all five notes, but sells note number 5 to *A*, *A* automatically acquires a first lien on the land, and the first four notes automatically become subject and subordinate to note number 5. In effect, the original mortgagee is left holding a second mortgage on the land. *Lawson v. Warren*, 34 Okla. 94, 124 P. 46, 42 L.R.A.(NS) 183. Most courts would give *A* priority if the mortgagee guarantees payment of the note sold to *A* or if the mortgagee endorses the note, so that he becomes liable for payment in case of the mortgagor's default. *In re Phillippi*, 329 Pa. 581, 198 A 16.

3. However, the rule followed in most states is that where a mortgage secures a number of notes, all the notes have equal lien regardless of their maturity dates or the dates of their assignment.

Special or local rules differing from the above rules exist in a number of states. Whenever a mortgage secures more than one note, it is important that the mortgage contain a clause to the effect that all notes are equally secured by the mortgage without any preference or priority by reason of priority in time of maturity, negotiation, or otherwise. This is known as the *parity* clause or *preference and priority clause*. Under such a clause, all notes have equal lien. Failure to understand these rules has led to much trouble. Many printed mortgage forms are only intended for use when the mortgage secures one note, and if such a form is used when the mortgage secures several notes, the results may be disastrous.

§ 233. **Marshalling of assets.** There is danger for the mortgagee in releasing personal liability of either the mortgagor or an assuming grantee.

EXAMPLE: *R* executed a mortgage and note to *E*. *R* then sold the land to *X*. *E* then with full knowledge of the sale to *X*, released *R*'s personal liability on the mortgage note. The court held that this removed any incentive on *R*'s part to pay the debt and the mortgage lien was therefore extinguished. *Coyle v. Davis,* 20 Wis. 593: 2 Jones, *Mortgages,* 238.

EXAMPLE: *R* executed a mortgage and note to *E*. *R* conveyed the land to *X*, who assumed the mortgage debt. *E* then released *X*'s personal liability. This automatically discharged *R*'s personal liability on his note. *Insley v. Webb,* 122 Wash. 98, 209 P 1093; 41 ALR 277.

EXAMPLE: *R* executed a note and mortgage to *E*. Thereafter he executed a junior mortgage to *X*. *E* knew of this transaction. *E* thereafter released *R*'s personal liability. The court held that this gave *X* priority of lien over *E*. *X*'s mortgage became a first mortgage. *Minneapolis Ins. Co. v. Nat. Sec. Ins. Co.,* 178 Minn. 50, 226 NW 189; *Sexton v. Pickett,* 24 Wisc. 346.

In all these cases a mortgagee having actual knowledge of another's rights has taken action the courts consider prejudicial to those rights and they punish the mortgagee accordingly.

A senior mortgagee who releases part of his land may thereby lose his priority to a junior mortgagee.

EXAMPLE: *R* mortgages Lots 1 and 2 to *E*. Thereafter *R* gives a junior mortgage on Lot 1 to *E-2*. Having actual knowledge of *E-2*'s mortgage, *E* releases his mortgage as to Lot 2, thereby throwing the entire burden of his mortgage on Lot 1. This seems unfair to *E-2*, who, normally, would have assumed that both Lots 1 and 2 would stand as security for the first mortgage debt. *E* will suffer some subordination of his mortgage to *E-2*'s. This is an aspect of the law of *marshalling of assets*. It is applicable when there are *two funds* (Lots 1 and 2) in the hands of a common debtor, and one of those funds is released by a senior creditor to the detriment of a junior creditor. 35 Am. Jur. 386. By the weight of authority, *E-2* moves into the first lien position only to the extent of the value of the Lot 1, the released lot. 2 Glenn, *Mortgages*, 1253; 72 ALR 389. In principle, the same rule should apply to a release by a senior mortgagee of the mortgagor's personal liability. If the mortgagor's personal liability is worth little or nothing, a release totally of this worthless asset ought not deprive the senior mortgagee of his priority.

Many mortgage attorneys argue that marshalling of assets will never be resorted to if the intention is clearly expressed that there shall be no marshalling. 2 Glenn, *Mortgages*, 1239. Thus they include in the first mortgage an express clause that under no circumstances shall there by any marshalling of assets upon any foreclosure or to other enforcement of the senior mortgage. This is a common provision in railroad mortgages. One who acquires a junior lien on the land with notice of this clause in the senior mortgage, can hardly complain of any act done by the senior mortgagee. *Platte Valley Bank v. Kracl*, 174 NW2d 724 (Neb. 1970).

A form of clause that pulls the teeth of the marshalling of assets rules as to partial releases of land is as follows:

> The right is hereby given by the Mortgagors and reserved by the Mortgagee to make partial release or releases of security hereunder, agreeable to the Mortgagee without notice to, or the consent, approval or agreement of others in interest, which partial release or releases shall not impair in any manner the validity of or priority of this mortgage on the security remaining, nor release the personal liability of the Mortgagors for the debt hereby secured.

There is also the *inverse order of alienation rule.*

EXAMPLE: *R* mortgages Lots 1 and 2 to *E*. The mortgage is recorded. *R* sells Lot 1 to *E-2*. *E-2* pays full value without examining the county records and believes he is buying an unencumbered lot. When E forecloses, the court, to protect E-2, will order Lot 2 sold first, to see if it will bring enough to satisfy the mortgage debt. If it does, there is no need to sell Lot 1. 2 Glenn, *Mortgages,* 1230.

This coin has a reverse side.

EXAMPLE: R Mortgages Lots 1 and 2 to E and the mortgage is recorded. R sells Lot 1 to E-2, and the deed recites that E-2 takes subject to the mortgage, which E-2 assumes and agrees to pay. When foreclosure occurs, the court will order this lot sold first, and if it brings enough to satisfy the mortgage, Lot 2 will not be sold.

Since purchasers today invariably search the records, the rule has little importance.

A question of marshalling *in favor of the mortgagor* arises mainly in homestead cases.

EXAMPLE: R mortgages Lot 1 (his homestead) and Lot 2 (non-homestead land) to E-1. The mortgage contains a valid waiver of homestead rights. Later R makes a mortgage of Lot 2 to E-2. By the weight of authority E-2 cannot compel E-1 to sell Lot 1 first at the foreclosure sale. The policy in favor of protecting homesteads forbids this result. There are a few cases *contra.* 44 ALR 758, 761; 46 Harv. L. Rev. 1035; 12 Tex. L. Rev. 514.

Cross-reference: § 461.

§ 234. Failure to foreclose—loss of priority. Failure of the mortgagee to proceed diligently with foreclosure may impair the mortgagee's rights if rights of third parties are present.

EXAMPLE: R mortgaged land to E. R conveyed the land to X, who assumed the mortgage. E filed suit to foreclose the mortgage, but later dismissed the suit. X's personal liability to E was extinguished. *Fed. Land Bank v. Shoemaker,* 263 NYS 653. Here the theory is that by his inaction E may cause the property to lose value, thus prejudicing X.

§ 235. Circuity of lien. This is a problem without a solution. There are several versions of the problem, but one will suffice to illustrate its complexity.

EXAMPLE: R makes a mortgage to E in 1968, which E fails to record. R makes a second mortgage to X in 1969, which X records. X knows of E's mortgage. Therefore he takes subject to E's mortgage, since he is not an innocent mortgagee. R makes a third mortgage to Y in 1970, which Y records. He has no knowledge of E's mortgage. Thus E has priority over X, because of X's knowledge. X has priority over Y because of the prior filing of X's mortgage. Y has priority over E because Y had no knowledge of E's mortgage. There is no agreement at all as to how this difficult situation should be handled. There will be a foreclosure suit that wipes out all three liens and the proceeds of sale will be available for distribution. But how does one distribute them? According to one formula:

1. Pay *Y* the amount of the fund less *X*'s claim.
2. Pay *X* the amount of the fund less *E*'s claim.
3. Pay the residue to *E*.

71 Yale L.J. 53 discusses the Dixon formula in *Hoag v. Layre*, 33 NJ Eq. 552. There are other solutions. 71 Yale L.J. 58 *et seq*. This problem is also referred to as the problem of circular priority. There is a good deal of literature. 19 Minn.L.Rev. 139; 29 Ill.L.Rev. 952; 66 Yale L.J. 784; 38 Colum.L.Rev. 1267.

19

Purchase Money Mortgages

§ 236. In general. The traditional purchase money mortgage is one taken back by the seller for part of the purchase money.

EXAMPLE: A conveys to B for $20,000, $10,000 cash and balance of $10,000 in the form of a mortgage by B to A. This is a purchase money mortgage.

§ 237. Funds advanced by third party. While most purchase money mortgages are those given back to the seller as part of the purchase price, a mortgage given to a lending institution or lender is also treated as a purchase money mortgage if the entire net proceeds are paid to seller as part of the purchase price. 41 CJS 531, 532. A few states limit the priority of purchase money mortgages to the traditional type described in the first paragraph of this section. *Ibid.* It is best to have the lender's check run directly to the seller (at the mortgagor's direction, of course) so that the money does not pass through the hands of the mortgagor. Otherwise a few states will refuse to treat it as a purchase money mortgage. *Austin v. Underwood,* 37 Ill. 438.

§ 238. Priorities. The law relating to the superiority of purchase money mortgages is well settled. Purchase money mortgages generally take priority over any other prior or subsequent claims or liens attaching to the property through the mortgagor. Purchase money mortgages are recognized as being senior to claims of dower and homestead as well as to earlier judgments and earlier mortgages on after-acquired property. *County of Pinellas v. Clearwater Fed.Sav. & L. Ass'n.,* 214 So.2d 525 (Fla. 1968); Osborne, *Mortgages* § 213.

EXAMPLE: A conveys land to B who gives A a purchase money mortgage not signed by B's wife. A's purchase money mortgage has priority over the dower rights of B's wife and over all homestead rights of B or his wife.

159

EXAMPLE: *X* obtains a judgment against *B* in 1969. *A* conveys land to *B* in 1970 and *B* gives *A* a purchase money mortgage. The mortgage has priority of lien over the judgment.

EXAMPLE: *X Corporation* gives *E* a mortgage in 1969 on Lot 1, with an after-acquired property clause. In 1970 *A* conveys Lot 2 to *X Corporation*, which gives *A* a purchase money mortgage. It has priority over *E's* mortgage.

A purchase money mortgage can lose priority.

EXAMPLE: In 1969 *A* gives a deed to *B* and *B* gives back a purchase money mortgage. The deed is recorded, but the mortgage is not. In 1970 *B* gives a mortgage to *C*. In 1971 the purchase money mortgage is recorded. It is junior to *C's* mortgage. Purchase money mortgages are not excused from the recording law. The same would be true if in 1970 *C* gets a judgment against *B*. The judgment would have priority over the purchase money mortgage. Of course, if the later lienor has actual notice of the purchase money mortgage, the purchase money mortgage has priority. *Truesdale v. Brennan,* 153 Mo. 600, 55 SW 147.

§ 239. Deficiency decree or judgment. Some state laws forbid entry of a deficiency judgment or decree on a purchase money mortgage.

20

Condominium and Planned Unit Developments—Priorities Problems

§ 240. **The** condominium and the planned unit development seem to have acquired a firm grip on the imagination of today's home seeker. So far as the legal mechanics of these types of development are concerned, they have much in common. Kratovil, *Real Estate Law* (5th ed. 1969), Chapters 32 and 33. An important document, placed of record at the inception of the project, is the *declaration of restrictions, easements, liens and covenants,* referred to hereafter as the *declaration.* Kratovil *Real Estate Law* (5th ed. 1969) § 579. The planned unit development is referred to as the *PUD.* Both in the condominium and the PUD, the home association will want a provision in the declaration giving it the right to levy assessments on the homeowner for maintenance of the common areas. Again, this can be done in the declaration, since the law requires no great formality for the creation of equitable or contractual liens. *Prudential Ins. Co. v. Wetzel,* 212 Wis. 100, 248 NW 791. Such assessment liens are enforceable by foreclosure, like a mortgage. *Rodruck v. Sand Point,* 48 Wash.2d 565, 295 P2d 714. The lien serves an important purpose. The declaration creates covenants which give the association the right to sue the homeowner for assessments, and to get a judgment against him. The covenants, in other words, create personal liability. But where the homeowner is financially irresponsible, or simply disappears, so that summons cannot be served upon him, the lien for his delinquent assessments can be foreclosed. Both methods of enforcement should be provided for. The declaration should state that any delinquent assessment bears interest at the highest legal rate and that attorney's fees are collectible as part of the assessment.

In both the condominium and the PUD there will usually be two liens, the lien of the mortgage on the home or apartment, and the lien of the assessments. Obviously a question will arise as to whether foreclosure of a mortgage will wipe out delinquent assessment liens or vice versa. A mortgage recorded subsequent to the recording of the deed and declaration creating the lien is subject and subordinate to such lien, even as to assessments accruing subsequent to the recording of the mortgage. *Prudential Ins. Co. v. Wetzel,* 212 Wis. 100, 248 NW 791. Foreclosure of the assessment lien wipes out the mortgage. Mortgages that antedate the effective date of the declaration or deeds will be prior and superior to the assessment liens (*Kennilwood Owners' Ass'n. v. Kennilwood,* 28 NYS2d 239), so that foreclosure of the mortgage will cut out all unpaid assessments and the future liability of the lot to pay assessments. This creates a potential conflict. Mortgagees, especially those who are required by law to loan only on first mortgages, will insist that the lien of all assessments, even those created by an earlier declaration, be subordinated to the lien of their mortgages. The wishes of the mortgagee must prevail, since otherwise financing cannot be obtained. However, once the mortgage is foreclosed and the mortgagee has become the owner of the lot, the lien of future assessments should be binding on the mortgagee, as they would be on any other homeowner. This can be accomplished by a clause in the declaration as follows:

SUGGESTED FORM: The lien of the assessments provided for herein shall be subordinate to the lien of any mortgages now or hereafter placed upon the properties subject to assessments and running to a bank, savings and loan association, insurance company or other institutional lender; provided, however, such subordination shall apply only to the assessments which have become due and payable prior to a sale or transfer of such property pursuant to a decree of foreclosure, or any other proceeding in lieu of foreclosure. Such sale or transfer shall not relieve such property from liability for any assessments thereafter becoming due nor from the lien of any such subsequent assessment.[1]

---

[1] Kratovil, *Real Estate Law,* 5th ed. (Englewood Cliffs, N.J.: Prentice-Hall, Inc., 1969), p. 371, © 1969.

21

Subordinations

§ 241. In general. Once priority has been established, it sometimes becomes desirable or necessary to reverse such priority by the voluntary act of the parties. In many cases, this is accomplished by the release or extinguishment of the prior interest and its re-creation subsequent to the date of the creation of the interest intended to be prior.

EXAMPLE: *R* gives *E-1* a mortgage in 1970. In 1971 *R* gives another mortgage on the same land to *E-2*. *E-2* insists on a first mortgage. *E-1* is induced to release his mortgage. Now *E-2* has a first mortgage on the property. Thereafter *R* gives a junior mortgage on the property to *E-1*.

It may be desirable, however, to maintain the existence of the prior interest, but to have its owner agree that its priority has been shifted to an inferior position with relation to another later created interest. Such an agreement is generally called a *subordination agreement*. Thus in the example given above, *E-1* could subordinate his mortgage to *E-2*'s mortgage.

While the situations where these agreements are obtained are varied, common examples are as follows:

EXAMPLE: *A* sells an orange grove to *B* and *B* gives *A* a purchase money mortgage. It is intended that *B* will subdivide the land and build residences on the land. The purchase money mortgage provides that it is subordinate to mortgages put on residential lots by homebuyers.

EXAMPLE: *R* leases land to *T* for a long term. *T* mortgages the leasehold to *E* to raise money to erect a building. *R* subordinates his title to *E*'s mortgage.

EXAMPLE: *R* leases a space in a building to *E*. The lease provides that it is subordinate to any mortgage *R* may later place on the property to an institutional lender.

§ 242. **Specific subordinations.** Where both the superior interest (that is to be subordinated) and the inferior interest (that is to be given priority) are in existence, no problems are presented.

EXAMPLE: *R* gives a mortgage to *E* in 1968. It is recorded. *R* gives a mortgage to *E-2* in 1970. It is recorded. *E* and *E-2* sign an agreement by which the mortgage given *E-2* is made a first lien on the land and *E*'s mortgage is the second lien. The agreement is recorded and a legend is typed on *E*'s mortgage and note indicating that it has been so subordinated. This is done to prevent *E* from selling the mortgage to an innocent purchaser having no knowledge of the subordination. Often *E* is paid a substantial sum to induce him to sign the subordination.

EXAMPLE: *R* gives *T* a lease in 1968. *R* gives *E* a mortgage in 1970. Again *T* and *E* can sign an agreement subordinating the lease to the mortgage so that foreclosure of the mortgage will extinguish the lease.

§ 243. **Automatic subordinations.** In many instances, however, the subordination agreement is prepared before the intended paramount interest has been created. Frequently the agreement for subordination is a provision in the instrument which creates, or retains, the interest which is to be subordinate. This instrument usually is a purchase money or other mortgage or a lease. If the agreement or provision states that the interest to be subordinate becomes so as soon as the subordinating interest is created, it commonly is referred to as an "automatic subordination."

EXAMPLE: *A* sells farm land to *B* in 1969 and *B* gives *A* a purchase money mortgage. The mortgage recites that *B* is to subdivide the land and to construct homes on the lots, also that the purchase money mortgage is to be subordinate to any construction loan for such purposes given to an institutional lender for a sum not to exceed $20,000 per house at 8% interest. This is an automatic subordination.

§ 244. **Agreements for future subordination.** There are also agreements for future subordination.

EXAMPLE: *A* sells a farm to *B*. *B* gives *A* a purchase money mortgage. *B* and *B* enter into an agreement that *A* will subordinate his mortgage to construction loans not to exceed $20,000 per home at interest not to exceed 8% interest, or such a clause is included in the mortgage.

§ 245. **Issues arising where new mortgage or new interest is not involved.** In automatic subordination situations and agreements for future subordination litigation may ensue that does not involve the new mortgage that is to be given priority. The litigation is between other parties.

EXAMPLE: In the example last given *B* puts a construction loan on a lot and comes to *A* for a subordination. *A* refuses. *B* files litigation in the nature of a specific performance suit. The same kind of litigation can arise in an automatic subordination situation where a dispute arises between *A* and *B*.

If the subordination provisions are poorly drafted, and lack completeness or certainty, *A* may prevail. For example, if the subordination provisions do not give the amount of the construction loan that is to achieve priority, *A* will often prevail on the ground that the subordination is too indefinite to be enforced. *Tarses v. Miller Fruit and Produce Co.,* 155 Md. 448, 142 A 522; *Bruggeman v. Sokol,* 122 Cal.App.2d 876, 265 P2d 575; *Wright v. Fred Heydon Industries, Inc.,* 6 Cal.Rptr. 392 (Cal.App.); *Magna Development Company v. Reed,* 228 Cal.App.2d 230, 39 Cal.Rptr. 284; *Lahaina-Maui Corp. v. Tau Tet Heu,* 362 F2d 419 (9th Cir); Miller, Starr and Regalia, *Subordination Agreements in California,* 13 U.C.L.A. L. Rev. 1298; *Subordination of Purchase-Money Security,* 52 Calif. L. Rev. 157. *See* 26 ALR3rd 855.

Or the subordination provision may have omitted the interest rate or other terms of the construction loan. *Gould v. Callan,* 127 Cal.App.2d 1, 273 P2d 93; *Kessier v. Sapp,* 169 Cal.App.2d 818, 338 P2d 34; *Spellman v. Dixon,* 63 Cal.Rptr. 668 (Cal.App.); *Standard American Homes v. Pasadena Corp.,* 147 P2d 729 (Md.). The following cases, however, have held that specifying *all* the terms is not necessary: *Simmons v. Dryer,* 216 Cal.App2d 733, 31 Cal.Rptr. 199 (only amount of loan stated); *Burrows v. Timmsen,* 223 Cal.App2d 283, 35 Cal.Rptr. 668 (maximum amount, interest rate and maturity stated); *Stockwell v. Lindeman,* 229 Cal.App2d 750, 40 Cal.Rptr. 555 (maximum amount and interest rate stated); *Cummins v. Gates,* 235 Cal.App2d 532, 45 Cal.Rptr. 417 (maximum amount, interest rate and purpose stated). Some decisions permit rather general subordinations. *White & Ballard v. Goodinow,* 58 Wash.2d 180, 361 P2d 571; *Pac.Mut. Life Ins. Co. v. Westglen* Park, 160 Tex. 1, 325 SW2d 113.

There is some indication that rather general automatic subordination language will be sustained where the subordination is to some future institutional mortgagee.

EXAMPLE: A mortgage contained a clause subordinating its lien to a future mortgage of $225,000 to a savings bank, trust company, or insurance company. This was held valid. *Exchange Place Corp. v. Tarvan Realty Inc.,* 255 N.Y.S.2d 1002, 44 Misc2d 988. Evidently the courts trust regulated, institutional lenders to impose reasonable terms.

Oddly, there is little litigation involving the mortgage that was supposed to be given priority by an automatic subordination. In other words if the land developer actually puts a construction loan on a lot and such a mortgage goes into foreclosure, claiming priority over the purchase money mortgage, there is very little law involving cases of this character. Nevertheless, the lesson is obvious. Automatic subordinations and agreements for future subordinations ought to go into considerable detail as to the construction loan.

One who intends to rely on a subordination must usually bring his title search down to the date of the subordination.

EXAMPLE: *R* gives *E* a long-term lease on *R*'s land in 1969. *E* mortgages the leasehold to *E-2* in 1970. *E-2* wants *R*'s ownership subordinated to the leasehold mortgage. Obviously a title search will be needed to make sure that *R* is still the owner of the land, that there are no other liens against him, and so on. *R* can only subordinate his ownership in the condition in which it is at the time of the subordination.

246. Subordination of the fee to leasehold mortgage. This last proposition brings up the question of "subordinations" of the fee ownership. Many lawyers dislike the whole idea. They argue, for example, that it is proper for the owner of the fee simple title to the land (that is, the landowner) to "subordinate" his fee title to a leasehold mortgage is to join in the leasehold mortgage. *Liens* can be subordinated, they argue, but not ownership. There is a very little law on this subject. Probably such subordinations are valid. *Mays v. Middle Iowa Realty Corp.,* 202 Kan.. 712, 452 P2d 279. *Appelfield v. Fidelitity S. & L. Assn.,* 137 So.2d 259 (Fla.); *Cambridge Acceptance Corp. v. Hockstein,* 246 A2d 138. Obviously, such subordinations should be used only where the local court decisions sanction them. There are situations where genuine problems seem to exist.

EXAMPLE: *R* gives a lease to *E*. *E* puts a mortgage deed of trust on the leasehold to *T*, as trustee, to secure a note payable to *E-2*. *R* now "subordinates" his ownership to the deed of trust. Some lawyers find difficulty in seeing how *T* can sell the land at a foreclosure sale if it has not been conveyed to him. Perhaps this argument can be met by including in the subordination a conveyance by *R* and his wife to *T* for mortgage purposes on the same terms as in the leasehold mortgage, expressly excluding liability on *R*'s part for payment of the debt or observance of the covenants in the deed of trust. See *also* § 387.

§ 247. Bringing the fee under a leasehold mortgage. The advantage to the lender of getting a mortgage on both fee and leasehold is obvious. His foreclosure will give him full ownership of the land. The advantage to the tenant is that he can get a bigger loan and there are more lenders to choose from, since some lenders will loan only on land, not leaseholds. The advantage to the landowner is that he gets a valuable building constructed on his land and a lease made in contemplation of such a deal will call for rent based on the full value of the land. The disadvantages to the landlord consist of the danger that he may lose his land if foreclosure ensues and the difficulty of evaluating the extra compensation he ought to receive for the subordination. To protect himself against loss of his land by foreclosure, the landlord should insist that the documents give him the right to see that the construction loan money actually goes into the building.

§ 248. Form of mortgage covering land and leasehold. Where a long lease exists, the construction mortgage may cover the land and leasehold because (1) both landlord and tenant join in the mortgage; (2) the tenant signs the mortgage and the landlord signs a separate document subordinating his land title to the mortgage; or (3) the tenant only signs the mortgage but the lease gives him power to subject the land title to the leasehold mortgage. There is a dearth of authority on method (3) and it therefore presents all the hazards that attend the unknown.

In situation (3) obviously the mortgage should state that the tenant is exercising his power to subject the land title to the leasehold mortgage. This is under the rule that one who exercises a power must make reference to the power.

In general, it is best for the mortgage to describe the land and the leasehold as separate parcels, and give the mortgagee the option of foreclosing on either or both. The mortgage should state that the landowner has no right to have the leasehold sold first at the foreclosure sale, and that the tenant has no right to have the land sold first. This last clause is sometimes called the *anti-marshalling of assets clause. See* § 377.

In situation (3) also, the mortgagee must be at pains to see that the mortgage conforms meticulously to all the requirements of the lease, which should supply adequate detail.

§ 249. Leases, mortgages, and subordinations. The courts appear to be relatively liberal in sustaining blanket automatic subordinations relative to leases and mortgages.

EXAMPLE: A lease provided that it was subordinate "to all present and future mortgages." The court gave this provision full effect. *Kirkeby Corp. v. Cross Bridge Towers Inc.,* 91 N.J.S. 126, 219 A2d 343; *In re American Pile Fabric,* 85 F2d 961.

EXAMPLE: A mortgage provided that it was subject to future leases made by the mortgagor. This was held valid. *Sammons v. Kearney Power Co.,* 77 Neb. 580, 110 NW 308.

If a subordination of a mortgage to a lease requires the tenant to pay a specified part of the rent to the mortgagee, this is binding on the tenant if he claims the benefit of the subordination. *Bank of America v. Hirsch Mercantile Co.,* 64 Cal.App.2d 446, 148 P2d 110.

If a prior lease is subordinated to a mortgage that forbids payment of rent in advance, this provision is binding on the landlord and tenant. *Matthews v Hinton,* 44 Cal.Rptr. 694.

Where the mortgagee by an instrument joined in by the lessee and mortgagee subordinates his mortgage to a lease executed subsequent to the mortgage, most lawyers feel that this, for all purposes, puts the lease ahead of the mortgage for all purposes, just as if the lease had been in existence when the mortgage was signed. However, it is customary to state in the subordination that this is the intention of the parties. Plainly, this course has advantages to both parties. The lease will not be extinguished by foreclosure of the mortgage and the lessee can proceed to erect valuable improvements with this assurance. The mortgagee will be able to hold the lessee (in title and intermediate states and in all states where there is an assignment of leases and rents) liable on his covenants to pay rent and perform under the lease. *See* §§ 301, 303. Concurrently with execution of the subordination, the mortgagee is likely to insist that the lessee and mortgagor sign representations that the lease has not been amended, that rent has been paid as required by the lease but has not been prepaid, and that there are no breaches of covenant under the lease.

If the mortgagee attempts unilaterally, by a document signed by him alone, to subordinate his mortgage to the lease, it is doubtful that he can thus lift himself by his bootstraps. He cannot put himself behind the lease in this fashion so as to be able to hold the lessee as though the lease antedated the mortgage.

A landlord giving a lease often gives thought to the possibility that if he wishes to mortgage the land thereafter, the lender may insist that his mortgage be prior and superior to all leases. The lessee, on the other hand, fears that if he signs a lease that subordinates his lease to all future mortgages, he might wind up junior to some outrageous mortgage held by a relative or nominee of the landlord, and that his lease could be extinguished by foreclosure after he had made valuable improvements and built up a good business. A compromise is to state that the lease will be subordinate only to a first mortgage running to an institutional lender. Other clauses that are sometimes found in this subordination include the "non-disturbance" agreement, which permits the tenant to remain in possession despite foreclosure of the mortgage as long as he pays the rent reserved by the lease.

§ 250. Non-disturbance clause. The *non-disturbance clause* or agreement appears in a variety of forms. In one form it occurs in a lease. The lease states that it is subject to a future mortgage to an institutional lender (bank, savings and loan association, insurance company) provided the possession of the lessee shall not be disturbed by the mortgagee. Friedman, *Preparation of Leases* (1962), 61; 2 Fleck, *Abstract and Title Practice* (2d ed. 1958) § 1565.5. Or there may be an agreement between a mortgagee and a prior lessee subordinating the lease to the mortgage, again with the *non-disturbance clause*. Hyde, "The Real Estate Lease as a Credit Instrument," *The Business Lawyer,* July 1965, p. 359. Most likely these clauses are employed where there is doubt, under the state law, whether an institutional lender would violate the investment laws that govern such lender if he loaned on property where the lease enjoys priority over the mortgage. Many of these investment laws are rather vague as to mortgage investments, simply stating that an insurance company, for example, can invest in first mortgages. These laws, by and large, are unsophisticated from the standpoint of mortgage law, since they do not take account of the technical problems that make prior leases superior, from a security standpoint, to junior leases. *See* § 301. At all events the non-disturbance clause attempts to solve the problem by making the lease subject to the mortgages (this satisfies the state regulatory bodies) and assuring the lessee that he will not be ousted as long as he pays his rent, which satisfies the lessee. The party who is not satisfied is the attorney who must advise a client in these circumstances. It is difficult to understand how a lease can be subordinate to a mortgage (which means that it can be extinguished by foreclosure) and yet have the tenant's right to possession continue despite foreclosure as long as he pays his rent. Many lawyers are witholding judgment until court decisions reveal the answer to this problem. 10 U. of Fla. L.Rev. 495.

§ **251. Parties to subordinations.** If there is a first mortgage on land, and a second mortgage is later placed thereon, the mortgagees can achieve subordination without participation by the landowner. *Putnam v. Broten,* 60 N.D. 97, 232 NW 749. On the other hand, the mortgagor and mortgagee can agree that a mortgage to a third party has the benefit of this agreement although he was not party thereto. *Rose v. Provident S & L Assn.,* 28 Ind.App. 25, 62 NE 293.

At times, however, participation by another is necessary. *See* § 249.

§ **252. Authority to subordinate.** Where a corporation purports to subordinate its interest in the property to a mortgage, a question inevitably arises as to the authority of the corporate officers to execute the subordination. The step entails such drastic consequences that the decisions appear to require sanction of the subordination by the board of directors of the corporation. Even the president of the corporation seems to lack the power to subordinate. 53 ALR2d 1421. In view of these decisions it is surprising to find subordination provisions commonly inserted in mortgages that are not even signed by the mortgagee doing the subordinating. At best such documents are authorized by the mortgagee's loan committee. Perhaps these can be accepted as customary transactions falling within the competence of the loan committee. Where a corporation is one that under the laws regulating it can only invest in first mortgages, it is doubtful that it has the power to subordinate its first mortgage to another mortgage on the same property. It seems that one who holds a negotiable note secured by a mortgage has apparent or ostensible authority to subordinate it to another mortgage even though actual authority to do so is lacking. *First-Trust Joint Stock Bank v. Hickock,* 367 Ill. 144, 10 NE2d 646.

§ **253. Diversion of construction proceeds.** When a mortgage, (for example, a purchase money mortgage given when a developer acquires vacant land) is subordinated to a "construction mortgage," a question that arises relates to the situation where the proceeds of the construction loan are diverted, in whole or in part, to purposes other than construction on the land. Some decisions proceed on the theory that the mortgagee in the subordinated mortgage has no right to have the funds so applied unless the loan documents so state. *Mathews v. Hinton,* 234 Cal.App.2d 736, 44 Cal.Rptr. 692; *Iowa Loan & Trust Co. v. Plewe,* 202 Ia. 79, 209 NW 399; *Darst v. Bates,* 95 Ill. 493; 42 Yale L. J. 980. Indeed, this is said to be the rule supported by a majority of the decisions. *See* cases cited in *Cambridge Acceptance Corp. v. Hockstein,* 102 N.J.S. 435, 246 A2d 138.

The result is likely to be the same where the subordination binds only the *borrower* to see that the loan funds are used for construction.

EXAMPLE: *R* gave a mortgage to *E. R* and *E* entered into a subordination agreement subordinating this mortgage to a later mortgage, the proceeds of which were to be used in constructing an apartment building and garage. *R* gave a mortgage to *E-2* and the proceeds were used in constructing an apartment building, but no garage was constructed. The court held that the subordination was effective. Only the borrower, not the new mortgagee, had the obligation to build the buildings described in the subordination. *Brooklyn Trust Co. v. Fairfield Gardens,* 260 N.Y. 16, 182 NE 231.

Where the later *mortgagee* contracts with the earlier mortgagee to see that the proceeds are used in construction, this must be done if the subordination is to be effective. *See* cases cited in *Cambridge Acceptance Corp. v. Hockstein,* 102 N.J.S. 435, 246 A2d 138.

Other courts have taken the view that a construction lender who fails to police the loan disbursement in this respect deserves to be punished by losing his loan priority to the extent that the construction proceeds are diverted to non-construction purposes, such as loan commissions. *Cambridge Accept. Corp. v. Hockstein,* 102 N.J.S. 426, 246 A2d 138.

The courts are not always clear as to the precise legal principle involved. At times the decision appears to turn on implications they read into the subordination document.

EXAMPLE: *R* gave a mortgage to *E-1*. This mortgage contained a provision that it was to remain subordinate to the lien of any "building loan bond and mortgage." Thereafter *R* gave a mortgage to *E-2*, which purported to be a building loan mortgage for the construction of dwellings on the land, but the proceeds were not used for construction. The court held that *E-2*'s mortgage did not meet the requirements of *E-1*'s mortgage and was ineffective. *York Mortgage Corp. v. Clotar Const. Corp.,* 254 N.Y. 128, 172 NE 265.

EXAMPLE: A mortgage recited that it would be subject to any "construction loan mortgage." A construction loan mortgage was placed on the property thereafter, and the proceeds were used for construction except a portion used to pay the lender a commission. It was held that the commission portion did not enjoy the benefit of the subordination. *Claypool v. German Fire Ins. Co.,* 32 Ind. App. 540. *Accord: Lehnert v. Notlin Realty Corp.,* 251 N.Y. 340, 167 NE 463.

The moral is obvious. The mortgagee had better police disbursement.

The fact that all of the construction mortgage is not disbursed is unimportant so long as what was disbursed went for construction. *Johnson v. Florida Bank*, 153 Fla. 120, 13 So.2d 799.[1]

§ 254. **Intervening liens.** This problem can best be explained by an illustration.

EXAMPLE: *R* gives a mortgage to *E-1* in 1968 for $5,000. *X* obtains a judgment against *R* in 1969 which is a lien on the land. *R* gives a mortgage to *E-2* in 1970 for $10,000. *E-1* subordinates his mortgage to *E-2's* mortgage. *E-2* has priority over the judgment only to the extent of $5,000. *Wayne Int. B & L Assn. v. Moats*, 149 Ind. 123, 48 NE 793.

§ 255. **Subordination by estoppel.** Equity always retains the power to declare a lien subordinated where the holder thereof has been guilty of inequitable conduct.

EXAMPLE: *XYZ Bank* sold a bond issue to its customers and continued to function as collection agent. The mortgagor defaulted. *XYZ Bank* advanced its own funds to acquire the defaulted bonds to conceal the existence of defaults. In a subsequent foreclosure, the court declared these bonds subordinate to the remaining bonds. *Lake View T. & S. Bank v. Rice*, 279 Ill.App. 538; 30 Ill.L. Rev. 493.

EXAMPLE: The guarantor of payment of mortgage notes acquired some of such notes. They were held subordinate to the other notes. *Robbins v. Slavin*, 292 Ill.App. 479, 11 NE2d 651.

ADDITIONAL REFERENCES: See *Middlebrook-Anderson* Co. *v. Southwest S. & L. Assn.*, 96 Cal. Reptr. 338 (Comprehensive review of authorities).

---

[1] Turner, "Subordination Agreements" (Chicago, Ill.: Chicago Title & Trust Co., *The Guarantor*, Oct. 1968, pp. 1–7). © 1968.

22

Subrogation

§ 256. Equitable subrogation in favor of mortgage. Courts of equity have evolved a doctrine known as *equitable subrogation*, also sometimes called *legal subrogation*. Most often it is applied in favor of refunding mortgages.

EXAMPLE: In 1968 R mortgages land to E. In 1969 R places a second mortgage on the land to E-2 which is recorded. In 1970 E's mortgage falls due. R borrows money from E-3 to pay off E's mortgage, which is done, and E's mortgage is released. Thereafter E-3 learns of E-2's mortgage. E-3 forecloses, claiming priority over E-2's mortgage. By the great weight of authority E-3 will be accorded priority. Osborne, *Mortgages* § 282. Various reasons are offered in the decisions for this rule. At times courts speak of *mistake*, pointing out that E-3 undoubtedly was mistaken as to the true condition of the title. At other times courts express the notion that E-3's *intention* must have been to succeed to E's position. Such a statement is usually accompanied by the statement that one who lends on the general credit of the mortgagor is never granted subrogation. In point of fact, the real reason for the rule is the simple justice it accomplishes. E-2 remains in exactly the same position he occupied when he made his loan. He is subject to a prior lien of the same amount or less that existed when he made his loan. The fact that E-3 demanded a mortgage shows he was not loaning on the general credit of the mortgagor. A few courts refuse to give E-3 relief, pointing out that to do so would be to reward negligence. *Fort Dodge B & L. Assn. v. Scott*, 86 Ia. 431, 53 NW 283. Negligence in searching the title or in omitting a title search altogether is commonly present in these cases. Nevertheless, the great weight of authority supports the rule stated. Negligence of this sort should not be penalized. *HOLC v. Collins*, 120 NJEq. 266, 184 A 621; *Martin v. Hickinlooper*, 90 Utah 150, 59 P2d 1139. To do so would unjustly enrich E-2. Subrogation is gaining in favor. *Martin v. Hickenlooper*, 90 Utah 150, 59 P2d 1139. It is likely that the minority rule will disappear in time.

The rule of subrogation is invoked for reasons other than the presence of an intervening lien. For example, there could have been, in the example given, some defect in *E-3*'s mortgage. 43 ALR 1393. Perhaps it was a forgery. Perhaps the mortgagor's wife failed to join, so that in the absence of subrogation her dower would be outstanding. Whatever the defect, subrogation cures it as long as *E*'s mortgage was free from any defect. *Serial B.L. & S. I. v. Ehrhardt*, 95 NJEq. 607, 124 A 56; *Davies v. Pugh*, 81 Ark. 253, 99 SW 78; *Everston v. Central Bank*, 33 Kan. 352, 6 P 606; *Helm v. Lynchburg T. & S. Bk*, 106 Va. 603, 56 SE 596.

Equity also recognizes the doctrine of *conventional subrogation*. The word *conventional* refers to the fact that subrogation is accomplished here by agreement. One of the secondary meanings of *convention* is an *agreement*.

EXAMPLE: R makes a mortgage to E-1 in 1968, and a second mortgage to E-2 in 1969. In 1970 E-1's mortgage falls due. E-3 is willing to advance the funds to pay E-1's mortgage but demands a first mortgage and E-1 is unwilling to assign his mortgage. In short, E-1 demands payment. R and E-3 sign a contract reciting the facts and containing an agreement that E-3 will succeed to E-1's lien the moment his funds go into E-1's hands. This sounds a little strange to laymen. They are puzzled over the fact that an agreement to which E-2 is not a party can affect his lien. Nevertheless, conventional subrogation is universally recognized in countless decisions. 50 Am. Jur. *Subrogation* § 3. The agreement serves several purposes. It shows that E-3 was not loaning on R's general credit. It shows his intention to succeed to E-1's lien. Osborne, *Mortgages* § 281. In other words, it shows that the transaction involving E-3 was not a "mere payment," which some cases denounce as not giving rise to subrogation. And it shows that E-3 was not a *volunteer* and that he was not *officious*. These epithets are also encountered in the cases that refuse subrogation. See *Martin v. Hickenlooper*, 90 Utah 150, 59 P2d 1139, 107 ALR 762. There are elements of sophistry and semantics in the decisions. It is said, on occasion, as in the *Hickenlooper* case, that the courts are not enforcing the contract but only look to it to see that E-3 is not a volunteer and that it was E-3's "understanding" that he was to succeed to E-1's lien. Osborne, *Mortgages* § 281. If courts are willing to protect and enforce an "understanding," certainly they ought to be much more willing to do so when that "understanding" is embodied in a contract. In short, it is clear that at times lawyers and judges are as puzzled as laymen at the operation of this principle, yet its simple justice is self-evident.

Conventional subrogation is also useful in connection with the wrap-around mortgage. *See* § 393.

It is also useful in connection with a permanent takeout of a construction loan.

EXAMPLE: In 1968 R mortgages his land to E to raise funds for the construction of a building on the land. The mortgage is recorded on July 1, 1969. At this date construction has not begun. This occurs in a priority state, where this set of facts gives E priority over mechanic's liens arising in the course of construction. See § 214. S, a subcontractor, does work that entitles him to a mechanic's lien, but is not paid. In 1970 *R* gives a permanent mortgage to *E-2*, all of the proceeds of which are used to pay *E*'s mortgage. *E-2* is entitled to equitable subrogation, giving him priority over *S*'s mechanic's lien. *Peterman-Donnelly Corp. v. First Nat. Bank*, 2 Ariz. App. 321, 408 P2d 841; *Planters Lumber Co. v. Wilson*, 241 Ark. 1005, 413 SW 55; *Hoagland v. Decker*, 118 Neb. 194, 224 NW 14; *City Realty Co. v. Tallapoosa*, 231 Ala. 238, 164 So 55.

While the cases cited in the foregoing example apply the doctrine of equitable subrogation, it would be helpful to invoke the doctrine of conventional subrogation as well, for example, by including a clause in the permanent mortgage.

SUGGESTED CLAUSE: The lender is hereby subrogated to the lien of any mortgage or or other lien discharged, in whole or in part, by the proceeds of the loan hereby secured.

Obviously, the institutional lender does not often have need of equitable subrogation. Routinely he demands evidence of title that will reveal the presence of intervening liens. The exception, of course, is the mechanic's lien, which, in most states, is a secret lien for some period of time. It would be a good idea for every permanent takeout lender to insist routinely on a conventional subrogation agreement. It can do no harm and might do a great deal of good. If the title search at the time the permanent mortgage is made reveals an intervening lien, obviously it would be advantageous to attempt to persuade the construction lender to assign his mortgage to the permanent lender. The construction mortgage would not be released of record.

A point of some difficulty, not discussed with frequency, unfortunately, involves the case where the new mortgage secures a greater debt than was secured by the earlier mortgage. It is equitable, arguably, to subject an intervening lien to a debt no greater than that existing when he acquired his lien. That portion of the new mortgage undoubtedly should have priority. Normally this suffices to extinguish the intervening lien even though the balance of the new mortgage might technically be subject and subordinate to the intervening lien.

§ 257. Subrogation in favor of junior mortgages. There will be many instances when a junior mortgagee claims subrogation. At times his claim will prevail and at times it will not.

EXAMPLE: In 1969 *R* mortgages land to *E*. In 1970 *R* mortgages the same land to *E-2*. *R* fails to pay the real estate taxes. In the state in question real estate taxes have a lien prior to all other liens on the land. *E-2* pays the taxes and now claims subrogation to the lien for taxes. That is, to this extent he claims priority over *E*'s mortgage. In most states this claim will not succeed. Money so paid is simply added to *E-2*'s mortgage and has the same lien as the mortgage. Other authorities permit the junior lienor to be subrogated to the paramount lien of the taxes. Osborne, *Mortgages* § 179.

§ 258. Subrogation in favor of mortgagor who conveys. Subrogation can arise in favor of a mortgagor who has conveyed.

EXAMPLE: *R* mortgages his land to *E*. *R* then conveys the land to *X*, the deed reciting that it is subject to the mortgage. *X* fails to pay the mortgage, and *E* demands payment of *R*, who remains liable on the promissory note that always accompanies a mortgage. *R* pays. He is now subrogated to *E*'s mortgage and may foreclose against *X*. If the deed had contained an assumption clause, *R* would also be subrogated to *E*'s right to seek a deficiency decree against *X*. Usually in such situations *E* will be quite happy to assign his mortgage and note to *R*, but if he refuses to do so, subrogation is available.

§ 259. Subrogation in favor of mortgagee for advancements. There are many situations in which a mortgagee feels under an economic compulsion to make advances to protect his mortgage.

EXAMPLE: *E*, a mortgagee, pays taxes or redeems from a tax sale in order to protect his mortgage from extinguishment under local law, where the mortgagor has discontinued all payments. The mortgagee will be able to add such payments to his mortgage debt. Often this result is described in terms of subrogation. Osborne, *Mortgages* § 173.

However, a mortgagee is often confronted with the need for making expenditures that offer doubtful prospect of subrogation; for example, expenditures for hazard insurance, liability insurance, repairs, management fees where he has taken possession and hired a management firm, commissions of rental agents, payments to complete a building under construction, payments for water taxes, sewer taxes, statutory liens such as mechanics' liens, special assessments and like advancements. The mortgage should authorize the mortgagee to make such expenditures and provide that all such payments become part of the mortgage debt of equal lien and dignity with the money originally advanced.

23

Property Covered

§ 260. **Description of the mortgaged property.** An accurate description of the mortgaged land is of great importance. Even greater care must be exercised in this regard than is necessary in the case of deeds. A purchaser usually goes into possession of the land under his deed and thereby gives all the world notice of his rights, since possession imparts constructive notice, whereas a mortgagee rarely goes into possession and therefore depends entirely on the recording of his mortgage to give all subsequent purchasers and mortgagees notice of his rights.

EXAMPLE: *R* owns the Northwest Quarter of Section 14 in a particular township. He executes a mortgage to *E* but through mistake the land is described as the Northwest Quarter of Section 15. Obviously persons searching the title have no way of knowing that the mortgage was intended for land in Section 14. A subsequent purchaser will take title free and clear of the mortgage.

EXAMPLE: *R* owns Lot 1 in Block 1 in Sunnyside Heights, a subdivision in the Northwest Quarter of Section 14 in a particular township. He executes a mortgage which describes the land as Lot 1 in Block 1 in Sunnyside Heights, a subdivision in the Northwest Quarter of Section 15 in the township. Again, purchasers will take title free and clear of the mortgage. *Thorpe v. Helmer*, 275 Ill. 86, 113 NE 554.

Where the question of an inaccurate description arises between the mortgagor and mortgagee, the courts apply liberal rules and will even "reform" a hopelessly bad description if convincing parol evidence is offered as to the land intended to be covered by the mortgage. But where the rights of third parties are involved, notably purchasers who buy in reliance on the condition of the title as revealed by the public records, then the mortgage as it appears on the record must pass fairly rigid tests of accuracy. *Thorpe v. Helmer,* 275 Ill. 86, 113 NE 554; 4 American Law of Property § 17.23; 8 Thompson, *Real Property* § 4302.

The rule applicable to a public road that a description of adjoining land runs to the center of the road is, in most states, applicable to land abutting on a private street or other private right of way, such as railroad, canal, ditch, or storm drain channel. *Rio Bravo Oil Co. v. Weed,* 121 Tex. 427, 50 SW2d 1080, 85 ALR 404; 11 CJS 593; 1 Patton, *Titles,* 381.

EXAMPLE: The right of way of the West Suburban Railroad ran east and west through the center of R's land. He also owned the land in the right of way, subject to the railroad company's easement for street railroad purposes. He made a mortgage to E of that part of his land "bounded on the north by the West Suburban Railroad." This description actually includes the south half of the right of way. *Talbot v. Mass. Mut. Life Ins. Co.,* 183 Va. 882. 14 SE2d 335.

In a few states, this rule is not followed. *Stuart v. Fox,* 129 Me. 407, 152 Atl. 413. It is therefore preferable that a mortgage or other document conveying land bounded on private way make reference to the private way. Thus the description in a mortgage of lot abutting on a private alley might conclude with a phrase like: "also the east half of the private alley lying west of, and adjoining, said lot."

There is a conflict of authority as to the effect of a mortgage that conveys land abutting on a vacated street or alley. 49 ALR2d 982, 1002. Some cases hold that the vacated street or alley does not pass unless mentioned in the mortgage. However, normally the mortgagee intends to acquire this area. Hence the mortgage should describe the premises conveyed as "Lot 1 and the West half of vacated alley lying East of and adjoining Lot 1."

It is not always clear that a description of the mortgaged land carries title to the adjoining streets, especially where a metes and bounds description is used. 19 ALR2d 982. Hence it seems desirable to insert language reflecting such an intention.

> Suggested clause following property description: TOGETHER with all right, title and interest of the Mortgagor, or Mortgagor's successor in title, if any, in and to any land lying in the bed of any street, road, avenue, alley or right-of-way opened or proposed, or hereafter vacated, in front of or adjoining the above described real estate.

§ 261. Chattels and fixtures—the package mortgage. When a mortgage is foreclosed, the mortgagee should be in a position to take over the mortgaged building as a functioning and operating unit. This is something that requires thought at the time the mortgage is made. For example, if the building contains personal property needed for its proper functioning, such as furniture in a furnished apartment building, some arrangement must be made to enable the mortgagee to take over these items in the event the mortgage is foreclosed. To accomplish this, it may be necessary to have the mortgagor create a lien on such chattels, for a real estate mortgage, although it automatically covers fixtures, does not cover personal property.

Under the package mortgage method of financing, the loan that finances the purchase of a home also finances the purchase of equipment—stoves, refrigerators, dishwashers, or washing machines—essential to the livability of the property. Following the legal description in the mortgage is a clause containing a general catch-all enumeration of the common items and a provision reciting that all such items are fixtures and thus part of the real estate. Under the basic rule of fixtures law, ordinary fixtures are treated as real estate, because from all outward appearances they satisfy the intention test as an average person would understand it. Kratovil, *Real Estate Law* 9 (5th ed. 1969). The package mortgage, however, attempts to make certain articles fixtures by means of an agreement between the mortgagor and mortgagee, even though in the absence of such agreement the articles might be considered chattels.

The practical advantages of the package mortgage are obvious. Installation of equipment by the builder makes the house more saleable. Moreover, it may enable the home buyer to finance the purchase of such equipment at a lower interest rate and over a longer term than would be the case if the purchase were made separately from a department store.

The legal objection to the use of the real estate mortgage to cover these articles is that the efficacy of the agreement that certain chattels shall be deemed fixtures has yet to be tested in the courts. If the article is actually removed from the mortgaged premises and then sold to a bona fide purchaser, it is, to all appearances a chattel, and in some states such a purchaser will acquire good title to the article. Kratovil, *Real Estate Law,* 213 (5th ed. 1969). If this were not the law, any purchaser of chattels would incur the risk of losing them if it should later develop that they were wrongfully removed from mortgaged land. In other states, particularly title theory states, the real estate mortgagee is permitted to reclaim such articles, even when he finds them in the possession of an innocent purchaser. Kratovil, *Fixtures and the Real Estate Mortgagee.* 97 U.Pa.L.Rev. 180, 210. And generally a purchaser of such articles who buys them while they are still installed on the mortgaged land will not be protected. *First Mortgaged Bond Co. v. London,* 259 Mich. 688, 244 NW 203; *Dorr v. Dudderar,* 88 Ill. 107. To prevent such articles from passing into the hands of a bona fide purchaser, some mortgagees have initiated the practice of pasting a notice on the equipment stating that the article is covered by the real estate mortgage. Purchasers of articles so marked would not be protected if they saw the notice since they would not be purchasers without notice, but it will be difficult to prove that a purchaser saw the notice. Some courts, moreover, speak of certain chattels as *inherent chattels,* meaning that they will not enforce any agreement to treat such articles as real estate. *Madfes v. Beverly Development Corp.,* 251 N.Y. 12, 166 NE 787. In the case of a mortgage on a furnished apartment, for example, these courts might frown upon any agreement that the linens and silverware are to be deemed real estate. This being the case, the question will always arise whether any given article is an *inherent chattel.*

Hence it is by no means certain that a real estate mortgage, recorded only as a real estate mortgage, can create a dependable lien on chattels. For this reason, where the loan includes chattels that are important to the mortgage lender, he will insist that the mortgagor execute a security agreement that complies with the Uniform Commercial Code. A financing statement that complies with the code will also be prepared and filed. Some states provide for local filing of financing statements as to consumer goods and central filing of financing statements on equipment. Often doubt will exist as to the category in which particular chattels fall. Every possible doubt should be resolved in favor of filing duplicates in all the code offices. Customarily a search of Code filings will be ordered prior to disbursement of the mortgage money to see if there are prior filings covering the chattels in question.

Where a separate chattel lien is not contemplated, a clause covering appliances and equipment may be useful. Such a clause follows:

> TOGETHER with all fixtures and articles used in occupying, operating or renting the building on the premises, including but not limited to gas and electric fixtures, radiators, heaters, washers, driers, engines and machinery, boilers, ranges, elevators, escalators, incinerators, motors, dynamos, bathtubs, sinks, water closets, basins, pipes, faucets and other plumbing and heating fixtures, tools and equipment, ventilating apparatus, air-conditioning equipment, mirrors, mantels, panelling, cabinets, refrigerating plants, refrigerators, whether mechanical or otherwise, stoves, cooking apparatus and utensils, fire prevention and extinguishing apparatus, furniture, shades, blinds, curtains, curtain rods, draperies, awnings, screens, screendoors, storm windows and doors, blinds, rugs, carpets and other floor coverings, lamps, draperies, curtains, hangings, pictures and other furnishings, and all replacements thereof and additions thereto, all of which shall be deemed to be and remain and form a part of the realty and are hereby covered by the lien of this mortgage.[1]

In determining whether an article is a fixture, courts customarily apply a number of tests, namely: (1) Is the article attached or annexed to the building in some more or less permanent manner? This is the *annexation test.* (2)

---

[1] Kratovil, *The Guarantor* (Chicago, Ill.: Chicago Title & Trust Co., April, 1969, pp. 5–6). © April, 1969.

Is the article well adapted to the particular structure? This is the *adaptation test.* (3) Was it the obvious intent of the party who caused the article to be installed that it form a permanent part of the structure? This is the *intention test.* Kratovil, *Real Estate Law* (5th ed. 1969) § 11.

With respect to the package kitchen, some items are weak with respect to the annexation test. For example, refrigerators and ranges are connected to the house only by electric cord or pipe. Laundry equipment and garbage disposals are built in, and have good annexation.

With respect to adaptation, ranges, refrigerators, and kitchen cabinets have great adaptation value in efficiency apartments.

In almost all package mortgages the items covered in the general language of the mortgage are obviously intended to be fixtures and, indeed, are expressly declared so.

A question nevertheless remains as to the attitude in some states where declarations of intention are ineffective if the courts consider the articles to be basically of a chattel nature.

§ 262. Fixtures attached after execution of real estate mortgage. When only the landowner and the real estate mortgagee are involved, the rule is that fixtures bought, paid for, and installed by the landowner after the execution of a mortgage on the land become subject to the lien of the mortgage and cannot thereafter be removed by the landowner. In this situation, in other words, the mortgage lien attaches to all fixtures thereafter installed by the mortgagor on the mortgaged premises. Such fixtures must not be removed without the mortgagee's consent. *Bowen v. Wood,* 35 Ind. 268. However, except in a few states, trade fixtures installed by a tenant, whether installed before or after the mortgage, are removable by the tenant. *Standard Oil Co. v. LaCrosse Super Auto Service,* 217 Wis. 237, 258 NW 791. Trade fixtures are those used by the tenant in his business, such as barber chairs, soda foundations, bars and mirrors, etc. Kratovil, *Real Estate Law* (5th ed. 1969) § 12.

§ 263. Easements. When *A* owns Lots 1 and 2 and mortgages Lot 1 to *B,* he may, at *B*'s insistence, include in the mortgage a grant of easement over part of Lot 2. Such a clause may run somewhat as follows:

> And as further security for payment of the debt above described, the mortgagor mortgages and grants to the mortgagee, his heirs and assigns, as an easement appurtenant to Lot 1 aforesaid, a perpetual easement for ingress and egress over and across the south ten feet of Lot 2 in the subdivision aforesaid.

When *A* owns Lots 1 and 2 and is mortgaging Lot 1 to *B, A* may wish to reserve, for the benefit of Lot 2, an easement over part of Lot 1. In such case, an appropriate clause of reservation may be included in the mortgage.

The foregoing illustrations show how a mortgage can create an easement. When such a mortgage is foreclosed, ownership of the dominant and servient tenements passes into separate hands, and the real existence of the easement begins. Suppose, however, that *A* owns a lot that enjoys the benefit of a previously created easement. He mortgages the lot, and in the mortgage nothing is said concerning the easement. The mortgage is foreclosed. The purchaser at the foreclosure sale enjoys the benefit of the easement, for an appurtenant easement runs with the land even though it is not mentioned in the mortgage or in the foreclosure proceedings. Kratovil, *Easement Draftsmanship and Conveyancing,* 38 Cal.L.Rev. 426.

Also, an easement acquired by a mortgagor subsequent to the giving of a mortgage automatically comes under the lien of the mortgage and passes to the purchaser at any mortgage foreclosure sale. *First Nat. Bank v. Smith,* 284 Mich. 579, 280 NW 57, 116 ALR 1078.

Suppose one mortgages his land in 1964 to *A*, and the mortgage is duly recorded. In 1965 he gives *B*, his neighbor, an easement across the same land. Since the easement is given after a mortgage has been recorded against the property, it will be extinguished if *A* forecloses his mortgage. *Kling v. Ghilarducci,* 3 Ill.2d 455, 121 NE2d 752. Similarly, if he gives *B*, his neighbor, an easement over his land, which is properly recorded, and thereafter he mortgages his land to *A*, foreclosure of *A*'s mortgage will not cut out the easement. 46 ALR2d 1197.

Often when the owner of two tracts of land sells or mortgages one of them, there is no mention at all of easements, and yet as a result of the transaction an easement is created. In such cases, the situation of the land is such that the courts feel the parties intended to create an easement even though they did not actually say so. Such easements are called *implied easements.* They are created by *implied grant* and *implied reservation.* Where a landowner uses one part of his land for the benefit of another part, and this use is such that, if the parts were owned by different persons, the right to make such a use would constitute an easement, then upon a sale or mortgage of either of such parts an implied easement is created.

EXAMPLE: *R* owns two adjoining lots, Lots 1 and 2. He constructs a building on Lot 1, but the entrance walk is located on Lot 2. *R* mortgages Lot 1 to *E.* Nothing is said about the walk. *E* forecloses the mortgage. *E* now has an implied easement over the walk on Lot 2. *Liberty Bank v. Lux,* 378 Ill. 329, 38 NE2d 6.

In today's land transactions property rights of considerable complexity are generated. This is true particularly of the condominium, the planned unit development, the shopping center, and the town house. Supplementing the local zoning ordinance in such developments there will be found a scheme of private building covenants, easements, liens and restrictions. The landowner in a condominium or PUD will covenant to do a number of things, for example, to pay maintenance assessments, which are foreclosable liens on the homesites or apartments. Each landowner in a condominium, shopping center or town house will enjoy a number of valuable easements over his neighbor's property, and his own property will be subject to easements in favor of his neighbors. There is general agreement among property lawyers that these detailed rights should be set forth in a *declaration of restrictions, easements, liens, and covenants,* and that only relatively brief reference should be made to them in the deeds of conveyance. The legality of this device rests upon the rule that if a recorded document, such as a deed, makes reference to another document recorded in the same office, the two are read together. Thus the provisions of the declaration are treated legally as "set out" in the deed. 82 ALR 412, 416. This document is discussed in Kratovil, *Real Estate Law,* (5th ed. 1969), Chapter 34.

§ 264. **Covenants running with the land.** The mortgagee will also wish to enjoy the benefits of covenants running with the land. For example, some adjoining building may have agreed to furnish heat and air conditioning to the mortgaged property, and the mortgagee wishes to be able to enforce this agreement. This, of course, requires the mortgagee to examine the instrument creating the covenant to be sure that the covenants, in fact, run with the land. The problem really has two aspects: (1) the mortgagee wants the covenants to run at law, so that the mortgagee, when he becomes the owner through foreclosure, can sue the adjoining owner if he breaches the covenants; and (2) the mortgagee will wish to satisfy himself that the agreement creates an equitable servitude that equity will enforce against any subsequent purchaser of the land that furnishes the heat and air conditioning.

Where the owner of the mortgaged land and the owner of the adjoining land enter into an agreement for the furnishing of heat and air conditioning to the land that is to be mortgaged, it is necessary that the agreement create cross-easements for the passage of heat and cold air through pipes and ducts in both buildings. This seems like a higly technical requirement. Yet it must be done. For a covenant to run with the land, there must be *privity of estate.* This means that the covenant must be found in a deed, lease, or easement grant. An agreement between two property owners creates no privity of estate. *Wheeler v. Schad,* 7 Nev. 204. Since neither a deed nor lease is adapted to our situation, we must contrive an easement, which is simple enough. An easement will do the trick. 3 Tiffany, *Real Property* § 853; Kratovil, *Easement Draftsmanship,* 38 Calif.L. Rev. 447.

As to the creation of an equitable servitude, all that is needed is a document that is recordable under local law. 4 Pomeroy, *Equity Jurisprudence* § 1295.

§ 265. Description of easements and covenants in mortgage. The mortgage, of itself, will pass the benefit of all covenants running with the land. However, the mortgagee may prefer to add, after the property description, a description of the easements and covenants that benefit the mortgaged land. At times this is done somewhat formally. The land and its appurtenances and chattels are described as Parcel 1. The easements are then described in detail as Parcel 2. Following this is Parcel 3, which describes the covenants. Mortgagees seem to be reassured by this, and it certainly does no harm.

§ 266. Property bounded on highway. The usual rules governing deeds of land abutting on streets or highways govern mortgages. Thus a mortgage and foreclosure thereof, where the mortgaged land is a lot abutting on a street, carries title to the center of the street. *Brackney v. Boyd,* 71 Ind. 592, 123 NE 695; 49 ALR2d 982. *See* § 260.

§ 267. After-acquired property. Corporate mortgages, particularly railroad mortgages, often contain clauses extending the lien of the mortgage to land subsequently acquired by the mortgagor. On one of several theories, such clauses are sustained as valid. 12 Boston U.L.Rev. 653; 40 Harv.L.Rev. 225; 13 Minn. L.Rev. 82; 87 U.Pa.L.Rev. 635.

But if a merger or consolidation takes place, the lien of the mortgage usually does not extend to lands contributed by the corporation merging into the mortgagor corporation.

EXAMPLE: *R Corporation* owns Lot 1. *R* executes to *E* a mortgage conveying Lot 1 and all property *R* may thereafter acquire. *R-1 Corporation* which owns Lot 2 merges into *R Corporation.* The mortgage lien does not attach to Lot 2. *Metropolitan Trust Company v. Railroad,* 253 F 868; *Irving Trust Co. v. Rwy.,* 292 F 429.

Of course, the mortgage is outside of the *chain of title* as to after-acquired property and a deed to a bona fide purchaser will defeat the mortgage as to such after-acquired property.

EXAMPLE: *R Corporation* owns Lot 1 and on February 1, 1970, mortgages it to *E* together with all property it may thereafter acquire. The mortgage is recorded the same day. On February 1, 1971, *R Corporation* acquires Lot 2. The mortgage lien immediately attaches to Lot 2. On March 1, 1971, *R Corporation* sells and conveys Lot 2 to *BFP,* a bona fide purchaser. *BFP* takes title free and clear of the mortgage. He need only begin his search as to mortgages made by *R Corporation* on February 1, 1971, the date the records show *R Corporation* acquired Lot 2. This search will not reveal the mortgage. *First Nat. Bank v. South-western Lumber Co.,* 75 F2d 814; 59 CJS 326.

By similar reasoning, a purchase money mortgage executed by *R Corporation* when it acquires Lot 2 will always enjoy priority over the mortgage with the after-acquired property clause. *US v. New Orleans Rrd.,* 12 Wall(U.S.) 362; 25 ALR 92.

Because of the chain of title problem with respect to the after-acquired property clause, some lenders provide in the mortgage or deed of trust that immediately upon acquisition of such after-acquired property, the mortgagee will be notified of its acquisition and the mortgagor will execute, in form satisfactory to the mortgagee, a supplemental mortgage or deed of trust evidencing the fact that the after-acquired property has come under the lien of the mortgage. This supplemental document, when recorded, brings the original mortgage into the chain of title.

§ 268. **Crops and trees.** Growing crops form a part of the real estate to which they attach and follow the title thereto. Therefore, a purchaser who has acquired title to the land through a foreclosure sale on the mortgage is entitled to the growing crops sown after the execution of the mortgage and not harvested before the purchaser acquires title to the land. *Chicago Bank v. McCambridge,* 343 Ill. 456, 175 NE 834; 2 Glenn, *Mortgages,* 1023. In a few states a mortgagor's tenant will be permitted even after the foreclosure sale to harvest crops he has sown, and in a few states a chattel mortgage to a country banker of growing crops will prevail against the purchaser at the foreclosure sale. 2 Glenn, *Mortgages,* 1024. Trees and shrubs planted in a nursery garden pass by a mortgage of the land to the purchaser at the foreclosure sale. *Colonial Land Co. v. Joplin,* 184 SW 537 (Tex.Civ.App.). Crops that are harvested before the foreclosure sale belong to the mortgagor. *Ahern v. Little,* 90 NJEq. 72, 105 A 597. In some agricultural states statutes govern this problem.

Much of the law with respect to security interests in crops is now found in the Uniform Commercial Code.

Formerly the courts made a distinction between annual crops, such as potatoes, corn or wheat, (fructus industrialis) and perennials (fructus naturales), which led to problems with respect to fruit crops, which seem to be both annual and perennial in their nature. Perhaps this distinction has been abolished by UCC § 2–105 which indicates that all commercially grown perennial crops, such as citrus crops, are to be treated identically under the Code. 49 Ia.L.Rev. 1270.

Loaning money on crops not yet planted is a familiar transaction to the country banker. Under the UCC (§ 9–204) a simple crop security in future crops is good only for one year. This paternalistic limitation, intended to protect farmers against the folly of mortgaging their future, follows the pattern of pre-code legislation passed during the 1930's at the instance of the federal government. 2 Gilmore, *Security Interests on Personal Property* § 32.4. Some states prescribe a period longer than one year. 49 Ia.L.Rev. 1274. The provision has been criticized. 49 Ia.L.Rev. 1275. However, it will invalidate a crop security interest that violates the section, thus strengthening the position of a real estate mortgagee who is laying claim to the crops. Seemingly, the one-year period must relate to the year prior to the *planting* of the seed, for the time of germination is a fact difficult to establish. 49 Ia.L.Rev. 1272. *See also* UCC § 9–312(2). Local statutes may also invalidate security interests in unharvested crops. 44 N.D.L. Rev. 561.

The one-year limitation has no application to a purchase money real estate mortgage covering a farm, and it has been speculated that all real estate farm mortgages are immune from the one-year limitation. 49 Ia.L.Rev. 1276, 1277. In farm states competition for priority between farmer and real estate mortgage or between crop security interests and the real estate mortgage has produced considerable litigation. 49 Ia.L.Rev. 1278; 2 Gilmore, *Security Interests in Personal Property* §§ 32.3, 32.4.

Of course, the crop security interest is subject to the Code requirements as to perfection and filing. 2 Gilmore, *Security Interests in Personal Property* § 32.4; 49 Ia.L.Rev. 1281; 44 N.D.L.Rev. 558. In addition, special local requirements as to filing may exist. 44 N.D.L.Rev. 559. *See also* Chapter 25.

24

Conveyance of Mortgaged Land

§ 269. In general. There is nothing about the existence of a mortgage on land that prevents sale of the land. Of course, the mortgage being recorded, it follows that any purchaser acquires ownership subject to the mortgage, and if the mortgage debt is not paid, it will be foreclosed, and the purchaser will be wiped out.

Likewise, there is the possibility that the mortgage may contain a clause providing for acceleration of the mortgage debt if the conveyance is not consented to by the mortgage. *See* § 125.

§ 270. Deed with seller to pay mortgage debt. Assume that I own land worth $15,000, on which there is a mortgage securing a debt of $5,000. In theory, I may sell the land to you for $15,000 and receive the entire amount of the sale price. In such a situation, no doubt the understanding will be that I am to pay the mortgage debt when it matures, and to evidence this arrangement I will probably convey to you by warranty deed, omitting all mention of the mortgage. I thereby become liable to you on the covenants of warranty. Such an arrangement is extremely rare. Normally if the mortgage is not paid at closing of sale, the arrangement between the seller and buyer will result in a payment to the seller of the sale price ($15,000) less the amount of the mortgage debt ($5,000), namely, $10,000.

§ 271. Personal liability for mortgage debt after deed made. Obviously where the mortgagor sells mortgaged land he does not thereby rid himself of personal liability for the mortgage debt. Remember that when the mortgage was signed, the mortgagor also signed a promissory note or other obligation that imposed upon him personal liability for the mortgage debt. If I owned a note and mortgage signed by General Motors Corporation, it is hardly likely that I would ever bother with foreclosure. I would simply demand that this highly solvent corporation pay its note.

However, two considerations come up in connection with sales of mortgaged land and the problem of personal liability: (1) Was the transaction so framed that in addition to the mortgagor the purchaser also became personally liable for payment of the mortgage debt? This is the problem of *assumption*. (2) Did some event occur that resulted in extinguishment of the mortgagor's personal liability?

There is a less important aspect of assumption, but it should be mentioned. The assumption clause in the deed is also a contract which the mortgagor-grantor can enforce. The grantee becomes personally obligated to the mortgagor-grantor to pay the mortgage debt.

In this connection we shall be looking at a number of documents, among them: (1) the contract by the mortgagor to sell the land to the purchaser; (2) the deed from the mortgagor to the purchaser; (3) documents signed after the sale was consummated, such as extension agreements; and (4) the original mortgage documents to see how they anticipated and dealt with this question of personal liability of mortgagor and purchaser.

§ 272. Assumption by grantee—contract of sale. Where the contract of sale between the mortgagor and the purchaser requires the purchaser to assume and agree to pay the mortgage, but the deed from the mortgagor to the purchaser omits any assumption clause, some cases hold that the grantee is not liable, on the theory that the contract is merged in the deed. Other cases are *contra*. *Wayne International Bldg. & Loan Ass'n. v. Becker,* 191 Ind. 664, 143 NE 273; *Buchsbaum v. Halper,* 265 Ill. App. 226; 89 ALR. 1041. This question does not often arise because the contract of sale is seldom recorded and the mortgagee does not know what it contains. For this reason, when a mortgagee asserts a personal liability on the part of the purchaser it is usually because of some provision in a recorded document, usually the deed.

§ 273. Assumption by grantee—provision in deed. Personal liability of the purchaser to pay the mortgage debt is usually created by a clause in the deed.

EXAMPLE: *R,* a mortgagor in a mortgage to *E,* conveys the mortgaged land to *P,* a purchaser, by a deed which recites: "The premises are subject to a mortgage recorded in Book 143, Page 256, which the grantee assumes and agrees to pay." By acceptance of this deed *P* becomes personally liable to *E* for payment of the mortgage debt. This means that *E,* without foreclosing the mortgage, can, in many states, obtain a judgment against *P* in case of default, can garnishee his wages, levy on his car, and so forth. It also means that if the foreclosure does not bring enough cash to pay the mortgage debt in full, *E* can obtain a deficiency judgment against *P* and garnishee by means of this judgment.

It may seem odd that by means of deed to which the mortgagee is not a party and which the purchaser does not even sign, such a personal liability to the mortgagee can be created. Nevertheless, the rule exists and must be understood.

§ 274. Personal liability of grantee—"subject clause." The general rule is that a conveyance of real estate in which the instrument merely refers to the fact that there is a mortgage lien, or which refers to the transfer as being "subject to" a certain mortgage, imposes no personal liability on the buyer-grantee without additional proof of intent to assume. The mortgagor and the land remain liable for the debt, but the grantee is not. The phrase "subject to" is treated as a limiting or qualifying term, and is not a covenant on the part of the grantee. 2 Glenn *Mortgages,* 1152; Osborne, *Mortgages,* 507. *But see* § 277.

§ 275. Assumption by grantee—theories of liability—differing consequences depending on the theory employed. Where the deed contains an assumption clause, this is, in legal effect, a contract between the grantor and grantee that the grantee will pay the mortgage debt. For breach of this contract, the grantee may become liable to (1) the grantor in the deed, who sues as a party to the contract (21 ALR 504, 507, 76 *id.* 1191, 1194; 97 *id.* 1076, 1077, 13 Minn.L.Rev. 737) and (2) the mortgagee, who, it is obvious, is not a party to the contract. *Green Properties Inc. v. Livingston,* 230 Md. 193, 186 A2d 475.

There is a difference of opinion as to the theory on which the mortgagee (who is naturally not a party to the deed containing the assumption clause) may maintain a personal action against the assuming grantee. These theories are as follows:

A. The mortgagee sues as the third-party beneficiary of a contract made for his benefit, under the rule of *Lawrence v. Fox,* 20 N.Y. 268. *Green Properties Inc. v. Livingston,* 230 Md. 193, 186 A 2d 475; 21 ALR 439, 454, 57 *id* 339, 341; 17 Va.L.Rev. 844; 25 Ill.L.Rev. 721, 723; 38 Cornell L.Q. 197. Usually, enforcement of this right is by means of a deficiency judgment.

B. The assumption clause creates a suretyship situation, in which the assuming grantee is the principal debtor, the mortgagor-grantor is the surety, and the mortgagee is the principal creditor. In suretyship situations the creditor is entitled to make use of all securities that the principal debtor may have given to the surety for the surety's indemnity. 27 Yale L.J. 1008. If the mortgagor were forced (because of his direct personal liability on the mortgage note) to pay the mortgage debt, he could sue the assuming grantee, who is obligated under the assumption clause to indemnify the grantor. This right of the grantor-mortgagor is an equitable asset in the hands of the mortgagor-grantor which the mortgagee-creditor can reach by direct proceedings against the assuming grantee, thus avoiding circuity of action. *Y.M.C.A. v. Craft,* 34 Ore. 106, 114, 55 P 439, 441.

The difference in theory between the third-party beneficiary states and the suretyship theory states results in conflicting decisions in certain situations:

A. In third-party beneficiary states, as soon as the mortgage debt is due, the mortgagee may sue the assuming grantee at law, without having to resort first to foreclosure proceedings. *Burr v. Beers,* 24 N.Y. 178. In suretyship states, since the contract is one of indemnity against actual loss, the mortgagee cannot sue the assuming grantee at law, but may join him as a defendant in the foreclosure suit and obtain a personal judgment against him for any deficiency which may remain after applying the proceeds of the foreclosure sale to the mortgage debt.

B. Where the grantor in a deed containing an assumption clause is not the mortgagor, and is not himself personally liable for the payment of the mortgage debt (for example, he might be a purchaser who bought from the mortgagor by quitclaim deed), most third-party beneficiary states hold the grantee liable to the mortgagee on the theory that a contract has been made for the mortgagee's benefit and he may sue on it. *Scott v. Wharton,* 226 Ala. 601, 148 So 308. In suretyship states, such a grantee is not liable to the mortgagee, since there is no suretyship situation in such cases. The grantor in the deed has no personal liability to the mortgagee; therefore he cannot suffer any loss; therefore there can be no indemnity against loss, for loss is impossible. One or two third-party beneficiary states follow this rule. 2 Glenn, *Mortgages,* 1185.

C. The suretyship and third-party beneficiary states differ as to the right of the grantor to release the grantee from the liability created by the assumption clause. In suretyship states the liability of the grantee may be released in good faith at any time before the mortgagee files his foreclosure suit. *Young v. Trustees,* 31 NJEq. 290. In third-party beneficiary states two different rules are followed:

   1. The third-party beneficiary acquires a vested right the moment the assumption contract goes into effect, and thereafter the grantor has no right to take away this property right by releasing the grantee or conveying without an assumption. *Kuzemchak v. Pitchford,* (N.M) 431 P2d 756.

   2. The more generally accepted rule in third-party beneficiary states is that the grantor cannot release the assuming grantee after the mortgagee has learned of the assumption contract and has assented to it. *Gifford v. Corrigan,* 117 N.Y. 257, 22 NE 756.

D. The assumption clause creates a liability running from the grantee to the grantor. In third-party beneficiary states, the grantor is allowed to sue the grantee as soon as the grantee breaches the contract by failing to pay the mortgage debt as it becomes due. 21 ALR 508; *Gustavson v. Koehler,* 177 Minn. 115, 224 NW 599. In suretyship states, since the contract is one of indemnity against loss actually suffered, some decisions deny the mortgagor the right to sue the assuming grantee until the mortgagor has himself paid the debt to the mortgagee and thus suffered a loss. 21 ALR 514, 76 ALR 1191, 97 ALR 1076.

§ 276. **Assumption by grantee—parol evidence as to assumption.** Controversies may arise as to the admission of parol evidence with respect to assumption of the mortgage debt by the grantee:

A. Suppose the deed contains an assumption clause and *the mortgagee* sues the grantee. Since deeds are signed by the grantor only, not by the grantee, the grantee has not signed the deed in question. He seeks to prove by parol evidence that he did not know the clause was there and the actual agreement was that he would not be personally liable. Most states admit such evidence on the theory that the parol evidence rule is not applicable to strangers to the contract, and the mortgagee is a stranger. *Hafford v. Smith,* 369 SW2d 290 (Mo.); *Ludlum v. Pickard,* 304 Ill. 449, 136 NE 725; Stowers v. Stuck, 131 Neb. 409, 268 NW 310, 12 Wis.L.Rev. 405; 50 ALR 1220, 1226; 37 Am.Jur. 328;. In Illinois, it has been held that any payment on the mortgage debt by the grantee is an assent to the assumption clause. *Ludlum v. Pickard,* 304 Ill. 449, 136 NE 725. Where the parol evidence is sought to be introduced between the grantor and the grantee, some cases exclude parol evidence that no assumption was intended. 37 Am.Jur. 328; 50 ALR 1220, 1224. Others do not. Osborne, *Mortgages,* 512.

B. Suppose the deed is a warranty deed and recites that it is "subject to" the mortgage, but no assumption clause is included. Or suppose the deed is a quitclaim deed and contains no assumption clause. The mortgagee may sue the grantee and seek to prove by parol that the grantee agreed to assume the mortgage. It is generally held that parol evidence is admissible, either on the theory that the parol evidence rule is not applicable to strangers to the contract, or on the theory that parol is always admissible to show the consideration for a deed, and the assumption agreement is part of the consideration. 37 Am.Jur. 327; *White v. Schader,* 185 Cal. 606, 198 P 19, 21 ALR 499.

C. Suppose the deed is a warranty deed and does not contain any mention of the mortgage. Here the deed on its face seems to convey the notion of personal liability on the part of the grantor because of his covenant against encumbrances. Here the authorities are in conflict. Some cases admit parol evidence to rebut as assumption of the mortgage by the grantee, both where the mortgagee is suing the grantee and where the grantor is suing the grantee. 37 Am.Jur. 327. There are decisions to the contrary. The authorities are collected in 4 Tiffany, *Real Property,* 75, 76.

§ 277. **Implied assumption.** Even in the absence of an assumption clause in the deed, some states imply an assumption agreement from the fact that the purchase price fixed between the grantor and grantee was the full value of the land, but in closing the deal the amount of the mortgage debt was deducted from the purchase money paid to the grantor. This is the doctrine of "implied assumption." The deed in question usually recites simply that it is "subject to" the mortgage. 37 Am.Jur. 324; Osborne, *Mortgages* § 257. Most courts reject this doctrine. *Fuller v. McCallum,* 22 Tenn.App. 143, 118 SW2d 1028; 2 Glenn, *Mortgages,* 1152. *See* § 274. The trend is away from the rule. New York, Pennsylvania, and California have statutes abolishing implied assumption.

§ 278. **Assumption—insurance.** Where mortgage insurance exists (VA, for example), the mortgagee may lose his coverage if he fails to pursue an assuming grantee.

§ 279. **Assumption by grantee—extension of time to grantee as discharging mortgagor's personal liability.** Where the grantee has assumed the mortgage, in all states the situation is treated for some purposes as a suretyship situation, the assuming grantee being the principal debtor, the mortgagor-grantor being the surety and the mortgagee being the creditor. The courts therefore apply the suretyship rule that where the principal and creditor, without the surety's consent, make a binding agreement to extend the time of payment by the principal, the surety is discharged of all personal liability. 41 ALR 277, 282; 43 *id.* 89; 71 *id.* 389, 390; 81 *id.* 1016, 1018; 112 *id.* 1324, 1327; 7 N.Y.U.L.Q.R. 214; 13 NCLR. 337; 4 U.Chi. L.Rev. 469, 476; 19 Va.L.Rev. 618. The main reason for the rule is that the surety's right of subrogation is impaired. If the mortgagor had been called upon to pay the debt at its original maturity, he could have paid and immediately filed foreclosure proceedings, since he would be subrogated to the mortgagee's rights. The extension agreement protects the assuming grantee against foreclosure until the extended maturity arrives. This impairs the mortgagor's right of subrogation. *Zastrow v. Knight,* 56 SD 554, 229 NW 925, 72 ALR 379. Where the mortgage secures a negotiable instrument, there were many decisions under the old law that looked to the Negotiable Instruments Act for guidance on this topic. These courts would now look to the Uniform Commercial Code. *See* § 3–606.

The discharge by extension rule does not apply unless the mortgagee knew of the assumption clause at the time the extension agreement was signed (41 ALR 277, 282), but in Illinois the mortgagee's knowledge of the assumption is inferred from the fact that the mortgagee accepts mortgage payments from the grantee. *Prudential Ins. Co. v. Bass,* 357 Ill. 72, 191 NE 284. And a few states reject the "discharge by extension" rule altogether. 2 Glenn, *Mortgages,* 1201.

Mere delay in foreclosure does not release the mortgagor. There must be a binding extension agreement.

Where the mortgage contains a *subject clause, but no assumption clause,* some states hold that the extension agreement rule is inapplicable. However, the majority rule is that the mortgagor's liability is discharged to the extent of the value of the land at the time of the extension. *Kazunas v. Wright,* 286

Ill.App. 554. A few states say that extension totally discharges the mortgagor in such cases. 112 ALR 1324.

Instead of entering into extension agreement, the mortgagee and the assuming grantee may enter into forebearance agreement, which postpones for a period of time the mortgagee's right to foreclose. This has the same effect as an extension agreement and results in a discharge of the mortgagor's personal liability. *United States Building & Loan Assoc. v. Burns,* 90 Mont. 402, 4 P2d 703; *Thompson v. Wilson,* 51 NYS2d 665.

§ 280. Subrogation. Whether the deed by the mortgagors is simply "subject to the mortgage," or, in addition, contains an assumption clause, subrogation rights are created in favor of the mortgagor in both situations. The land becomes the primary fund for the payment of the mortgage debt. As between the grantor and grantee a sort of suretyship situation results, under which, if the mortgage debt is not paid by the grantee and the grantor-mortgagor is compelled to pay the mortgage debt because of his personal liability created by the mortgage note, such grantor-mortgagor is subrogated to the rights of the mortgagee, and may foreclose the mortgage in order to reimburse himself. 38 Cornell L.Q. 196.

§ 281. Deed to impede foreclosure. Every once in a while, some cunning mortgagor who has defaulted in his mortgage payments records a deed running to a great number of persons, hoping thereby to discourage the mortgagee from foreclosing, for, especially in states where foreclosure is by court proceedings, all landowners must be made parties to the proceeding and served with process. This device is ineffective.

EXAMPLE: *R,* a defaulting mortgagor, recorded a deed running to "each and every member of the American Legion of Iowa, each and every member of the Independent Order of Odd Fellows of Iowa, and each and every member of the Knights of Pythias of Iowa, and each and every attorney at law in Iowa." The court held the deed void. *State v. McGee,* 100 Ia 329, 204 NW 408.

25

The Uniform Commercial Code

§ 282. **In general.** The Uniform Commercial Code, which has been adopted throughout the United States, is a law of considerable importance to the mortgage lender. While it does not deal with *land,* it deals extensively with fixtures, which are often the mortgagee's chief security.

§ 283. **Code documents.** The code, particularly Article 9, which deals with chattel security, abolishes much pre-Code terminology and many pre-Code distinctions. Any lien upon chattels, including chattels intended to be affixed to land as fixtures, is now created by means of a document called a *security agreement.* Instead of recording the security agreement, however, the Code provides for filing a notice (*financing statement*) of the existence of the security agreement. This is something of a novelty to the real property lawyer. In real property law nothing but the recording of the original instrument will satisfy our familiar recording law and serve to impart constructive notice. Under the Code, however, it is not the original instrument that is recorded but rather a brief notice called a financing statement which gives notice of the existence of the security agreement. This should be a welcome innovation, for it means that all the "fine print" provisions can be eliminated from the public records. This method of filing is called *notice filing.*

Surprisingly, the statutory form financing statement does not require the financing statement to state the amount of the debt. No doubt this information is to be obtained from the secured party. A lien filing that does not state the amount of the debt is, again, something of a novelty to the real property lawyer, for under some decisions, a real estate mortgage that does not give the amount of the debt does not impart constructive notice.

193

Section 9–402 sets forth a number of requirements that must be complied with when one seeks to file a financing statement. Naturally, questions will arise with respect to financing statements that do not comply with this section in one or more particulars. It has been held that where a financing statement was offered for filing, but it did not contain the mailing address of the debtors, as required by the Code, it was not entitled to be filed. *In re Smith,* 205 F.Supp. 27. Hence, if filed, it would not impart constructive notice. In another case, a financing statement was held invalid because it lacked the address of the secured party. *Strevell Paterson Finance Co. v. May,* 77 N.M. 331, 422 P2d 366.

Where a photocopy of a signed financing statement was filed, it was held that this was an ineffective filing and did not impart constructive notice. *In re Kane,* 55 Berks County L.J. 1. This point is of importance because often the person filing a financing statement is in doubt as to whether or not the article in question is a fixture or a chattel. He may therefore wish to file the document both in the recorder's office and in the office or offices where chattel filings are made. This case appears to indicate that the document must be executed in duplicate or triplicate so that a signed original can be filed in each office.

Whether this idea, that the financing statement must bear an original signature in order to impart constructive notice, will generally be accepted is a difficult question to answer. Nothing in the Code requires a manual signature on a financing statement so long as the signer has accepted or adopted a printed signature or some other type or signature in question as his own.

One feels misgivings, however, about a photographed document. If *A* signs a document and hands it to *B*, and *B* chooses to photograph it so that he can file it in two places, it can, with considerable force and logic, be argued that *A* signed only one document and had no intention of signing the other or of adopting the photograph as his signature.

As to the signature of the secured party on the financing statement, the courts are already rewriting the Code. In *Strevell-Paterson Financing Co. v. May,* 77 N.M. 331, 422 P2d 366, the court held the signature of the secured party not necessary (though Section 9–402 expressly requires it), and in *Benedict v. Lebowitz,* 346 F2d 120, the court stated that it suffices if the name of the secured party is typed in the body of the instrument.

The mere presence on the public records of a perfected fixture financing statement does not establish the existence of a valid fixture security transaction. A filed financing statement not supported by an existing security agreement and lacking the essentials of a security agreement is void.

§ 284. Amendments proposed. Because a number of states have adopted their own versions of various sections of Article 9 of the Uniform Commercial Code, a Review Committee (hereafter referred to as the Committee) has been working on a revision that might overcome criticisms of the existing version of

Article 9 and bring the Article back into uniformity. Preliminary Draft No. 2 has been published by the Committee and will be found in the April, 1970, issue of *Business Lawyer,* Vol. 25, No. 3. In the remainder of this chapter, page references are to Vol. 25 of *Business Lawyer.* It is accompanied by a report that will also be found in this periodical. Considerable time will elapse before agreement is reached on a final draft. Hence, space must be devoted to existing problems, since they will be with us for some time. For additional discussion of the fixture problem, see Leary and Rucci, *Fixing Up the Fixture Section of the UCC,* 42 Temple L.Q. 355 (Summer 1969).

§ 285. Articles purchased on credit and stored for future use. A question of major concern under the present code can best be given by example:

> Suppose the collateral consists of 100 hot water tanks purchased by a professional builder on credit and warehoused. He has no idea at the time where these tanks will ultimately be installed. That being the case, the creditor can only file the financing statement with the chattel filings, usually with the Secretary of State and additionally, in some states, where the debtor resides or has a place of business. What happens after the hot water tanks have been installed in various buildings throughout the state? Must the purchaser or mortgagee search the records of the Secretary of State to see whether or not financing statements were filed covering such hot water tanks? It is obvious that one of two innocent parties must suffer here. Where the building containing the hot water tanks is sold to an innocent purchaser, if he gets title free and clear of the financing statement, the creditor is hurt. If, on the other hand, the financing statement is good against the purchaser of the real estate, the purchaser is hurt.

The answer to this question cannot be given quickly. The antecedents of the Code must be examined. In the first place, case law in the old chattel mortgage days taught us that, by the majority rule, persons buying chattels were required to examine only the chattel records. Persons buying land were required to check only the land records. 1 Patton, *Titles* 147 (2d ed.).

Under the Uniform Conditional Sales Act, fixture filings were governed by Section 7 thereof, which required a filing in the land records.

The reasons for this were given by the draftsman of the Section as follows:

> "The conditional seller of the fixture should not get protection by filing the contract with ordinary conditional sale contracts and making a record similar to that made in the case of chattel mortgages. It is unreasonable to ask purchasers and mortgagees of realty to search in the personal property records regarding every article connected with a building which might have been sold separately." 2A Unif. L. Annot. 98.

The official text to the Uniform Commercial Code in its comments to Section 9–401 says:

"Fortunately there is general agreement that the proper filing place for security interests in fixtures is in the office where a mortgage on the real estate concerned would be filed or recorded, and . . . subsection (1) (b) . . . so provides. This provision follows the Uniform Conditional Sales Act. Note that there is no requirement for an additional filing with the chattel records."

And in its comments to Section 9–313 said:

"Under this article, as under the Uniform Conditional Sales Act, the place of filing with respect to goods affixed or to be affixed to realty is with the real estate records and not with the chattel records."

This means that under the Code, as under the Uniform Conditional Sales Act and the common law, purchasers and mortgagees of real estate need not concern themselves with those records that relate only to personal property, such as those that are filed under the Code with the Secretary of State. In other words, if there is no filing in the local recorder's office, there is no constructive notice. People dealing with land need not search the office where only chattel liens are filed.

Nevertheless, it must be conceded that some lawyers do not concur in these views. In particular some point to Section 9–401(3) which provides that:

"A filing which is made in the proper place in this state continues effective even though . . . the location of the collateral . . . is thereafter changed."

The case of the hot water heaters is put at rest by the proposed Amendments. The Amendments require in Section 9–313(4) that a code filing to be good as to fixtures and binding on purchasers or mortgagees of the land be filed as a fixture filing and in Section 9–402(5) that fixture filings be filed in the land records.

Thus if a record search made to cover recording of a new deed or mortgage shows no fixture filing, the grantee or mortgagee takes free of any fixture liens.

§ 286. Financing statement where debtor is a party not in the chain of title.
A problem that has been repeatedly cited as a matter of concern under the present code is the problem of articles purchased by a general contractor. A filing is made in the fixture filings, but names the general contractor as debtor. Even though the land is appropriately described in the financing statement, subsequent purchasers and mortgagees checking the Code Index will not discover the filing because it is made and indexed in the name of a person whose name does not appear in the chain of title. The Code does not specifically require that the name of the record owner be included in the financing statement. It has therefore been argued that the filing is good even though a real estate title examiner would regard it as a "wild filing." Motivated by this fear, a number of legislatures have departed from the Uniform Code and specifically included a require-

ment that the financing statement in such case contain the name of the record owner.

Our first task, of course, is to deal with the Uniform Code as drafted. Let us consider the language of our old recording laws relating to deeds. They provide, in most states, for an official grantor-grantee index. They do not provide, in so many words, that a "wild" deed or mortgage does not impart constructive notice. The cases say so, but the statutes do not. The recording law simply says that deeds, mortgages and other real estate documents shall be indexed according to the names of the parties. The courts, taking it from there, evolved the notion that an orderly, chronological sequence of instruments was required with names therein sufficiently similar so that they were deemed idem sonans. *Harris v. Reed,* 21 Idaho 463, 121 P 780 (1912). This is the familiar chain of title theory.

Under this theory a "wild deed," where the grantor is a stranger to the chain of title, does not impart notice. Is there any reason to suppose that the court will not arrive at the same conclusion with respect to the provisions of the Code? What possible reason would exist for requiring indexing in the name of the debtor, unless this had some significant relation to the land in question? In holding that purchasers of land need not search the personal property records and that "wild" deeds do not impart constructive notice, the courts, without benefit of any legislative crutch, took a practical, sensible approach to the problem.

With respect to chattel mortgages, it was well established that the chain of title theory was applicable. *New England National Bank v. Northwestern National Bank,* 171 Mo. 307, 71 SW 191 (1902).

The same was true of conditional sale contracts. *Industrial Bank of Commerce v. Packard Yonkers Corp.,* 279 App. Div. 125, 108 NYS2d 249, aff'd. 304 NY 622, 107 NE2d 96 (1952).

Thus although the statutes say a deed gives notice from the date it is filed, the courts say this is not so when the deed is a "wild" deed. The chattel mortgage statutes and the conditional sales acts were construed the same way. Nothing in the Official Text with Comments indicates a disposition to depart from this inveterate and unbending interpretation of the law. Will the courts, therefore, take the literal language of the Code, so similar to that of our other recording laws, and from this contrive a truly revolutionary innovation in the law? This certainly seems unlikely.

To cure this seeming defect, the Amendments in Section 9–313(4) require that to qualify as a fixture filing the financing statement must be one where the debtor has an interest in the real estate.

§ 287. Construction loans. The Code in its present form leaves some question as to whether a real estate construction lender obtains priority over fixture filings made in the course of construction. 2 Gilmore, *Security Interests in Personal Property* § 30.6. The Amendments make it clear that the construction lender does indeed enjoy such priority and that any refinancing of the construction mortgage succeeds to this priority.

While Section 9–313 as re-drafted is clearly intended to protect construction lenders against fixture filings occurring during the course of construction, a question has been suggested concerning the definition in this section of a "construction mortgage." A mortgage is defined in the proposed amendments as a construction mortgage "to the extent that it secures an obligation incurred for the construction of an improvement on land." Not all of the proceeds of the typical construction mortgage go for brick and mortar. Loan commissions and title charges are common disbursements from the loan fund. Even the cost of acquiring the vacant land may be financed in part by the construction loan. The Committee has this aspect under consideration and some further amendment seems likely.

§ 288. **Open-end advances.** With respect to mortgages given to secure in part open-end advances, the criticism was made by the United States Savings and Loan League that the Code put the mortgagee to a great deal of trouble as measured against the amount of the usual open-end advance. Section 9–313(4) states that a security interest does not take priority over a prior encumbrancer to the extent that he makes subsequent advances, where the advance is made before the security interest is perfected. But before making the advance the open-end lender must search for perfected security interests. Again we have the problem of the code filings as to fixtures being mingled with other code filings, thus creating the necessity of sifting through a vast number of informal documents to justify the making of a small open-end advance. The Amendments make it clear that a mortgagee making such an advance need only search the fixture filings. It seems, however, that the advance would be vulnerable to the ten-day gap period allowed by this section.

§ 289. **Protection of the landowner.** Possibly as a result of oversight, the present Code seems to extend no protection to a landowner against fixture financing that may take place subsequent to his acquisition to the land. The instance that has been cited is that of a landowner who hires a general contractor to construct a building on his property. Some of the articles installed in the building by the general contractor are purchased by him on credit. The landowner, after checking the records for mechanics' liens and taking such other documentation as is normal in such case, makes final disbursement of the contract price to the general contractor. Thereafter the secured parties demand payment of the balance due them on pain of removal of the articles financed. It would seem that the security interests would prevail in such a case because of the following language found in present Section 9–313(2):

"A security interest which attaches to goods before they become fixtures takes priority as to the goods over the claims of all persons who
have an interest in the real estate except as stated in subsection (4)."

In the Amendments this situation seems to be covered by the language of
new Section 9–313(4), which extends protection to the landowner against
unfiled fixture liens.

§ 290. **Description of fixtures in financing statement.** A problem that exists
under the present version of the Code is accurately described in the following
statement made by the Committee:

> ". . . Practices are too loose in the use of the term 'fixture' in
> financing statements as a catchall phrase as in descriptions like 'all
> machinery, equipment, tools and fixtures situated at 14 Digby Road,
> Chicago.' This leads to a question whether a fixture filing is intended
> and whether a possible objection to the title to the real estate men-
> tioned should be noted." (p. 1109)

This problem is aggravated by a circumstance the draftsmen of the Code
could have not foreseen. If you glance at present Section 9–402(3) you will
see that the suggested form of financing statement allocates a separately num-
bered paragraph for fixtures. It is obvious that this was done in recognition of
the extraordinary difficulties attending the determination of whether particular
articles are fixtures or chattels. The draftsmen were aware, of course, that all
Code filings in the local Recorder's Office would be filed and indexed together,
since Section 9–403(4) specifies that the filing officer shall mark each statement with a consecutive file number. Thus the numerous filings relating to consumer goods, for example, find their way into the same file and index as the
less numerous filings relating to fixtures. The Code draftsmen, one would infer,
intended to make searching the Code records less time-consuming for those
checking for fixture filings by pin-pointing on the form one particular place at
which the searcher could glance quickly if non-farm real property was the subject of the search.

Unfortunately, in adopting official forms, the various secretaries of state
have substantially deviated from the suggested Code form. *Business Lawyer,*
July 1968, p. 1210. Thus in many states (including, for example, Alabama,
Colorado, Connecticut, Delaware, Florida, Illinois, Indiana, Iowa, Kansas,
Massachusetts, Michigan, Nevada, New Hampshire, New Jersey, New Mexico,
North Carolina, North Dakota, Ohio, Oklahoma, Oregon and Pennsylvania), a
form is used that provides one box for describing every type of collateral, chattels,
fixtures, or what have you.

As a means of curing this defect the Amendments introduce changes in
Section 9–402. In existing 9–402(3), which sets forth a proposed form of
financing statement, the paragraph relating to goods which are or are to become

fixtures simply states that the above-described goods are affixed or to be affixed to the real estate. The Amendments propose that this paragraph of the form shall read:

> "3. The above goods are to become fixtures on (*Describe Real Estate*) . . . . and this financing statement is to be filed for record in the real estate records." (p. 1131)

In Section 9–402(5) the Amendments require that if a financing statement is filed as a fixture filing it must show that it covers this type of collateral and must recite that it is to be filed in the real estate records.

This Amendment will compel abandonment of the present form of financing statement generally used throughout the country. It is likely, further, to compel adoption of a form that more closely follows the form set forth in the Code. Indeed, it is a pity that the secretaries of state throughout the country deviated from the Code form in the first place.

§ 291. **Filing in the land records.** The present Code in Section 9–401 provides that where a financing statement covers a fixture, filing is to be in the office where a mortgage on real estate would be filed. There is no requirement that filings be indexed in the land records. Many recorders index fixture filings in the Code Index only, citing as authority Section 9–403 requiring code filings to be marked with a consecutive file number. Since this lumps into one category all code filings received by any given filing officer, it is contended that no special treatment is indicated for fixture filings. The real estate fraternity was unhappy over this, and as a result quite a number of states deviated from the Official Code. They added requirements that fixture filings be indexed with real estate documents. Thus they found their way into the grantor-grantor indexes.

The Amendments provide in Section 9–313 as follows:

> "(b) A 'fixture filing' is the filing in the office where a mortgage on the real estate would be filed or recorded of a financing statement covering goods which are or are to become fixtures and which conforms to the requirements of subsection (5) of Section 9–402." (p. 1126)

In Section 9–402 they provide that a fixture filing must be filed in the real estate records.

The Committee comments:

> "The term 'fixture filing' has been introduced and defined. It helps to emphasize a point that was intended but not clearly set forth in the existing Code—that when a filing is intended to give the priority advantages herein discussed against real estate interests, the filing must be for record in the real estate records and indexed therein, so that it will be found in a real estate search (except as stated in paragraphs A-11 to A-13)." (p. 1077)

§ 292. Description of land. The problem of inadequate land descriptions in fixture financing statements has been an acute one. Street addresses or other vague descriptions are commonplace in such documents. The Committee was aware of this problem. It says:

"The difficulty asserted by real estate lenders and title companies in locating relevant fixture security interests applicable to particular parcels of real estate has been cured by new provisions as to real estate description in fixture filings, the indexing thereof, and other related provisions in Part 4 of Article 9." (p. 1078)

Thus in new Section 9–402(5), setting forth the form of a fixture filing, the following language occurs:

"(5) A financing statement . . . filed as a fixture filing (Section 9–313) must show that it covers this type of collateral, must recite that it is to be filed [[for record]] in the real estate records, and where the debtor is not a transmitting utility the financing statement must contain a description of the real estate [[sufficient if it were contained in a mortgage of the real estate to give constructive notice of the mortgage under the law of this state]]. (p. 1131)

Beneath it is this note:

"Note: Language in double brackets is optional."

"Note: Where the state has any special recording system for real estate other than the usual grantor-grantee index (as, for instance, a tract system or a title registration or Torrens system) local adaptations of subsection (5) and Section 9–403(7) may be necessary. See Mass. Gen. Laws Chapter 106, Section 9–409."

Contrast this with present Section 9–110 of the Code which states a description of real estate is sufficient whether or not it is specific if it reasonably identifies what is described. The Amendment's optional language in Section 9–402(5) requires a fixture filing to contain a description of the real estate sufficient if it were contained in a mortgage of the real estate to give constructive notice of the mortgage under the law of the state. This, obviously, is a more stringent requirement. *See* Patton, *Titles* (2d ed. 1957) § 122, stating that for a street address description to be effective for recording purposes the records must contain a description, probably a specific description, of the tract in question.

If the last statement is correct, then in a state adopting the Amendments a drastic change in documentation would be required, for apparently the great majority of today's fixture filings contain street addresses only. The requirements for a description to impart constructive notice of record is a topic which the decisions leave shrouded in some uncertainty. 4 Am. Law of Property § 17.23; 45 Am. Jur. *Records and Recording Laws* § 127. The Amendment appears to be derived from a Mississippi variation of the U.C.C.

The Committee adds the comment that the Amendments do not go so far as requiring full "legal description" of the real estate (p. 1078). But if the optional language in Section 9–402(5) is employed, it will push fixture security interests a long way toward using descriptions taken from deeds, abstracts or title policies.

§ 293. **Utilities and railroads.** Another problem under the existing version of the Code is described by the following statement of the Committee:

> "Far-flung railroad and other public utility corporations may have signalling systems or other chattels strung along their rights of way, and the chattels may be encumbered with a combined real estate and chattel indenture on the whole utility plant. Where the chattels are non-fixtures, the Code would require one or at most two chattel filings. But where the chattels may be fixtures, the Code would require a filing in each county where the chattels exist, and with a fixture filing including real estate descriptions. This is clearly unduly onerous." (p. 1106)

The Amendments propose to deal with this problem by adding to Section 9–105 a definition of "transmitting utility" which definition is as follows:

> "(n) 'Transmitting Utility' means any person primarily engaged in the railroad or street railway business, the electric or electronics communications transmission business, the transmission of goods by pipeline, or the transmission or the production and transmission of electricity, steam, gas or water, or the provision of sewer service." (p. 1117)

A financing statement covering collateral including fixtures of a transmitting utility is to be filed in the Office of the Secretary of State and this filing will constitute a fixture filing as well as a chattel filing (Section 9–401(5).)[1]

POINTS TO REMEMBER: If (1) no financing statement has been filed; or (2) if a financing statement has been filed but it is fatally defective; or (3) if a proper financing statement has been filed but not in the county where the land is located; or (4) if the name on the financing statement deviates so substantially from the debtor's true name that it must be considered a "wild" instrument, then a bona fide purchaser or mortgagee of the real estate is protected against the security interest and the fixture cannot be removed without his consent. Additionally, if the local law deviates from the code, for example, if it requires that the financing statement be filed in the land records, a bona fide purchaser or mortgage will be protected if this has not been done. However, if a bona fide purchaser or mortgagee is not protected, as where the fixture installation on credit is done with proper Code documentation, then if the code security is defaulted, the holder of the security may remove the fixture but must pay for physical damage to the building.

---

[1] Kratovil, "Problems of Title Examiner under UCC," (Chicago, Ill.: ABA Real Property 5, Probate & Trust Journal #3, pp. 281–289). © 1970.

If a fixture is installed on Code credit *after* a real estate mortgage has been recorded, the fixture may be removed if default is made in the Code security, but the remover is liable for physical damage to the building.

Until the Code is amended court decisions will give conflicting interpretations of the Code. For example, some hold a financing statement is fatally defective if it fails to contain the signature of the secured party. *Maine League Credit Union v. Atlantic Motors*, 250 A2d 497 (Me.); *Hillman's Equipment Inc. v. Central Realty Inc.*, 242 NE2d 522. Other decisions are *contra*. *Strevell-Paterson Financing Co. v. May*, 77 N.M. 331, 422 P2d 366; *Benedict v. Lebowitz*, 346 F2d 120. As is evident, some court decisions depart from the plain language of the Code. Another instance of this is a holding that lack of addresses on the financing statement (which the Code requires) is not a fatal defect. *Rooney v. Mason*, 394 F2d 250.

26

Possession and Rents

294. Title and lien theories. The difference in viewpoint between title theory and lien theory states (*see* § 6) is of greatest importance with respect to the mortgagee's right to the possession and rents of the mortgaged property. To illustrate the significance of this statement, let us list, in chronological order, some important dates in a mortgage situation: (1) the date when the mortgage is signed by the mortgagor, (2) the date when the mortgagor first defaults, (3) the date when the mortgagee files his foreclosure suit, (4) the date of the foreclosure sale, and (5) the date when the statutory redemption period expires and the mortgagee receives the deed under which he becomes the owner of the mortgaged property.

Let us first make our broad generalizations and thereafter list the particular points of difference that exist. In general, the title theory states regard the mortgage as retaining some of its early character, that is, they view it as a conveyance of the land, so that immediately on the signing of the mortgage, the mortgagee has the right to take possession of the property and collect the rents thereof. On the other hand, the lien theory states regard the mortgage as merely creating the right to acquire the land through foreclosure of the mortgage, so that the mortgagor remains the full owner of the land with the right to possession and rents until the statutory redemption period has expired and the foreclosure deed has issued to the mortgagee. In other words, at its most extreme, this difference in point of view represents to the mortgagee the difference between dates 1 and 5 in the list so far as the right to possession and rents is concerned. In title states, therefore, rents are an important part of the mortgagee's security. In lien states, this is not so. *Grether v. Nick,* 193 Wis. 503, 213 NW 304, 215 NW 571.

Now let us analyze the situation in somewhat greater detail, from the point of view just expressed:

1. In a number of title theory states, Alabama, Maine, Maryland, and Tennessee, for example, the mortgagee, immediately upon execution of the mortgage, has the right to take possession and collect the rents of the mortgaged property. *Darling Shop v. Nelson Realty Co.* 262 Ala. 495, 79 So2d 793. The right exists even though the mortgage is silent on this point. There are two exceptions: (1) In recent times laws have been passed in some title states giving the mortgagor the right of possession until default occurs. In effect, these laws convert such states into intermediate states. (2) Many mortgage forms used in title states give the mortgagor the right of possession until default.

2. In intermediate theory states, Illinois, New Jersey, North Carolina, and Ohio, for example, the mortgagor has the right of possession until his first default, but after default the mortgagee has the right to take possession. *Kranz v. Uedelhofen,* 193 Ill. 477, 62 NE 239.

3. In lien theory states, in the absence of a contrary provision in the mortgage, the mortgagor is entitled to possession and rents at least until the foreclosure sale.

4. In some lien theory states, either by express provision in the mortgage or by a separate assignment of rents signed at the time that the mortgage is signed, the mortgagor may give the mortgagee the right to take possession and collect rents as soon as a default occurs, and such provisions are valid. *Penn Mutual Life Ins. Co. v. Katz,* 139 Neb. 501, 297 NW 899; *Kinnison v. Guaranty Corp.,* 18 Cal.2d 256, 115 P2d 450; *Dick & Reuteman Co. v. Jem Realty Co.,* 225 Wis. 428, 274 NW 416. However, some of these lien theory states make special rules as to owner-occupied homes. In New York, for example, a home owner cannot be compelled to pay rent pending foreclosure. *Holmes v. Gravenhorst,* 263 N.Y. 148, 188 NE 285.

5. In other lien theory states, the provisions described in Number 4 are considered void as against public policy. *Rives v. Mincks Hotel,* 167 Okla. 500, 30 P2d 911; *Mutual Inc. Co. v. Canby Inv. Co.,* 190 Minn. 144, 251 NW 129; *Hart v. Bingham,* 171 Okla. 429, 43 P2d 447.

6. In all states, if the mortgagor, after defaulting in his mortgage payments, voluntarily turns over possession to the mortgagee, the mortgagee has the legal right to remain in possession. Notice that in Number 5 it is the clause in the mortgage binding the mortgagor to give up possession at some future time when default occurs that is held void. The same agreement made after default is valid. The mortgagee is then called a *mortgagee in possession.*

7. Whenever a mortgagee takes possession before he has acquired ownership of the property by foreclosure, the rents he collects must be applied in reduction

of the mortgage debt. A mortgagee does not become the owner of the property by taking possession. Foreclosure is still necessary.

8. Whenever a mortgagee has the right to possession and fails to exercise that right, allowing the mortgagor to remain in possession and to collect rents, the rents so collected belong to the mortgagor.

9. In many states, there is a statutory period of redemption. No general rule can be laid down as to the right of possession during this period, for each state has its own rule.

§ 295. Practical aspects of the possession problem. A mortgage lender seeks a regular return on a safe investment and does not wish to assume the responsibilities of management. A lender is most unlikely to make a loan that will require him to go into immediate possession of the land, and this right is therefore seldom exercised. On the mortgagor's default, however, it is imperative that prompt action be taken to seize the rents so that they will not be diverted to the mortgagor's own personal use. An eviction suit to enforce the mortgagee's right to possession is often a long, drawn-out affair, especially when the mortgagor is interposing all the legal obstacles available to him. However, if the mortgagee files a foreclosure suit, he can often have a receiver appointed in a matter of days, and this is the course usually preferred.

A receiver's leases are approved by the court, and he therefore assumes no personal responsibility. Again, as will hereafter appear (*see* § 302), entry by the mortgagee may automatically terminate leases executed by the mortgagor, and if these leases are favorable to the landlord, such a course is to be avoided if possible. Appointment of a receiver will ordinarily not have such a result. *First Nat. Bank v. Gordon,* 287 Ill.App. 83, 4 NE2d. 504. Also, though there is some question as to the right of a mortgagee to retain possession during the redemption period, courts will often allow a receiver to collect the rents during this period if the foreclosure sale is for less than the mortgage debt. *Haas v. Chicago Bldg. Assn.,* 89 Ill. 498.

However, the mortgagee's right to possession is of value to the mortgagee in overthrowing prepaid leases and other devices employed by a mortgagor who is on the brink of default. Also, when the mortgagee forecloses but because of some defect in the foreclosure fails to acquire good title, the purchaser at the foreclosure sale, who is usually the mortgagee, on obtaining his deed and taking possession, is regarded as a mortgagee in possession. He has the right to retain this possession until the mortgage debt is paid, even though the debt has in the meantime become outlawed by lapse of time so that it would be impossible for the mortgagee to file a new foreclosure suit. *Stouffer v. Harlan,* 68 Kan. 135, 74 P. 610; *Pettit v. Louis,* 88 Neb. 496, 129 NW 1005.

Appointment of a receiver has other advantages. In most lien theory states, even though the receiver has been appointed only to preserve the property from destruction, the courts will apply in reduction of the mortgage debt the rents collected by the receiver, despite the absence of an assignment of rents. *Grether v. Nick,* 193 Wis. 503, 213 NW 304, 215 NW 571. However, in other states, the courts will not allow the receiver to apply rents to payment of the mortgage. *Windom Nat. Bank v. Reno,* 172 Minn. 193, 214 NW 886. Some states permit a receiver to collect past due rents. 2 Glenn, *Mortgages,* 944.

Where the mortgaged property is occupied by the mortgagor as his home, courts are reluctant to order him to pay rent to a receiver, especially in lien theory states. *Holmes v. Gravenhorst,* 263 N.Y. 148, 188 NE 285.

Courts differ as to the grounds for appointment of a receiver. Some say it is enough that the property be inadequate security for the mortgage debt. Other courts require a showing that the security is inadequate and that the mortgagor is insolvent. Still others appoint a receiver only when the property is in danger of destruction. 2 Glenn, *Mortgages,* 925; 26 ALR 33.[1]

§ 296. Possession—equitable mortgages. An equitable mortgage gives the mortgagee no right of possession. *McFarland v. Cornwell,* 151 N.C. 428, 66 SE 454.

§ 297. Possession after foreclosure sale—effect of mortgage provisions. It is difficult to generalize concerning the efficacy of mortgage provisions to give any right of possession to the purchaser at the foreclosure sale. To a considerable extent the local redemption statutes will control the situation. There is, of course, some case law. For example, it has been held that any provision in the mortgage giving the purchaser at the foreclosure sale the right of possession is merged in the decree of foreclosure and therefore void. *Schaeppi v. Bartholomae,* 217 Ill. 105, 75 NE 447. Some decisions sustain a clause that the mortgagor automatically becomes a tenant at will of the purchaser at the foreclosure sale. *Griffith v. Brackman,* 97 Tenn. 387, 37 SW 273; 103 A.L.R. 981. If the language of the mortgage or deed of trust is broad enough, it will be binding on the mortgagor's grantee. *Criswell v. Southwestern Fidelity Life Ins. Co.,* 337 SW2d 893 (Tex.Civ.App.). At all events it is unlikely that provisions of this sort will override a clearly expressed statute giving the owner the right of possession during the redemption period. *See also* § 297.

§ 298. Mortgagee in possession—lien theory states. The old maxim is that right to possession follows legal title. This poses a conceptual difficulty in lien states. However, while some such states hedge the rule with some conditions, all follow the rule recognizing the rights and status of a mortgagee in possession. Osborne, *Mortgages,* 280.

§ 299. Mortgagee in possession—accounting for rents. A mortgagee in possession must account to the mortgagor for rents received, and some decisions

---

[1] Kratovil, *Real Estate Law,* 4th ed. (Englewood Cliffs, N.J.: Prentice-Hall, Inc., 1964), pp. 226–229, © 1964.

go further and require the mortgagee to account for rents he might have received by the use of reasonable diligence. *Carter v. McHaney* 373 SW2d 82 (Tex.Civ. App.); 2 Glenn, *Mortgages*, 1056. All such rents are credited against the mortgage debt. If a mortgagee in possession allows any of the rents to be paid to the mortgagor, this is obviously prejudicial to any junior lienor. The rents should be held, to be applied ultimately, in reduction of the first mortgage. The mortgagee in possession is subordinated to junior liens to the extent of rents thus diverted. *Branch v. Barnes,* 19 Ill.App.2d 472, 154 NE2d 337; *Ganried v. Hansen,* 210 Minn. 125, 297 NW 730, 26 Minn.L.Rev. 730.

A deterrent to a mortgagee's resorting to the remedy of taking possession, is the extreme stringency of the accounting problems that face a mortgagee who pursues this course. Osborne, *Mortgages, 285.*

§ 300. Missouri lease clause in deed of trust. The Missouri realty mortgage or deed of trust frequently contains a clause providing that the trustee leases the mortgaged premises to the mortgagor. The usual provision states that the trustee lease the mortgaged premises to the mortgagor until the instrument be satisfied and released, or until default, at a rental of one cent per month, payable on demand, and that the mortgagor will surrender peaceable possession to the trustee or purchaser at foreclosure sale within ten days after the foreclosure sale, without notice or demand. The primary significance of this leasing clause in Missouri is to permit the trustee or purchaser at foreclosure sale to recover possession of the mortgaged premises utilizing the statutory action of unlawful detainer. 24 Mo.L.Rev. 524.

ADDITIONAL REFERENCES: 3 Powell, *Real Property,* § 457 (discussing various state statutes declaring that mortgagee is not entitled to possession).

27

Leases—Rent Problems—Assignment of Leases and Rents

§ 301. Leases antedating mortgage. It is important to distinguish between the rights of a tenant under a lease made prior to the mortgage and those of a tenant under a lease made subsequent to the mortgage. When the lease is made subsequent to the mortgage, the mortgagee can, by foreclosing his mortgage, extinguish the rights of the tenant under his lease. When the lease antedates the mortgage, then, unless the lease contains a clause making it subject to all mortgages on the land, the mortgagee must respect the tenant's rights, and, regardless of foreclosure, the tenant cannot be evicted prior to the expiration of the lease, unless, of course, he fails to pay his rent. 14 ALR 678.

Again, in title theory states, if the lease antedates the mortgage, then immediately upon the mortgagor's default, the mortgagor may serve a demand upon the tenant that he pay all rents to the mortgagee. Thereafter, the tenant must pay all rents to the mortgagee. *King v. Housatonic R.R. Co.,* 45 Conn. 226; LRA (1915C) 200. Of course the tenant may continue to pay rents to the mortgagor until such demand has been served upon him.

In lien theory states, the mortgagee ordinarily is not entitled to make such a demand on the tenant. LRA (1915C) 200.

Because a lease that antedates the mortgage is binding on the mortgagee, he will scrutinize it carefully, noting: (1) whether the rent is adequate in his opinion; (2) whether the computations of percentage rent and minimum rentals are satisfactory; (3) whether the rent can be diminished in any way, for example, by partial condemnations, too liberal abatement of rent provisions in case of fire damage, etc.; (4) whether the lease contains an option to purchase, for if it does, this must be subordinated to the mortgage; (5) whether the tenant had been given too liberal a right to terminate the lease, e.g,, in case of fire damage; (6) whether the lease imposes obligations on the lessor that the mortgage would find objectionable if he became the landlord by foreclosure; or (7) whether the lease is too liberal in giving the lessee the right to remove buildings, fixtures, etc., erected or installed by him.

§ 302. **Leases subsequent or subject to mortgage.** Obviously, a mortgagor cannot make any leases that will give the tenant greater rights than he, the mortgagor, possesses. In title and intermediate states, the mortgagor has no right to retain possession after default. Tenants who occupy by virtue of leases made after the making of the mortgage also have no right to retain possession of the premises after the mortgagor's default, and the mortgagee may evict such tenants. To avoid eviction, the tenant, upon the mortgagee's making demand for possession, may agree to pay rent to the mortgagee, and the mortgagor will have no right to collect further rent from such tenant. *West Side Trust & Savings Bank v. Lopoten,* 358 Ill. 631, 193 NE 462; *Del-New Co. v. James,* 111 NJL. 157, 167 A 747; *Anderson v. Robbins,* 82 Me. 422, 19 A 910. One disadvantage of this course in title and intermediate states is that such action automatically terminates the lease, and the tenant becomes a tenant either from month to month or from year to year. *N.Y. Life Ins. Co. v. Simplex Products Corp.,* 135 Ohio St. 501, 21 NE2d 585; *Anderson v. Robbins,* 82 Me. 422, 19 A 910; *Burke v. Willard,* 283 Mass. 547, 137 NE 744; *Hale v. Nashua Rrd,* 60 N.H. 333; *Gartside v. Outley,* 58 Ill. 210, 17 Wash.L.Rev. 39. If the lease is one favorable to the landlord, the mortgagee will prefer to have a receiver appointed, since in many states the receiver can hold the tenant to his lease.

In lien theory states, in the absence of some provision in the mortgage, the mortgagee is not entitled to collect rents even under leases made after the making of the mortgage.

As stated, there are a number of decisions holding that where a lease is subject to the mortgage, then, if the mortgagee takes possession on default in the mortgage payments, the inevitable result is a termination of the lease. Either the mortgagee has a right to possession or he doesn't. It he does, the lessee obviously cannot have the right to possession. Therefore, so these decisions reason, the lease must have been terminated. *Am. Freehold Land Co. v. Turner,* 95 Ala. 272, 11 So 211; *Mercantile Tr. Co. v. Union Oil Co.,* 176 Cal. 461, 168 P 1037; *Merchants Union Tr. Co. v. New Philadelphia Graphite Co.,* 10 Del. Ch. 18, 83 A 520; *Gartside v. Outley,* 58 Ill. 210. At times the cases say that when the mortgagee exercises his right to possession, this *relates back* to the date of the mortgage. Again the result is the same. The lease is destroyed. These decisions tend to upset mortgage lenders. Mortgage loans are made in reliance on leases. When default occurs, perhaps the last thing a mortgagee wants is to be looking around for new tenants. Therefore, the mortgagee will want the key leases to be *prior* to the mortgage, so that this termination does not take place. *See* § 301. Or he may seek the protection of assignment of leases and rents. *See* § 303.

If the mortgagee does not seek to take possession, but instead files a foreclosure and obtains the appointment of a receiver, he may be able to preserve subordinate leases by omitting lessees from the foreclosure suit.

The statutes and decisions are in hopeless confusion as to the power of a mortgagee to keep junior leases alive by manipulating his foreclosure toward that end. In some states, where foreclosure is by judicial proceedings, junior leases can be preserved from extinction by omitting the tenants from the foreclosure suit and by including statements in the complaint to foreclose and decree of foreclosure that it is subject to such lease. The tenant must then pay rent to the grantee in the foreclosure deed. *Met. Life Ins. Co. v. Childs Co.,* 230 N.Y. 285, 130 NE 295; *Davis v. Boyajian Inc.,* 229 NE2d 116; 109 ALR 457. In other states this stratagem is ineffective. The lease is nevertheless extinguished. 109 ALR 455.

In a power of sale foreclosure it is difficult to avoid extinguishment of junior leases. *Kage v. 1795 Dun Road Inc.,* 428 SW2d 735.

This is an important consideration. Where a lease is an important source of revenue to the mortgagee, he may, for the reasons herein set forth, insist that all valuable leases be prior and superior to the mortgage, for in such case, foreclosure does not extinguish the lease.

In the following states the mortgagee may keep a junior lease alive after foreclosure: Pennsylvania, Nebraska, Florida, New Jersey, Illinois, Arkansas, Colorado, Arizona, New York. This result is reached in some cases by statute and in some cases by court decision. *Metrop. Life Ins. Co. v. Childs* 230 N.Y. 285 130 NE 295, 14 ALR 638. In judicial foreclosures it is usually necessary to omit the tenant as a party to the foreclosure and to state in the complaint and decree of foreclosure that the foreclosure is subject to the lease. In power of sale foreclosures, the notice of sale states that foreclosure is subject to the lease and no notice is given to the lessee.

Contra: North Carolina, Minnesota, Kentucky, California, Michigan, Ohio, Connecticut, Delaware, Virginia, Louisiana, Missouri, New Hampshire, Iowa, all holding that foreclosure extinguishes a junior lease.

The assignment of leases and rents is helpful in this situation.

As is obvious, a mortgage is subject to a lease in the usual case where the lease is executed and recorded prior to the recording of the mortgage, but it is also possible that a mortgage that antedates a lease can become subordinate to the lease as a result of the execution of a subordination. And a lease that is prior and superior to a mortgage can become subject to it in the same fashion. This is discussed in the chapter on subordinations. *See* Chapter 21.

§ 303. Assignment of leases and rents—rent reductions—advance payment of rents. At the time the mortgage is signed, the mortgagee should require the mortgagor to sign a separate assignment of leases and rents. *Franzen v. G. R. Kinney Co.,* 218 Wis. 53, 259 NW 850; 50 Harv. L. Rev. 1322. This document assigns to the mortgagee the mortgagor's interest in all existing leases and all leases to be executed in the future, also all rents falling due after the date of the mortgage, all as additional security for payment of the mortgage debt. Lawyers have found that there is magic in the argument that the mortgage creates a lien on the land and that the assignment creates a lien on the rents. All existing tenants are notified of the making of the assignment. The assignment is recorded. The following rules are applicable:

1. In most lien theory states, an assignment of rents enables the mortgagee to reach the rents accruing prior to foreclosure sale and to treat them as part of the security for his debt. This gives the mortgagee in a lien theory state virtually as favorable a position with regard to rents as the mortgagee has in title and intermediate states. In one or two lien states, an assignment of rents, like the mortgage clause giving the right to take possession on default, is held invalid as being opposed to public policy. *Hart v. Bingham,* 171 Okla. 429, 43 P2d 447. Also, in a few lien states, an assignment signed contemporaneously with the mortgage is given only limited recognition. In these states, after a default occurs and the assignment has been activated, rents collected by the mortgagee can be applied only to maintain the property or to pay taxes or insurance. They cannot be applied in reduction of the mortgage debt. *Mutual Benefit Life Ins. Co. v. Canby,* 190 Minn. 144, 251 NW 129.

2. Since the assignment does not contemplate that the mortgagee will begin collecting rents immediately upon the signing of the assignment, but only after a default occurs, the assignment is inoperative until it is activated by some action of the mortgagee. *Ivor B. Clark Co. v. Hogan,* 296 FSupp.398; 2 Glenn, *Mortgages,* 940. Rents collected by the mortgagor before the assignment is activated belong to the mortgagor. *Sullivan v. Rosson,* 223 NY 217, 119 NE 405. Or they may become the property of a junior mortgagee who exercises greater diligence. If *A* holds a first mortgage and *B* a second mortgage on the same property, and if default occurs and *B* activates his assignment but *A* does not, *B* gets the rents. *Stevens v. Blue,* 388 Ill. 92, 57 NE2d 451. Even specific language that the assignment will operate automatically on default has been held insufficient to activate the assignment. *Dime Savings Bank of Brooklyn v. Lubart,* 38 NYS2d 252. There are a number of cases which contain the statement that an assignment can be drafted to operate automatically, and one or two cases appear to so hold. *New Jersey Nat. Bank & Trust Co. v. Wolf,* 108 NJEq. 412, 155 A 372. A number of cases stating this rule are cited in *Kinninson v. Guaranty Liquidating Corp.,* 18 Cal2d 256, 115 P2d 450. But as you read these cases, almost

invariably there is some circumstance present that reveals some demand, suit for rent, voluntary payment of rent by mortgagor, or other action taken by the mortgagee to activate the assignment. It must be deemed unsafe as a business proposition to rely on an automatic operation of the assignment. Michigan has a statute that may create a special situation.

3. Everywhere the assignment is properly activated if, after default and pursuant to the assignment, the mortgagor consents to collection of the rent and the tenants begin paying rent to the mortgagee.

4. In title and intermediate theory states, the assignment is activated on default by the mortgagee's serving notice on the tenants to pay rent to the mortgagee. The mortgagor's consent is unnecessary. *Randal v. Jersey Mortgage Inv. Co.,* 306 Pa. 1, 158 A 865; *Grannis-Blair Audit Co., v. Maddux,* 167 Tenn. 297, 69 SW2d 238.

5. In some lien theory states, the assignment can be activated in the same manner as in title theory states. *Kinnison v. Guaranty Liquidating Corp.,* 18 Cal2d 256, 115 P2d 450; *Long Island Bond & Mortgage Guaranty Co. v. Brown,* 11 NYS2d 793.

6. In other lien theory states, the assignment can be activated only by the mortgagee's filing a foreclosure suit and applying for the appointment of a receiver. *Dick & Reuteman Co. v. Jem Realty Co.,* 225 Wis. 428, 274 NW 416; *Hall v. Goldsworthy,* 136 Kan. 247, 14 P2d 659. Of course these same steps will serve to activate an assignment in a title or intermediate state.

7. In one or two lien theory states, an assignment can be activated only by the mortgagor's voluntarily turning over possession to the mortgagee or allowing the mortgagee to collect rents. *Hart v. Bingham,* 171 Okla. 429, 43P2d 447.[1]

8. Rents collected by the mortgagee under an activated assignment must be applied to taxes, repairs, insurance, and, in most states, the mortgage debt.

9. Whenever a mortgagee acts under an activated assignment, he does not destroy existing leases, as sometimes occurs when a mortgagee takes possession under his mortgage. An assignment preserves valuable leases.

10. A mortgagee acting under an assignment is accountable to the mortgagor only for rents actually collected.

11. When a mortgagee who holds an assignment of rents sells and assigns his mortgage, he should also assign the assignment of rents to the assignee of the mortgage. *Koury v. Sood,* 74 R.I. 486, 62 A2d 649.

With respect to the language of the assignment, some suggestions might be pertinent:

1. It should be a document separate from the mortgage. It should assign the mortgagor's interest in all existing leases and the interest of the mortgagor, or any subsequent landowner in leases that may be executed in the future

---

[1] Kratovil, *Real Estate Law,* 4th ed. (Englewood Cliffs, N.J.: Prentice-Hall, Inc., 1964), © 1964.

by the mortgagor, or any subsequent landowner. Leases of any importance should be specifically set forth in the assignment. Some mortgages include a provision whereby the mortgagor covenants, on the mortgagee's demand, to execute a separate assignment, in specified form, as and when any new lease is executed by the mortgagor.

2. It might be helpful not to state that the assignment will become operative only on default, but instead make the assignment a presently operative assignment, giving the mortgagor the privilege of collecting and keeping rent until default.

SUGGESTED CLAUSE: Notwithstanding that this instrument is a present assignment of said rents, it is understood and agreed that the undersigned has permission to collect the same and manage said real estate and improvements the same as if this assignment had not been given, if and so long only, as the undersigned shall not be in any default whatever with respect to the payments of principal and/or interest due on said loan, or in the performance of any other obligation on our part to be performed thereunder, but this permission terminates automatically on the occurrence of default or breach of covenant.

3. The mortgage should refer to the assignment of rents and the assignment of rents to the mortgage, so that the mortgagee can resort to one or the other as convenience dictates, and should permit entry under mortgage as to part of the premises and under assignment as to other parts of the premises.

EXAMPLE: As to one store in the building a lease junior to the mortgage is so unfavorable that it should be terminated and the tenant ousted. Enter under the mortgage.

EXAMPLE: As to another store a lease junior to the mortgage is very favorable. Enter under the assignment.

4. The right to cancel or alter existing leases should be included.

5. The assignment should include the right to the use and possession of furniture, appliances, and so forth. While such a provision will be helpful, neither a rent assignment nor the appointment of a receiver is a substitute for a chattel security interest under the Uniform Commercial Code. In other words, if there is valuable personal property on the mortgaged premises, for example, a hotel, the mortgagee may not have the legal right to the possession of such personal property unless he has a chattel security interest. 44 Yale L.J. 701.

6. The assignment should include the right to operate the business and to take possession of books and records.

7. The assignment should confer the right to apply rents to the payments on furniture bought on credit, to insurance premiums on personal property, and so forth.

8. The assignee should be given the right to apply rents to the mortgage debt. Otherwise some states limit application of rents collected to taxes and maintenance. Western Loan Co. v. Mifflin, 162 Wash. 33, 297 P 743.

9. The document should provide that the assignee shall not be accountable for more monies than he actually receives from the mortgaged premises, nor shall he be liable for failure to collect rents.

10. The document should forbid any cancellation or modification of leases by the mortgagor and should also forbid any prepayment of rent except the normal prepayment of monthly rent on the first of the month.

11. Authority should be given the assignee to sign the name of the mortgagor on all papers and documents in connection with the operation and management of the premises.

12. The assignment should provide that any assignee of the assignment shall have all the powers of the original assignee.

13. It should contain a recital that (a) all rents due to date have been collected and no concessions granted and that (b) no rents have been collected in advance.

14. The assignment should contain a schedule setting forth all existing guarantees of payment of rent by third parties and all securities for rent held by the mortgagor. This is done so that the mortgagee can insist on separate assignments of these guarantees and securities to the mortgagee.

15. It should provide that the assignee may execute new leases, including leases that extend beyond the redemption period.

Of course neither an assignment of rents nor any other device can make a good lease out of a bad one.

EXAMPLE: A shopping center lease to a department store provides that if 5% or more of the parking lot is condemned, the tenant may terminate the lease. This is a key lease, providing revenue for retirement of the mortgage. It must be amended, because if 5% or more of the parking lot is condemned, for example, for a street widening, and the tenant terminates the lease, the mortgage will go into default.

If the lease provides for a security deposit by the tenant with the landlord, an assignment of leases and rents standing alone gives the mortgagee no right to the security deposit. *Anuzis v. Gotowtt,* 248 Ill. App. 536; *Keusch v. Morrison,* 240 App.Div. 112, 269 N.Y.S. 169; 52 CJS. 473. Specific language should be included in the assignment transferring all rights in the security deposit.[2]

A problem of considerable importance is the extent to which a receiver or a mortgagee entering into possession is bound by rent reductions, prepayments of rents, and lease cancellations effected by the mortgagor for a cash consideration. Such agreements are standard devices by which hard-pressed mortgagors

---

[2] Kratovil, *Real Estate Law,* 5th ed. (Englewood Cliffs, N.J.: Prentice-Hall, Inc., 1969), pp. 227–229, © 1969.

pocket the future earning capacity of the land and deliver to the mortgagee the empty shell of the mortgaged asset. Again, differences exist between the theory and lien theory states. The following are some of the applicable rules:

1. In title and intermediate theory states, when the lease is made subsequent to the mortgage, the mortgagee is not bound by advance rent payments made by the tenant to the mortgagor, and upon appointment of a receiver or the mortgagee's taking possession of the land, the tenant will nevertheless have to pay rent thereafter to such receiver or mortgagee, even though he has already paid his rent in advance to the mortgagor. *Rohrer v. Deatherage,* 336 Ill. 450, 168 NE 266. This rule follows from the rule that recording of the mortgage gives all the world, including subsequent tenants, notice of the mortgagee's rights, and these rights include the right to take possession on default. This rule is of special importance to a tenant who pays a large sum of money for the privilege of receiving a lease, for example, a tenant in a co-operative apartment, a tenant of commercial space who pays a large "bonus" for receiving his lease, or a tenant who plans to make substantial investments in alterations in reliance on his lease.

2. In title and intermediate theory states, if the lease antedates the mortgage, recording of the mortgage does not give the tenant notice of the mortgagee's rights, for recording of the mortgage gives notice only to those persons who acquire rights in the property after recording of the document. The question therefore arises, if the tenant, acting in good faith and in ignorance of the mortgage, prepays his rent to the mortgagor, and the mortgagor thereafter defaults, is this prepayment binding on the mortgagee, or must the tenant pay his rent again to the mortgagee? Some cases hold for the mortgagee and some for the tenant. *Anno., 1916 D Ann. Cas.* 200; 55 L.R.A. (N.S.) 233; 2 Jones, *Mortgages* 362. Arguably the best rule is that no abnormal prepayment of rent is good against the mortgage. 2 Glenn, *Mortgages,* 952. The mortgagee can protect himself at the time the mortgage is signed, by procuring an assignment of all existing leases and giving tenants notice at that time of his rights under such assignment.

3. In many lien theory states, the mortgagee is bound by advance payments of rents made in good faith by the tenant to the mortgagor, and when the mortgagee's receiver takes possession, he will find himself unable to collect any rents from the tenant. *Smith v. Cushatt,* 199 Ia. 690, 202 NW 548; *Ottman v. Tilbury,* 204 Wis. 56, 234 NW 325.

4. But even in lien theory states following the rule stated in Number 3, if, at the time the mortgage is made, the mortgagee obtains from the mortgagor an assignment of rents and leases and notifies the tenants thereof, the mortgagee will not be bound by any advance payments of rent made by the tenant to the mortgagor. Also, no rent reduction granted by the mortgagor after the tenant has notice of this assignment will be effective. *Franzen v. G. R. Kinney Co.,* 218 Wis. 53, 259 NW 850.

5. Where, at the time of making the mortgage, the mortgagor, by a separate instrument, assigns an existing lease to the mortgagee, and the lessee is notified of the assignment, the tenant and mortgagor cannot thereafter cancel the lease or reduce the rent so far as the mortgagee is concerned. On the mortgagee's taking possession, or on the appointment of a receiver, the tenant can be held to his lease. *Metropolitan Life Ins. Co. v. W. T. Grant Co.,* 321 Ill. App. 487, 53 NE2d 255; *Mercantile & Theatres Properties v. Stanley Co.,* 346 Pa. 343, 30 A2d 136; *Franzen v. G. R. Kinney Co.,* 218 Wis. 53, 25 NW 850, *Darling Shop v. Nelson Realty Co.,* 262 Ala. 495, 79 So2d 793. If there is no assignment of rents, and the lease is prior to the mortgage, a cancellation of the lease made by the mortgagor and lessee may be valid. *Metropolitan Life Ins. Co. v. W. T. Grant Co.,* 321 Ill. App. 487, 53 NE2d 255.

6. The courts are less likely to be sympathetic toward advance payments of rent made pursuant to a conspiracy entered into between the mortgagor and the tenant in an effort to deprive the mortgagee of the rents. *Boteler v. Leber,* 112 NJEq. 441, 164 A 572.

7. The courts are also very unsympathetic toward last-minute rent reductions granted by the mortgagor to the tenant on the eve of foreclosure. *First Nat. Bank v. Gordon,* 287 Ill. App. 83, 4 NE2d 504.[3]

§ 304. Pledge of rents. There is a curious decision holding that if the mortgagor conveys the land together with the rents thereof, the mortgage is nothing more than a "pledge" of the rents, without effect until the morgagee takes possession or has a receiver appointed. On the other hand, the court held, an *assignment* of the rents contained in the mortgage gives the mortgagee's receiver an immediate right in the rents. *Paramount B & L Assn v. Sarks,* 107 NJEq. 328, 152 A 457 (1930). This seems to exalt form over substance. Possibly it can be explained by the desire of courts to help the mortgagor during the trying days of the Great Depression. At all events it again illustrates the need for careful documentation where rents are involved.

§ 305. Modern active assignment of lease. In recent times mortgage lenders have turned to a device that has certain advantages. Where a building is to be constructed with mortgage funds for a high-credit tenant, as soon as the lease is made, the landlord assigns his interest in the lease and all rents thereunder to the mortgage lender. The assignment calls for the mortgage lender to begin collecting rents *immediately* on completion of the building. The lease refers to the assignment, and it also is recorded, thus making certain that the mortgagee's rights are treated as recorded rights, good against the whole world. The lease is a "net" lease under which all taxes, insurance premiums, etc., are borne by the lessee, and no burdens or payments are borne by the lessor or the mortgagee.

---

[3] Kratovil, *Real Estate Law,* 4th ed. (Englewood Cliffs, N.J.: Prentice-Hall, Inc., 1964), pp. 235–236, © 1964.

The rent payments exactly equal the mortgage payments. A mortgage accompanies the transaction, but the main security is the assignment. The loan is for the full cost of construction of the building. With a high-credit tenant like Sears, Woolworth, etc., a lender can lend with complete security on a transaction of this sort. The assignment is good against a subsequent bankruptcy of the lessor. It also prevails over subsequent federal liens, subsequent creditors of the mortgagor, subsequent attempts of the mortgagor to cancel the lease or obtain prepayment of the rent. In short, virtually nothing can occur that will prevent full collection by the lender. The typical assignment of rents is not considered quite as foolproof legally as this *active assignment*.[4]

Reference: Rents after default, state by state study. Journal of ABA Real Property Section (Winter 1967), p. 603.

ADDITIONAL REFERENCES: 27 Ia. L. Rev. 626; 52 Mich. L. Rev. 1085; 14 Mich. S.B.J. 331; 24 Mo. L. Rev. 524; 89 U. Pa. L. Rev. 679; 7 U. Pittsb. L. Rev. 345.

---

[4] Kratovil, *Real Estate Law*, 5th ed. (Englewood Cliffs, N.J.: Prentice-Hall, Inc., 1969), p. 229, © 1969.

28

Lease Drafting for the Purposes
of a Mortgage on the Fee

§ **306. In general—interim and permanent lenders.** In many large loans the mortgage lender looks to lease revenue to furnish the cash flow for debt service. The terms of the lease, in consequence, have become a matter of grave concern to the lender. The lender wants the assurance of income to retire the mortgage, which, in turn, requires unconditional liability of triple-A tenants. He wants protection against the landowner's acts or defaults that might destroy the lease.

As between lenders, the interim lender, who finances the contruction of a project, is concerned with construction and completion of improvements and his rights with respect to tenants until completion of the project and acceptance of leased quarters by the tenants. But the takeout lender steps in after the tenants have accepted their leases and premises in writing, and has little interest in construction problems. On the other hand, the interim lender has no interest in rental income because he steps out of the picture as the tenants step in. *See* § 209. The shopping center offers illustrations of the problems encountered and much of this chapter deals with this situation.

As for the landlord, he must satisfy the interim lender, the permanent lender, and the triple-A tenant if he is to get his financing, so he must defer to these parties to a great extent so far as lease clauses are concerned. Compared with the triple-A tenant, who has triple-A bargaining power, and the big insurance company that will be the permanent investor, the landlord-promoter is likely to be low man on the document totem pole.

§ **307. Rent.** Obviously every lease should contain a covenant by the tenant to pay rent and should state that this covenant runs with the land. The time of payment of rent should be set forth.

§ 308. Date of commencement of occupancy. The tenant will wish to defer his occupancy and commencement of rent payment until construction of the building in the leased premises has been completed and the other neighboring tenants are prepared to commence their occupancy. The landlord, however, will wish the tenant to begin his occupancy as soon as his store is completed. A compromise may require the tenant to occupy before the building is completed, but to pay only a percentage rent during that period.

The lease may define the commencement of its term as the date construction of an entire shopping center is completed. This is dangerous because of the rule against perpetuities, for completion is technically an indefinite date in the future, and the rule against perpetuities makes such indefinite documents void. *See,* however, *Wong v. D. Grazia,* 60 Cal.2d 525, 386 P2d 817. *See* § 344. This threat is met by providing that the commencement of lease and completion of center shall be not more than five years from date of lease, otherwise the lease to be void.

§ 309. Duration of leases. The key leases must continue in force at least as long as the mortgage debt remains unpaid so that the mortgage debt dwindles to nothing by the time the lease has run out. Small tenants can have shorter leases so that, if the key tenants wish to expand, space will be available for them to do so.

§ 310. Subordination clauses. There are legal advantages to the lender in having the key leases prior and therefore superior to the mortgage. For one thing, in some states foreclosure of a senior mortgage automatically terminates a junior lease and the lender is powerless to prevent this. For a like reason the lender objects to a lease clause subordinating the lease "to all institutional mortgages now or hereafter on said premises." The lender is not consoled by the fact that the lease also provides (in the so-called *non-disturbance clause*) that despite foreclosure the possession of the tenant will not be disturbed as long as he pays his rent. This protects the tenant but not the landlord, for the tenant may seek to contend that this clause is one he may, but need not, take advantage of. Also the lease should prohibit any subordination by the tenant to a junior mortgage, since foreclosure of the junior mortgage might then wipe out the lease.

§ 311. Description of leased premises. Often a building in a shopping center is leased while the project is still on the drawing board. Here, preparing the description of the leased premises will pose problems. While the leased site may not be too definitely settled, the lease can nevertheless give an exact description of the total area of the center, taken from the title policy, abstract, or other evidence of the landlord's title. The leased site will then be described by reference to a sketch, preferably drawn to scale, attached to the lease. Usually this gives a complete layout of the center, with the location of the leased premises in the layout being indicated by crosshatching. The landlord will wish to reserve the right to make some changes in the layout of the shopping center and location of the store at least until the center is substantially rented. The tenant will probably demand covenants that: (1) parking area will not be reduced, (2) no change will be made that will reduce the visibility of tenant's store front, (3) no store will be allowed to project beyond tenant's store, and (4) tenant's space will not be reduced below certain minimum dimensions.

§ 312. Construction of building by developer. The lease may contain a covenant by the developer to build the building in accordance with the site plan, subject to such changes as the lease specifically permits.

Since the project may have only reached the stage of general overall design, final working drawings of the tenant's store may not be available at the time the lease is executed. A workable way to handle the situation is to attach to the lease a synopsis setting forth the construction to be performed. Where the landlord is to do both interior and interior construction, the tenant must covenant to furnish the landlord a store and fixture layout in sufficient detail so that the landlord can prepare drawings and specifications for the construction work. The landlord should covenant to furnish, when construction is completed, an architect's certificate that the premises have been completed according to the synopsis.

The lease should require the tenant to give the landlord an acceptance letter when the landlord has completed all required construction work on the leased premises. The permanent mortgage lender will insist on seeing such acceptances, for he counts on revenue from the tenants to pay off the mortgage and wants to know that the tenants have no excuse for seeking to be relieved of their leases. The landlord will find that if he allows the tenant to take possession before the acceptance is given, the tenant, knowing that the landlord must furnish the mortgage lender these acceptances, may demand additional work he is not entitled to under the lease.

§ 313. Construction of interior by tenant. Some leases will simply require the developer to construct the exterior of the building and will require the tenant to construct all the interior work. Here the lease should: (1) furnish at least some sort of outline specifications of the building if final plans and specifications are unavailable, for the tenant cannot intelligently decide how much rent he can agree to pay unless he knows what the construction work will cost him; (2) require the tenant to protect the landlord against mechanics' liens by furnishing a deposit, surety bond, etc., though a lease covenant by a triple-A tenant to pay all mechanics' liens may be sufficient; (3) require the tenant to carry builder's risk, workmen's compensation, and other insurance during construction; (4) require the tenant to hire labor that will not cause controversies with the developer's construction crew.

§ 314. Cancellation clauses. The lease should give either party the right to cancel if certain stages of the construction work have not been started by a specified date.

§ 315. Key tenants. The smaller tenant in a shopping center will want the landlord to covenant: (1) that there are leases with stated key tenants, (2) that the leases are not cancellable, and (3) that the leases run for a specified period of time, and prohibit these tenants from discontinuing business. The lease of a small tenant may further provide that if a named key tenant discontinues operations, the small tenant may cancel his lease. This is sometimes called the *follow-the-leader clause*. It is dangerous, for if a key tenant moves, the shopping center may collapse. Alternatively, it may provide that the small tenant pays a lower rent until operations are resumed by a major tenant of caliber equal to that of the tenant who moved out.

§ 316. Evidence of title. The lease requires the landlord to furnish the tenant evidence of good title to the leased premises, preferably a leasehold title insurance policy. The tenant checks this policy to make sure there are no building restrictions forbidding the use he plans to make of the premises. In addition, the landlord covenants that he has good title to the remainder of the center and affords the tenant's lawyer an opportunity to check the landlord's title policy covering the entire shopping center.

§ 317. Radius clause. Objection can be raised to a clause which forbids the landlord to rent premises within a specified radius of the shopping center for a purpose that competes with the tenant's business. The shopping center promoter might sell the center, and set up a competing use outside the center, and the lender would be powerless to prevent a cancellation of the lease by the tenant for this breach of the landlord's covenant. Perhaps the lender can get the tenant to sign a side agreement that he will not cancel the lease for such cause as long as the mortgage remains unpaid.

§ 318. Exclusives. Commonly, certain tenants are given the exclusive right to operate a certain type of business in the center. The fact that the tenant is given an exclusive imposes a restraint on the activities permitted other tenants. Hence it is important that the lease be recorded so that all other tenants are given notice of this restraint, and it is better for the exclusive clause to describe the center accurately, so that subsequent lessees are put on notice of the extent of the restricted area. 51(C) CJS 625.

An exclusive should be carefully drafted or litigation (in which the lender will become embroiled if he acquires the center by foreclosure) will result. 97 ALR2d 4.

EXAMPLE: A lease to a delicatessen forbids "other delicatessen shops" in the center. Would this bar a supermarket from handling delicatessen items? One court has said "Yes." *Parker v. Levin,* 285 Mass. 125, 188 NE2d 502. Another court has said "No." *Mook v. Weaver Bros.,* 59 F.2d 1028.

In general, where they are asked to enforce an exclusive, courts look for substantial overlapping of products and substantial competition. 97 ALR2d 46.

EXAMPLE: A junior department store that operates a variety department violates, to that extent, an earlier exclusive given to a variety store. *Variety, Inc. v. Hustad Corp.*, 145 Mont. 358, 400 P2d 408; 51(C) CJS. 635.

A landlord's violation of an exclusive may entail drastic consequences.

EXAMPLE: The developer gave *A* an exclusive for a variety store and later leased another site in the center to *B* for a variety store. When *A* stopped *B*'s operations, *B* successfully contended that there was a constructive eviction. This released *B* of all liability on his lease. *Variety, Inc. v. Hustad Corp.*, 145 Mont. 358, 400 P2d 408.

Where the lease gives the tenant an "exclusive," the lender will want the lease to provide that this can only be enforced by an injunction suit restraining another tenant from using the premises for the purpose in question. In other words, the lender will not want the tenant to have the right to terminate the lease for violation of the "exclusives" clause. It is not sufficient that the lease does not specifically give the tenant the right to terminate the lease for violation of the exclusive clause. Some courts, as the last example shows, have allowed the tenant to terminate his lease where the exclusives clause is violated on the ground that this was a "constructive eviction" of the tenant.

An exclusive may apply to additions to the shopping center as well as to the original center. 51(C) CJS. 623.

§ 319. **Use of premises.** The lease should state the use which the tenant is to make of the premises and contain a covenant not to use the premises for other purposes. Both provisions are necessary. If this protection is lacking, a tenant who would like to "jump his lease" simply puts the premises to a use offensive to the other tenants and the landlord will be compelled to agree to a cancellation of the lease. Or, just as bad, the tenant may use the premises for a use for which another tenant has an "exclusive." Surprisingly, leases have been encountered which gave the tenant an "exclusive" but did not forbid him to use the premises for other purposes! Obviously the use must be one which is not forbidden by local zoning.

§ 320. **Parking area and malls—easements and covenants.** The lease should contain a covenant by the landlord to furnish a parking area of prescribed size. The landlord should also covenant not to diminish the area of the parking lot or to materially increase the store area that uses it. The lease should grant the tenant an easement for customer and employee parking in common with customers and employees of the other tenants. Care must be exercised to make this an easement and not a license. It is customary to include a provision barring a tenant's employees from certain choice areas of the lot. Employees arrive early in the day, before shoppers arrive, and are in a position to usurp preferred parking places unless the lease forbids this. The landlord customarily covenants to pave, light, and strip the parking area; to police it; to keep it lighted, in repair, and free of ice and snow. Parking is only one of many easements that are important to the high-credit tenant. Ingress and egress over the drives, walks, and malls, for example, is another. Indeed, the tenant's right to enjoyment of all the common areas should be set out in some detail. This prevents the landlord from curtailing improvidently the basic rights of the high-credit tenant so important to the successful operation of the tenant's business. Once an easement has been granted, it cannot be moved without the tenant's consent. To maintain a degree of flexibility, it is well to reserve to the landlord (and this right will accrue to the lender in the event of foreclosure, if the clause so states) the right to make reasonable changes in the location of the easements without curtailing their area or availability to the lessee.

§ 321. **Assignment of lease.** The perfect commercial lease from the landlord's point of view contains an absolute prohibition against an assignment or sublease of the demised premises by the tenant, since this assures the landlord (and, incidentally, the mortgage lender) that the original triple-A tenant will remain in possession. But the tenant who wants to move will try to contrive subterfuges to get around the prohibition. Accordingly, assignment clauses are written to prevent subterfuges. The clause should forbid the tenant to assign, mortgage, encumber, or sublet without the lessor's consent. A prohibition should also be included against permitting the demised premises to be used by others through concessions or even through occupation by others. In the event the tenant is a corporation, it should be spelled out that any transfer, sale, pledge, or other disposition of the corporate stock or voting securities shall be deemed a prohibited assignment, though such a provision is obviously impossible in the case of corporations having numerous stockholders. A lease to a chain store may, at the chain's request, permit assignment to a subsidiary of the chain so long as the chain is willing to sign a guarantee of payment of rent and so long as the operation will continue in substantially the same fashion and without changes of signs or other physical features that "pull" shoppers to the area.

Before consenting to an assignment, the landlord and his mortgagee must determine that the assignee's operation will not violate an "exclusive." If the lease is a percentage lease, they should not consent to an assignment to a tenant whose gross volume of business is substantially smaller than that of the present tenant, for percentage rents are based on gross receipts, not net receipts.

§ 322. **Covenants in general.** Every shopping center lease contains covenants on the part of the landlord and covenants on the part of the tenant. Among the provisions the lender hopes and expects to find are the following tenant's covenants: to operate his business continuously; to remain open a certain number of hours per day; to keep his quarters illuminated until some specified hour each night; to pay a proportionate share of maintaining, policing, lighting, and insuring the parking area and other common areas; to pay for central services such as air-conditioning, heat, water, janitorial service, and utilities, if landlord is to furnish same; to pay a share of any increase in real estate taxes over the amount levied when the center becomes operational; to repair and maintain the store interior including doors and windows and be responsible for glass break-age, while the landlord covenants to maintain the exterior; to avoid trash accumu-lation; to submit proposed signs and awnings for landlord's approval (which chain stores will resist); and to maintain membership in a merchants' association.

Ordinarily the parties contemplate that any party who succeeds to the land-lord's ownership or the tenant's leasehold will enjoy the benefit of and be bound by the covenants. It is best to spell this out in the lease. This insures the right of the lender to enforce these covenants against the tenant in the event he acquires ownership through foreclosure. By the same token, the tenant will have the right to enforce covenants on the part of the lessor. Hence the lender must analyze the lease covenants that place duties on the landlord to determine whether they are unduly burdensome, such as covenants to rebuild or repair, regardless of cost. It may be possible to negotiate a side-agreement with the tenant that specific burdensome covenants will not be enforceable against the lender.

The covenants on the landlord's part should be covenants that the lender is able to perform, if necessary, so that if the landlord defaults, the lender can step in and perform and thus prevent termination of the leases by the tenant.

EXAMPLE: A landlord who happens to own a nearby "Kiddieland" can covenant to furnish complimentary tickets to a tenant who sells children's shoes. A lender succeeding to ownership of the center could not perform this covenant, and so it must not be included in the "covenants that run with the land."

EXAMPLE: A mortgage covers part of a shopping center. A lease to a tenant in this part of the center requires the landlord to restore or replace *any building in the center* damaged by fire, etc. If the mortgagee forecloses he cannot restore any building in the other portion of the center and yet, as the new landlord, if he fails to do so he will be in default under the lease.

§ 323. Cancellation clauses. Any clause giving the tenant a right to termi-nate the lease because of events other than the landlord's breach of covenant is disturbing to a lender. For example, the value of the lease is affected by any clause giving the right to cancel if any part of the parking lot is condemned, for example, for road widening or if the tenant's sales do not average a specified dollar amount.

If possible, the lease should provide that any lender will receive notice from the tenant of the landlord's breach of covenant and be given an opportunity to cure it before the tenant cancels the lease. There should be no objection to this if the notice is required only if the lender first informs the lessee in writing of his name and address. This is analogous to the situation in a leasehold mortgage where the landlord agrees to notify the lender of a tenant's default and to give the lender the right to cure it before the landlord declares a forfeiture of the lease. Alternatively, the lender may be able to procure a side-agreement with the tenant under which the tenant waives, as to the lender, the right to cancel the lease because of landlord's breaches of covenant, either altogether or until the lender has acquired ownership by foreclosure and can then control the situation. In one way or another, in other words, the lender should endeavor to insulate himself against the tenant's wriggling out of the lease because of the landlord's defaults, as the tenant will try to do if the lease proves economically disadvantageous.

§ 324. **Abatement of rent.** The lease, or the state law even in the absence of a lease provision, may give the lessee the right to an abatement of rent because of the landlord's breach of covenant. This is objectionable to the lender. The tenant conceivably could advance large sums of money to build an addition the landlord was obligated to build, and when the lender takes over the property by foreclosure he may be unable to collect rent until the tenant has recouped his expenditures. A good lease would forbid withholding of rent by the tenant under any conditions, at least as to a lender.

§ 325. **Option to purchase.** A lease clause giving a prior lessee an option to purchase the premises is a troublesome clause to the lender. In the first place, some fine lawyers believe such an option is a prior "encumbrance" that makes the mortgage an illegal investment for an institutional lender. In the second place, no one can be certain of the consequences where there is an exercise of the option, with payment of the purchase price to the lessor. In many cases the courts have said that exercise of the option relates back to the date of the option. 50 ALR 1314; 66 CJ 487. If exercise of the option relates back, it might wipe out the mortgage. *Kansas State Bank v. Bourgeois*, 14 Utah 2d 188, 380 P2d 931. At best, exercise of the option results in prepayment of the mortgage with no prepayment premium. And if the option is in the form of a "pre-emption right" to purchase the property at a price the mortgagor is willing to accept from a third party, some court decisions hold that this gives the tenant the right to buy from the lender at a price equal to the foreclosure sale price if the mortgage is foreclosed. 17 ALR 3rd 962. Finally it certainly is objectionable to take subject to an option where the option price is or could be less than the mortgage debt. The option to purchase, therefore, should be subordinated to the mortgage. It is perfectly possible to subordinate the option without subordinating the lease. In the document subordinating the option to the mortgage it should also be provided that if the tenant exercises his option and thus becomes the owner of the property, the lease shall nevertheless remain in existence for the benefit of the lender, so that he can collect rent thereunder if default occurs under the mortgage.

§ 326. Tenant's lien. The tenant may have a lien on the land for some purpose, as for example, to insure return of a security deposit or because the tenant made some repairs or performed some other act that was legally the obligation of the landlord. This lien, in the case of a prior lease, may be prior and superior to the lien of the mortgage, and may possibly make the investment illegal in some states. This lien and, indeed, any other lien the tenant may have by virtue of his status as a tenant, should be subordinated to the lien of the mortgage, or the lease should contain a general clause making all the tenants' liens subordinate to any mortgage thereafter placed on the property to an institutional lender.[1]

§ 327. Expansion provisions. Some high-credit tenants take the position that their merchandising experience is such that they should be allowed to make the judgment that an expansion of their premises is needed. If the lease contains such a clause, the mortgagee examining such a lease will look for a clause to the effect that if the landlord fails to build the addition and the tenant is forced to do so at his expense any lien the tenant thus acquires will be subordinate to any mortgage held by an institutional lender. It may well be that the lease will contain covenant binding the landlord to erect any such addition. The mortgagee will want a clause in the lease or in a side agreement with the tenant that such covenant does not obligate the mortgagee to erect the addition. And finally the lease should make it clear that if the landlord fails to erect the addition, this does not give the tenant the right to terminate the lease.

§ 328. Percentage leases. Leases of retail locations often provide for a percentage rent. Such a lease usually provides a minimum fixed rent. Over and above this minimum, the rental is fixed at a percentage of the tenant's gross sales. The percentage of gross income that is to be charged usually presents no great problem, for commonly accepted percentages for each type of retail establishment are published periodically by the National Association of Real Estate Boards. However, is it obvious that if such a lease is prepared for a department store in a shopping center, it will be necessary to fix different percentages for different departments within the single store. Deductions from gross sales are usually allowed for sales and luxury taxes and merchandise returned by the shopper. Care should be exercised to include in gross sales all income from vending machines, telephone booths, pay toilets, lockers, weighing machines, stamp machines, and so on; and also services rendered on the premises, hairdressing and the like. Services rendered at cost, clothing alterations and employees' cafeteria, for example, are usually excluded. Income from subtenants

[1] Kratovil, *Real Estate Law*, 5th ed. (Englewood Cliffs, N.J.: Prentice-Hall, Inc., 1969), pp. 347–352, © 1969.

and concessionaires is included. The lease should state whether gross income includes sales made by mail and sales to employees. The lease should require the tenant to conduct business throughout the year, for obviously, if the store is closed, the percentage rent stops or drops. Further, the lease should fix the hours and days on which the store is to be open. A provision should also be included forbidding the establishment of a competing store within a specified radius. Since the landlord is depending on the particular tenant's ability to run a profitable business, the lease should forbid any assignment or sublease or even the occupancy of the premises by anyone other than the tenant, unless the landlord consents.

For the landlord's convenience, all percentage leases in the project should be uniform with respect to the time of month when monthly statements of gross sales are to be furnished by the tenants.

§ 329. Net leases. Attorneys for mortgage lenders ought to have some familiarity with the jargon lenders employ with respect to leases. In general, a *net lease* is one in which, in addition to rent, the tenant pays real estate taxes and special assessments. If, in addition, he pays insurance premiums, the lease is a *net-net lease*. And, if in addition to all this, the tenant pays the cost of repairs and maintenance, even to the extent of replacing a damaged or destroyed building, it is a *net-net-net lease*. The definitions are not universal or precise and are totally lacking in legal significance.

§ 330. Eminent domain clauses. Among the clauses in leases one encounters relating to condemnation is one providing that if there is any detrimental change in the roads giving access to a shopping center, the tenant may terminate the lease. Obviously the mortgagee would look at this with a jaundiced eye. Or a lease may provide that if the landlord conveys part or all of the leased premises of the shopping center to a condemning body, this gives the tenant the right to terminate. The landlord faced with the obvious power of a public body to condemn may decide to convey voluntarily. This is just as objectionable to a mortgagee as a clause giving the right to terminate in case of condemnation. Or the lease may give the tenant the right to terminate where condemnations or conveyances to a condemnor take place with respect to adjoining property. Where blighted areas are being cleared, obviously a tenant dislikes remaining in business when neighboring stores are being demolished. All these clauses affect the mortgagee's assessment of the risk.

Other clauses may provide for withholding of the tenant's share of a condemnation award in case of a partial taking. This is good from the mortgagee's point of view, since it provides assurance that rent will be paid. The tenant may insist that this money be held by a third party and that he receive interest.

§ 331. Default clause. Any landlord or prospective landlord (like a mortgagee) is vitally interested in the default clause in the lease. Many such clauses follow some ancient form and are inadequate for today's purposes. To take one aspect, a lease form may provide that the landlord may terminate upon bankruptcy or other default by the lessee, leaving open the question whether the right to terminate applies to a bankruptcy of an assignee, sublessee or guarantor. Or the lease may refer to an adjudication of bankruptcy, which might not include arrangements, for example, under Chapter XI.

SUGGESTION: Use the form set forth in American Bar Assn., Proceedings of Section of Real Property, Probate and Trust Law (August 1964), p. 109.

§ **332. Survival clause.** Where the landlord evicts the tenant because of the tenant's defaults, the tenant's liability for future rent is ended unless the lease contains a clause (called the *survival clause*) to the effect that the tenant's liability shall survive such eviction. Such lease clauses are now commonplace. Under these clauses the courses open to the landlord are much the same as in cases of abandonment by the tenant. *Broniewicz v. Wysocki,* 306 Ill.App. 187, 28 NE2d 283, 2 Ill.Bar.J. 269. If the landlord intends to hold the tenant liable after eviction for default, the landlord should not, in his notice to the tenant to quit the premises, include any statement to the effect that the lease is forfeited or terminated because of the tenant's defaults. If such a forfeiture statement is included, some states hold that the tenant is not liable for further rent, the theory being that further rent cannot accrue under a lease that the landlord has himself declared at an end. 99 ALR 42. However, in some states this is regarded as a mere technicality, and the tenant's liability for rent continues under the survival clause even though the landlord has declared the lease forfeited. *Central Investment Co. v. Melick,* 267 Ill. 564, 108 NE 681.

A clause similar to the *survival clause* is included in the portion of the lease dealing with abandonment of the premises by the tenant.

Courts tend to distinguish between a tenant's liability for rent and his liability for damages provided for in the lease, where the tenant abandons the premises or is evicted for default. Rent is compensation for the use of land. The tenant may also be liable under the lease for *damages* if he abandons or is evicted for default, but damages are not rent. The point is of importance. A landlord and tenant can agree on any *rent* they choose. The law will not interfere. But the moment the parties start contracting about *damages* they are in a new ball game. Contract provisions regarding damages are subject to court scrutiny. Among the rules applied is the rule distinguishing between liquidated damages and penalties.

EXAMPLE: *L* leases to *T* for 99 years with a provision that in case of default *L* may declare a forfeiture of the lease and hold *T* liable for damages equal to the rent for the remainder of the term. Here if *T* defaulted in the first year of the lease he would be saddled with a damage claim equal to rent for 98 years. No court would sanction this. It is an obvious penalty. *Commissioner v. Mass. Accident Co.*, 310 Mass. 769, 39 NE2d 759. Quite commonly the dispute may center upon a security deposit made by *T* with *L*. If the lease provision for which the deposit stands as security is illegal, the security transaction is illegal. As a corollary, the security provision would not be binding on *T* and his trustee in bankruptcy, who, at a minimum, succeeds to all of *T*'s rights.

It may be said at this point that the law discussed here is interwoven with the law concerning the impact of bankruptcy where a landlord and tenant relationship exists. *See* Chapter 34.

EXAMPLE: Under state law in the particular state a *survival clause* would be valid. Nevertheless, if the bankruptcy court considers the clause in the nature of a penalty it will strike it down. *Kothe v. Taylor Trust*, 280 US 724. When it does this, the trustee in bankruptcy is entitled to the securities.

If the lease is rejected by the lessee's trustee in bankruptcy, the measure of damages is fixed by the Bankruptcy Act. *City Bank Farmers Trust Co. v. Irving Trust Co.*, 299 US 433.

§ 333. Security deposits, advance payments of rent. Of interest to the mortgagee are the several different kinds of security devices employed by landlords to protect against loss caused by the tenant's abandonment of the property or default in the payment of rent:

1. The lease may require the tenant to deposit securities with the landlord. The deposit is called a *security deposit*. Often it is provided in the lease that interest will be paid the tenant on such deposit. If the tenant abandons the premises or is evicted for default in rent, the landlord is authorized by the lease provision to sell the securities and apply the proceeds to the damages suffered by the landlord as a result of the tenant's defaults. By and large such provisions are valid. 45 Yale L.J. 537; 43 Yale L.J. 307; 25 Ill.L.Rev. 716.

As is always true with all security transactions, a security deposit stands as security for rent or damages that can be legally collected by the landlord.

EXAMPLE: The lease expires and the tenant has paid all rent and other sums due the landlord. The security deposit must be returned to the tenant.

Of course, the problems that arise are never so simple.

EXAMPLE: *L* leases to *T*. *T* makes a security deposit with *L*. The lease does not contain *survival clause*. *T* defaults and *L* declares a forfeiture under the lease. *L* cannot hold the security for rent or damages accruing after the forfeiture because forfeiture in such case wipes the slate clean.

EXAMPLE: *L* leases to *T* with a security deposit and with a provision for *ipso facto* termination of the lease if *T* files a petition in bankruptcy. There is no survival clause. *T* files bankruptcy. *T*'s trustee in bankruptcy is entitled to the security deposit. *T*'s bankruptcy wiped the slate clean as to *L*.

As has already been mentioned in connection with the survival clause (*see* § 332), there is a distinction between *rent* and *damages* suffered by the landlord as a result of the tenant's eviction for default. The security deposit can stand as security only for amounts the landlord is legally entitled to collect. Moreover, as in the case of other security transactions, the security deposit is security only for those items described in the security instrument as being within the protection of the security deposit.

EXAMPLE: A security deposit states that it is security for *rent* not paid by tenant. It cannot be used to compensate the landlord for cost of repairs the tenant is supposed to make under the lease.

The cases are in conflict as to the exact nature of the relationship between landlord and tenant created by the security deposit. When there is an actual deposit or securities, some courts treat the relationship with respect thereto as pledgor-pledgee. 2 Powell, *Real Property* § 229; 1 Real Property, Probate and Trust Journal of A.B.A. 416 (Winter 1966) (dealing extensively with nature of security deposits); 12 So. Calif.L.Rev. 416. In New York such a deposit, by statute, is a trust.

Where the deposit is a pledge of securities, enforcement of the pledge should follow pledge law. There should be a pledgee's sale with notice to the pledgor, etc. Obviously the lease should contain language similar to that found in a collateral note, giving the landlord-pledgee the right to sell at a public or private sale or on a stock exchange, to dispense with public notice of the sale, to bid in at his own sale and so on. 1 Real Property, Probate and Trust Journal of ABA (Winter 1966) p. 427. Obviously the courts will strike down any clause to the effect that in case of default the securities belong to the landlord without any sale.

Whether the deposit is a pledge or trust, the landlord has no right to commingle the securities with his own or to pocket the interest or dividends generated by the securities. Real Property, Probate and Trust Journal of A.B.A. (Winter 1966) 412. The clause should cover these matters.

If the lease contains a survival clause, the security deposit will, if the lease so provides, stand as security for the damages spelled out in this clause. *In re Hamann,* 45 F 481.

2. The lease may provide for a deposit of cash which is to be retained by the landlord as *"liquidated damages"* in case the tenant abandons the property or the landlord is forced to evict the tenant for default in rent. This deposit differs from a true security deposit in that there is no effort here to wait out the natural life of the lease to see what actual damages are sustained on a reletting to new tenants. It is obvious that such a deposit is not a serious attempt actually to approximate a sum that would compensate the landlord for the tenant's default, for a default in the early months of the lease might damage

the landlord considerably, when he cannot promptly obtain a new, responsible tenant, whereas a default in the last month's rent would harm the landlord very little. Since the same sum of money is forfeited whether the default occurs early or late, it is obvious that the landlord is simply trying, through the threat of a penalty, to induce faithful performance by the tenant. Therefore, some courts say this is not a valid provision for liquidated damages and compel the landlord to return the deposit to the tenant less any rent actually due at the time the tenant abandons the property or is evicted. 45 Yale L.J. 537; 25 Ill.L.Rev. 716. However, the court decisions on this point are quite conflicting, and it is difficult to establish any general rule. 106 ALR 292.

3. The lease may require the tenant to pay a lump sum at the time the lease is signed as a bonus for the privilege of receiving the lease. This is universally held valid on the theory that a man can legally "buy" a lease just as he can buy a car. 45 Yale L.J. 537. The money belongs to the landlord no matter what the tenant does. Of course, such clauses are often coupled with other clauses by which the rent is reduced in the last months of the lease if the tenant pays his rent faithfully, so in practical effect, though not in legal contemplation, the clause is a security device to insure faithful performance.

4. The lease may require the tenant, at the signing of the lease, to pay the last several months rent "in advance." If the tenant abandons the premises or is evicted for default in rent, the landlord is allowed to retain the rent. Mostly such clauses are held valid. 25 Ill.L.Rev. 716. Some authorities perceive in this situation an analogy to the case of vendor and purchaser, where a defaulting purchaser forfeits all payments he has made. *Claude v. Sheppard,* 122 N.Y. 397, 25 NE 358. Again, however, other courts regard them as being essentially identical with the "liquidated damages" clauses discussed in Paragraph 2, and accordingly the clause will be held valid or invalid depending upon whether a liquidated damages clause would be valid or invalid. *Burns Trading Co. v. Welborn,* 81 F2d 691; 106 ALR 285; 25 Ill.L.Rev. 716.

5. The lease may provide that securities or money deposited by the tenant shall be held *as an indemnity* against loss suffered by the landlord for loss of rent, breach of covenant or because of the termination of the lease for the tenant's fault. There are said to be advantages to the landlord in the event of the tenant's bankruptcy where the clause assumes this form. *Ghote Estates v. Freeda's Capri Restaurant,* 332 Mass. 17, 123 NE2d 232; Real Property, Probate and Trust Law Journal of ABA Real Property Division, August 10–12, 1964, pp. 108–109. There are also certain disadvantages. *Id.* pp. 108–109, 126. These disadvantages can be minimized by competent draftsmanship. *Ibid.*

6. The protection may take the form of guarantee of payment of rent and performance of leasee's covenants by a third party, usually a parent corporation.

1 Real Property, Probate and Trust Journal (Winter 1966) 428–430; Real Property, Probate and Trust Law Journal of ABA, Real Property Division (August 10–12 1964) p. 124 *et seq. See* § 410.

The advance payment of rent and bonus payment clauses involve a tax disadvantage. Such items are treated as income taxable to the landlord in the year received.

Where a bonus or true payment of rent in advance is involved, obviously the landlord is at liberty to commingle these funds with his other funds. The money belongs to him. And for the same reason, he need not pay interest on the money.

When a tenant who has deposited funds with his landlord as security or as an advance payment of rent later assigns his lease, the tenant's right to a refund of this money does not pass by the assignment. A separate assignment is necessary, or language assigning the deposit must be included in the assignment of the lease. *Anuzes v. Gotowtt,* 248 Ill.App. 536; *Reidy v. Miller,* 85 Cal.App. 764, 260 P 861.

To some considerable extent the law in this area reflects an effort by bankruptcy courts to salvage more assets for the general creditors. The landlord's lawyers have reacted by resorting to more sophisticated drafting devices. 18 Mo.L.Rev. 1. The Bankruptcy Act has been amended from time to time in this area as the fortunes of war have shifted from one combatant to the other. One result is that the decisions must always be examined with reference to the form of statute in effect at the time.

Cross reference: Chapter 29.

29

Lease Draftmanship for Leasehold Mortgage Purposes

§ 334. **Introduction.** Since mortgages on leaseholds have become relatively common, lawyers have become conscious of the need for preparing every long-term lease with a view to qualifying it for such a loan. Often the lease and mortgage thereon are drafted almost simultaneously. There are provisions the lender wants included for his protection. Other common provisions must be omitted altogether or tailored to his needs. The problem is one that has often confronted attorneys for landlord, tenant and lender. Anderson, *The Mortgagee Looks at the Ground Lease,* 10 U. Fla.L.Rev. 1; Gunning, *A Primer for Mortgageable Ground Leases,* The Mortgage Banker (March 1967) 35, Harth, *Mortgaging the Leasehold Interest,* 26 *Legal Bulletin* of the U.S. Savings & Loan League 89; Kelly, *Some Aspects of Leasehold Mortgages—Some Practical Considerations,* 14 Business Lawyer 609; Mendel, *Financing Commercial Structures—Essentials of Documentation,* 12 Business Lawyer 30; Thomas, *The Mortgaging of Long Term Leases,* 30 Dicta 363; Wayte, *Drafting a Lease Which Is Mortgageable,* Los Angeles Bar Bulletin (Dec. 1966) p. 62.

§ 335. **Mortgage covering fee and leasehold.** Not uncommonly the owner of the reversion will join in a leasehold mortgage. This, of course, converts the mortgage into one on the fee. Or the reversioner may "subordinate" his fee title to the leasehold mortgage. *Applefield v. Fidelity Fed. S & L Assn.,* 137 So2d 259 (Fla.).

§ 336. **Statutes regulating investments by institutional lenders.** Requirements concerning the leasehold estate to be mortgaged may occur in statutes regulating investments of institutional lenders. For example, in Arizona the statute provides that if an insurance company is to invest in a leasehold mort-gage, the lease must have an unexpired term of not less than 21 years inclusive of the term which may be provided by an enforceable option of renewal. Arizona Stat. Annot. Sec. 20–553 (A). The Arizona Statutes continue with a provision forbidding any condition or right of re-entry or forfeiture under which the lender is unable to continue the lease in force for the duration of the loan. Arizona Stat. Annot. Sec. 20–553 (B). Moreover, the loan must not exceed 75% of the value of the leasehold. Arizona Stat. Annot. Sec. (C). This last requirement as to percentage of value will, in turn, compel the mortgagee to make an accurate appraisal of the value of the leasehold. Boyer and Wilcox, *An Economic Appraisal of Leasehold Valuation in Condemnation Proceedings,* 17 U. Miami L. Rev. 245; Dalgety, *The Appraisal of Long-Term Leaseholds,* The Appraisal Journal (April 1948) pp. 165-173; Hitchings *The Valuation of Leasehold Interests and Some Elements of Damage Thereto,* Southwestern Legal Foundation, Second Annual Institute on Eminent Domain 61 (1960); Horgan, *Some Legal and Appraisal Considerations in Leasehold Valuation under Eminent Domain,* 5 Hastings L.J. 34; McMichael, *Appraising Leasehold Estates,* American Institute of Real Estate Appraisers, Selected Readings in Real Estate Appraisals, 33 Appraisals J. 563 (1965). In Florida the statutes regulating insurance company investments provide with respect to leasehold mortgages that there must not be any condition or right of re-entry or forfeiture "not insured against" under which the insurer is unable to continue the lease in force for the duration of the loan. Florida Stat. Annot. Sec. 625.0125 (1). The prudence which institutional lenders are required to exercise would seem to preclude loaning where the mort-gage lien is exposed to extinguishment by enforcement of a condition whether contained in some earlier deed in the chain of title or in the lease itself. Title companies can at times provide insurance against conditions contained in prior deeds. Conditions contained in the lease itself are dealt with later. In Minnesota the statutes permit leasehold mortgages by insurance companies only where 40 years or more of the term of the lease remain unexpired. Minn. Stat. Annot. Sec. 61A.28 (3). In Iowa the comparable requirement is that 50 years or more of the term "including renewals" remain unexpired. Iowa Code Annot. Sec. 508.

With respect to loans made by savings and loan associations, the Arizona law specifies that the leasehold shall extend not less than ten years beyond the contractual term of the mortgage loan. Arizona Stat. Annot. Sec. 6–445 (2). A similar provision will be found in California. Calif. Fin. Code Annot. Sec. 7100. In Illinois the lease must continue at least 14 years beyond the maturity of a savings and loan association loan. Ill. Rev. Stat. Ch. 32, Sec. 793.

In general the laws of the domicile of the lender are the laws governing the propriety of an investment. However, there are some exceptions. New York, for example, requires that investments of foreign life companies doing business in New York comply in substance with the limitations imposed by New York law on domestic insurers. Insurance Code § 90.

At all events, the investment statutes must be carefully analyzed where a loan of this type is contemplated.

§ 337. Parties—joinder of lessor's spouse. In many states, dower or some statutory marital interest may exist that will make it necessary for the lessor's spouse to join the lease. *Fargo v. Bennett,* 35 Ida. 359, 206 P 692; *Benson v. Dritch,* 244 SW2d 339 (Tex.Civ.App.).

§ 338. Parties—lessor a corporation. Where the lease is made by a corporation as lessor, the requirements are much the same as with respect to a deed or mortgage made by a corporation. *See* § 71.

A lease by a municipal corporation is unacceptable unless a statute specifically authorizes it and the statutory procedure has been followed. Even where this is done, questions exist as to the right of the municipal corporation to include an option to renew or other features desired by the parties. *Cf. Whitworth College v. Brookhave,* 161 FSupp. 775 (D.C.S.C. Miss.) (holding option bad), and *Wring v. City of Jefferson,* 413 SW2d 292 (Mo.) (holding option good).

§ 339. Parties—trustee as lessor or lessee. A trustee-lessor may not have the power to make a lease extending beyond the term of the trust. 3 Scott, *Trusts* § 189.2; 67 ALR2d 978. The same may well be true of a trustee-lessee. Local statutes should be consulted on this score. 3 A.B.A. Section of Real Property, Probate and Trust Law 295 (Fall, 1968). Where the trustee cannot lease for a term beyond the expiration of the trust, he cannot give an option to renew that will extend beyond the term. *Hallin v. Hallin,* 2 Ill.App.2d 118, 118 NE2d 612. A trustee, absent specific authorization, cannot make a lease to begin *in futuro.* 3 Scott, *Trusts* § 189.6.

§ 340. Demised premises. Of course the lease will demise the land as well as any improvements thereon. The description will be taken from a title policy, abstract caption or other reliable source. The description will usually conclude with a conveyance of the landlord's interest in adjoining streets, alleys and rights of way thereafter vacated or abandoned, and including vault rights in adjoining ways.

§ 341. Easements. Where the demised premises are to be serviced by easements, either easements antedating the lease or created contemporaneously therewith out of adjoining land owned by the lessor, it is best to divide the description of the demised premises into two paragraphs; for example:

PARCEL I

Lot 1 in Block 1 in Sheffield's Addition to Chicago in Section 2, Township 40 North, Range 14 East of the Third Principal Meridian, in Cook County Illinois.

PARCEL II

Easement for ingress and egress over, under and across the East
40 feet of lot 2 in Block 1 aforesaid created by Grant dated_____
_____recorded_____in Book____Page_____ad Document No.
_____as an easement appurtenant to Parcel 1.

Where the easement is of current vintage, all the standard guides in the
draftsmanship of easements should be observed. Kratovil, *Easement Draftsmanship and Conveyancing, 38 Calif. L.Rev. 426* (1950). Likewise title insurance
should be requested covering the easement as well as the demised premises, both
for the lessee and his mortgagee.

§ 342. **Grants of rights or affirmative covenants by landlord.** If the tenant
is to receive other rights necessary for proper enjoyment of the premises, such as
grants of licenses by the landlord or to the tenant, or there is to be joinder by the
landlord in applications for zoning dispensations (variances, conditional use
permits), these rights should be set forth in the lease.

§ 343. **Use of premises.** The lessor obviously will insist on some limitation
of the uses to which the leasehold premises can be put. The leasehold mortgagee
will argue for some leeway. Care must be exercised not to prohibit incidental
activities, such as the operation of a cafeteria for employees. And utmost care
must be used to avoid restrictions on use that would be unacceptable to subtenants. Obviously these are matters of negotiation, depending largely on the
circumstances of each case. A limitation on use acceptable while the tenant is
in possession and operating may be unacceptable to a mortgagee who has foreclosed and is now in possession and operating or seeking a purchaser who will
acquire the leasehold and operate.

§ 344. **Perpetuities—perpetual leases—duration of lease.** Although there
are occasional statements that a perpetual lease is void (*Green v. Dietrich,* 114
Ill. 636), many holdings that perpetual leases are not favored (*Rutland Amusement Co. v. Seward,* 127 Vt. 324, 248 A2d 731), and some authority to the
effect that a perpetual lease is not a lease at all but a fee simple title (*Piper v.
Meredith,* 83 N.H. 107, 139 A 294), the great weight of authority is to the
effect that perpetual leases are valid. Thus, if a lease commences at once, the
fact that it has a perpetual duration does not create a violation of the rule against
perpetuities. 66 ALR2d 733. A good many leases, however, provide that the
term of the lease is to have its inception at some time in the future, the most
usual provision being that the lease will begin when construction of a building
has been completed. This perpetuities problem has been fully explored. *Wong
v. DiGrazia,* 35 Cal.Rptr. 241, 386 P2d 817, 1964 Duke L.J. 645, 16 Hasting
L.J. 470, 24 Md. L.Rev. 356, 12 UCLA L.Rev. 246, 9 Vill. L. Rev. 545.
See also 66 ALR2d 733, 735. Lawyers choose different methods of meeting

this particular perpetuities problem. Some lawyers will put a clause in the lease to the effect that if the building is not completed within a stated period of time, for example, five years, the lease is to become void. This eliminates any chance that the term could begin beyond the period permitted by the rule. Recently statutes have been enacted making the rule against perpetuities inapplicable in these cases. Ill.Rev.Stat. 1969, Ch. 30, § 194. Properly handled at all events, this point presents no problem. *See also* § 308.

Another question in this area relates to *attorment agreements.* They are normally entered into by a sublessee with a fee owner of the land and a mortgagee holding a mortgage thereon or on the prime leasehold estate, which mortgage occupies a paramount position to the subleasehold estate. These agreements are made by the subtenant to protect his leasehold estate from destruction by reason of the premature termination of the prime leasehold estate upon which his own estate depends, or from the loss of his estate by reason of the foreclosure of the paramount mortgage. To protect his subleasehold estate from being terminated upon the happening of either of these events, the sublessee provides for its continued existence, if one of these events should occur, by entering into agreements with the fee owner and the mortgage holding the paramount mortgage on the fee or on the prime leasehold estate. Such agreements, in general, provide that if the prime leasehold estate shall prematurely terminate, or the mortgagee shall acquire ownership of the fee or prime leasehold estate, as the case may be, through foreclosure, the sublease shall continue with the same force and effect as if the fee owner or mortgagee, as lessor, and the sublessee had entered into a lease for a term equal to the unexpired term of the sublease and containing the same provisions as those contained in the sublease. In effect, therefore, these agreements could be construed as creating a lease to commence in the future based on conditions precedent which may or may not occur within the perpetuity period. Under this construction, the agreement might be in violation of the rule against perpetuities. In some jurisdictions this problem has been solved by statute. Ill. Rev. Stat. 1969, Ch. 30, § 194. This statute provides that the rule is to have no applicability to commitments by a lessor to enter into a lease with a subtenant or with the holder of a leasehold mortgage or by a lessee or sublessee to enter into a lease with the holder of a mortgage.

Apart from statutes regulating investments, which tend to fix a minimum acceptable duration; apart, also, from statutes that limit the duration of farm leases; and apart, finally, from the problems created by rules relating to perpetuities, the leasehold mortgagee will insist on a lease of sufficient length to give him the security he requires. Obviously the lease must continue beyond the expiration of the projected mortgage. Moreover, the duration must be such that the leasehold will appraise out at a figure that will satisfy both the lender's investment department and the state supervisory authorities.

§ 345. Restrictions on assignment. Lease provisions vary with respect to restrictions imposed on the mortgaging of the leasehold. These are important to the leasehold mortgagee from two standpoints: (1) The leasehold mortgage itself may fall within the terms of the restriction. (2) The leasehold mortgagee must consider that he may become the owner of the leasehold by foreclosure and analyze these clauses to see if they will unduly fetter his disposition of the leasehold thus acquired. Examples of such clauses are as follows:

(1) The lease may expressly permit the mortgaging of the leasehold, without limitation whatever. These provisions are growing more common and should be included.

(2) The lease may expressly forbid the mortgaging of the leasehold. Such provisions are rare.

(3) The lease may forbid assignment of the leasehold or forbid assignment without consent of the lessor. In this situation it becomes necessary to distinguish between title and lien theory states in determining the legal significance of this restraint. Kratovil, *Real Estate Law* (5th ed., 1969) § 356. In title theory states a mortgage of the entire leasehold estate is viewed as an assignment of the leasehold. Hence if the lease forbids assignment of the leasehold without the landlord's consent, in title theory states this would be regarded as forbidding a mortgage of the leasehold without the landlord's consent. *Becker v. Werner*, 98 Pa. 555. This consent, by the prevailing rule, may be arbitrarily withheld. 55 Mich. L. Rev. 1029; 41 Minn. L. Rev. 355. In lien theory states, since a mortgage merely creates a lien, mortgage of the leasehold is not viewed as an assignment of the leasehold: hence a covenant against assignment is not broken by a mortgage of the leasehold. *Chapman v. Great Western Gypsum Co.,* 216 Cal. 420, 14 P2d 758; *Great South Aircraft Corp. v. Kraus,* 132 So2d 608, appeal dismissed, 133 So2d 788 (Fla.); *Riggs v. Pursell,* 66 N.Y. 193. It follows, moreover, that in lien states transfer of the leasehold to the mortgagee in consequence of default and foreclosure should likewise be viewed as falling without the purview of the assignment clause. Foreclosure should be viewed as an involuntary transfer, and lease restrictions on assignment do not restrict involuntary assignment through foreclosure unless the lease specifically so provides. *Crouse v. Mitchell,* 130 Mich. 347, 90 NW32; 1 Am. Law Ppty. 302. In one intermediate state it has been held that while a mortgage of the lease does not violate the clause forbidding assignment without the mortgagee's consent, a transfer taking place through foreclosure of the leasehold mortgage does constitute a violation. *Feldman v. Urban Commercial Inc.,* 64 N.J.S. 364, 165 A2d 854. This view is singularly wanting in logic. 1 Am. Law Ppty. 303. It denies protection to the mortgagee at the moment of greatest need. A final complication arises from the view taken in some lien states that while a mortgage creates only a lien, a mortgage deed of trust transfers the legal title, operating in much the same way as a mortgage in

title states. *People v. Nogarr,* 164 Cal. App.2d 591, 330 P2d 858, 11 Stanford L. Rev. 572. It is barely conceivable that in such jurisdictions a deed of trust conveying the leasehold would be viewed as a security assignment of the leasehold.

(4) The lease may forbid sublease as well as assignment without the landlord's consent. But where the restriction on subleasing is absent, the restriction on assignment can be circumvented by mortgaging the leasehold except the last day of the term, since a transfer of anything less than the entire leasehold estate is a sublease rather than an assignment. A restriction on assignment does not preclude a sublease. *Burns v. Dufresne,* 67 Wash. 158, 121 P 46; 74 ALR. 1018. Likewise a covenant against a sublease is not violated by an assignment. *Goldman v. Daniel Feder & Co.,* 84 W.Va. 600, 100 SE 400, 7 ALR. 246, 20 Colum. L. Rev. 233, 68 U. Pa. L. Rev. 189, 29 Yale L. J. 568; 7 ALR 249.

(5) The lease may forbid assignment or sublease, whether absolute or by way of security or any transfer voluntary or involuntary of part or all of the leasehold estate, without the landlord's consent. Absent such all-inclusive language a restriction upon assignment or sublease will always be construed as referring to a voluntary transfer on the lessee's part. Hanmer, *Option of the Lessor to Terminate a Lease Because of Involuntary Assignment,* 9 Chicago-Kent Review 268. An involuntary transfer, such as one to the lessee's trustee in bankruptcy, or by sale on execution or foreclosure of a mortgage, is not violated by a simple covenant against assignment. *Gazlay v. Williams,* 210 US 41, 28 S.Ct. 687, 52 L.Ed. 950, 22 Harv. L. Rev. 146; *In re Prudential Lithograph Co.,* 270 F 469, 69 U. Pa. L. Rev. 182; *Miller v. Fredeking,* 101 W.Va. 643, 133 SE 375, 46 ALR 842. The type of lease discussed in this paragraph is not mortgageable.

(6) The lease may require an assignee to assume all the covenants in the lease. The difficulty with this is that this personal liability continues even after the assignee transfers the leasehold estate to a purchaser, for assumption creates privity of contract. Hence a provision is needed that such personal liability terminates with an assignment by the assuming assignee. A problem is also posed where the assignee is a trustee who insists on an exculpation from personal liability.

(7) Some store leases contain a provision forbidding assignment without the lessor's consent coupled with a clause that consent will not unreasonably be withheld. This clause is not acceptable to some leasehold lenders. *See* e.g., 3 ALR2d 831, 835.

A question may remain as to disposition of the leasehold by a mortgagee who has acquired the leasehold by foreclosure. Provisions in the lease authorizing mortgages of the leasehold have now spent their force, and, in title theory states, if the lease contains a provision requiring the landlord's consent to an assignment, the mortgagee has no choice but to seek that consent. From the standpoint of the leasehold mortgagee, then, nothing is quite as satisfactory as the entire absence from the lease of any restriction on assignment of the lease.

In a few states statutes exist restricting the tenant's right to assign, *e.g.,* Texas Rev. Stat., Title 84, Landlord & Tenant Art. 5237, § 33. Such a statutory restriction may be waived in the lease if the intention to do so is clearly expressed. *Young v. De La Garga,* 368 SW2d 667 (Tex.Civ.App.).

§ 346. Personal liability of mortgagee. The leasehold mortgagee cannot legitimately object to being personally liable for payment of rent if and when he acquires ownership of the leasehold estate by foreclosure of his mortgage. At that time he is everywhere deemed an assignee of the leasehold estate with the necessary privity of estate that creates liability upon those covenants that run with the land, such as a covenant to pay rent. 51 CJS 585. However, there is danger in title theory states that the mortgage itself would be considered an assignment of the leasehold estate that would fasten personal liability on the leasehold mortgagee from the date of the mortgage. *Williams v. Safe Deposit Co.,* 167 Md. 499, 175 A 331; 73 ALR2d 1118. To eliminate personal liability, the leasehold mortgage might omit the last day of the term, converting the mortgage into a sublease, rather than assignment. There is, of course, no privity of estate between the owner of the reversion and a sublessee; hence no liability on the part of the sublessee. Failure to enjoy ownership of the last day of the term, however, is a matter of concern to leasehold lenders, particularly with respect to ownership of improvements, for the lease may confer "on the lessee at the termination of the lease" ownership of improvements erected by tenants. Such ownership might well be restricted to one who answers the description of lessee at the very moment of termination of the lease. Hence leasehold mortgages tend to couple the sublease method with an option in the mortgagee to acquire the last day of the term for some nominal amount. This, in turn, offers courts the opportunity to brand the entire transaction as an assignment rather than a sublease. There is no acceptable alternative to inclusion of a clause in the lease permitting a mortgage of the leasehold and negating personal liability of any leasehold mortgagee until he becomes the owner of the leasehold by foreclosure or assignment in lieu of foreclosure. As a further precaution, some mortgage lenders ask that the clause also provide that the mortgagee's personal liability shall continue only during his ownership of the leasehold estate and shall end when he transfers such ownership to another. Preferably a like limitation on liability should be extended to all subsequent assignees. Attorneys for assignees like to see this spelled out. The absence of such a contingent liability may assist a corporation in effecting a plan of liquidation under Sec. 337 (a) of the Internal Revenue Code.

Some questions may arise with respect to the problem of continuing breaches. For example, if the lease provides that the tenant will not permit the premises to be in disrepair, a breach in this respect on the part of the original tenant may be a breach on the part of the leasehold mortgagee who acquires the leasehold while the premises continue in disrepair, 51 CJS *Landlord and Tenant* § 117(6). Obviously the mortgagee and the landlord are likely to approach this problem from differing points of view. The leasehold mortgagee would prefer to assume liability for only those breaches that have their inception during his ownership.

Even where the lease expressly permits assignment or mortgage of the lease, a question arises where it is contemplated that the leasehold will be divided for development purposes with separate leasehold mortgages on each portion. The lease must provide for such division. Else default by any one of the tenants of a portion of the leasehold might cause forfeiture of the entire lease. Or if the same developer is to retain the entire leasehold, but wishes to mortgage separate portions, provision should be included in the lease for such separate mortgages and allocation of rents to such portions.

§ 347. **Covenants.** The mortgagee should carefully examine the lease covenants that run with the land. If there are covenants with which he might be unable to comply (e.g., a covenant to maintain affiliation with a franchised operation) or covenants he deems too onerous, he may wish to negotiate freedom from these covenants with the landlord.

§ 348. **Burdens falling on lessee.** Since the mortgagee must anticipate that he may be compelled to acquire the leasehold by foreclosure, he is interested in lease clauses that allocate financial burdens as between lessor and lessee, *e.g.,* taxes, special assessments, insurance premiums, repairs, and as to those burdens falling on the lessee he will wish to see the unforeseen contingencies clause, which states that the lessee is not in default where performance is delayed or prevented by Acts of God, war, civil commotion, strikes, labor disputes, etc.

Rent, of course, is a burden that will fall on the leasehold mortgagee if he forecloses. He must analyze rent escalation clauses carefully to see if they create an objectionable burden.

§ 349. **Bankruptcy of the lessor.** The impact on the leasehold of the lessor's bankruptcy is a question the statute and cases leave shrouded in doubt. Section 70 (b) of the Bankruptcy Act says that the trustee's rejection of the lease shall not "deprive the lessee of his estate." One court has conjectured that this gives leave to the bankruptcy court to adjust the rental and covenants of the lease according to the equities of the case. *In re Freeman,* 49 FSupp. 163. This seems to strip the quoted language of significance. The rental and covenants of the lease are the heart of the leasehold bargain. To the extent that the Bankruptcy Act requires respect for the estate of the lessee it should command respect for the ingredients that are at the heart of the leasehold contract. 6 Collier, *Bank-*

ruptcy (14th ed., 1965) 598; Report, Committee on Mortgage Law and Practice, A.B.A. Section on Real Property, Probate and Trust Law, August 10, 1964, p. 124.

Another writer suggests that the trustee is bound by the rental covenants and the other covenants that run with the land. Silverstein, *Rejection of Executory Contracts in Bankruptcy*, 31 U. Chi. L. Rev. 467, 491. This is a view favored by many knowledgeable property lawyers. However, this problem does leave an area for conjecture. Gottesman, *The Onus of Executory Contracts in Bank ruptcy: Focus on Vendors and Lessors*, 4 Practical Lawyer 65. See excellent treatment in 26 Bus. Law 1391.

§ 350. **Options.** If there is a renewal option or option to purchase in the lease it should be exercisable by the mortgagee on behalf of the lessee. Caution is urged in relying on such options because of the bankruptcy problem. The lessor's trustee in bankruptcy, it has been held, may reject the lessor's contracts, including an option of renewal. *Coy v. Title Guarantee & Trust Co.,* 198 F 275. See also *Ground Leases & Their Financing*, 4 A.B.A. Real Property Probate and Trust Journal 437, 457 (1969), and Turner, *Bankruptcy and Executory Contracts,* 41 Title News 144. The same holding can be anticipated with respect to an option to purchase. *In re New York Investors Mut. Group,* 143 FSupp. 51. Some mortgagees require that the lessee immediately exercise the option to renew, so that the leasehold mortgage and the title policy thereon cover the extended term from the outset.

There is also the problem of relation back. When a option is exercised, it relates back so as to cut off intervening rights acquired with knowledge or constructive notice of the option. This is the rule favored by the weight of authority. 91 CJS *Vendor & Purchaser* § 13; 50 ALR. 1314. There is, however, some authority expressing a contrary view as to some types of intervening inter ests. *Ibid.* There is law to the effect that where an option to purchase contained in a lease is exercised by the tenant, the leasehold mortgage automatically attaches to the fee. *Chapman v. Great Western Co.,* 216 Cal. 420, 14 P2d 758 (1932). A careful draftsman would prefer to spell out this consequence. It would do no harm to add that the lien on the fee thus created shall be superior to all liens and encumbrances created subsequent to the recording of the lease.

On FHA insured loans, FHA requires that the Secretary of HUD have an option to purchase the fee within 12 months after FHA has acquired the lease hold by foreclosure. *Ground Leases and Their Financing,* 4 A.B.A. Real Prop erty Probate and Trust Journal 437, 461 (1969).

§ 351. **Defaults or breach of covenant by tenant.** A standard lease provi sion is to the effect that in the event of default in payment of rent or in the event of breach of covenant the lessor may terminate the lease. In addition, the lease may specify certain events, over which the tenant or the leasehold mort-

gagee has no control but which will give rise to a right on the landlord's part
to forfeit or terminate the lease; for example, the filing of an involuntary petition in bankruptcy against the tenant. These provisions are matters of major
concern to the mortgagee, since termination of the lease terminates the leasehold
estate and, in consequence, the mortgagee's estate as well. Automatic termination clauses like the bankruptcy clause simply must be omitted from the lease.
Nonpayment of taxes by the tenant may be a default under the lease language
unless some qualifying language is added giving the tenant the right to contest
a levy he considers illegal or excessive. If the event leading to forfeiture is one
that the mortgagee can cure, e.g. failure to pay rent or taxes, the mortgagee
may be content if the lease provides for notice of the default by the landlord
to the mortgagee, followed by a reasonable period during which the mortgagee
may cure it. What is a reasonable period is a matter of negotiation, but one
must keep in mind that large corporations tend to move rather slowly. To avoid
mishap, it is certainly appropriate to specify in the lease a specific department
in the mortgagee's home office to which the notice should be directed. A grada-
tion of time schedules for curing defaults in also indicated. For example, the
landlord may quite reasonably require prompt cure by the mortgagee of the
tenant's default in rent payment. If the alleged breach is failure to repair, the
mortgagee should be given a reasonable time to investigate the situation and to
take steps to remedy it, for at the worst, the mortgagee may have to oust the
tenant or even foreclose his mortgage in order to take the necessary action.
Obviously in states where foreclosure is by judicial sale followed by a redemption period, the suspension of the landlord's right to declare a forfeiture may
continue for a prolonged period. There is no feasible alternative. Of course, the
landlord is entitled to a covenant that the mortgagee will press his foreclosure
with all reasonable dispatch, meanwhile paying rent under the lease. Some mortgagees seem to prefer an agreement that on termination of the lease because of
the tenant's default or breach, the landlord will give a new lease on identical
terms for the balance of the term to the mortgagee. This can be accomplished
by a separate contract between the landlord and the mortgagee, for a contract
to give a lease is specifically enforceable. To avoid any contention on the part
of the tenant that the landlord and mortgagee conspired to freeze out the tenant,
a lease may give the landlord the right to enter into such a contract with the
mortgagee. An advantage of a separate contract is that it may eliminate the
delay and expense of foreclosing the leasehold mortgage. However, in the event
of the landlord's bankruptcy, this contract, like his other contracts, may be
subject to disaffirmance by the trustee in bankruptcy. Moreover, if the mortgagee
chooses to make this provision an option to purchase a lease, rather than a contract, questions will arise as to liens or other events occurring between the date
of the option and the date of its exercise. Again we encounter the problem of

relation back. Some question has also been raised as to the possibility that such a contingent contract might violate the rule against perpetuities.

In short, the mortgagee enjoys greater security if he makes his plans on the basis of foreclosure of the leasehold, with appropriate provisions in the lease giving him the necessary grace period to complete the foreclosure and to remedy the defaults thereunder. A mortgagee who plans to go the foreclosure route may nevertheless request the inclusion of a clause in the lease that in the event of forfeiture of the lease, through accident or otherwise, the lessor will execute a new lease to the mortgagee. This is, in essence, a precaution against an event that may possibly occur. This clause is in effect a contract to make a lease and must spell out the details of the transaction. For example, the lease will provide, most likely, that in case of forfeiture the tenant's improvements become the property of the landlord. In the new lease, the new mortgagee-tenant will want to be the owner of such improvements. He will want to step in as landlord under valuable subleases. And so on.

§ 352. **Estoppel certificate.** It is usual for the mortgagee of a leasehold to require production of an estoppel certificate from the lessor stating that there are no defaults or breaches of covenant or condition by the tenant under the lease. The mortgagee disburses its loan in reliance on this assurance, and the lessor is estopped to deny the truth of the statements. To be assured that this certificate will be forthcoming, the lessee insists on a lease covenant requiring the lessor or his assigns to furnish such a certificate.

§ 353. **Subleases.** The lender, of course, would like to obtain legally enforceable rights in substantial subleases. This poses a problem. No doubt the lender will receive from the lessee an assignment of the sub-lessor's interest in all present and future subleases, the assignment will be recorded, and notice of the assignment given to all existing sublessees. One difficulty with this arrangement is that in some jurisdictions such an assignment is not an instrument entitled to be recorded. 71 ALR 270. Another fear is that such an assignment might have no legal effect until activated, leaving the lessee and sublessee free in the meantime, it has been argued, to modify the terms of the sublease, which might, in turn, create a Benedict v. Ratner problem. Mark, *Assignment of Leases to Mortgagees,* 134 N.Y. Law Journal Numbers 67 and 68 (October 5 and 6, 1955). As to *Benedict v. Ratner,* 268 US 353, *see* excellent discussion in 1 Gilmore, *Security Interests in Personal Property,* 253 *et seq.* Hence it has been suggested that, in addition to the assignment aforesaid, the lender's protection as to subleases should be built into the ground lease. Provision would be included in the lease giving the leasehold mortgagee rights in future subleases. Covenants could be included that the lessee-sublessor will not amend the terms of such subleases, reduce the rent thereunder, or accept prepayments of rent or surrenders without the consent of any leasehold mortgagee, and that covenants to this effect will be included in each sublease. Some leases contain covenants that all subleases must be approved by the leasehold mortgagee as to rent, term and the provisions of the lease. The lease may also contain a covenant requiring that all subleases contain an agreement by the subtenant to attorn to the leasehold mortgagee if it becomes the holder of a new ground lease or that subleases will be subject to such new ground lease.

Where the ground lease is extinguished by merger into the reversion or by surrender thereof to the reversioner, there is authority for the proposition that the subtenant may remain in possession with no payment of rent whatever. This is the scholastic logic of the old common law at its worst. The reasons given are that there is no privity of contract or estate between the fee owner and the subtenant or, alternatively, that rent under the sublease is incident to the sub-reversion, which has ceased to exist. 1 Tiffany, *Real Property* § 150; 13 Colum. L.Rev. 245; 37 Yale L.J. 16. This rule has been abrogated by statute in a few states. Ill. Rev. Stat. 1967, Ch. 30 § 39. In other states courts have declined to perpetuate this medieval nonsense. *Hessell v. Johnston,* 129 Pa. St. 174 18 A 945; 32 Am.Jur., Landlord and Tenant § 425. But occasionally the rule is still followed. *McDonald v. May,* 96 Mo. App. 236, 69 SW 1059. It seems prudent to require an assignment to the mortgagee of the lessee's interest in all present and future subleases, it being expressly covenanted that such assignment will survive the extinction of the ground lease.

§ 354. Merger and surrender. The leasehold mortgagee may desire protection against the possibility that if the lessee acquires the fee in the leased premises the lease will terminate by merger. The lease should provide that neither the conveyance of the lessor's interest to the lessee nor the conveyance of the lessee's interest to the lessor shall result in any merger so as to affect the rights of a leasehold mortgagee.

It seems desirable to include a clause forbidding the lessor to accept a surrender of the lease while the leasehold mortgage remains a lien.

§ 355. Improvements—lessee's ownership of building—remodeling. The lease clause concerning ownership of improvements installed by the tenant must be carefully scrutinized. The common store lease clause that all installations by the tenant become the property of the landlord is unacceptable to the mortgagee. A landlord and tenant may covenant respecting the ownership of improvements during the lease. *Commissioner v. Hills Corp.,* 115 F2d 322 (CCA 10th). The ownership of the building erected by the tenant and the tenant's right to remove it at the end of the term should be clearly stated. Although large structures are seldom moved, the right to do so may create a bargaining position if any economic value remains in the building at the end of the term. *Lawrence v. F. W. Woolworth Co.,* 45 Cal.Rptr. 140, 403 P2d 396. Likewise, ownership of the improvements enters into the appraisal of the value of the leasehold. Ownership of the improvements also is of importance in determining depreciation questions for tax purposes.

Where the lessee owns the building, as is often the case, this poses a problem at the expiration of the lease, since physical removal is not feasible. Some leases handle this by giving the landlord an option toward the end of the term to purchase the building at a price fixed by a three-man appraisal. If he fails to exercise this option within the time specified, the lease may give the lessee the option to purchase the reversion, again at a price fixed by a three-man appraisal. This last is a true option to purchase and should be reasonably detailed as to marketability of title, evidence of title, type of deed, etc. As has been pointed out, all options are subject to the infirmities occasioned by the bankruptcy problems and by uncertainties connected with the doctrine of relation back.

At times a leasehold mortgage occurs in connection with a transaction whereby the fee owner conveys the land "except fee title to the building located thereon" to a grantee. The grantee thereupon leases the fee to the grantor. This transaction, with its tax benefits, involves some unanswered questions. *See* § 395.

The law of waste holds the lessee in a pretty tight vise so far as remodeling of the landlord's building is concerned. *F.W. Woolworth Co. v. Nelson,* 204 Ala. 172, 85 So 449 (1920). Since the mortgagee who has foreclosed may be compelled to put the building to a new use, the lease shoud provide for remodeling or demolition where the building remains the property of the landlord. Even where the tenant owns the building, his right to remodel or demolish without the landlord's consent should be spelled out.

§ 356. Condemnation. The clause common in store lease forms that the entry of a condemnation judgment results in an ipso facto termination of the lease is unacceptable to a leasehold mortgagee. There is also considerable reluctance to leave this question to the dubious mercy of case law. 3 ALR2d 286. Hence the lease will contain a condemnation clause. This clause is difficult to negotiate. The mortgagee obviously wants some provision giving him the right to be heard in the condemnation proceedings and to participate in any settlement. If the taking is total, some formula must be agreed upon for paying the landlord the value attributable to his interest. See, *e.g.* Anderson, *The Mortgagee Looks at the Ground Lease,* 10 U. Fla. L.Rev. 1, 12–13. This should leave a sufficient sum to pay the leasehold mortgage in full. If the taking is partial, or if only an easement is taken, the lease will contain some formula for reduction of rent and for distribution of the award, but the formulas adopted display considerable variety and apparently depend upon the bargaining skills of the parties and their attorneys. Anderson, *The Mortgagee Looks at the Ground Lease,* 10 U. Fla. L.Rev. 1, 14 et seq.,; *Condemnation of Leasehold Interests,* 3 ABA Real Property, Probate and Trust Journal 226 (1968).

§ 357. Insurance. The insurance clauses of the lease should be drafted so as to be acceptable to the mortgage lender. For example, a lease clause making hazard insurance payable to the landlord in case of loss would be unacceptable. On the other hand, all might agree to a provision for rebuilding, with progress payments on certificates of architects approved by landlord, tenant, and lender, with appropriate retentions and with title company endorsements insuring against mechanics' liens as disbursements are made. Application of the insurance proceeds should be without regard to ownership of the improvements damaged or destroyed. Payment under some leases is made to a trust company that will disburse for the benefit of all concerned, though with a responsible institutional lender as mortgagee the landlord and tenant may agree on disbursement by such lender. The mortgagee will wish to participate in adjustment of the loss figure. Provision should be made for business interruption insurance and rent insurance to compensate for loss of rent under subleases that provide for rent abatement while the premises are untenantable. The ground lease will contain no such abatement clause.

Where restoration of the building is impossible, as where zoning ordinances prohibit restoration, any provision awarding a prior lien on the insurance proceeds to the leasehold mortgagee may be unfair to the landlord. A formula for valuing the landlord's interest for this purpose may be similar to that employed for condemnation purposes. Anderson, *The Mortgagee Looks at the Ground Lease,* 10 U. Fla. L.Rev. 1, 20; 1957 Law Forum 289. Again, whether the mortgage lender will accept anything but a full prior lien on the condemnation award is a question negotiation must decide. The landlord may wind up with a prior lien only to the extent of rent in arrears.

It is also difficult to do justice to all parties where a casualty loss occurs near the end of the term, since using the insurance proceeds to build a new building gives the landlord a bonus. Various formulas have been envolved to cover this situation. Anderson, *The Mortgagee Looks at the Ground Lease,* 10 U. Fla. L.Rev. 1, 21–22.

§ 358. Mortgages on the fee—landlord's liens. The title search covering recording of the lease will enable the mortgagee to determine that the leasehold estate was unencumbered at that time. The lease itself should not permit or create any encumbrance that primes the leasehold mortgagee's rights. For example, the lease should not specifically subordinate the lease to mortgages on the fee title subsequently executed by the landlord. Such a provision, even coupled with provision for non-disturbance of the lessee by the mortgagee, is likely to upset a leasehold lender. In the first place, there is no respectable authority providing definitive legal analysis of a non-disturbance agreement. Anderson, *The Mortgagee Looks at the Commercial Lease,* 10 U. Fla. L.Rev. 484 at p. 495; Friedman, *Preparation of Leases,* 62. In the second place, if a mortgage that gains priority by virtue of a subordination clause in the lease is foreclosed, what remains of the lease? Is the lessee's right of possession a bare skeleton, the simple right to remain in possession by paying the rent reserved in the lease? What becomes of the lease covenants? Do they survive foreclosure? If they do, what was subordinated? In the third place, is the non-disturbance agreement an executory contract that a trustee in bankruptcy of the lessor or his mortgagee might repudiate? Finally, some investment statutes permit a mortgage loan only where the lease is on an "unincumbered fee."

The leasehold mortgagee would hope to find a clause that any and all landlord's liens whether created by the lease or by operation of law are subordinate to the leasehold mortgage.

§ 359. Purchase money mortgage after acquisition of leasehold by foreclosure. Since any given mortgage may ultimately be foreclosed, the leasehold mortgagee must look ahead to that time when he may become the owner of the leasehold estate by foreclosure or by assignment in lieu of foreclosure. Logically the mortgagee will seek a purchaser of the leasehold, and, to facilitate the sale, may agree to take back a mortgage on the leasehold for part of the purchase price. Again he is cast in the role of leasehold mortgagee and again he needs all the protective devices he has sought in connection with the original financing. Perhaps it would suffice to include in the lease some general language that in such event all rights, privileges, and protections extended by the lease to the original financing would extend to the purchase money mortgage financing.

§ 360. Amendments and modifications of the lease. Where the identity of the mortgagee is known at the time the lease is drafted, the lease can provide that it shall not be amended or modified without the written consent of the mortgagee. This creates a valid third-party beneficiary enforcement right in the mortgagee. It also insures that there will be no tampering with the lease clauses that provide the mortgagee with needed protection.

§ 361. Multiple encumbrances. Special problems are presented where the project is divided into separate tracts, with construction funds furnished by several lenders. *Ground Leases and Their Financing,* 4 A.B.A. Real Property Probate and Trust Journal 437, 462 (1969).

§ 362. Legal opinions. One encounters lease covenants by the tenant to furnish supporting legal opinions as to the validity and efficacy of documents of importance to the mortgage lender, e.g., subleases. The utility of such clauses is obvious.

§ 363. Recording. Normally the lease and mortgage thereon are recorded. This protects the lessee and the mortgagee against unrecorded instruments that the recording act requires to be recorded and gives constructive notice of the mortgagee's rights. This protection is indispensable. In a few states the law permits a memorandum of the lease to be recorded. Sec. 291-C N.Y. Real Property Law. At times a question has been raised whether the recording of a memorandum imparts constructive notice in the absence of a statute so providing. *Motels of Md. Inc. v. Baltimore County,* 244 Md. 306, 223 A2d 609; *MacMotor Sales, Inc. v. Pate,* 148 Me. 72, 90 A2d 460. It is the belief of able lawyers that the memorandum imparts constructive notice where it is a present demise rather than a mere informational statement indicating that a lease exists. If the lease contains an option to purchase, it is unclear whether a recorded memorandum that speaks only in terms of leasing gives constructive notice of the option. By the majority rule a tenant's possession is notice of an option to purchase or contract to purchase contained in the lease. 17 ALR2d 331 and 37 ALR2d 1112. Recording of a memorandum might well have a like result. But it would be preferable to set out all options and contracts in full in the memorandum. Moreover, a lease of the kind under discussion may well incorporate other legal concepts, such as a contract or option running from the landlord to a mortgagee giving the mortgagee the right to receive a new lease for the balance of the term if the mortgaged lease is forfeited. Does a recorded memorandum of lease impart constructive notice of rights under such clauses? It might be prudent, in cases like these, to record the entire lease.

Because a lease is that peculiar type of property known as a "chattel real," partaking of the character of personal property and real property both, a question has sometimes been raised regarding the proper place to record a lease or a mortgage on a leasehold. It seems that such documents should be recorded in the land records. *Willoughby v. Lawrence,* 116 Ill. 11 (1886); *Lincoln Nat. Bank & Trust Co., v. Nathan* 215 Ind. 178, 19 NE2d 243 (1939). However local law should be consulted.

§ 364. Title search and title insurance. The title search should be continued to cover the recording of the lease. This establishes that the lessor then owned the fee title and that there were no prior mortgages or other liens. Such a search might reveal the existence of a condition subsequent antedating the lease. This would make the leasehold mortgage an unauthorized investment in some states. A prior recorded non-reverter building restriction revealed by the title search should be carefully analyzed to ascertain that it does not forbid the carrying on of the business the lessee proposes to operate on the demised premises or that the mortgagee's purchaser would wish to carry on if he acquires the leasehold by foreclosure. A recorded ingress easement running through the area on which the lessee proposes to establish his business likewise might prevent consummation of the deal. But the title search cannot stop with the recording of the lease, for events occurring thereafter may affect the leasehold or even destroy it, for example, a tax sale. Many mortgage lenders insist on title insurance covering the mortgage on the leasehold and brought down to the date of disbursement of the loan. Demands for comprehensive title insurance continue to increase. Insurance against mechanics' liens as construction goes forward is demanded at times, likewise insurance against survey matters, unrecorded easements, or violations of building restrictions. A leasehold mortgagee may demand insurance as to the validity and priority of a key sublease.

§ 365. **Covenants of title.** Instead of relying on covenants as to quiet enjoyment that the courts may read into the leases (3 Thompson, *Real Property* § 1129), or statutory language like "convey and warrant" that is found in statutes relating to deeds, (Ill. Rev. Stat. 1969, Ch. 30, Par. 8), the lessee and his mortgagee are best served by insertion of specific covenants of title of the landlord with a specific "subject clause" listing encumbrances to which the leased title is subject. This has the virtue of certainty. Likewise it gives protection against matters not covered by the abstract and opinion or other methods of evidencing title, e.g., easement not of record, questions of survey, etc.[1]

Cross reference: Chapters 28 and 30.

---

[1] Kratovil, Lease Draftsmanship: Problems of Lessees and Their Lenders, *The Guarantor*, April, 1970, (Chicago, Ill.: Chicago Title & Trust Co.) pp. 1–18, © 1970.

30

Leasehold Mortgages

§ 366. The institutional mortgage. The great majority of leasehold mortgages run to institutional lenders. Liberalization of their investment statutes in recent years simplifies their problems somewhat. Nevertheless the law should be checked when a leasehold mortgage is involved.

EXAMPLE: The investiment statute requires mortgage loans to be on an "unencumbered fee title." The company cannot invest in a leasehold mortgage.

§ 367. Basic requirements of a leasehold mortgage. The requirements for a valid leasehold mortgage do not differ much from the requirements for mortgages generally. A corporate mortgage requires corporate resolutions, a trustee-mortgagor must have power under the trust instrument to borrow money and execute mortgages, and so on. *See* Chapter 7. In most states, however, a leasehold is treated as personal property, and an individual lessee may find it possible to execute such a mortgage without his spouse's joinder, there being no dower in personal property. It is nevertheless customary for the spouse to join, and, in some states, it is necessary as well as customary. The lease and mortgage should be duly acknowledged and recorded. The examination of title should be continued past the date of the mortgage and down to the present time.

EXAMPLE: *L* gives a lease to *T*, which is recorded on July 1, 1969. *T* mortgages the leasehold to *E* by a mortgage recorded July 1, 1970. True, once the leasehold mortgage has been recorded there is little that *T* can do to disturb the lien of the mortgage. But there are some matters that could affect the leasehold mortgage. Suppose *T* fails to pay the real estate taxes. A tax sale could wipe out the lease and the mortgage thereon. The same consequence could take place as a result of mechanic's liens. *E* should demand a title policy on his mortgage dated as of the current date.

§ 368. Modifications of the lease. Where the leasehold mortgagee cannot live with the lease as executed, it may be possible to procure a modification. Mortgagees prefer this to take the form of *an amended and supplemental lease.* If it takes the form of a contract between the lessor and mortgagee, questions arise that already have been discussed. *See* § 349. In addition there are the usual questions of recordability of such a document, what remedies are available for breach of contract, and the like.

Courts have held that if there are both a first mortgage and a second mortgage on a leasehold, the first mortgagee may lose his priority if he consents to a modification of the lease after he has learned of the existence of the junior mortgage. *Empire Tr. Co. v. Lewington,* 276 NYS 586.

§ 369. Right under lease to mortgage the leasehold. Lease restrictions upon the right of a lessee to mortgage the leasehold is a topic already discussed. *See* § 345. Of course, if the lease is one already in existence, not one tailored for the present transaction, its clauses relative to mortgage, assignment or sublease must be carefully studied, and all questions resolved in favor of compliance.

EXAMPLE: A lease states that if it is assigned by the lessee a copy of the assignment must be sent to the lessor by registered mail. Doubt should be resolved in favor of sending the lessor a copy of the mortgage. The accompanying letter may disclaim any admission that the mortgage is tantamount to an assignment. For similar reasons one would send the lessor a copy of the foreclosure deed.

This problem will recur if the mortgagee forecloses, acquires the leasehold, and seeks to sell and assign it, or to sublease. Here there is no question but that the mortgagee must comply with the terms of the lease relative to assignments and subleases. And if the mortgagee sells the leasehold and takes back a purchase money mortgage, we again encounter the problem.

§ 370. Description of the mortgaged estate. In a leasehold mortgage, the description of the mortgaged premises should read somewhat as follows:

> Leasehold estate created by lease dated May 1, 19__ and recorded in the Recorder's Office of_____County, _____, on May 2, 19 __, as Document 1,000,000 from John Smith, as Lessor, to Henry Brown as Lessee, demising for a term of years commencing on May 1, 19 __, and ending on April 30, 19 __, the premises described as follows, to wit: (here insert description of leased premises).

In addition, the description clause should mortgage, transfer, and assign any option to renew, extend or purchase contained in the lease, any after-acquired fee title, including title to any adjoining streets or alleys that may "hereafter" be vacated and the benefit of all covenants contained in the lease whether running covenants or otherwise.

EXAMPLE: *L* leases to *T*. *L* covenants to give children patronizing *T*'s store admission passes and free rides in *L*'s adjoining amusement park. This is probably not a running covenant. But it can be assigned.

Quite likely a fee title acquired by the lessee, whether by exercise of an option to purchase or otherwise, would "feed" the leasehold mortgage and be covered by it. *Garner v. Union Tr. Co.*, 45 A2d 106, 163 ALR 431 (Md.); *Chinn v. Sheridan*, 229 Ore. 123, 366 P2d 321; *Chapman v. Great Western Gypsum Co.*, 216 Cal. 420, 14 P2d 758, 85 ALR 917. But good draftsmanship dictates that this be spelled out in the lease.

The mortgage might well transfer to the mortgagee security deposits made with the lessor.

§ 371. Possession on default. It is important for the mortgagee to be able to take possession of the premises in case of breach of covenant under the lease.

EXAMPLE: The lease provides that in case the premises are allowed to fall into disrepair, the lessor may terminate the lease. The premises do fall into disrepair. The leasehold mortgagee should have the right under his mortgage to take possession and cure the defaults. The state law should be carefully checked to see that it permits this. If it does not, the leasehold mortgagee will have to foreclose and wait until the redemption period expires before he can take possession and correct the situation. Whether the lessor will be patient enough to sit this out is a question. If values and rents are rising rapidly, the lessor may be tempted to terminate the lease. It is for this reason that leasehold mortgagees want the lease drafted or amended to cover this contingency. The leasehold mortgagee cannot count on a court receiver as supplying the answer. He is a court officer, and may not be given court authority to make the repairs.

As has been observed, the lessor may have a side agreement that in such cases the lessor will terminate the lease, oust the lessee, and put the mortgagee in possession under an identical lease for the balance of the term. This has legal drawbacks. *See* § 351.

§ 372. Liability of leasehold mortgagee. Particularly in title states, a mortgage of the entire leasehold estate is apt to be regarded as a security assignment. Hence, from the moment the mortgage is made, the leasehold mortgagee will be liable on lease covenants that run with the land, including the covenant to pay rents. 73 ALR2d 1118. Again, the mortgagee likes to have the lease drafted or amended to exclude this liability until he has foreclosed. At least liability should be postponed until the mortgagee can take possession and control the situation.

This problem may recur if the mortgagee forecloses, acquires the leasehold, sells and assigns it, and takes back a purchase money mortgage.

The lease should be carefully examined for specific clauses pinning personal liability on a mortgagee of the leasehold. Again, a side agreement may be obtainable to water down this liability.

Of course, once the mortgagee becomes the owner of the leasehold by foreclosure, he acquires liability on all running covenants. *State v. Martin,* 82 Tenn. 92.

§ 373. Acceleration clause. Obviously the usual printed mortgage forms contain no reference to performance by the mortgagor of leasehold covenants. This means that the acceleration clause must be re-drafted to provide that the mortgagor will pay all the rent and observe all the covenants of the lease, and in case of his default in this regard the leasehold mortgagee may accelerate.

§ 374. Landlord's cooperation where he refuses to join in leasehold mortgage. In many situations the landlord may categorically refuse to subject his title to the leasehold mortgage. Indeed, this is a common situation. This does not dispose of the negotiations, however. He may be quite content to go half-way or less, even where he is determined not to go all the way. He may, for example, agree to a provision in the ground lease that in the event a default occurs in the payments in the leasehold mortgage, rent under the ground lease will abate in whole or in part, until the leasehold mortgage debt or some specified part thereof has been paid, either from the leasehold mortgagee's collection of rents (probably under an assignment of leases and rents) or by payments of the leasehold mortgagor or his guarantor. This certainly "sweetens" the deal from the standpoint of the leasehold mortgagee. It should enable the developer to obtain a larger leasehold mortgage.

§ 375. Economic disadvantages. Even where the ground lease contains provisions requiring the landlord to subject his fee title to the construction mortgage on the leasehold estate, the developer's situation presents aspects of vulnerability. For example, suppose after a lapse of time, modernization of the improvement becomes imperative. New financing is needed. Now it becomes necessary to bargain with the fee owner for his joinder in the new mortgage, but he is now free to dictate the terms on which he will join. This is particularly important in condominium situations where the condominium is set up on a long-term lease rather than a fee title. The one single legal fact that sells the condominium is the assurance that if the condominium owner keeps up his payments on his individual mortgage, he will never lose his apartment. This means that to continue this assurance the fee owner *must* be brought into the new financing. This poses a truly difficult choice: (1) The landlord will balk at a clause in the ground lease that compels him to join at some future time in some future leasehold mortgage that will endanger his fee position. (2) The developer will balk at a lease that omits such a provision and exposes him to the greed of the fee owner when refinancing becomes necessary. Indeed, he may be unable to sell condominium apartments to prospects represented by sophisticated counsel unless the lease binds the fee owner to join in the new financing.

§ 376. Joinder by fee owner in tenant's leasehold mortgage. Obviously a mortgage on a leasehold creates problems that would not be present if the mortgagee held a mortgage on the fee title. The ground lease may, therefore, contain one of several provisions designed to bring the landlord's fee title under the leasehold mortgage.

EXAMPLE: A ground lease from *R* to *E* provides that *R* will join with *E* in any mortgage provided: (1) the mortgage is a construction mortgage designed to construct a specified type of building; (2) the mortgagee is an institutional lender; (3) the mortgage does not exceed a stated principal amount, stated interest, and stated maturity; (4) the mortgage relieves *R* of all personal liability whatever; and (5) the lease is in good standing at the time.

EXAMPLE: A ground lease from *R* to *E* provides that the title and interest of *R* will be subordinate to any leasehold mortgage executed by *E*, the conditions being much the same as those set forth in the preceding example. See Chapter 21.

§ 377. Marshalling of assets. A problem in this area is perhaps best illustrated by an example:

EXAMPLE: *R* makes a ground lease to *E*. *E* mortgages the leasehold to *E-2*. *R* joins in the leasehold mortgage. There are several ways of doing this, but it is doubtful that procedure affects the present problem. At all events, let us suppose that the mortgage names *R* and *E* as mortgagors and in the description of the mortgaged property sets up two separate parcels in two separate paragraphs, Parcel I being the leasehold estate and Parcel II being the landlord's fee title. When foreclosure ensues, *R* may argue the "two funds" doctrine well-known in the law of marshalling of assets. *E-2* has two funds to which he can look as security, the leasehold being the primary fund and the fee title being a secondary security. He argues that the leasehold should be sold first, and the fee should be sold only if the leasehold fails to bring in enough to pay off the mortgage. There is authority to support this position. See § 388.

The decisions accepting this doctrine are difficult to defend. In truth and fact, two funds do not exist. There is only one fund, the fee title. The mortgagee wants to acquire the fee title unencumbered by the lease when foreclosure becomes necessary. It is truly difficult to comprehend how this completely obvious fact can be ignored. At all events, attorneys for *E-2* anticipate this problem and include in the mortgage a specific provision that marshalling of assets principles shall not govern the foreclosure sale and that the fee, unencumbered by the leasehold, is to be the asset sold at the foreclosure sale.

31

Sale and Buy-Back

§ 378. **In the sale and buy-back,** a landowner sells and conveys his land to an investor and the investor enters into a contract to sell the land back to the grantor in the deed. After a period of time stated in the contract, the grantor-purchaser has the option of paying the balance due and taking a deed from the investor. The right of the grantor-purchaser to deduct depreciation and interest paid to the investor offers an income tax advantage.

A question that has been raised is whether usury is present. It has been stated that in the old-fashioned cases arising between individuals, the courts were likely to hold usury not present when a party presently acquiring land conveys it to another and takes back an installment contract in the process, but the courts would be more suspicious of a transaction where one who has been the owner of land for some time conveys it and receives an installment contract back. See §§ 26–28. This new financing technique flies in the face of this distinction. Nevertheless, there is a pronounced tendency in recent cases to avoid finding usury present where sophisticated parties bargain on equal terms for economic advantages, like tax advantages. Hence, it is doubtful that usury will be found to be present. *Meridian Bowling Lanes Inc. v. Brown,* 90 Ida. 403, 412 P2d 586. Having reasoned that usury is not present, the courts should take the next logical step and hold that this is a true contract of sale situation, not a mortgage situation. This will result in holding that the contract can be forfeited for default, like any other installment contract, and need not be foreclosed like a mortgage. *See also* § 27.

32

Sale and Leaseback

§ 379. **In general.** Suppose an industrial corporation wants money to use in its business. It sells its plant to an investor, receiving the full cash value. The investor then leases the land back to the industrial corporation. Hence the term *sale and leaseback*. The lease is usually for a term ranging between 20 and 30 years, and the tenant is given an option to renew the lease for an additional period. The rental on the original term pays back to the buyer an amount equal to the purchase price plus a return higher than could be obtained on a conventional mortgage loan. The lessee is required to pay all real estate taxes, fire insurance, repairs, and so forth, so that all rental paid is "net" to the landlord.

Among the advantages to the lessee of such an arrangement are the following:

1. A tax advantage. In computing its income for income tax purposes, the lessee deducts its rent payments under the lease. Were the lessee merely a mortgagor, the only permitted deductions would be interest and depreciation. Also, if the building is not newly constructed, it may be that the current value and sale price are substantially less than the price paid when the seller lessee bought the building, and the sale to the investor represents an income tax loss to the seller-lessee.

2. By selling the property for its full value to the lessor, the lessee obtains much more cash money than it could raise on a mortgage, for no mortgagee will loan up to 100 per cent of the value of the property.

3. Existing mortgages, corporate charters, debenture agreements, or other documents binding on the lessee may place restrictions on its right to borrow money. Since a lease is not a loan, the leaseback arrangement provides a method of getting around these restrictions.

4. A mortgage note would appear as a liability on the mortgagor's financial statement. Liability for rent under a lease is a fixed and certain legal liability. Yet under accounting practice, it is not shown as a liability. It appears on the financial statement, if at all, only as a footnote. This facilitates borrowing, sale of stock, and so forth.

The chief disadvantages to the lessee are:

1. If the building goes up in value, the investor, not the lessee, will reap the benefit of this increase once the lease expires.
2. The lessee has all the burdens of ownership, for the lease requires the lessee to pay taxes, insurance, and so on. But the lessee lacks the freedom of action that an owner enjoys. Under the terms of the lease, the lessee cannot sell the leasehold without the consent of the investor. Even if the investor consents, there are many prospective purchasers who are reluctant to buy leaseholds. Moreover, the lessee cannot tear down or remodel buildings as business needs dictate unless the investor consents. Likewise, to erect new buildings would be foolish, for they would belong to the landlord at the end of the lease period.

Transactions of this sort are entered into only after careful scrutiny by tax counsel. There are different tax consequences, for example, where the building is a fully depreciated building than there are where the building is a relatively new one. The latter situation sometimes produces one of the most thorny problems known to the real property lawyer.

EXAMPLE: *R* owns Lot 1 on which he has recently erected a valuable building. His tax counsel evolves a deal under which he sells and conveys Lot 1 to *E*, but reserves fee simple ownership of the building. *E* now makes a 99 year lease of the land to *R*. Many articles have been written about this type of deal. *See* §355.

§ 380. Sale and leaseback as a disguised mortgage. At times the courts have found a transaction of this sort to be nothing but a disguised mortgage.

EXAMPLE: *A*, a landowner, desiring to refinance an existing indebtedness, applied to *B*, a trust company, for a loan. A plan was adopted under which *A* conveyed his land, appraised at $2,000,000, to the trust company. The trust company contemporaneously executed a lease of the land to *A* for 99 years, renewable forever. Contemporaneously, also, the trust company executed a declaration of trust reciting that it held the land in trust for the benefit of the owners of certain land certificates, and that the holder of each certificate was entitled to $55 per year as income on the certificate. The trust company issued 1,000 of these certificates, each representing a 1/1000th undivided interest in the land. These certificates were delivered to *A*, who sold them to an investment banker for $955,000, and the banker, in turn, sold them to the public. *A* had the right after ten years to "repurchase" the certificates at the rate of $1,000 each, plus an additional sum ranging from $50 to $25 depending on the time the certificate was outstanding. The original rental of the land under the lease was fixed at $55,000 per year, and, assuming from the repurchase price that each certificate had a face value of $1,000, this $55,000 would be equivalent to 5 1/2% interest on the total certificate issue, there being 1,000 certificates. As certificates were purchased, the rent was to be reduced proportionately, and A was also given the option to re- purchase the land. The court held that this was a mortgage transaction rather than a sale of the property. The "rent" stipulated in the lease was really intended as a promise to pay 5 1/2% interest on the loan. The "repurchase" of the certifi- cates was equivalent to a redemption of bonds similar to that provided for in corporate trust deeds securing issues of bonds. The "purchase" of the land from A by the trust company was clearly not intended as such, since it was for a price far below the value of the land. All these things stamped the transaction as a mortgage transaction. *Commissioner v. H.F. Neighbors R. Co.*, 81 F2d 173. The same view was later adopted by the United States Supreme Court. *Helvering v. Lazarus & Co.*, 308 US 252, 84 L.Ed. 226. Keep in mind the fact that if the transaction is really a mortgage transaction, the lease cannot be forfeited if the lessee defaults. Instead, a regular foreclosure proceeding must be instituted. In Minnesota, these transactions are not regarded as mortgage transactions. *Nitkey v. Ward*, 199 Minn. 334, 271 NW 873.

At other times, when the issue seemed equally close, the courts have found that the transaction represented a genuine sale.

EXAMPLE: *B* purchased land located in California to improve as an industrial park. Being in need of approximately $4,000,000 to construct the park, it applied to *J*, an insurance company, for the money, and *J* offered *B* a package deal con- sisting of the purchase of the land for $1,000,000, a leaseback of the land to *B*, a commitment for construction loan of $3,000,000 and an option to *B* to repurchase the land. The $1,000,000 purchase price for the land included $250,000 for certain off-site improvements to be performed by *B*. The approximate value of the land at that time was $2,000,000. *B* accepted *J*'s proposition. The agreement executed by the parties provided for the sale of the land to *J* for $1,000,000, a lease of the land by *J* to *B* for a term of 50 years at an annual rental of $65,000 (6 1/2% on the $1,000,000 purchase price), with the option to renew for an additional 25 years at an annual rental of 5% of the market value of the land or $65,000, whichever should be greater, an option to *B* to repurchase land for $1,000,000 or for 75% of its fair market value at the time of the exercise of the option, whichever sum should be greater, the option to be exercisable only after the ex- piration of 25 years and thereafter to be exercisable for the term of the lease. The agreement also provided for construction loans of up to $3,000,000. *B* realized a profit of $200,000 on the sale of the land to *J*. The court found that this transac- tion was not a disguised loan. The parties were sophisticated parties, dealing at arm's length. No one was taken advantage of. There were financial advantages to both. *In re San Francisco Industrial Park, Inc.*, 307 FSupp. 271 *See also* § 386.

As always, when it is contended that a deed is a disguised mortgage, courts hear evidence as to all the circumstances. For example, the fact that the grantor initially applied to the grantee-lessor for a loan is a circumstance indicating the transaction was really a loan. *Farther v. Clark,* 67 Md. 18, 8 A 740. See Chapter 3.

Again the absence of a debt on the part of the purported "mortgagor" weighs heavily with the courts.

EXAMPLE: *B*, having purchased land for $200,000, $165,000 of which was to be secured by mortgage, paid $10,000 cash, but was unable to raise the remaining cash payment of $25,000, and therefore induced defendants to pay the $25,000, in return for which the property was transferred to them by absolute deed, under a five-year agreement whereby *B* guaranteed them net rents from the property of $2,100 a year, which was equal to 6% upon $35,000, and they agreed that, if they sold their interest in the property before the maturity of the $165,000 mortgage, he should receive from the proceeds of such sale all in excess of the sum of $35,000, plus arrears of guaranteed rental. The transaction was a sale, and not a mortgage. It was held that since *B* was under no obligation to repay the $25,000 paid, there was no mortgage. *Bailey v. Poe*, 142 Md. 57, 120 A 242.

§ 381. Usury aspects. Where the sale price in a sale and leaseback is substantially less than the market value of the property, and the lease grants an option to purchase at a figure near the sale price, the economic compulsion to exercise the option is so great that some courts might regard the transaction as a security transaction, there being an "economic obligation" to repurchase. That result seems more probable where there is a contract by the seller-tenant to repurchase. The effort to defend these transactions from usury consequences by means of the *time-price rule* seems doomed to failure. A seller of goods or real estate can charge more on a time or installment sale than on a cash sale, and no usury is present as a result, but the sale and leaseback can never fall in this category. The time-price rule applies only to a true sale to a person who never previously owned the goods or real estate. However, there is a pronounced tendency to hold usury is not present where sophisticated parties of equal bargaining power bargain for economic advantage. This should protect these transactions from the taint of usury.

§ 382. Junior and other financing. Some mortgages forbid junior financing and allow acceleration if such financing takes place. If the property is overloaded with debt, the possibility of default is increased.

Corporate mortgages tend to place some limit on borrowing, secured or unsecured. At times a corporation can circumvent this limitation by means of a sale and leaseback.

EXAMPLE: *Corporation A* mortgages Lot 1 to *E* by a mortgage that forbids further borrowing of any kind. *Corporation A*, needing additional working capital, makes a sale and leaseback to *E-1* of Lot 2, another property it owns. The mortgage clause is not violated. A sale and leaseback is not "borrowing." Modern corporate mortgages tend to forbid sale and leaseback as well as other borrowing.

§ **383. Recording.** All these transactions are big deals. Yet the parties persist in methods that involve risks. As has been noted, there is at least some doubt in many states as to the recordability of a memorandum of a lease. *See* § 363. In these transactions the lease should be acknowledged by the parties and recorded.

§ **384. Title requirements of the investor.** In the investor's mind the sale and leaseback is somewhat akin to a mortgage. The investor has put as much money into the deal as it proposes to risk, and wants no further expenditures or risks. Hence, the investor will demand an owner's title insurance policy that protects against mechanics' liens, survey problems, and unrecorded easements. An ordinary purchaser who proposes to take possession and utilize the property can be depended upon to inquire into these matters for himself and for his own protection. But an investor who is simply putting money into a deal wants protection against such matters.

ADDITIONAL REFERENCES: Anderson, *Tight-Money Real Estate Financing,* 24 U. of Miami L. Rev. 642.

33

Mortgages in Large Scale Transactions

§ 385. In general. Every big mortgage loan today is a tailor-made job. Because money is tight, the lender is often in a position to dictate the terms on which the loan will be made. But exacting high return may put the lender in fear of usury. Hence, rather complex techniques have been divised.

§ 386. Sale and leaseback. The sale and leaseback, on the surface, offers advantages other than those ordinarily connected with that transaction. *See* Chapter 32. Usually the lease can call for any rental the investor can negotiate with the tenant, and no usury problem is presented. There is no loan of money involved, and in most states usury is presented only where there is a loan. Another thing heavily in favor of the investor in usury cases such as these, is the fact that both parties to the transaction are sophisticated and represented by counsel. Usury laws were never intended for the protection of this kind of venture capital. But the investor may want to have his cake and eat it too. He may insist that the lease include a contract to repurchase the premises at an agreed price. Here an argument can be made that this is a debt by another name and usury rears its ugly head. If the tenant is simply given an option to purchase, this makes it less likely that usury will be found, unless the economics of the situation are such that the tenant cannot afford to pass up exercise of the option. Nevertheless, for income tax purposes even the option to purchase invites the IRS to find that the transaction is a mortgage for income tax purposes. To guard against this consequence, the tenant may be given a *rejectable option* to buy the property back at a figure not less than the investor's unamortized investment in the property, but usually at a higher figure, with the option in the tenant to cancel the lease if the investor declines to accept the offer. *See also* § 380.

§ 387. Leasehold mortgage—ground lease. A fee owner may agree to subordinate his fee title to a leasehold mortgage by his tenant. This increases the amount of the mortgage, because the mortgage is of the entire fee ownership. There are also income tax advantages. There are a number of forms of this transaction.

EXAMPLE: *L* leases ground to *T*. *T* mortgages his leasehold to *E*. *L* joins in the mortgage with a clause exculpating him from all liability and stating he joins in the mortgage solely to subject his fee to the mortgage. This is legally air-tight. Some title companies are likely to insist on the transaction taking this form.

EXAMPLE: *L* leases ground to *T*. *T* mortgages his leasehold to *E*. *L* executes a document "subordinating" his fee to the mortgage. He does this because he is suspicious of any attempt to get him to sign a mortgage. Probably this will stand up. It certainly ought to be good as an equitable mortgage. Lawyers argue whether it conveys the legal title, which is important for rent collection purposes. Perhaps this fault can be cured by adding a clause that "*L* conveys his fee title to *E* for the purposes of the subordination." This might also calm the nerves of mortgagee's lawyers in power of sale foreclosure states who argue that a subordination does not bring the fee title under the power of sale. Again additional language in the subordination stating that the power of sale extends to the fee title would be helpful. Nevertheless, some title companies may object to this document. See § 247.

EXAMPLE: *L* gives a ground lease to *T* with a clause automatically subordinating his fee to a leasehold mortgage later put on by *T*, or the lease may contain a covenant requiring *L* to join in the leasehold mortgage. This situation raises all the questions discussed in Chapter 21. The subordination clause would have to give the details of the leasehold mortgage in such detail that it could be capable of specific performance. And the subordination should state that it is effective notwithstanding diversion of the leasehold mortgage proceeds from the purposes stated in the subordination clause. Probably all title companies find automatic subordinations objectionable to some degree.

See 4 ABA *Real Property, Probate and Trust Journal* 466 et seq for documentation.

Obviously a landlord who subordinates wants many protective features; for example, forbidding modification of the lease, and limiting the subordination to a period until the debt is paid down to a stated figure, after which the mortgage is on the leasehold only.

Obviously, also, subordinations to a construction loan should also extend to the permanent takeout and to refinancing of the takeout.

§ 388. Marshalling of assets—fee and leasehold in one mortgage. Where the fee and leasehold are covered by the same mortgage, there are two funds, and the doctrine of marshalling of assets arguably is applicable.

EXAMPLE: *L* gives a ground lease to *T*, and *L* and *T* join in a mortgage to *E*. *E* forecloses. *J*, a judgment creditor of *L*, argues that the leasehold should be sold first, and if this raises enough to pay the mortgage debt, there is no need to sell the fee. This is unfair to the mortgage lender. He bargained for a mortgage on the fee title. Hence the mortgage needs an *anti-marshalling of assets clause.* See 4 ABA Real Property Probate and Trust Journal 471. See § 377.

§ 389. **Leasehold mortgages—subleaseholds.** Another variation in this area can be illustrated by an example.

EXAMPLE: *R* makes a ground lease to *E*. The lease provides that rent due *R* will abate during default under a leasehold mortgage made by *E*. This "sweetens" the leasehold mortgage. *E* makes a leasehold mortgage to *E-2*, this mortgage being subordinate to a sublease to be executed by *E* to *E-3*. *E* makes a sublease to *E-3*. This sublease, being prior and superior to the leasehold mortgage, has value, and *E-3* can mortgage his sublease to *E-4*.

§ 390. **Non-disturbance clauses.** In all big financing transactions, high credit sublessees are involved, and they are likely to insist on non-disturbance clauses, which leave them in possession as long as they pay their rent, no matter what happens to the ground lease. As explained elsewhere, the nature of this document remains something of a mystery. *See* § 250.

§ 391. **Holding companies.** Giving the investor flexibility in investing is the holding company device. Large life insurance companies and banks are now owned by holding companies. The holding company has other subsidiaries, one or more of which have the power to invest in land. This gives the organization great flexibility in investment operations. To a lesser degree, a life company can achieve flexibility by forming a subsidiary with assets taken from the "basket." Life companies are regulated closely as to their investments. But a substantial portion of each company's assets is free by law to go into unregulated investments. This portion of the assets is called the "basket." A subsidiary formed out of basket investment funds is free to invest in opportunities denied to the parent life company. By illustration, a life company financing a large shopping center might suggest participation by its investment subsidiary, so that 50% of the equity is owned by this subsidiary and 50% by the developer, subject to a mortgage or mortgages held by the life company. Thus the life company participates in profits (through its subsidiary) and has a hedge against inflation as real estate values rise.

§ 392. **Joint ventures—the unanticipated joint adventure.** The joint adventure described in the preceding section is harmless to the investor, except to the extent that all joint ventures may fail. Success is not a foregone conclusion. In quite another vein is the possibility, however remote, that the contention may be advanced that the investor-mortgagee is also a party to the joint venture. Among the unpleasant consequences envisioned in horror story bull sessions of mortgagee's counsel are the possibility that the mortgagee as a member of a joint venture might be liable for the joint venture's debts. This curse is not removed by an indemnity agreement from the developer. He may be insolvent. Even worse, other lienors and creditors may argue the proposition that partners lending money to the partnership are subordinate to all other creditors and joint ventures are nothing but partners. *See* § 78. Finally, if the mortgagor is a corporation (exempt from usury laws) but there is also a lease or other transaction running to the corporation's individual shareholders, some may argue that it's all one ball of wax and the total return to the lender must be considered, and that usury is present. This particular skeleton, it seems clear, will never emerge from the closet. No joint venture is intended as between the mortgagee and the developer. This intention is an indispensable agreement for the existence of a joint venture. *Mortgage Associates v. Monona Shores,* 177 NW2d 340 (Wis.). Every construction lender and the developer share an interest in the success of the project. To ensure its success, the lender engages in those activities that will protect its investment, like watching to see that loan disbursements go into this project, not some other project of the developer, and that all subcontractor's bills are paid. These are time-honored activities common to all responsible construction lenders. Except to the extent that the lender acts to protect his investment, neither lender nor borrower has the right to direct or control the conduct of the other, as is true in typical joint ventures. *Gainesville Carpet Mart v. First Federal Savings and Loan Association,* 121 Ga. 450, 174 SE2d 230.

Nevertheless, probably because of the prudence one has come to expect of wise investors, some life companies insist that where one of its satellite corporations engages in a joint venture in the equity, the mortgage loan must be procured by the joint venture from some other investor. This, of course, is commendable. But in modern law the separate-entities status of corporations is respected, especially in the parent and subsidiary situation. The decisions are innumerable. Hence, fears that the courts will identify the subsidiary investment corporation with the subsidiary life company simply because they have a common parent seems unfounded. *See also* § 80.

§ 393. **Wrap-around mortgage.** There is a new financing arrangement called the *wrap-around mortgage.*

EXAMPLE: *R* has mortgaged a shopping center to *E* for $5,000,000 at 6% interest. The loan has been paid down to $4,000,000. He now would like to borrow an additional $5,000,000 to expand the center. The going rate of interest in the area on commercial loans is 10% and this rate is permitted by law on business loans. *R* makes a second mortgage to *X* of $9,000,000 at 10% interest. *X* advances only $5,000,000. However, the mortgage provides that *R* will make all his payments to *X* and *X* will make the mortgage payments to *E*. *R* will pay interest at 10% on the money actually loaned to him by *X* and on the advances *X* makes to retire the mortgage to *E*. But *X* pays *E* only 6% interest. The result is a yield to *X* greatly in excess of 10%. *R* should not be in a position to complain, it is argued, because he is paying 6% on his old mortgage and 10%, as agreed, on his new mortgage. Healey, *A Legal View of "Wrap-Around" Mortgages*, N.Y. Law Journal (October 14, 1970).

A number of questions arise. One is the question of usury. Of course, if the borrower is exempt (e.g., borrower is a corporation), or the lender is exempt (e.g., lender is a bank and local law exempts bank lenders from usury loans), or the loan is exempt (e.g., the loan is a business loan and is exempt under local law), no problems arise. But if there is no local exemption, the question of usury may arise in states that consider usury is present if the lender *receives* more than the statutory maximum. *Mindlin v. Davis,* 74 So2d 789. *See also* Chapter 14.

Another question that arises is that of intervening liens. If, for example, R places a third mortgage on the property, does this obtain priority over subsequent advances made by X? In wrap-around mortgages, it is uncommon for X to obligate himself to make all the advances. Hence he does not have the protection of obligatory advances rule. *See* § 115. And the third mortgagee will no doubt notify X of his third mortgage, so that X seems, at first blush, to suffer the exposure to risk and loss that is involved in making optional advances.

Actually, this risk can be eliminated.

EXAMPLE: At the time the mortgage to X is executed, R and X enter into an agreement providing that X will be subrogated to E's prior lien position as to all payments made by X to E. This is called *conventional subrogation*. It is a technical concept, but is widely recognized. *See* § 256. It gives X all the priority that E's mortgage enjoys over intervening liens, that is total priority. 50 Am. Jur. *Subrogation* § 95, 107; Osborne, *Mortagages* § 282. The fact that X knows of the third mortgage is immaterial. *Wilkins v. Gibson,* 113 Ga. 31, 38 SE 374. There is an apparent but not an actual problem caused by the rule that subrogation, as a rule, is allowed only when the party claiming the benefit of subrogation makes full payment of the first lien. That rule is inapplicable to situations like the wrap-around mortgage. Partial payments are fully protected. *Marks v. Baum Bldg. Co.,* 73 Okla. 264, 175 P 818; *Rouse v. Zimmerman,* 51 N.D. 94, 212 NW 515. Also where the mortgage to X provides, as it invariably will, that all payments made by X to E shall be protected and secured by the mortgage to X to the same extent as any previous disbursements and advances made by X, this is valid and binding. *Boone v. Clark,* 129 Ill. 466, 21 NE 850. This is the rule of *tacking*. Mortgagees often pay real estate taxes and insurance premiums under such covenants, and the courts hold that such payments give the mortgagee a lien equal in dignity to the mortgage debt. *Rusman. v. Jacobs,* 107 Ga. App. 200, 129 SE2d 338.

Another problem relates to acceleration. If default is made by R, X can accelerate his mortgage and foreclose. But he cannot force E to accelerate.

Despite the problems, the making of wrap-around mortgages seems to continue.

§ 394. UCC filings. If any mortgage in a large-scale transaction is to give the lender a lien on chattels, obviously the lender will order a chattel search at the same time he orders his title search, and will make Uniform Commercial Code filings on the chattels when he files his mortgage on the land.

§ **395. Sale or reservation of building combined with lease of land.** One of the transactions made popular by our tax laws calls for a landowner selling to an investor, to receive a leaseback of the land and to reserve, in the deed to the investor, ownership of the building.

EXAMPLE: *R*, a landowner, sells and conveys the land to *E*. In the deed *R* reserves to himself the fee simple title to the "building" on the premises conveyed. *E* contemporaneously leases the land to *R* for a term of years, with specified renewal options, the lease providing that at the termination of the lease, for any cause whatever, the building is to be the property of *E*. For income tax purposes, *R* will have the benefit of depreciation of the entire value of the building over the period of the lease, which can be a valuable right if the building is a relatively new one.

There are a number of problems. By and large, these problems spring from the fact that the deal is put together by tax lawyers, to suit their purposes, and the property lawyers are left with problems:

1. When the grantor in a deed reserves to himself the "building," does he reserve to himself only the bricks and mortar, which do depreciate, or does he also reserve to himself the space occupied by the building? There are, of course, many decisions holding that when a grantor conveys a building, he automatically conveys the land occupied by the building. *Cross v. Weare Comm.*, 153 Ill.499, 38 NE 1038. Arguably, the same result should follow in the example given. The question could be set at rest by expressly stating the grantor's intention; for example, stating that the grantor reserves fee title to the building on the premises conveyed "and the air, land, and space occupied by the building." This must be the intention, since occupants of the building occupy the space within it.

2. The deed leaves unanswered some questions concerning the possible existence of implied easements. If the grantor conveys land, reserving ownership of the building, the law of implied easements might create easements of support of the building by the land, easements to enter over the land, easements to use the adjoining air space, for window washing, painting, tuck pointing, for example. Since the grantor receives a lease of the land, no doubt he has no particular desire to enjoy implied easements. This question could be set at rest by stating in the deed that it is not the intention of the parties to create any implied easements.

3. When the grantor reserves *fee title* to the building and the space it occupies, one would hope that the documents would make some formal provision for conveying the fee title. The early arrangements of this sort were informal. After all, it is basic deed law that any conveyance of the fee title must contain words of grant. Modern decisions are liberal on this score. *Ross v. Ross,*

406 Ill. 598, 94 NE2d 885. One solution to this problem might be to put in the lease a clause whereby the tenant conveys to the landlord the fee simple title to the building on the termination of the lease for any cause whatever. There is no reason why a deed cannot be combined with a lease. And the fact that the fee title springs or shifts at some future time causes no problem in deed law, since enactment of the Statute of Uses. *Harder v. Matthews,* 309 Ill. 548, 141 NE 442.

4. In the law of future interests, however, a problem arises, because the rule against perpetuities applies to "executory interests." Arguably, this rule does not apply nowadays to commercial transactions. *Wong v. DiGrazia,* (Cal.), 60 Cal.2d 525, 386 P2d 817. Nor does it apply, under modern concepts, where all interests are vested, though one or more are postponed as to the time of enjoyment. Simes and Smith, *Law of Future Interests* (2d ed.) § 1236; *Restatement, Property* § 370. Moreover, there are many long-term leases that call for the tenant to erect a building, which shall become the property of the landlord at the termination of the lease. Such "executory interests" have never been challenged as violating the rule.

5. Again, a question has been raised as to conversion of the building into personalty by constructive severance. This question seems of minor importance. As a problem of the law of fixtures, it is governed by the modern test of intention. Thus a specific covenant in the deed that the building is real property seems to answer that question. *Young v. Consolidated Implement Co.,* 23 Utah 586, 65 P 720 (1901). Indeed it has been held that substantial buildings are real property despite a covenant that they are to be treated as personalty. *U.S. v. 15.2 Acres of Land,* 154 FSupp. 770.

6. There is the contention, from the viewpoint of the property lawyer, that the talk of a "fee simple" in the building simply will not stand scrutiny. A fee simple, the old books say, is an estate that potentially has the ability to last forever. 28 Am.Jur.2d, *Estates* § 10. This is what distinguished an estate in fee simple from a life estate or a term for years. An estate "in fee simple" that ends when the lease ends is not a fee estate at all, so the argument goes, but an estate for years. As such, it ends when its life expires, leaving the building owned by the then owner of the fee without resort to any concept of springing or shifting uses. This view cannot be accepted in modern times. Since the enactment of the Statute of Uses it is perfectly possible to have a fee simple that springs up in the future. Simes and Smith, *Law of Future Interests* (2d ed.) § 502.

EXAMPLE: R makes a deed to E to take effect ten years after the date of the deed. R has a fee simple for ten years and then E's fee simple springs into being. R's fee title has the quality of a fee simple for ten years but then comes to an end.

This does not alter the fact that R's fee simple is, in fact, a fee that will inevitably end. But it is best to spell out precisely what R's rights are with respect to demolition or alternation of the building during his ten-year period.

7. There is the problem of intervening liens. The lessee, let us assume, contracts to convey fee title to the building to the landlord when the lease terminates. Suppose that judgments, junior mortgages, and federal liens intervene against the lessee during the term of the lease. This is but the restatement, in a different context, of a perennial problem in property law.

EXAMPLE: A judgment lien against the lessee under a lease ends when the lease ends. A judgment lien against a contract purchaser ends when the contract is lawfully terminated. Arguably liens against a fee simple title that expires by its terms should also expire at that time.

34

Bankruptcy and Reorganization

§ 396. In general. Bankruptcies are commonplace. The bankruptcy of the mortgagor can pose some serious problems to the mortgagee.

§ 397. Filing a claim. Ordinarily it is pointless and unwise for the mortgagee to attempt to file a claim against the bankrupt estate. Filing as an unsecured creditor may destroy the mortgage. In any case, there seldom are enough assets to pay off the mortgage.

§ 398. Foreclosure. In ordinary bankruptcies the rule is that if the bankruptcy is pending before foreclosure is filed, the mortgagee must obtain consent of the foreclosure court before he files a judicial foreclosure. *Straton v. New,* 283 US 318; *Emil v. Hanley,* 318 US 515. If he fails to do this, the foreclosure may be totally void. As a rule, if the court is satisfied that there is little or no equity, over and above the amount due on the mortgage, it will readily give its consent to the filing of the foreclosure.

If a foreclosure proceeding has been initiated prior to the filing of a petition in bankruptcy by or against the landowner, the bankruptcy offers no obstacle to prosecution of the bankruptcy. *Smith v. Hill,* 317 F2d 539. True, at times, the bankruptcy court will issue a *stay order,* temporarily halting all action by creditors. *In re Lustron,* 184 F2d 789. But when the bankruptcy court perceives that there is little or no equity in the property over and above the mortgage debt, it will release its stay order and the foreclosure proceeds. 8A CJS *Bankruptcy* § 256(3).

Before giving leave to the mortgagee to foreclose in a state court, the bankruptcy court will require proof of the value of the property. It may also grant a conditional leave to foreclose. For example, the bankruptcy court may put a condition in its order requiring the mortgagee to pay to the trustee in bankruptcy

271

any excess in the foreclosure sale price over and above the amount of the mortgagee's debt and expenses of foreclosure.

Where the foreclosure is by power of sale, the picture is not clear. The cases are in conflict. 112 ALR. 508. The sounder rule appears to be the one holding that the mortgagee does not automatically acquire the right to proceed with his foreclosure from the simple fact that advertising the foreclosure sale began before the bankruptcy was filed. *In re Bowden,* 274 FSupp. 729. At all events the bankruptcy court may enjoin such a sale from proceeding. *In re Victor Builders v. C.J.S. Carlson,* 418 F2d 880. Of course, if the bankruptcy is filed before foreclosure begins, the mortgagee must obtain leave to foreclose from the bankruptcy court.

§ 399. Foreclosure of fee mortgage where junior lessee is in bankruptcy. Where a mortgage covers the fee title, and thereafter the landowner gives a lease to a tenant who goes into bankruptcy, the bankruptcy court has no power to interfere with a foreclosure of the mortgage. The mortgagee's lien is superior to the rights of the tenant and his trustee in bankruptcy. *In re Holiday Lodge Inc.,* 300 F2d 516.

§ 400. Trustee's deed in lieu of foreclosure. If the bankruptcy court gives him leave to do so, the trustee in bankruptcy may give a deed to the mortgagee for such consideration as they can agree upon. *In re National Public Service Corp.,* 88 F2d 19. This may save the mortgagee the expense of foreclosure, if there are no junior liens and no problems of dower or homestead.

§ 401. Notice of the bankruptcy as affecting the mortgagee. The mortgagee is concerned legally with possible existence of the mortgagor's bankruptcy from several angles. Of course, if the mortgagee knows that bankruptcy was imminent, he would not make the loan to the mortgagor in the first place. Putting this matter aside, there are other legal problems. If the mortgagee has legal notice that a bankruptcy is pending against the mortgagor, any mortgage given by the mortgagor would be invalid, because the trustee in bankruptcy becomes the owner of the bankrupt's real estate as of the date the bankruptcy petition was filed. And if the mortgagee has previously given a mortgage loan to the mortgagor, which is now in default, the mortgagee must obtain permission from the bankruptcy court to file his foreclosure if the bankruptcy antedates the foreclosure.

Under Section 47c of the Bankruptcy Act, the trustee must, within ten days after his qualification, record a certified copy of the order approving his bond in every recorder's office where the bankrupt owns land. Section 21g contains a somewhat similar requirement, but excludes from the filing requirements the county in which the bankruptcy proceeding is pending. These two sections are somewhat contradictory. To the extent that they are contradictory, the mortgagee had best be guided by Section 21g.

EXAMPLE: *R* mortgages land in Cook County, Illinois, to *E*. *R* thereafter files bankruptcy in the federal court that sits in Cook County. Under Section 21g (though not under Section 47c) *E* has legal notice of this bankruptcy even though the trustee has made no filing in the recorder's office in Cook County. Thus, before filing any foreclosure, *E* must ask permission of the bankruptcy court. In any case, as a mortgagor approaches bankruptcy, his condition becomes common knowledge to his creditors, and it will be difficult for a mortgagee to prove that he had no notice of knowledge of the bankruptcy. Hence a mortgagee who goes ahead with his foreclosure, for example, on the theory that no bankruptcy filing has been made in the local recorder's office, is doing so on the basis of calculated risk. If the bankruptcy court later attacks the foreclosure, the mortgagee may expect tough sledding.

Prior to 1938 the equivalent of present Section 21(g) of the Bankruptcy Act was old Section 44(e). This section spoke simply in terms of the trustee filing in the recorder's office where the bankrupt owned land of a certified copy of the order approving his bond. The court decisions treated these provisions as valid. *Vombrack v. Wavra,* 331 Ill. 508, 163 NE 340. However, in the Chandler Act revision of the Bankruptcy Act in 1938 a new concept emerged. Congress evidently concluded that only *state law* could determine what instruments were entitled to recording. Hence at that time Section 21(g) was given its present form. It provides for recordings by the trustee in bankruptcy in the proper county "in any State whose laws authorize such recording." Hence, it seems necessary for the state to specifically provide in its recording law for such documents to be recordable. Patton, *Titles* § 653. Such legislation has been enacted in Colorado, Florida, Georgia, Illinois, Iowa, Kansas, Kentucky, Massachusetts, Minnesota, New Jersey, New York, North Carolina, Ohio, South Carolina, and Washington. In other states a serious question remains whether a mortgagee would be protected in taking a mortgage from a mortgagor against whom a bankruptcy has been filed elsewhere in the country.

§ 402. Sale by trustee—subject to or free and clear of mortgages. Usually in a bankruptcy there is no equity over the mortgage debt, bankruptcy often being the result of borrowing in excess of value. In such case the bankruptcy court will either simply sell the bankrupt's equity for whatever it can get, usually a nominal amount, or the court may, in effect, abandon the asset by giving the mortgagee leave to foreclose. *Dodson v. Beaty,* 144 SW2d 609 (Tex.Civ.App.). This should be done only on notice to all secured creditors. *National Bank & Tr. Co. v. Allied Supply Co.,* 386 F2d 225. If there is already a foreclosure suit pending, such leave permits the state court to proceed. *Morristown F.S. & L. Assn. v. Erwin,* 140 A2d 458.

But if there is a definite equity over and above the amount of the mortgage debt and other liens, the proper course for the bankruptcy court is to take jurisdiction over the property and order a sale free and clear of liens. *Van Huffel v. Harkelrode,* 284 US 225.

In such a proceeding, special notice must be given to the mortgagee and all lien creditors that the sale is to be free and clear of liens. *Ray v. Norseworthy,* 23 Wall. 128. If any lien creditor believes there is no equity above the liens, he may appeal from any such order.

At such sale, the purchaser receives ownership of the property free and clear of liens, and the claims of the lien claimants, including the mortgagee, are transferred to the proceeds of sale. Care must be exercised, however, for such sale may turn out to be subject to homestead rights. *Lockwood v. Bank,* 190 US 294.

Just as a mortgagee may purchase at a judicial foreclosure sale of his own mortgage and bid up to the amount of his mortgage debt, so in a sale free and clear of liens, a mortgagee who has a first lien on the land may purchase at such sale and bid up to the amount of his mortgage debt without producing any cash. 4A Collier, *Bankruptcy* § 70, 99 (8).

§ 403. **Sale free and clear—objections by the mortgagee.** While the court decisions are somewhat conflicting, there are decisions that, in effect, require the mortgagee to make formal protest to a sale free and clear of liens. If he fails to make this formal protest, the court will charge against the mortgagee's share of the sale proceeds a proportionate share of the costs and expenses of the bankruptcy, which can run into a substantial amount. 4 Collier, *Bankruptcy* § 70. 99 (6).

§ 404. **Sale free and clear—encumbrances other than liens.** The law is well settled that the bankruptcy court can sell free and clear of liens. However, occasionally the bankruptcy court will purport to sell the land free and clear of leases, easements or other interests that are not technically *liens.* The power of the bankruptcy court to do this is not clear, and a mortgagee who plans to purchase at such a sale must weigh this matter carefully. Moreover, the bankruptcy law speaks only in terms of notice of sale to "creditors," leaving a further doubt as to the manner in which the trustee should notify a party other than a creditor. Personal service of a rule to show cause is recommended.

§ 405. **Sale by trustee—protection of mortgagee.** Where the trustee proposes to sell free and clear of all liens, the mortgagee has no choice but to prepare himself for bidding at the sale. If no outside bidder is willing to bid as much as the amount of the mortgage debt, obviously the mortgagee will take a loss unless he himself is willing to bid in the property. Having these things in mind, the mortgagee must start his preparations before the mortgage is signed. He wants a provision in the mortgage that in case of the landowner's bankruptcy, the mortgage may declare an acceleration of the mortgage debt. He also wants a provision in the mortgage that in such case the mortgagee's attorney's fees and expenses occasioned by the bankruptcy become part of the mortgagee debt. When bankruptcy occurs and a sale is ordered, either the trustee or the mortgagee should order a title search from a title company to make sure that *all* lien holders receive notice of the sale if the sale is to be free of liens. The title company should be requested to make a further search at the time the order of sale is entered, for in the course of this search the title company can determine that proper notice was, in fact, given to all parties. In this connection, the title company is likely to insist that if the sale is to cut off interests that are not liens (leases, easements, etc.), personal service of a rule to show cause be served on the holders of each of such interests. 6 Remington, *Bankruptcy* § 2586 (5th ed. 1956). A certified copy of the order of sale should be filed in every recorder's office where the land lies. This is to make certain that the land is not sold to an innocent purchaser, who might claim he had no knowledge or notice of the bankruptcy.

On rare occasions, at the mortgagee's request, the bankruptcy court will fix an upset price equal to the mortgage debt, this being the minimum price at which the trustee can sell the property.

If the bankruptcy court sells the mortgaged land free and clear of a mortgage, ordinarily the mortgagee is entitled to receive interest on his mortgage debt up to the time of distribution of proceeds of sale if the proceeds are sufficient to pay such interest. *Palo Alto Mutual S. & L. Assn. v. Williams,* 245 F2d 77; *In re Mood,* 59 FSupp. 828. Obviously this is part of the mortgagee's lien and certainly is entitled to come ahead of the claims of unsecured creditors. Probably the mortgagee will have less trouble on this score if the mortgage spells out that such interest is part of the mortgage debt.

Protecting the mortgagee's rights in the rents of the property is a difficult matter. In the first place, the rights of the mortgagee in this regard are bound to differ from state to state. Obviously, the fact that the mortgagor goes into bankruptcy will not give the mortgagee any right to rents if the state law does not permit this in the absence of bankruptcy. Assuming, however, that the state law does give the mortgagee some protection (*see* Chapter 27), there still remains the difficulty that even with the best of documentation, the mortgagee's right to rents does not ripen until he activates his assignment of rents. And the pendency of the bankruptcy precludes any request for a receivership in the state courts. Hence, it seems to most lawyers that the proper remedy for the mortgagee is to file a petition in the bankruptcy court for this court to sequester the rents of the property for the benefit of the mortgagee. This should be done promptly. The trustee may contend that rents accruing prior to the filing of this petition belong to unsecured creditors. Hence, when an attorney is consulted about a mortgagor's default, he ought immediately to order a bankruptcy search to see if any such bankruptcy has been filed.

§ 406. Leases—security deposits. When the trustee, pursuant to his statutory authority, terminates the lease of a bankrupt lessee, he will lay claim to any security deposit made by the tenant and held by the landlord. As has previously been noted (*see* § 333), the claim of the landlord against the bankrupt estate is limited to an amount not exceeding the rent reserved by the lease for the year succeeding the date the landlord resumes possession of the premises plus any unpaid rent accrued. The landlord's claim against the security deposit is also limited to this amount. 4A Collier, *Bankruptcy* (14th ed.) § 70.44(5). But if the lease provides for an *advance payment of rent* rather than a security deposit, this money can be retained by the landlord. *Ibid.* This is also true where a gross sum was paid by the tenant as consideration for receiving the lease. *In re Sun Drug Co.,* 4 F2d 843. These distinctions are important to a mortgagee. He must take account of them before placing too much reliance on receipt of a security deposit.

If the permitted amount of the landlord's claim for rent exceeds the amount of the security deposit, the landlord may apply the security deposit in reduction of the amount due him and prove up his claim for the balance. *In re Plywood Co.,* 425 F2d 151. However, if the lease provides that the landlord is to retain the security deposit as "liquidated damages," the bankruptcy court may refuse to permit the landlord to file any claim for rent, the theory being that retention of such "liquidated damages" is complete compensation to the landlord for the extinquishment of the lease. *In re Plywood Co.,* 425 F2d 151. *See also* § 333.

§ 407. Lease terminations by bankruptcy. A rather common provision in leases is to the effect that if the tenant is adjudged a bankrupt or if any bankruptcy petition or petition for arrangement is filed by the tenant, the lease shall automatically end. This clause has been held to be effective not only with respect to ordinary bankruptcies but also with respect to proceedings under Chapter X or Chapter XII, if the clause is broad enough. *Finn v. Meighan,* 325 US 300.

The Bankruptcy Act in Section 70th gives the trustee in bankruptcy the power in ordinary bankruptcies to reject an ordinary lease within 60 days after the adjudication of the bankrupt or within 30 days of the qualification of the trustee, whichever is later. As to a bankrupt lessor the act provides, in cryptic and ambiguous language, that such rejection shall not deprive the lessee of his "estate." It has never been decided whether this gives the bankruptcy court the power to rewrite the rent provisions and other covenants of the lease. Learned writers differ as to the meaning of this ambiguous clause. The better opinion appears to be that the bankruptcy court does not have this power. 31 U. Chi. L.Rev. 484 and 26 Bus.Law. 1391. *See also* § 349.

Mortgagees who make their loans in reliance on the credit of a lease to a substantial tenant have an obvious concern in the power of the bankruptcy court over leases.

§ 408. Lease subordinate to mortgage—bankruptcy of fee owner. Where a lease is subject to a pre-existing mortgage on the fee, there is an added danger to a leasehold mortgage. If the fee owner goes into bankruptcy, his trustee in bankruptcy may choose to sell the premises free of the mortgage, which, in turn, may automatically involve an extinguishment of all interests subject to the mortgage, including the lease. *In re Bowen,* 35 FSupp 60. It has been suggested that this danger can be met by having the mortgagee, if he can be persuaded, sign a *springing subordination* subordinating his mortgage to the lease effective upon bankruptcy of the fee owner. Real Property, Probate and Trust Law Journal (Real Property Div. of ABA), August 10–12, 1964, p. 125.

§ 409. Protection of a leasehold mortgagee. Protecting a leasehold mortgagee against the problem of bankruptcy is a difficult matter. Suppose that the lease contains an option to renew or an option to purchase. The trustee in bankruptcy of the landlord may argue that he has the right to disaffirm or reject such options. *In re New York Investors Mutual Group,* 153 FSupp 172, aff'd 258 F2d 14; *Coy v. Title Guarantee & Tr. Co.,* 198 F 275. The mortgagee can protect himself on the renewal option by requiring the lease to be for the full extended term or by requiring the lessee to exercise his option to renew before the mortgage is made. No protection is possible as to the option to purchase.

§ 410. Protection of mortgagee on guarantees of payment of rent. Often a mortgagee makes a mortgage in reliance on a lease to a high credit tenant. The mortgagor-lessor gives the mortgagee an assignment of leases and rents, and the mortgagee expects to be able to step in and collect rents if the mortgagor defaults. At times the actual tenant is a subsidiary of a high credit parent corporation. In this case the mortgagee is also likely to demand that the parent corporation give the mortgagee a guarantee of payment of rent by the lessee— subsidiary. There is a case holding that such a guarantee will not survive termination of the lease by the trustee in bankruptcy. *Hippodrome Building Co. v. Irving Trust Co.,* 91 F2d 753. To pull the teeth of this case, the mortgagee should require that the guarantee contain a primary obligation by the parent company to pay in cash the present cash value of the rent stipulated in the lease in case of bankruptcy. This language is not language of guarantee, but an actual covenant to pay money.

§ 411. Chapter X. Since the object of Chapter X is to reorganize corporate situations with a degree of flexibility impossible under the old equity receivership or foreclosure of corporate indentures, it is possible for a plan of reorganization to call for extinguishment of existing mortgages with stock in the reorganized corporation being substituted for the mortgage notes or bonds.

In the case of junior mortgages or stockholders of the corporation, where there is no equity over and above the senior mortgage, the junior mortgagees and stockholders may be wiped out without receiving anything under the plan. *In re*

620 Church St. Corp., 299 US 24; *In re Chicago Railways,* 160 F2d 59; *Country Life Apts v. Buckley,* 145 F2d 935.

The court may also order a sale of mortgaged land, subject to or free and clear of mortgages. The sale may be pursuant to the plan of reorganization. *In re Lorraine Castle Apts.,* 149 F2d 55. Or the sale may be made independently of the plan. *In re Air and Space Mfg. Inc.,* 394 F2d 900. *See* 6 Collier, *Bankruptcy* (14th ed.) § 3.27.

Or the court may even give leave to the mortgagee to foreclose, thereby abandoning the asset. *In re Southern Land Title Corp.,* 301 FSupp. 368.

Section 148 of the Bankruptcy Act provides that the entry of an order approving a Chapter X petition as filed in good faith operates as an automatic stay of any prior pending mortgage foreclosure or any other proceeding to enforce a lien. Obviously, every mortgagee must arrange, at some point before a mortgage foreclosure on valuable property goes to sale, to check for such a bankruptcy order.

§ 412. Chapter XI—stay of pending mortgage foreclosure. Under Chapter XI the situation is much the same as under straight bankruptcy so far as mortgage foreclosures are concerned. Under Section 311 the bankruptcy court acquires exclusive jurisdiction of the debtor's property. This means that after a petition has been filed under Chapter XI, a mortgagee planning to foreclose should obtain leave of the bankruptcy court.

§ 413. Chapter XII—stay of pending mortgagee foreclosure. Under Section 428 of the Bankruptcy Act, upon hearing and after notice to the debtor and all other parties in interest, the filing of a petition under Chapter XII operates as a stay of any proceeding to enforce a lien on real estate.

§ 414. Chapter XIII—wage earner's bankruptcies. In a proceeding under Chapter XIII, the bankruptcy court again has exclusive jurisdiction of the bankrupt's property. This again suggests that, as in ordinary bankruptcy, the mortgagee should obtain leave of the bankruptcy court to initiate foreclosure. *Hollenbeck v. Penn. Mutual Life Ins. Co.,* 323 F2d 566.

§ 415. The strong-arm clause. In 1910 a clause was added to the Bankruptcy Act commonly known as the *strong-arm clause.* This gives the trustee greater rights than the bankrupt had. In its present form Section 70(c) gives the trustee the rights of a judgment creditor, an execution creditor, and a creditor having a lien by legal or equitable proceedings. This has important consequences.

EXAMPLE: In *State A* judgment creditors are protected by the recording act. *R* gives *E* a mortgage, which is recorded, but the acknowledgment is fatally defective. Thus the mortgage must be treated as an unrecorded instrument, for in most states a valid acknowledgment is a pre-requisite to recording. *R* goes into bankruptcy. The mortgage is invalid as to the trustee in bankruptcy. Collier, *Bankruptcy* §§ 70.55, 70.80.

§ 416. **Preferences.** A mortgage given to secure an antecedent debt may be a preference under the Bankruptcy Act. Bankruptcy Act, Section 60 (a) (1).

EXAMPLE: In 1969 *R* borrows $10,000 from *E* on an unsecured note. On November 1, 1970, *R* gives *E* a mortgage to secure the debt, which *E* records on that day. The mortgage is a preference. If *R* goes into bankruptcy within four months of the recording of the mortgage, bankruptcy court can set the mortgage aside as a preference. *First Nat. Bank v. N.Y. Title Insurance Co.,* 12 NYS 2d 703.

EXAMPLE: *R* gives *E* a mortgage, which is recorded on February 1, 1969. On November 1, 1969, *R* gives *E* a deed in satisfaction of the mortgage debt. On December 1, 1969, *R* goes into bankruptcy. The deed, being given within four months of bankruptcy, can be set aside as a preference if there is an equity over and above the amount of the mortgage debt at the time the deed was given. *Russell's Trustee v. Mayfield Lumber Co.,* 158 Ky. 219, 164 SE 783.

The elements of a preference, as that term is used in Section 60 of the Bankruptcy Act, are set out in subdivision (a) (1) of that section, 11 U.S.C. § 96 (a) (1). To constitute such a preference there must be (1) a transfer of the debtor's property, (2) to or for the benefit of a creditor, (3) for or on account of an antecedent debt, (4) made within four months before the filing by or against him of the petition in bankruptcy, and (5) the effect of which transfer enables such creditor to obtain a greater percentage of his debt than some other creditor of the same class. The absence of any one of the requisite elements set forth in § 60(a) (1) precludes a finding of a Bankruptcy Act "preference." *Thomas v. Gulfway Shopping Center, Inc.,* 320 FSupp. 756. The law places the burden of establishing each of these elements in § 60(a) (1) and (b) squarely upon the shoulders of the Trustee. A transfer for a present consideration cannot be preferential because the transferee is not being preferred over other creditors. In that situation there is no depletion or diminution of the estate. A transfer made in satisfaction of an unassailable mortgage, pledge, trust receipt, mechanic's lien or other valid lien is supported by a present consideration where the property subject to lien is at least equal to the amount of the payment. Hence such a transfer cannot be preferential.

§ 417. **Certificates of indebtedness.** In various circumstances, but most often in connection with corporate reorganizations, bankruptcy courts have found it necessary to borrow money, which is done by means of issuance of certificates of indebtedness to the lender. If this is done on proper notice to the mortgagee, indicating that the certificates will have priority of lien over the mortgagee, such an order is valid, and the mortgage becomes a junior lien. *In re Prima Co.,* 88 F2d 785, 116 ALR 774, 23 Cornell L.Q. 434.

It has been held that certificates of indebtedness issued in a Chapter XI proceeding can be given priority over a mortgage. *White Chemical Co. v. Moradian,* 417 F2d 1015.

§ 418. Redemption rights. The trustee in bankruptcy succeeds to any redemption rights the mortgagor may have. Thus he may redeem from a foreclosure sale, using funds of the bankrupt estate for that purpose. *In re Argyle-Lake Shore Bldg. Corp.,* 78 F2d 491.

§ 419. FHA loans. Section 263 provides that Chapter X shall not apply to an FHA insured mortgage. Hence in a Chapter X proceedings the bankruptcy court cannot enjoin foreclosure of an FHA insured mortgage. *Monta Vista Lodge v. Guardian Life Ins. Co.,* 384 F2d 126.

Sec. 517 provides that Chapter XII shall not apply to any FHA insured mortgage. This is parallel to Section 263, which applies to Chapter X.

§ 420. Waiver of mortgage. The bankruptcy court has been quick to find that some action on the mortgagee's part has resulted in a waiver of the mortgage lien. For example, if, through inadvertence, the mortgagee files a claim in bankruptcy as an unsecured creditor, this will be interpreted as a waiver of the mortgage. It is best that the mortgagee avoid filing any claim whatever. If the mortgagee takes any action whatever, such as accepting receiver's certificates, it is best that he make an express reservation of his lien at the time to avoid any inference that the mortgage lien has been waived.

§ 421. Interest disallowed because inequitable. A court of bankruptcy may refuse to allow a mortgagee interest after the date of the bankruptcy if allowance of interest would be inequitable, for example, where the rate of interest is inequitably high. *In re Leeds Homes,* 222 FSupp. 20; *Vanston Committee v. Green,* 329 US 156.

35

Federal Liens

§ 422. **In general.** The federal government holds untold thousands of liens against taxpayers, chiefly for unpaid income tax. This lien arises the moment the tax is assessed. The assessment, of course, is a matter that does not appear on the public records in the county. However, under federal and state law provision has been made for filing notice of the lien in the local recorder's office.

§ 423. **Amendments of 1966.** Up to 1966 the law, as interpreted by the Supreme Court (wrongly, as most lawyers felt) was extremely harsh, unfair and oppressive with respect to real estate mortgages.

EXAMPLE: *R* mortgages land to *E* in 1963 and the mortgage is recorded. The government files a federal lien against *R* in 1964. *E* files a foreclosure in 1965. The federal lien would be given priority over the attorney's fees which *E* necessarily paid to have his mortgage foreclosed. As to the whole world except the United States such fees are part of the mortgage debt and enjoy the same priority as the mortgage. Under the Amendments passed by Congress in 1966 this inequity is corrected and the attorney's fees have priority over the federal lien.

EXAMPLE: *R* mortgages land to *E* in 1963 and the mortgage is recorded. The government files a federal lien against *R* in 1963. In 1964 *R* fails to pay the real estate taxes. To protect himself against extinguishment of his mortgage by a tax sale, *E* pays the real estate taxes. As against the whole world except the federal government this payment would be part of the mortgage debt and would enjoy the same priority as the mortgage. But the Supreme Court awarded the federal lien priority over the amount so paid by the mortgagee. The Amendments of 1966 correct this inequity and give such payment priority over the federal lien.

§ 424. **Mortgages made in routine sales or financing.** In ordinary mortgages, made, for example, in connection with the sale of real estate, the Amendments of 1966 give some new protection. The mortgagee is protected as to any disbursement made within 45 days after a tax lien is filed unless he has actual knowledge of such filing. Since actual knowledge is a rarity, the mortgagee seems to have good protection, for his title search covers the recording of the mortgage and normally will show the title clear of federal liens as of that date. Normally, again, the deal will be closed and mortgage money disbursed before 45 days after recording of the mortgage, and thus the loan will be protected against federal liens.

§ 425. **Construction loans.** The Amendments of 1966 also clarify the situation of a construction lender. As long as the construction mortgage is recorded prior to the filing of the federal lien, the mortgagee may continue to make cash disbursements to complete construction, and these will have priority over federal liens filed during the progress of construction. Because this protection is given only if the mortgagee would, in similar circumstances, be protected against a judgment lien against the mortgagor during the course of construction, it seems probable that a construction lender will gain best protection only if his loan is an obligatory advance loan. This offers no problem, for the construction lender routinely makes his construction loan into an obligatory advance loan to gain priority over other liens intervening during the course of construction. *See* § 115.

However, an assignment of rents given concurrently with the construction mortgage quite possibly enjoys priority only for advances made within 45 days after the filing of the federal lien. This is a thorny problem, as yet unresolved. 32 Business Lawyer 271.

Because of ambiguities in the Amendments of 1966, it is best for the construction lender to insist that the construction money coming from the mortgagor's purse be expended before the mortgagee's funds are used. If the mortgagor's money is simply deposited with the mortgagee, it may be vulnerable to a federal lien against the mortgagor until it is expended. 32 Business Lawyer 271.

§ 426. **Open-end advances.** Under the Amendments of 1966 a mortgagor making future advances under a mortgage is protected against federal liens filed after the recording of the mortgage only if the mortgage provides for future advances in accordance with local law, and the local law must be such that an open-end advance would be protected against a judgment lien. Since open-end advances are optional advances, the result appears to be that a mortgagee making open-end advances must take the same precautions against federal liens that he would against intervening judgment liens.

§ 427. **Power of sale foreclosure.** Prior to the Amendments of 1966, if a power of sale deed of trust was recorded prior to the filing of a federal lien against the mortgagor, foreclosure by exercise of the power of sale extinguished the federal lien. *U.S. v. Brosnan,* 363 US 237. The Amendments of 1966 give the government some protection against this consequence. The federal government now has the right to receive written notice of the foreclosure sale at least 25 days prior thereto if the federal lien was filed more than 30 days before the sale. 32 Business Lawyer 271, 293. This means, of course, that any mortgagee planning to hold such a sale must make a search for federal liens against the mortgagor covering any period up to 30 days before the sale. This provision applies only with respect to federal tax liens.

§ 428. Judicial foreclosure. It was always the practice for a mortgagee to name the United States as party defendant if any judicial foreclosure was filed after federal liens were filed against the mortgagor, and this is still necessary. Moreover, summons and a copy of the foreclosure complaint must be served on the United States District Attorney and the Attorney General in strict compliance with the law specifying conditions under which the United States may be sued.

However, prior to the Amendments of 1966 it was unclear whether a judicial foreclosure wiped out federal liens filed *during the pendency of the foreclosure.* The United States frequently took the position that the doctrine of *lis pendens* had no application to it. This created an almost impossible situation for real estate mortgages. Fortunately the Amendments of 1966 make it clear that in mortgage foreclosures the doctrine of lis pendens does apply to the United States.

§ 429. Redemption rights of the United States. Both with respect to judicial foreclosures and foreclosures under power of sale, the United States has a right to redeem for a period of 120 days after the sale. The sums appropriated for this purpose by Congress are nominal and the likelihood of such redemption seems small.

36

Soldiers and Sailors Civil Relief Act

§ 430. In general. The Soldiers and Sailors Civil Relief Act offers certain protections to persons in military service. For example, if, after placing a mortgage on his property, a mortgagor is brought into this country's military service, the law gives him certain protections until 90 days after he has been separated from military service. The court may halt foreclosure on the mortgage if the court finds that the borrower's ability to keep his loan current has been materially affected by his military service. In general, if the court finds that the mortgagor's income from his military career is substantially less than that he enjoyed as a civilian, the court may halt the foreclosure. Or the court may order the soldier to pay interest and taxes only during his military service. Likewise, if there is some genuine issue that requires the testimony of the soldier, for example, the existence of usurious payments exacted by the lender, the court may postpone foreclosure until the military service is over. The court has a great deal of discretion. *Cortland Savings Bank v. Ivory,* 27 NYS2d 313. One problem to the soldier is the necessity of clearing up all arrearages within 90 days after his separation from military service.

§ 431. Persons protected. This protection of the law is not confined to those whose rights on the property are shown on the public records.

EXAMPLE: *A,* being about to be called into military service, conveyed his land to his mother, *B.* They had an oral agreement that the land would be his if he came back from military service. A bank holding a power of sale mortgage on the land foreclosed its mortgage by exercise of the power. On his return from military service, *A* had the foreclosure set aside. *Hoffman v. Charlestown Bank,* 231 Mass. 324, 121 NE 15. This shows the length to which the courts will go to protect veterans and shows also the risk that a mortgagee runs by using the

284

power of sale unless he is sure that no one interested in the land is in military service.

However, the protection of the law does not extend to those who make military service a career. *King v. Zagorski,* 207 So2d 61 (Fla). Nor does it protect a serviceman who buys land after entering military service. *Ibid.*

§ 432. Interest after induction. After a mortgage is inducted into military service, the mortgage bears only 6% interest during the period of such service regardless of the rate stated in the mortgage. *State v. Warden,* 197 Okla. 97, 168 P2d 1010.

§ 433. Default judgments of foreclosure. If a mortgage foreclosure turns out to be a default situation, that is, no defendant bothers to file any defense to the suit, and this is quite normal in foreclosure, the law requires the mortgagee to file an affidavit setting forth that none of the defendants is in military service. 50 USCA § 520. However, failure to file such an affidavit does not invalidate the foreclosure. *Snapp v. Scott,* 196 Okla. 658, 167 P2d 870.

The Act also gives a person in military service 90 days after the termination of such service to have set aside a default judgment if he can show a meritorious defense, for example, that the mortgage was tainted with usury or was in fact paid. Institutional tenders have few worries on this score. Their mortgages are almost invariably *bona fide.* In any case, a purchaser of the property from a mortgagee who has acquired the land by foreclosure is protected against loss of his ownership under this section.

§ 434. Redemption period. The redemption period from any mortgage foreclosure sale is prolonged by the time of military service occurring during such redemption period. *Bank of Springfield v. Gwinn,* 390 Ill. 345, 61 NE2d 249.

§ 435. Power of sale foreclosures. If anyone having any interest in the land is in military service, foreclosure of a mortgage must be by court proceedings, not by exercise of a power of sale. *Hoffman v. Charlestown Bank,* 231 Mass. 324, 121 NE 15. The power of sale foreclosure will be invalid if made during the period of military service or within three months thereafter.

37

Payment

§ 436. **In general.** In the normal mortgage situation, where a financial institution is involved, the mortgagor makes his payments to the mortgagee who made the loan, having confidence that the loan is retained by the institution. Normally the payment is made by mail or at a teller's cage. No demand is made by the mortgagor to see the mortgage and note and to have his payments endorsed thereon. This is the way business is done, and on the whole it works out quite well. Problems are encountered, however, when the lender is an individual or where a financial institution encounters financial difficulties. Likewise problems are encountered where the mortgage lender originates the loan and promptly sells it to an investor, in which case the mortgagor may continue to make payments to the original lender, who may in turn fail to account to his investor. Payments are also made, at times, to agents who pocket the money. In all such cases the courts must place the loss on one of two innocent persons. A party making payment may have to make it over again, this time to one lawfully entitled to receive it. Or a party who bought a mortgage may find it extinguished without his having received any payments. These are difficult problems.

§ 437. **Payment to trustee in deed of trust.** The mere fact that a person or corporation is named as trustee in a deed of trust does not give such trustee who does not have possession of the deed of trust and the notes thereby secured power to receive payment. *Kennel v. Herbert,* 342 Ill. 464, 174 NE 558. But where, at or after the maturity of the debt, the trustee has possession of the deed of trust and the note thereby secured it may be inferred that he has authority to receive payment. *Kranz v. Uedelhoefen,* 193 Ill. 477, 61 NE 392.

§ 438. **Payment to one of several mortgagees.** Where a mortgage runs to two or more mortgagees, any one of the mortgagees is entitled to receive payment of the mortgage debt. 36 Am.Jur. 900; 59 CJS 694. And in such case any one of the several mortgagees may give a valid release of the mortgage. 4 Am. Law of Property 828.

§ **439. Assignment problems.** Many difficult problems arise in connection with an assignment of the mortgage, especially where the assignment has not been recorded. One such problem is involved in the *release rule. See* § 190.

Suppose, however, that we alter the facts of the release rule slightly to show *payment by the person procuring the release deed.*

EXAMPLE: *R* makes a mortgage to *E. E* assigns it to *A,* who fails to record his assignment. *R* sells and conveys the land to *P. P* makes payment of the mortgage debt to *E* and receives a release deed from him which he records. *P* is not protected in many states. The *release rule* protects a person who buys or loans in reliance on a release deed *already appearing on the records.* It does not protect *P* in this case. 2 Jones, *Mortgages,* 701; Osborne, *Mortgage* § 238. The argument for the rule denying protection to *P* is that he could prevent any loss by requiring production of the mortgage paper when he makes payment. This argument is pretty weak in most cases. However, the payment rule is quite generally followed.

Where the mortgage secures a non-negotiable note and payment is made *by the original mortgagor after an assignment has been recorded,* the problem is a difficult one.

EXAMPLE: *E,* mortgagee, assigns to *A,* who records his assignment. The mortgage and note are delivered to *A. R,* thereafter, makes payment to *E.* Here the question is a close one. Does recording of the assignment impart constructive notice to the mortgagor? The authorities are conflicting. In some states there is an express statute relieving the mortgagor of the duty of checking the records before making payment. In other states a like result is reached by interpretation of the general recording act. Some states (California and Utah, for example) have statutes that make recording of the assignment notice thereof to all parties. If it is held in the jurisdiction in question that recording of the assignment is constructive notice to the mortgagor, the rule will apply to all payments made after the recording of the assignment, whether partial or final payments. Since there are many cases on each side of the controversy, it is not possible to say that one or the other is the prevailing rule. 1 Jones, *Mortgages,* 819; 2 *id* 392; 89 ALR 196, 197. Certainly the rule protecting *R* is the better one, because it is more simple for an assignee of a mortgage to serve personal notice of his assignment on the mortgagor than for the mortgagor to check the records for assignments each month before he makes his payment.

The problem grows more complicated when payment is made by a *grantee* of the mortgagor.

EXAMPLE: *R* makes a mortgage to *E. E* assigns the mortgage to *A,* who records his assignment. *R* now sells the mortgaged land to *P. P* makes payment of the mortgage to *E*. This is not a good payment. At the time he bought the property, *P* should have checked the records. They would have shown the assignment. Moreover, while it is practical to require an assignee of a mortgage to serve notice of his assignment on the mortgagor, it is unreasonable to require him to keep checking the records constantly so that he might serve notice on subsequent purchasers of the land. 5 Tiffany, *Real Property,* 493; 1 Jones, *Mortgages,* 818; 2 *id.* 442.

As you can see from the last two examples, whether a payment is to be deemed a good and valid payment depends to a considerable extent on who is making payment. It certainly makes a good deal of sense to protect the original mortgagor. If you asked the ordinary homeowner who has a mortgage on his house whether he checks the public records before making his monthly mortgage payments, he would look at you in amazement. He assumes he can continue to make payments to the mortgagee who loaned him the money until he receives notice to make payments to some one else, and to some extent the law is going to protect him in this assumption. However, when you get into the situation where someone has purchased property subject to an existing mortgage, already this is something unusual, and it should not be surprising to find the courts applying different rules to this kind of a person making payment.

EXAMPLE: *R* makes a mortgage to *E*. *R* sells and conveys land to *P*, who records his deed. *Thereafter, E* assigns his mortgage to *A*, who records the assignment. Now *P* makes payment of the mortgage debt to *E*. This is not good payment, and *P* will have to pay over again to *E* in many states. 89 ALR 171. The rule protecting a payment made to the mortgagee extends only to the *mortgagor,* not to a *purchaser* from him. However, some states protect *P* on the ground that at the time of his purchase the records obviously would not reveal the later assignment. 5 Tiffany, *Real Property,* 493. Suppose that in this same case *A* had failed to record his assignment. The case is now stronger for protecting *P*. 5 Tiffany, *Real Property,* 494.

Where the mortgage secures a negotiable note, in all but a few states the purchaser of the negotiable note is protected against payment made to the original mortgagor.

EXAMPLE: *R* makes a mortgage to *E* securing a negotiable note. *E* transfers the note to *A*. *R* makes payment to *E*. The payment is not good. The same result occurs where a pre-payment of the note is made to *E* who thereafter, and before maturity of the note, transfers it to *A*. 1 Jones, *Mortgages,* 823; 89 ALR 193. Anyone paying a negotiable note must demand to see it. In Illinois and Minnesota, however, the mortgagor is apparently protected in making payment to the original mortgagee, so that the purchaser of the note must serve notice on the mortgagor to protect himself against such payment. *Napieralski v. Simon,* 198 Ill. 384, 64 NE. 1042; Osborne, *Mortgages* § 234. *See also* §§ 190, 191.

§ 440. Payment—date of payment—pre-payment. The mortgagors cannot be called upon to make payment before the date specified for payment nor can the mortgagee be called upon before such date to receive payment. The mortgagee is entitled to have his money out earning interest until the day of payment unless the mortgage or mortgage note specified otherwise. 2 Jones, *Mortgages,* 593, 603. However, rule 545. 6–12 relating to Federal Savings & Loan Associations states that the borrower has the right to prepay his loan unless the loan documents state otherwise. On VA loans the right to prepay also exists. As interest rates climb, various states have enacted laws giving the mortgagor the right to prepay, the assumption being that interest rates will turn downward some day, and the mortgagor should be entitled to refinance his mortgage at lower interest rates.

§ 441. **Payment to agent.** A mortgagor, before making payment to a pretended agent of the mortgagee, should ascertain the agent's authority by inquiry of the mortgagee or by requiring the agent to produce a power of attorney from the mortgagee. *Coxe v. Kriebel,* 323 Pa. 157, 185 A 770. It is the duty of a person paying money to an agent to know that he has authority to receive it. The fact that the agent falsely states that he has authority to receive the payment will not protect the mortgagor in making payment to him. Mere possession of the mortgage notes by the agent does not of itself confer authority on the agent to receive payment. But where an agent procured the loan for the mortgagee, and the mortgagee from the very beginning has left the mortgage notes in the agent's possession, then the mortgagor is warranted in inferring that the agent is authorized to collect principal and interest.

Suppose that *A* buys a mortgage from *B* and *B* delivers the mortgage papers to *A,* but *A* allows *B* to continue collecting principal and interest. This course of conduct would confer authority on *B* to continue making such collection. Such questions will become important if *B* should embezzle some of the payments made by mortgagor. The payments having been made to an authorized agent are good payments and reduce the mortgage debt accordingly. *A* must bear the loss. *Hoiden v. Kohout,* 12 Ill. App2d 161, 138 NE2d 852.

The mere fact that a mortgage owned by *X* is, by its language, made payable at the office *Y* does not give *Y* authority to receive payments on the mortgage. 2 CJS. 1280. Technically, *Y*'s office is merely the place where *X* will be present to receive the payments. But if *Y* also has possession of the mortgage and note, he has authority to receive payment. This rule, for some strange reason, is called the *scrivener's rule.*

§ 442. **Payment—final payment rule.** There is some support for the proposition that final payment is never good against the true owner of the debt unless the party making payment demands production of the mortgage papers. 1 Glenn, *Mortgages,* 343. Whether courts would apply this rule to today's amortized mortgage is doubtful. In any event, since the final payment is rarely much larger than previous payments on the amortized mortgage, the rule is unimportant here. If the mortgage had a substantial balloon at the end, possibly courts might invoke the rule. However, the balloon note is in disfavor these days and courts could readily find reasons to avoid invoking the final payment rule.

§ 443. **Payment—effect of.** When a mortgage has been paid in full it ceases to exist. *Am. Nat. Ins. Co. v. Murray,* 383 F2d 81; Thompson, *Real Property Law* § 4813. Any future advances made thereunder after that time are not secured by the mortgage. 1 Glenn, *Mortgages,* 329.

§ 444. **Purchase of mortgage by mortgagor.** When a mortgagor has sold the property, and has no obligation to his purchaser to see that the mortgage is paid, the mortgagor may purchase the mortgage from the mortgagee and this does not constitute payment. 2 Jones, *Mortgages,* 578.

EXAMPLE: *R* makes a mortgage to *E*. *R* conveys the land to *X*, who assumes and agrees to pay the mortgage. *R* buys the mortgage from *E*. He may enforce it. *Flagg v. Geltmacher,* 98 Ill. 293; *Singer-Fleischaker Royalty Co. v. Whisenhunt,* (Okla.) 402 P2d 886.

38

Limitations

§ 445. **In general.** All states have laws placing a time limit on the right to file suits. A law of this type is known as a *statute of limitations* or *limitations act*. Typically the state will place a short time limit on the right to file a suit for personal injuries. The right to file a suit on a written contract usually exists for a much longer period. In any case where the time allowed for filing a particular kind of suit has gone by, it is said that the suit or the document is *barred by limitations*. One problem relates to the fact that in the case of a mortgage there are two documents: the promissory note or other obligation evidencing the debt, and the mortgage securing the debt. Arguably, the note secured by the mortgage is a *"contract in writing"* within the meaning of the limitations acts, and when the time has passed for maintaining a suit on the note, the mortgage, which exists merely to insure payment of the note, ought also to be barred by limitations. Unfortunately, the decisions do not fall into a simple pattern. Moreover, some states have special laws relating to documents that bear a seal, which is usually the case with respect to mortgages. Complicating the situation is the tendency in some states to put mortgages in a special and illogical pigeon-hole.

After a period of time, often *20 years,* there may be a *presumption* that the mortgage is paid. This means that if the mortgagee attempts to foreclose, he must offer some proof that the mortgage debt, in fact, remains unpaid.

Further complicating the problem is the presence in each state of some general law stating that part payments of interest or principal, written acknowledgments that the debt remains due, or the borrower's absence from the state keep the debt alive although the statutory time limit has expired. The problem, of course, exists because these laws, by and large, are old-fashioned and in need of modernization and clarification.

The court decisions disagree as to the right to foreclose the mortgage lien where the note secured by the mortgage is barred by limitations. In a majority of the states (including virtually all the title theory states and a majority of lien theory states) the fact that the mortgage note is barred by limitations only prevents the obtaining of a personal judgment on the note and does not prevent foreclosure of the mortgage. 2 Jones, *Mortgages,* 1040. In these states the landowner seeking to prevent a foreclosure of the mortgage is left to the defense of presumption of payment which arises after 20 years. *Shaefer v. Woodside,* 257 Pa. 276, 101 A 753, 1 ALR 775. Or, in some states, to the statute of limitations applicable to sealed instruments. *Empire Trust Co. v. Heinze,* 242 N.Y. 475, 478, 152 NE 266, 267. A minority of the states follow the view that where the debt is barred the mortgage is barred. 2 Jones, *Mortgages,* 1045. In these states whatever keeps the debt alive, keeps the mortgage alive. Osborne, *Mortgages* § 296.

Both of these views leave an intending purchaser of land in doubt when an old unreleased mortgage appears on the records. Under the majority view, a purchaser of land must be wary of old mortgages because the 20-year presumption of payment can be rebutted by showing part payments, acknowledgments of the debt, etc. *Shaefer v. Woodside,* 257 Pa. 276, 101 A 753, 1 ALR 775. Under the minority rule the purchaser must also be wary, because even unrecorded matters (part payments, unrecorded extensions, absence of debtor from state) will prolong the life of the mortgage. This will be discussed later in this chapter.

§ 446. Part payments by mortgagor as prolonging life of mortgage. The problem of the effect of the mortgagor's part payments on subsequent grantees is a difficult one.

a. Where the mortgage on its face seems barred by limitations but the mortgagor has been keeping the debt alive by part payments, and *thereafter* he conveys the land, many states hold that the grantee is bound by such acts of the mortgagor. The theory is that the grantee takes title with constructive notice of all recorded, unreleased mortgages, and should make inquiry as to whether any apparently barred mortgage has been kept alive. 101 ALR 337, 339.

b. Where the debt is completely barred by limitations, *and after the debt is so barred* the mortgagor conveys the land, the cases generally hold that any part payment by the mortgagor *thereafter* will revive his personal liability but will not revive the mortgage. In other words, the grantee is protected. 101 ALR 337, 343.

c. Where the mortgagor conveys while the mortgage is still enforceable on its face, and thereafter makes payments on the debt so that the bar *of the statute never attaches as to such mortgagor, most cases hold that the grantee is bound and the mortgage is kept alive. 101 ALR 337, 346; Smith v. Busch,* 173

Okla. 172, 44 P2d 921; *Richey v. Sinclair,* 167 Ill. 184, 47 NE 364. Nevertheless, there are a few cases *contra.* These last decisions hold that any payments, extensions, absence from the state, etc., by the mortgagor after conveyance merely keep alive his personal liability; they do not keep the mortgage lien alive. 101 ALR 337; *Tate v. Hawkins,* 81 Ky. 577; *Kendall v. Clarke,* 90 Ky. 178, 13 SW 853; 26 LRA (N.S.) 898; 9 Columb. L. Rev. 718. This minority theory is that after the mortgagor conveys, he has no interest in keeping the lien alive.

d. Where the mortgagor conveys while the debt is still alive, and thereafter the bar of the statute attaches, and *thereafter* the mortgagor makes a part payment, some courts hold that this revival is not binding on the grantee. *Schmucker v. Sibert,* 18 Kan. 104. The theory is that the grantee has a vested right in the protection of the completed bar. The mortgagor cannot impose burdens on property he no longer owns. There is some authority *contra.*

The same problems arise with respect to junior liens.

a. Where the mortgagor has been keeping the debt alive or has revived a barred debt by part payment, etc., and thereafter a junior lien attaches to the land, the junior lienor is bound by the part payments. His lien can attach only to the mortgagor's equity. 38 ALR 833. 834; *Clark v. Grant,* 25 Okla. 398, 109 P2d 234; 28 L.R.A. (NS.) 519.

b. Where the mortgage debt is completely barred by limitations before the subsequent lien attaches, the better rule is that any part payment by the mortgagor *thereafter* does not revive the mortgage lien as against the subsequent lienor. In effect, the subsequent lien is a first lien on the land. *Burns v. Burns,* 11 NW2d 461 (Ia); 59 CJS 345, 339; 32 Ill.L.Rev. 750. There are some cases *contra.* 38 ALR 833, 834.

c. Where the subsequent lien attaches while the mortgage is still enforceable, and thereafter the mortgagor makes payments on the debt, so that the bar of the statute never attaches *as to the mortgagor,* many cases hold that the junior lienor is bound by these payments. 38 ALR 833. Were the rule otherwise, the mortgagee would hesitate to grant extensions to his mortgagor, for fear of losing his priority of lien. *Hess v. State Bank,* 130 Wash. 147, 226 P 257, 38 ALR 829. There are a number of cases *contra.* These cases hold that from and after the creation of the junior interest, the mortgagor is impotent to affect the running of the statute. 49 Harv. L. Rev. 639, 642. These cases argue that once a junior lien has attached it is not fair to permit the mortgagor to keep the senior mortgage alive.

d. Where the subsequent lien attaches while the mortgage is still alive, and thereafter the statute runs, and thereafter the mortgagor makes a part payment, the tendency is to hold that this revival is good against the subsequent lienor. *Burns v. Burns,* 11 NW2d 461 (Ia.). The theory is that the subsequent lienor is not harmed, since he merely retains the junior position he occupied when his lien attached. There are cases *contra. Lord v. Morris,* 18 Cal. 482.

§ 447. Part payments by grantee of part of mortgaged land. Payments by a grantee of part of the mortgaged land, made while he is the owner of the premises, may prolong the life of the mortgage as to a subsequent grantee.

> **EXAMPLE:** Mortgagor conveys part of mortgaged premises to A who assumes the debt, and conveys another part of B who does not assume. Some courts hold payments by A do not bind B. Other decisions are *contra.* 2 Jones, Mortgages, 1034.

§ 448. Payments by one of two or more mortgagors. . Where *A* and *B* execute a mortgage and note jointly, payments by either keep the mortgage lien alive, but do not prolong the existence of the personal liability of the other joint debtor. *Fohrman v. Laird,* 338 Ill.App. 393; *Ritzmueller v. Neuer,* 130 Ill.App. 383.

§ 449. Deed subject to mortgage. If the mortgagor conveys the land by deed that recites it as "subject to" the mortgage, this, according to most authorities, starts a new limitations period. If the mortgage had been barred by limitations before the deed, it is revived. 2 Glenn, *Mortgages,* 837; 37 CJ 1135.

§ 450. Notice to mortgagee of existence of grantee or junior lienor. At times the courts say that a mortgagee who acts with the mortgagor to prolong the life of his mortgage will succeed unless he has "notice" that the rights of a grantee or junior lienor have intervened. However, constructive notice by recording of the deed to the grantee or the mortgagor to the junior lienor satisfies the requirement. Hence it is meaningless.

§ 451. Mortgagee in possession. The statute of limitations does not run against a mortgagee in possession. This means that once the mortgagee has taken possession peaceably, he may retain that possession and cannot be ousted until his mortgage has been paid in full. The rule is of particular value to the mortgagee where there has been a defective foreclosure. No matter how defective the foreclosure proceedings have been, if the mortgagee is the highest bidder at the foreclosure sale, has received a deed and taken possession of the land, he cannot be ousted until has debt has been paid. But if the mortgagee takes possession, albeit peaceably, *after* the mortgage has been barred by limitations, this does not revive the mortgage. *Morford v. Wells.* 68 Kan. 122, 74 P 615; *Banning v. Sabin,* 45 Minn. 431, 48 NW 8. If the mortgagee takes possession of the mortgaged land and retains such possession for 20 years without accounting to the mortgagor for rents, the mortgagor's rights, including his equitable right of redemption, are terminated. *Locke v. Caldwell,* 91 Ill. 417. In some states a much shorter period will suffice.

§ 452. Statutes extinguishing mortgage lien. The ordinary statutes of limitation are virtually useless to an intending purchaser of the land, owing to the off-record matters that may prolong the life of the mortgage and owing to the rule that the presumption of payment may be overcome by proof of non-payment. Hence additional laws have been passed in recent times. In general, they fix some period, for example, 20 years after the maturity of the mortgage debt, when the mortgage becomes void for all purposes. *Livingston v. Meyers,* 6 Ill.2d 325, 129 NE2d 325; Basye, *Clearing Land Titles* § 76 *et seq.* Among the states having such laws are Alaska, Colorado, Florida, Georgia, Idaho, Illinois, Indiana, Iowa, Kansas, Massachusetts, Michigan, Minnesota, Missouri, Nebraska, Nevada, New Hampshire, New Mexico, Ohio, South Carolina, Tennessee, Texas, and Virginia.

§ **453. Marketable title acts.** In a number of states laws have been enacted declaring titles marketable and ridding them of stale claims. The period prescribed by law varies from state to state and the laws vary somewhat in their operation. 44 N.C.L. Rev. 99; 53 Cornell L.Q 45; 71 ALR 2d 846. In time laws of this sort will be enacted throughout the entire country and will also be helpful in clearing stale mortgages from the public records.

39

Merger

§ 454. In general. There are, in general, two situations that call into play the rules concerning merger.

EXAMPLE: *R* mortgages land to *E*. Later *R* sells and conveys the land to *E*. There being no reason for *E* to retain a security interest on the land, the mortgage is extinguished by merger.

EXAMPLE: *R* mortgages land to *E*. Later *E* sells and assigns the mortgage to *R*. Again, it is likely the courts will hold the mortgage is extinguished by merger.

Of course, the situation is rarely as simple as the examples indicate. The usual situation involves the presence of a lien of which *E* was ignorant.

EXAMPLE: *R* mortgages land to *E*. Later *X* obtains a judgment against *R* which, in the state in question, is a lien on the land. *R* fails to pay on the mortgage. To avoid the expense of foreclosure *E* buys *R*'s equity for a nominal sum. He receives a deed of the land and records a release of the mortgage. Later *E* discovers the existence of *X*'s judgment and seeks to foreclose his mortgage. *X* defends, contending that *E*'s mortgage was extinguished by merger. This contention will not prevail. The courts hold that merger is a question of intention of the parties, and where it develops that merger would work to the disadvantage of the mortgagee, the courts will take the view that merger was not intended. *Silliman v. Gammage,* 55 Tex. 365; 95 ALR 628.

Again, this is a situation in which an institutional lender will rarely be involved. *E* will insist on a title search before he accepts the deed from the mortgagor. Moreover, *E* will insist that the deal be closed in an escrow with a title company with a provision in the escrow that the deal can go forward only if the title company is willing to insure clear title in *E*.

There are situations where E is perfectly aware of the junior liens and nevertheless is willing to buy a deed from R. This is done so that E can go into possession and terminate any "milking" that is going on. E has a mortgage big enough to discourage any competitive bidding at the foreclosure sale. Hence he is willing to pay to get R out of the picture so that E can proceed with rehabilitation of the property. All that E needs to do here is insist that the deed contain a clause stating that no merger of the mortgage or extinguishment of the mortgage debt, complete or partial, is intended. This will prevent any junior lienor from raising merger as a nuisance defense to the foreclosure. Commonly, the mortgagee will have the mortgagor convey to a nominee of the mortgagee. This buttresses the mortgagee's position that no merger or extinguishment is intended. At a minimum, the mortgagee should cancel the mortgagor's note at this time, so that it cannot be contended that the deed was only a security deed. *See* Chapter 3.

Where the mortgage is planning to bid at a judicial or execution sale of the mortgagor's equity, the situation becomes a bit sticky. Obviously the mortgagee is in no position to insist that the sale proceedings recite that no merger is intended. Here, obviously, the use of a nominee as the purchaser is routine. At times, a mortgagee will record simultaneously with the sheriff's deed a declaration by the nominee reciting that no merger or extinguishment is created by acceptance or recording of the deed. In addition, a check of the local decisions must be made to determine if they make such a purchase hazardous. Osborne, *Mortgages* §§ 272 *et seq.*

If the mortgage holds a senior and junior mortgage on the same land, again merger problems arise when the mortgagee forecloses one mortgage and is the successful bidder at the foreclosure sale. The question that arises is whether the mortgage that was not foreclosed was merged or the mortgage debt extinguished. 2 Glenn, *Mortgages* 1409. Here it is probably best to foreclose the senior and junior mortgages in one judicial foreclosure. If the state is one where power of sale foreclosures are permitted the first deed of trust ought always to have a clause stating that it secures any additional debt of the mortgagor held by the lender. If it does not contain this clause, the mortgagee can insist on a supplemental deed of trust containing this clause at the time the junior loan is made. The mortgagee ought always to be in a situation where he can throw the weight of all the mortgage debt he holds into the foreclosure bidding.

The rule with respect to protection of a bona fide purchaser who relies on an apparent merger of the mortgage in the fee title is discussed elsewhere. *See* § 190.

40

Release of Mortgage

§ 455. Necessity for release. Under modern law, when the mortgage debt is paid, this automatically terminates all title or lien of the mortgagee. However, this payment does not appear on the public records, and therefore the mortgage still appears on the records, clouding the landowner's title. It is therefore necessary, when final payment is made, for the mortgagee in a regular mortgage to execute a document, variously called a *release, release deed, reconveyance, satisfaction* or *discharge* of mortgage debt. The fact that a release deed or reconveyance is used in some states is a throwback to the times when a mortgagee had pretty substantial title to the land (*see* § 6), which it was necessary to "reconvey" to the mortgagor when the debt was paid. 1 Glenn, *Mortgages,* 320.

§ 456. Who signs the release deed. The release deed is signed by the mortgagee. If an assignment of the mortgage has been recorded, the release deed is signed by the assignee. If there are two mortgagees, both usually sign. *See* however, § 438. If the mortgagee has died, the release deed is signed by his executor or administrator.

§ 457. Recording. The release deed must be recorded so as to clear the mortgage from the public records. Obviously the mortgage must have a proper acknowledgement on it. This is needed to entitle the release to recording.

§ 458. Release on margin of record. A few states still retain older laws permitting the recorder to endorse a release on the margin of the record of the mortgage when the cancelled note and mortgage are produced to him. In these days of photostat and microfilm recording this custom is just about dead.

§ 459. Defective releases. Since the discharge of a paid mortgage strikes the average layman as an informal transaction, many informalities occur in these transactions, notably lack of acknowledgments and witnesses, release executed by wrong party, and the like. Many states have enacted laws curing such defects. Basye, *Clearing Land Titles* § 353. In many states, also, bar associations have adopted Title Standards, that is, local rules for the guidance of attorneys, under which many technical defects in releases may be disregarded. *Ibid.*

§ 460. **Penalty for failure to release.** All states have some sort of statute imposing a penalty on a mortgagee who wrongfully refuses to release the mortgage. This penalty is collectible by the mortgagor. Oridinarily, it is a penalty in a nominal amount. However, in some states, Connecticut, for example, a substantial penalty is imposed, in that state running $50.00 per week during the period of refusal to execute the release.

§ 461. **Release of part of mortgage land.** If a mortgage covers several tracts, it may be released as to less than all of them. This is commonplace in land developments.

EXAMPLE: Farmer *A* sells 160 acres of land to *B*, a developer, who pays part cash and part by giving *A* a purchase money mortgage for $100,000. The mortgage provides that the land will be subdivided into 100 lots and any lot can be released by payment of $1,000. This is necessary, since as a house is built and sold the home buyer will need his own first mortgage. If the mortgage lacks a partial release provision, the mortgagor has no right to demand a partial release.

In a mortgage of land intended to be subdivided, this partial release clause is vital. In addition, where the mortgage is in the form of a deed of trust, it is desirable to include a recital that each release by the trustee shall be conclusive evidence in favor of any purchaser that all pre-conditions for the giving of such release have been satisfied. Since the courts are likely to treat the partial release clause as a contract to release land and a demand for a partial release as a demand for specific performance of the contract, the partial release clause must have all the elements of certainty and completeness that courts insist upon when they grant specific performance of a contract. *Lawrence v. Shatt,* 75 Cal.Rptr. 533; *White Point Co. v. Herrington,* 73 Cal.Rptr. 885.

If a mortgagee releases part of the mortgaged land after having learned of junior mortgages, he may lose his priority of lien.

EXAMPLE: *R* executed a mortgage to *E* on Lots 1 and 2. *R* thereafter executed a junior mortgage to *X* on Lot 1. *E* knew of this mortgage. *E* then released Lot 2 from his mortgage, throwing the entire burden of his mortgage on Lot 1. This gave *X* priority of lien over *E*'s mortgage. *Turner v. Ridge Heights* Co., 92 NJ Eq. 64, 111 A 675.

The same result can occur where the mortgagee releases the mortgage as to some valuable right in the mortgaged land.

EXAMPLE: The situation is the same as in the preceding example, but instead of releasing all of Lot 2, *E* releases the timber of Lot 2 from the lien of his mortgage. Again X gains priority over *E. Traverse v. Stevens,* 108 Fla. 11, 145 So. 851.

This is the so-called *two funds doctrine* in the law of *marshalling of assets.* *See* § 233. It is based on the proposition that the mortgagee, having actual knowledge of the rights of others, must not voluntarily take action that will harm them. It is not applicable unless the same mortgagor owns both tracts of land.

EXAMPLE: *H* and *W* owned Lot 1 and *H* owned Lot 2. *H* and *W* mortgaged both lots to *E*. *H* mortgages Lot 2 to *X*. The doctrine of marshalling of assets is not applicable. The same identical mortgagor must own both lots. *Miller Lumber Co. v. Berkheimer,* 20 A2d 772; 35 Am. Jur. Marshalling of Assets § 4.

It is a good idea to include in every mortgage a clause reserving to the holder of the mortgage the right to release part of the mortgaged premises or the personal liability of the mortgagor all without impairment of the priority of the lien of the mortgage, for, lacking this clause, such a release made with knowledge of the existence of a junior lien, may cause an impairment of the priority of the mortgage under the doctrine of marshalling of assets.

> Suggested marshalling of assets clause: The right is hereby reserved by the Mortgagee to make partial release or releases of the mortgaged premises hereunder without notice to, or the consent, approval or agreement of other parties in interest, including junior lienors, which partial release or releases shall not impair in any manner the validity of or priority of this mortgage on the mortgaged premises remaining, nor release the Mortgagor from personal liability for the indebtedness hereby secured.

Where the first mortgage and junior mortgage both cover the same identical land, the doctrine of marshalling of assets is inapplicable. By releasing part of the mortgaged land, the first mortgagee harms only himself. The junior mortgage becomes a first mortgage on the property. There is no prejudice to the junior mortgagee; hence no reason for marshalling.

By the great weight of authority, a clause in a mortgage providing for partial releases of portions of the mortgaged land on payment of amounts scheduled in the mortgage is for the benefit of subsequent purchasers or owner of the mortgaged land. It is not one that only the mortgagor can exercise. Osborne, *Mortgages* § 877. Moreover, unless the mortgage provides otherwise, the right to demand a partial release can be exercised even after a default has occurred in the mortgage payments unless the mortgage provides otherwise. 93 ALR 1027; 59 CJS 759.

SUGGESTION: Let the partial release clause provide that partial releases will be issued only if there is no default or breach of covenant under the mortgage.

§ 462. Release of mortgage as automatic release of assignment of rents. Quite often, a mortgage is accompanied by an assignment of leases and rents. *See* Chapter 27. When the mortgage is paid off, a release deed is recorded releasing the mortgage. Through negligence, the release fails to release the assignment of leases and rents. In some states, title standards, that is, rules of the local bar associations, permit attorneys to treat a release of a mortgage as a release of such assignment. Basye, *Clearing Land Titles* § 353.

§ 463. Title standards. In many states, also, bar associations have adopted Title Standards, that is, local rules for the guidance of attorneys, under which many technical defects in releases may be disregarded. *Ibid.*

§ 464. Wrongful release—protection given an innocent purchaser. Problems of wrongful release normally occur in connection with unrecorded assignments of the mortgage. *See* §§ 190 and 439. With respect to the release of a deed of trust, the problem of the wrongful release is more complex. *See* §§ 468. The issue is the extent to which a bona fide purchaser is protected by a recorded release where part or all of the mortgage debt remains unpaid.

41

Release of Deeds of Trust

§ 465. **Trustee executes release.** As has been mentioned, payment of the debt is made to the holder of the note. Typically the holder of the note secured by a deed of trust also has physical possession of the deed of trust. However, the note holder does not execute the release deed. Instead, upon receiving final payment, the note holder marks the note "*PAID,*" adding his signature and the date. He thereupon cancels the note and deed of trust. This can be done by pen, writing the word "*CANCELLED*" and adding the note holder's name or initials across the signatures on note and deed of trust. Or, in a financial institution, these are run through a cancelling machine. The landowner then takes the note and deed of trust to the trustee, who thereupon executes a *release deed*. In some areas this is called a *deed of reconveyance*. This last name stems from the fact that in some states, by reason of the title theory (*see* § 6), the trustee is regarded as having a sort of legal title to the land. In modern times the courts regard this title as automatically coming to an end with payment of the mortgage debt, but it is still the custom to procure this release deed. Oddly, it is the custom in some states for a mortgagee who receives final payment to execute a *satisfaction,* which merely recites payment and satisfaction of the note and mortgage. But even in these same states a trustee gives a release deed or deed of reconveyance. There is no substantial legal reason for this distinction, but it persists.

EXCEPTIONS TO RULE: In Virginia the release is executed by the note holder rather than the trustee. In Colorado there is an official known as the *public trustee* and he executes the release deed.

If there are two trustees, both must sign. If the trustee is an individual who has died, the release is executed by the successor trustee named in the deed of trust, and a recital is added that the trustee has died.

§ 466. Recording of release. The note holder then takes the release deed to the recorder's office and has it recorded. This is important, because it clears the record of the deed of trust. Obviously the release deed must have a proper acknowledgment on it. Otherwise in most states it will not be entitled to be recorded.

§ 467. Wrongful release. If a trustee executes a release deed without satisfying himself that the mortgage debt has been paid in full, he exposes himself to the risk of a lawsuit. Hence trustees tend to be cautious in this regard. Some corporate trustees will not execute a release unless the note was identified by them at the time the note and deed of trust were signed. *See* § 90. Then when a release is requested, the trustee checks his identification on the note before executing the release deed. This is done because in some cases dishonest lenders will have an ignorant borrower sign two (perhaps more) notes and sell these notes to different investors. If one of these notes is exhibited to the trustee marked cancelled and he executes a release deed, he may then face a lawsuit by another note holder.

If the ownership of the land has not changed and no other liens attach to the land after a wrongful release has been recorded, the note holder will file a suit to have the release deed set aside and the court will so order. Commonly, since the debt is in default, this type of suit is combined with a suit to foreclose the deed of trust, if this occurs in a state where foreclosure by court proceedings is common.

§ 468. Bona fide purchaser or lienor after recording of wrongful release. There will be instances where even a wrongful release will extinguish the deed of trust.

EXAMPLE: *R* borrows $100,000 from *E* and gives *E* his promissory note for that amount. He also signs a deed of trust to *T*, as trustee. This deed of trust secures the debt. Seeking to defraud *E*, *R* prepares a clever forgery of the note and exhibits it to *T* marked cancelled. *T* executes a release deed, which *R* records in the recorder's office. *R* now sells the land to *P*, who is an innocent purchaser having no knowledge of *R*'s fraud. *P* becomes owner of the land free and clear of the trust deed. This is a necessary rule, even though it may seem harsh to *E*. People must be allowed to deal with land in reliance on the land records.

Where the ownership of the land has not changed since the wrongful release was recorded, but another lien has attached to the land, the rule operates, but somewhat differently.

EXAMPLE: The facts are as in the last example, but only up to the recording of the release deed by *R*. Thereafter, instead of selling the land to *P*, *R* borrows $50,000 from *X* and gives *X* a mortgage to secure that debt. *X* records the mortgage. On discovering the fraud, *E* may have the release deed set aside, but *X*'s mortgage will remain as a first mortgage on the property. An innocent mortgage, like an innocent purchaser, is protected. These rules are akin to the *release role.* See § 190.

Of course, in both examples given above the trustee will be liable to *E* because of the giving of the wrongful release. And if the trustee is a corporate trustee, *E* will suffer no loss. And, of course, *R* remains liable on his promissory note. However, dishonest persons always seem to have no discoverable assets, so attempts to collect from *T* may prove fruitless.

In Illinois a special and peculiar rule is followed. A wrongful release by a trustee gives no protection to a subsequent purchaser or mortgagee unless the release deed is dated (1) at or after the maturity date of the debt as it appears on recorded deed of trust or (2) on a prepayment date stated in the recorded deed of trust. The theory is that a release deed dated on any other date should excite the suspicion of any intending purchaser or lender and he should demand to see the cancelled note and deed of trust. *Marsh v. Stover,* 363 Ill. 490 2 NE2d 559. *Lenartz v. Quilty,* 191 Ill. 174, 60 NE 913. This rule seems wanting in logic. It is common knowledge that mortgage debts are often prepaid, even though the debt contains no prepayment privilege. It is doubtful that any other state will follow the Illinois rule. 2 Glenn, *Mortgages,* 1420. However, it is a good practice to include in the deed of trust a statement that any release executed by the trustee will be conclusive evidence in favor of any subsequent purchaser or mortgagee that the mortgage debt was paid. In such case the release, when recorded, will protect a subsequent purchaser or mortgagee without the necessity of exhibiting the mortgage papers. This is a matter of convenience, since after a time it is possible some of the mortgage papers may be mislaid.

§ 469. Missing notes. At times, when a deed of trust secures a number of notes, one or more paid notes may be mislaid. When the debt is finally paid, and the trustee demands production of all the notes marked cancelled, the landowner will be unable to produce the missing note or notes. This will put him to the expense of procuring a corporate surety bond to protect the trustee. The trustee can legally demand such a bond. *O'Connor v. Brower,* 262 Ill.App. 621. The trustee is within his rights in demanding such a bond, for if the note is not actually outstanding and unpaid, the trustee would be liable in damages for executing a wrongful release. If, however, the notes were held by a reasonable financial institution which is willing to give the trustee its written statement that all notes were paid and cancelled, the trustee, in his discretion, may dispense with the surety bond. Surety companies usually demand collateral when they give bonds of this sort. Hence it is a pretty serious matter to lose or mislay a note secured by a deed of trust.

§ 470. Future advances. As has been observed, before a trustee is willing to execute a release of a trust deed he will insist on determining that the note secured by the trust deed is paid and cancelled. The cancelled note is physically produced and exhibited to trustee. There may be occasions where the trust deed in addition to securing a particular promissory note secures future advances that may be made to the mortgagor. This poses a problem to the trustee. It is difficult to determine in such case what future advances were made. Some trustees are unwilling to rely on a simple affidavit as to matters of this character. The best solution to this problem is to strike the language relating to future advances from the deed of trust and in such case the problem will not arise at all.

§ 471. **Provisions of deed of trust.** It is best for the protection of the trustee if the deed of trust sets forth in some detail the circumstances under which the trustee is to execute his release deed. Otherwise controversies may arise and the trustee may be confronted with personal liability.

EXAMPLE: R executed a note payable to E secured by a deed of trust to T. The deed of trust provided that it could be released on E's direction. R and E agreed on a modification of the loan. R conveyed the property to H at the direction of E, T then signed a release of the deed of trust, H then went into bankruptcy. This bankruptcy frustrated the plans for a refinancing of the deed of trust. E proceeded to sue R on the promissory note secured by the deed of trust and R paid. R now sued T for executing a release deed at a time when the note was unpaid. The court held for T because he acted in accordance with the provisions of the deed of trust. *Fisher v. Consolidated* Co., 30 Cal.Rptr.137.

§ 472. **Recitals.** If a trust deed provides that recitals of payment in the release deed shall be conclusive, then any release deed by the trustee containing such recital will protect a purchaser or mortgagee who acts in reliance on such release deed. *Firato v. Tuttle* 48 Cal. 2d 136, 308 P2d 333.

42

Foreclosure by Judicial Proceedings

§ 473. In general—information to be furnished the foreclosing attorney. In quite a number of states mortgage foreclosure must take place through a court proceeding. These states are motivated by a desire to protect the mortgagor. The thought is that since the foreclosure sale must be approved by the court, the property will not be sold below its value. There is some advantage to the mortgagee also, in that since the sale is approved by the court, it is difficult for the mortgagor to upset it later. Title thus acquired by the mortgagee is more readily marketable than title acquired by foreclosure through a power of sale.

As a rule, a mortgagee who has decided upon foreclosure, should turn over to the foreclosing attorney all documents the attorney will need. Obviously this includes the mortgage and note, since they must be introduced in evidence in the foreclosure suit. This may also be true of the assignment of leases and rents, and, in any case, the attorney will need this document if he is going to make demand on tenants to pay rent to the mortgagee. The mortgage title policy should also be included. A transmittal letter should contain certain basic information: (1) the dates and amounts of all defaults; (2) the balance due on principal as of date of transmittal; (3) the amounts of balances in escrow accounts for taxes and insurance, since these will probably be credited by the court against the mortgage debt; (4) the amounts of any advances made by the mortgagee on taxes, insurance, etc; (5) the status of possession, stating units occupied by mortgagor, units occupied by tenants, lease terms etc; (6) addresses of all persons who will be served with summons as known to mortgagee (mortgagor, purchaser from mortgagor, junior mortgagee), since the sheriff who is to serve summons will require this information.

§ 474. Defects in proceedings—nonjurisdictional defects. Mistakes are frequently made in foreclosure suits. However, it is a rarity for a mistake to invalidate the title of the purchaser at the foreclosure sale as long as (1) the foreclosure is brought in the proper court (which is *jurisdiction of the subject matter*), (2) the court has jurisdiction of the land (for example, a foreclosure on Illinois land cannot be filed in Indiana), (3) the foreclosure proceedings reveal that all necessary parties were made defendants, and (4) they do not reveal fatal defects in the service of process on the defendants (which is *jurisdiction of the parties*). Any defendant who claims he was prejudiced by some error of the trial court must take an appeal within the time allowed by law. If he fails to do so, the purchaser's title cannot be attacked by any other proceedings (*collateral attack*). 73 ALR 613. Error makes a judgment or decree erroneous, but not void. Of course, a mistake may be made that will invalidate the foreclosure, for example, where it describes the wrong tract of land throughout the foreclosure.

§ 475. Jurisdiction of the subject matter. *Jurisdiction of the subject matter* means that the mortgage must be foreclosed in a court that has power under local law to hear mortgage foreclosure cases. A mortgage could not be foreclosed, for example, in a justice of the peace court. No problems arise in this area, since in all states there is some court that has power to foreclose mortgages. Often it is called the *circuit court,* a name that harks back to the days when the judges actually rode the circuit of courts, as, indeed they still do in some areas.

§ 476. Jurisdiction of the parties—necessary parties—omitted parties. The purpose of foreclosure is to (1) establish the validity of the mortgage, (2) establish the amount due the mortgagee, and (3) produce a foreclosure sale that will wipe out all interests that are junior to the mortgage, so that the purchaser at the foreclosure sale will emerge with a marketable title. To achieve this object all interested parties whose interests are junior to the mortgage being foreclosed must be given their day in court. Legally this means that all interested parties must be named as defendants in the foreclosure. The landowner, that is the mortgagor, or his grantee, if he sold the property, is the chief party defendant.

His wife should be joined because of her dower, homestead, or other rights. Any junior mortgagee must be brought in, also any judgment creditor or other party claiming a lien on the land. To some extent requirements as to parties vary from state to state. Generally, even if he has sold the land, the mortgagor is brought into the foreclosure suit, so that a personal judgment or deficiency decree can be rendered against him.

The problem of unknown parties is a difficult and technical one.

EXAMPLE: *R* makes a mortgage to *E. R* later makes a deed of trust to *E,* as trustee, to secure a note payable to bearer. *E* has no way of knowing who holds this note. In many states the note holder can be made party under the designation *Unknown Owners, John Doe,* or some other such designation. Notice is published as to such party.

EXAMPLE: *R* makes a mortgage to *E*. Default occurs. *E* inspects the property and finds no occupants. The neighbors report *R* has died. In some states *E* will bring *R*'s heirs in as *Unknown Heirs or Devisees of R, Deceased*. The practice on this differs from state to state.

In determining who should be brought into the suit as necessary parties, the foreclosing attorney will make use of the evidence of title furnished him by the mortgagee. One precaution he will take is to check for subordinated items.

EXAMPLE: *R* gives a mortgage to *E* in 1970. There is a prior mortgage given by *R* to *X* in 1969, which *X* subordinates to *E*'s mortgage. Hence the mortgage title policy shows *E*'s mortgage as a first mortgage on the land. It may not even mention *X*'s mortgage, since it is subordinate to *E*'s mortgage. The attorney should routinely contact the title company and inquire whether such subordinate items exist.

The attorney must then determine what interests were acquired in the land after the recording of the mortgage that would require their owners to be made defendants to the foreclosure. In counties that are sparsely populated the attorney may make this search of the record himself. In areas where title insurance is used, the mortgagee may call upon the title company that issued his mortgage policy to make a search of the title from the date of the recording of the mortgage to the present time. Quite often the title company will simply furnish a list of the names (and addresses if they appear on the public records) of those holding interests that require them to be made parties to the foreclosure.

The attorney for the mortgagee thereupon prepares his foreclosure complaint naming such parties and files it. In many states he is also required to file notice of lis pendens in the recorder's office. He then proceeds to have all parties served with summons or by publication of notice.

As a rule, he will then return to the title company and request a supplementary search that will reveal the names of any parties who acquired interests in the property after the last title search but before the complaint to foreclose was filed.

EXAMPLE: *E*, a mortgagee holding a defaulted mortgage, goes to the title company and requests a title search for foreclosure purposes. The title company furnishes a search which shows *R* as the owner of the property on June 1, 1970, and listing junior liens. *E*'s attorney prepares his complaint, naming all such persons as defendants. It is filed on June 11, 1970. A notice of lis pendens is recorded in states that require this. Thereafter a new title search is ordered, which reveals that on June 10, 1970, *R* recorded a deed to *X*. *E*'s attorney must now file an amendment to his complaint bringing in *X* as a party defendant, since *X* was the owner on the day the complaint was filed. *X* is served with summons.

Where the mortgagee's attorney is meticulously careful, he will order a third search of the title at the time the judgment or decree of foreclosure is entered. At this time the title company's search will report back whether all the defendants were properly served with summons or by publication.

EXAMPLE: *E* files a foreclosure suit against *A, B, C,* and *D.* The court enters a judgment of foreclosure. The title company's search reveals that no summons was served on *D.* This can readily happen where the sheriff uses rubber stamps in showing his *return of service* on the summons. The rubber stamp showing that he could not serve a defendant superficially resembles the stamp showing service. *E* has the court vacate or set aside its judgment, which must be done within the time allowed by law. Summons is served on *D* and a new judgment of foreclosure is entered.

In areas where the methods of searching title to land are the abstract and opinion method or the attorney's search of the public records, the same double or triple check of the title is made.

The important consideration at all times is to conduct the foreclosure with meticulous care, so that the purchaser at the foreclosure sale will emerge with marketable title.

In addition to imposing the obligation of searching the public records in order to bring into the foreclosure all persons having interests of record that are junior to the mortgage being foreclosed, the law also imposes on the mortgagee the obligation of checking the possession, for in nearly all states possession imparts constructive notice.

EXAMPLE: *R* gives a mortgage to *E* in 1965. Default occurs in 1970. *E* checks the records and finds nothing since the date mortgage was recorded. However, he also checks the possession and finds *X* in possession. *X* claims that *R* had died, leaving *X* and a number of other children as his heirs. Now *E* has the duty of inquiring further in order to obtain the names of all the children and bringing them into the foreclosure suit.

The usual practice, then, of a mortgagee who plans to foreclose is to (1) search the records and (2) check the possession of the premises. All persons whose interest would be revealed by these searches are necessary parties to the foreclosure proceeding.

Nevertheless instances occur where there is a slip-up and some necessary party is omitted. In the first place, this does not invalidate the foreclosure. It is binding on all persons who were made parties to the foreclosure.

EXAMPLE: *R* makes a mortgage to *E. R* dies leaving *X* and *Y* as his heirs. *E* files a foreclosure suit, but, through error, names only *X* as a defendant. *Y,* if he acts promptly, may "redeem," that is, pay off the mortgage even after the foreclosure sale. The foreclosure sale cuts off all equitable rights of redemption of the defendants to the foreclosure. *It does not cut off the equitable redemption rights of those who should have been made parties defendant and were not.*

However, this right does not continue indefinitely. It can be lost by unreasonable delay, known technically as *laches.*

EXAMPLE: In the example given above Y delays for five years after the foreclosure sale. Meanwhile the property is rising sharply in value. Y now cannot redeem. He is barred by laches. *Walker v. Warner,* 179 Ill. 16, 53 NE 594.

Junior lienors who have not been made parties to foreclosure of a senior mortgagee retain their right to foreclose their liens. This is a rather tenuous right, since the senior mortgagee will instantly respond by bringing his own suit or counterclaim to extinguish the junior liens by strict foreclosure. Osborne, *Mortgages* § 324.

While ordinarily it is improper for a junior mortgagee to implead the first mortgagee in a foreclosure of the first mortgage, it is occasionally held this may properly be done for the sole purpose of obtaining an adjudication of the amount due on the first mortgage. 80 Am. Dec. 716.

To cut out a senior mortgage by foreclosure of a junior mortgage it does not suffice to make the senior mortgagee a party and make some general allegation that his interest is subordinate to the lien of the junior mortgage. Some rather specific allegation and prayer for relief is necessary to put the senior mortgagee on notice that the priority of his lien is under attack. *Jasper v. Rozinski,* 228 N.Y. 349, 127 NE 189.

§ 477. Omitted parties—foreclosure as an assignment of the mortgage. Since foreclosure is without effect as to necessary parties to the foreclosure whom the mortgagee failed to name as such, then if the mortgagee is the successful bidder at the foreclosure sale, he continues to own an unforeclosed mortgage as to such parties. He may, therefore, on discovering his mistake bring a new foreclosure suit against such parties. In many states he will be permitted to bring a strict foreclosure against an omitted junior lienor though not against an omitted equity owner. 1 Glenn, *Mortgages,* 427, 428. This forces the omitted party to pay the mortgage debt within a short time fixed by the court, in default of which the rights of the omitted party are barred.

If a stranger purchases at the foreclosure sale, the sale operates also as an assignment of the mortgage to such purchaser. *Rodman v. Quick,* 211 Ill. 546, 71 NE 1087; 73 ALR 630.

§ 478. Omitted parties—mortgagee in possession. When the purchaser at a foreclosure sale, whether it be the mortgagee or a third party, takes possession of the mortgaged land, then, as to omitted parties, the purchaser becomes a mortgagee in possession, 73 ALR 643. He cannot be ousted by the mortgagor unless the mortgagor offers to pay the mortgage debt. Moreover, the mortgage never outlaws as long as the purchaser retains this status of mortgagee in possession. And finally, in all states there comes a time when some local law bars the rights of the omitted parties.

§ 479. Lis pendens. Judicial foreclosure is subject to the doctrine of lis pendens.

EXAMPLE: *R* gives a mortgage to *E*. *E* files foreclosure against *R* in 1970 and files a notice of lis pendens. In 1971 *R* conveys to *X*. *X* is not a necessary party. He has acquired his title lis pendens.

§ 480. Exceeding jurisdiction. In general, the philosophy of foreclosure law has been that foreclosures are intended to cut out the rights of the mortgagor and all persons whose interests are junior to the mortgagee being foreclosed. A senior mortgagee is not a proper defendant in a suit to foreclose a junior mortgage. 1 Glenn, *Mortgages,* 504. A foreclosure is not intended as a means of deciding questions of title or cutting out lien paramount and superior to the lien of the mortgage foreclosed. However, laws and court decisions have grown so liberal that it is hard to generalize concerning these matters.

EXAMPLE: In 1969 *R* makes a mortgage to *E*. In 1970 *R* makes a mortgage to *X*. *X* files a foreclosure suit. He names *R* and *E* as defendants and claims, in his suit, that his mortgage is prior and superior to *E's* mortgage. Probably most courts today would permit this issue to be tried in this foreclosure. Some might not. Osborne, *Mortgages* § 323. If *E* makes no objection and allows the court to render a decree or judgment that his mortgage is junior to *X's* mortgage, the better rule is that this is binding on *E*. *Sielbeck v. Grothman,* 248 Ill. 435, 94 NE 67. *But See* § 476. Certainly it seems unreasonable to refuse *X* the opportunity of trying a genuine issue of priority of lien in the foreclosure suit. It is obviously difficult for outsiders to make an intelligent bid at the foreclosure sale if this issue cannot be resolved in advance. At the very least this issue should be included as a matter of declaratory judgment.

Likewise, a problem exists where there is an adverse claim of title that casts a cloud on the validity of the mortgage.

EXAMPLE: *R* makes a mortgage to *E*. Thereafter the land is sold at a tax sale to *X*. If this sale is valid, in this particular state it extinguishes the mortgage. *E* files a foreclosure, names *R* and *X* as defendants and claims, in his foreclosure, that *X's* tax deed is void. In some states, on *X's* request, he will be dismissed from the foreclosure suit on the theory that this is not the proper way to decide the validity of the tax title. Osborne, *Mortgages* § 323. In most states today the law makes liberal provision for joining in one suit all types of issues affecting the property, including requests for *declaratory judgment,* that is judgments declaratory of the rights of the parties. The old rule requiring piece-meal litigation of various issues is on the way out. Occasionally, however, some court will hold a foreclosure suit void as to some matter that the plaintiff improperly attempted to inject into the suit. The court says that the foreclosure court *exceeded its jurisdiction. Rheinberger v. Security Life Ins. Co.,* 146 F2d 680. This is bad law that is quite likely to disappear.

§ 481. Jurisdiction of the land. The foreclosure court must also acquire jurisdiction of the land.

EXAMPLE: A mortgage covers Lot 12 in a subdivision. The stenographer transposes the digits, and throughout the foreclosure the property is described as Lot 21. The foreclosure is void.

EXAMPLE: In the above example the foreclosure complaint refers to a photostatic copy of the recorded mortgage attached to the complaint, and throughout the foreclosure the mortgage is referred to as the "mortgage aforesaid." The foreclosure is valid. The defect in description is cured by reference to the copy attached. *Arapian v. Rice,* 296 F 891. Likewise, if the foreclosure complaint simply describes the premises as being the same as those described in a recorded deed or mortgage, this will suffice. *Sepulveda v. Baugh,* 16 P 223 (Cal.); *Sherman v. Harno,* 66 N.H. 160, 28 A 18; *Lumpkin v. Silliman,* 15 SW 231, 79 Tex. Civ. App. 165. Of if the complaint describes the premises by reference to a recorded plat that also will suffice, *Read v. Bartlett,* 255 Ill. 76, 99 NE 345. A mistake in the description of the land in the judgment or decree of foreclosure is cured by a statement in the judgment that these are the same premises described in the complaint, if the complaint correctly describes the land. *McNair v. Johnson,* 95 S.C. 176, 78 SE 892; *Thompson v. Crocker,* 18 Colo. 328, 32 P 831.

§ **482. Multistate mortgages.** With respect to mortgages covering land in a number of states, the question will arise as to the propriety of foreclosing the entire mortgage in one foreclosure suit. This, of course, confronts the plaintiff with the age-old jurisdictional problem of suing in *State A* where the land lies partly in *State B.* In some decisions this jurisdiction has been found to exist primarily as a matter of sheer necessity, because railroads, for example, cannot be foreclosed piece-meal. *Woodbury v. Allegheny & K.R. Co.,* 72 F 371; *Craft v. Indiana R. Co.,* 166 Ill. 580, 46 NE 1132. Such a suit may be filed in the federal court. However, some courts have held that a foreclosure suit filed in *State A* is totally void with respect to land in *State B. Widmann v. Hammack,* 110 Wash. 77, 187 P 1091, 42 ALR 468; *Hammond v. Wall,* 51 Utah 464, 171 P 148; 2 Glenn, *Mortgages,* 791. At times the foreclosure in *State A* has been sustained on the theory that process served on the mortgagor in that state enables the court to order the mortgagor to execute a deed to the purchaser at the foreclosure sale. 42 ALR 470. This leaves something to be desired. Junior lienors who cannot be served with process in *State A* are not disposed of by this procedure.

There seems to be no acceptable alternative to filing separate foreclosures in each state where the land lies. The courts recognize primary foreclosure in *State A* with ancillary foreclosure in State B. 2 Glenn, *Mortgages,* 799, 806. Obviously, the mortgage should contain clauses providing for such foreclosures.

§ **483. Multi-county foreclosures.** The problem is simple where the mortgage covers land in a number of counties in the same state. The foreclosure is valid if filed in any county where the land lies. *First Conn. Small Bus. Inv. Co. v. Hoffman,* 265 A2d 508 (Conn.).

§ 484. Filing of the foreclosure suit. The suit is filed by the mortgagee in a regular mortgage (or his assignee if an assignment has been made), and, in the case of a deed of trust, by the trustee or note holder. This party is the *plaintiff*. The suit is initiated by a *complaint* or *petition,* which sets forth (1) the name of the plaintiff; (2) the names of all defendants; (3) a description of the mortgage; (4) a description of the land; (5) the defaults that occurred; and (6) the plaintiff's acceleration of maturity. It concludes with a *prayer for relief,* that is, a request for foreclosure of the mortgage, for a deficiency judgment for appointment of a receiver, and the like.

§ 485. Hearing and judgment or decree. After all parties have been served with process, each defendant has the right to interpose any defense he may have. The mortgagor may contend that there was no default, that usury was present, that the mortgage was barred by limitations or is a forgery, and so on. Junior lienors may question the mortgagee's priority, as for example, where the mortgage failed to state the principal amount of the debt. *See* § 111.

Most first mortgage foreclosures are *default cases.* There is no doubt of the validity or priority of the mortgage or that default occurred. Hence no one files any defense. In those rare instances where a defense is interposed, in the great majority of the cases it is without substance and is overruled by the court. The court then enters a judgment or decree. This is a court order establishing the validity and priority of the mortgage and directing a sale of the property. It specifies the time and place of sale and the manner of advertising. A court officer is designated to make the sale.

§ 486. Appraisal statutes. A number of states have appraisal statutes. These require an appraisal of the value of the mortgaged property before it is exposed for foreclosure sale, and then the statute goes on to specify what percentage of the appraised value the property must bring at the sale in order for the sale to be confirmed. However, it is the universal practice in all these states to include in the mortgage or deed of trust a provision waiving appraisal, and, except in one or two states, such provisions are held to be valid. Jones, *Mortgages* § 2074; 59 CJS *Mortgages* § 722.

EXCEPTION: Under Section 4 Title 46 Okla. Statute Annot. if appraisement is waived the foreclosure sale is postponed for six months after the date of the judgment of foreclosure. Any waiver of appraisement clause in this state should state that appraisement is waived only if the lender so elects.

§ 487. Upset price. Since the court has power to refuse to confirm a sale where it deems the price inadequate, it may exercise its judgment in advance and set a price, called an *upset price,* which marks the lowest bid that will be acceptable. Any valid bid must be at this price or higher. *Levy v. Broadway-Carmen Building Corp.,* 366 Ill. 279, 8 NE2d 671.

§ 488. Sale. Very often there is no competitive bidding at the foreclosure sale. This is especially true where there is a redemption period following the sale. The "court house crowd" of land speculators that does the bidding at public sales stays away from foreclosure sales where a redemption period exists because there is no opportunity for a quick turnover of the investment. A speculator does not want his hands tied for a year.

If a third party is the successful bidder he is not permitted to withdraw his bid. 1 Glenn, *Mortgages,* 566.

§ 489. Cash bids—holder of mortgage debt. If a person other than the mortgagee makes the highest bid at the foreclosure sale, he is required to produce cash, although depending on the local practice he may be permitted to pay a down payment at the time of the sale and the balance when the sale is confirmed by the court. However, where the mortgagee is the highest bidder, he is permitted to bid up to the amount of the mortgage debt without producing cash. *Helvering v. Midland Ins. Co.,* 300 US 216. The reason, of course, is that the officer making the sale would immediately hand any cash over to the mortgagee, so that it would be pointless to have cash handed back and forth in this fashion.

§ 490. Title acquired. If a judicial foreclosure by sale is properly conducted, the mortgagor and all persons claiming under him (grantees, heirs, junior mortgagees, etc.) are bound by the proceeding and all their rights and title are extinguished. The title acquired by the purchaser at the foreclosure sale *relates back* to the recording of the foreclosed mortgage so as to extinguish all rights of the mortgagor and persons later acquiring interests in the property. *Cooley v. Marx,* 17 Mich.App. 470, 169 NW2d 655.

Reversal of the decree of foreclosure on appeal does not divest the title of a third party who acquires title through foreclosure. 155 ALR 1252. However, if the mortgagee is the owner of the land when reversal takes place, his title is automatically divested. *Ure v. Ure,* 223 Ill. 454, 79 NE 153.

If an appeal is taken from the decree of foreclosure, and the appeal becomes a supersedeas under local law, this blocks the foreclosure sale until the appeal has been disposed of.

As to fatally defective foreclosures, *see* §§ 498, 499.

§ 491. Sale en masse. Where the mortgage covers several distinct parcels of land, a question may arise as to whether the land should be offered for sale en masse or in separate parcels, the land to be struck off to the bidder or bidders offering the highest bid, depending on which method produces the highest bid. This is a source of annoyance to the mortgagee. It is often difficult to determine what are "separate parcels." The fact that they were acquired at different times does not mean that they are truly separate parcels, if, for example, one building occupies all parcels. 61 ALR2d 574; 2 Wiltsie, *Mortgage Foreclosure* § 881. Also keeping one set of bidders tied down while the property is being offered to another set of bidders poses problems. For this reason the mortgage form must contain a clause stating that the land *may* be sold en masse, without offering it for sale in separate parcels. As a rule, an attack on a judicial sale on the ground that it was held en masse only, is, in effect, an attack on the ground of inadequacy of price. *Summerhill v. March,* 142 Cal. 554, 76 P 388. As such it has little prospect of success once the sale has been confirmed.

§ 492. **Marshalling of assets.** Under the rule of marshalling of assets, sometimes the foreclosure sale on a multi-parcel mortgage is required to be in inverse order of alienation. This is disposed of by a clause in the mortgage making the doctrine of marshalling of assets inapplicable in foreclosure of the mortgage. *See* § 233.

§ 493. **Confirmation of sale—setting aside sale.** Like any other judicial sale, a foreclosure sale is incomplete until confirmed. The highest bid is merely an irrevocable offer to purchase the property. Acceptance of the offer takes place when the court confirms the sale. *Straus v. Anderson,* 366 Ill. 426, 9 NE2d 248. Until that occurs, there is no "sale" in a legal sense but only in a popular sense. *Levy v. Broadway-Carmen Building Corp.,* 366 Ill. 279, 8 NE2d 671; *Continental Oil Co. v. McNair Realty Co.,* 137 Mont. 410, 353 P2d 100; Osborne, *Mortgages* § 327. It is therefore inaccurate to speak of "setting aside" an unconfirmed sale, though the phrase occurs often enough in the decisions Actually what the decisions are discussing at this point is the propriety of a refusal to confirm.

In the typical sale held in foreclosure of an institutional mortgage there is little likelihood that the court will refuse to confirm. The sale is typically for a substantial amount. The court is likely to turn deaf ears to any complaint by the mortgagor that the sale price is inadequate unless he can persuade someone to bring in a cashier's check in an amount exceeding the mortgagee's bid. If such a check is produced, the court may reopen the bidding in open court. *Continental Oil Co. v. McNair Realty Co.,* 137 Mont. 410, 353 P2d 100. However, the court has a relatively broad discretion in refusing to confirm a sale, and if it does so, and orders new bidding, as it has the power to do, a reviewing court is not likely to disturb this order. *Levy v. Broadway-Carmen Bldg. Corp., supra.* Technically, it must be admitted, however, there are three different points of view: (1) the mere fact that a higher bid of a sufficient amount has been received in court is sufficient reason to refuse confirmation and open the bidding; (2) the mere fact that a higher bid has been received is not sufficient reason for refusal to confirm the sale; (3) the entire matter of confirmation is left with the court to be confirmed or not confirmed according to its discretion. *Continental Oil Co. v. McNair Realty Co.,* 137 Mont. 410, 353 P2d 100.

Once the sale has been confirmed, it becomes more difficult to set it aside on appeal from the order of confirmation. Again, the trial court has broad discretion in confirming the sale, and if it does confirm, the reviewing court is reluctant to disturb its judgment. The review court will reverse only if there has been an obvious abuse of discretion. *Central Savings Bank v. First Cadco Corp.,* 181 NW2d 260 (Neb. 1970).

After the sale has been confirmed, deed issued, and the time for vacating the order of sale on motion (usually a short period of time that varies under local practice acts), any proceeding to set aside the sale is a *collateral attack. Barnard v. Michael,* 392 Ill. 130, 63 NE2d 858. The order of confirmation cures a multitude of defects. Failure to appraise the property as required by law, defects in the publication of notice of sale, departures from the judgment or decree ordering sale are all cured by confirmation. Freeman, *Void Judicial Sales* (3rd ed.) § 44; Van Fleet, *Collateral Attack* § 787. The order is conclusive on all matters that might have come before the court when confirmation was sought. *Speck v. Pullman Palace Car Co.,* 121 Ill. 33, 12 NE 213.

Where an appeal is taken from the order confirming sale to the mortgagee, and the property is sold by the mortgagee to a purchaser while the appeal is pending, an extremely technical question is presented. There are decisions to the effect that a reversal of the confirmation will extinguish the purchaser's title. This is on the theory that the doctrine of *supersedeas* is inapplicable to the confirmation of a judicial sale because it is a self-executing judgment. *E Town Shopping Center Inc. v. Lexington Finance Co.,* 436 SW2d 267 (Ky.); *Central Tr. Co. v. Hubinger,* 87 F 3. This rule is followed despite the existence of a statute that a purchaser's title shall not be lost by the reversal of a decree. *Dunfee v. Childs,* 45 W. Va. 155, 30 SE 102. Whether these decisions are sound under modern practice acts and rules is debatable. Certainly it is arguable that some such statutes extend the doctrine of supersedeas to all appealable orders.

§ 494. **Purchase or repurchase by mortgagor or his grantee.** When the mortgagor or his grantee allows the mortgage to go into default and foreclosure, and then such mortgagor or grantee bids the property in at the foreclosure sale or causes it to be bid in by a nominee, there are a number of court decisions dealing with the effect of such a purchase on junior liens.

EXAMPLE: *R* makes a mortgage to *E* in 1968, for $20,000. *R* makes a junior mortgage to *X* in 1969 for $10,000. *R* defaults in both mortgages, and E forecloses. *R* bids the property in for $20,000, the amount due *E*. The question is whether *X* is wiped out. If he is, this certainly is a cheap way of getting rid of junior liens.

In the above example, typically the junior mortgage will contain covenants of warranty. Virtually all mortgages do. Some courts seize upon this fact to hold that the mortgagor must not destroy the title he has covenanted to keep good. They hold that the mortgagor acquires title subject to the junior mortgage. This is an instance where foreclosure of a first mortgage does not wipe out the second. *Martin v. Raleigh State Bank,* 146 Miss. 1, So 448; 51 ALR 442.

Other courts are less technical. Where the mortgagor's grantee has not signed the mortgages, but merely acquired the property with the liens thereon, the court nevertheless holds that his purchase is nothing more than a payment of the first mortgage, leaving the junior liens in full force and effect. *Knicker-bocker v. McKindly Coal Co.,* 172 Ill. 535, 50 NE 330.

But if the first mortgagee bids in at his own sale, and later he sells the property to the mortgagor, the authorities divide sharply. Here the old mortgagor is a logical customer for the property. He may be living in it. If it is business property, he knows how to run it. If his purchase will revive the junior liens, he will refuse to buy it, and the first mortgagee is deprived of a customer. Nevertheless some courts say that if the mortgagor signed the junior mortgage, his acquisition of the title revives it. *Dixieland Realty Co. v. Wyson,* 272 N.C. 172, 158 SE2d 7. *Thompson v. Lawson,* 132 F2d 21; 51 ALR 445, 111 ALR 1285. Other courts hold that the junior mortgage is not revived. Sometimes this ruling is put upon the ground that the junior mortgage recited that it was subject to the first mortgage. This, the courts contend, pulls the teeth of the covenants of warranty. 51 ALR 446. More likely they are influenced by the fact that the junior mortgagee could have protected his investment by bidding at the foreclosure sale. The sympathies of the court for the second mortgagee are not as strong in this situation as in the situation where the mortgagor, directly or through a nominee, has bid at the first mortgage foreclosure sale.

References: 52 Harv. L. Rev. 1177; 5 Houston L. Rev. 22; 12 Minn. L. Rev. 34; 13 St. John's L. Rev. 182.

§ 495. **Tax sale—purchase by mortgagor or mortgagee at senior lien sale.** This rule is best explained by illustratons.

EXAMPLE: *R* mortgages to *E. R* permits the real estate taxes to become delinquent and buys in at the tax sale. Under local law tax sales wipe out all mortgages. *E's* mortgage is not wiped out. *R* cannot get rid of his mortgage burden in this fashion. The same is true if *R* were to default in payments on a mortgage senior to *E's* mortgage.

EXAMPLE: *R* mortgages to *E. E* cannot purchase at a tax sale in order to cut out *R.* Courts feel that to permit this would permit a mortgagee to extinguish the mortgagor's equitable right of redemption.

§ 496. **Foreclosure sale as an incident triggering a pre-emption option.** There is a type of option commonly called a *pre-emption option* or *right of first refusal.*

EXAMPLE: *R* leases land to *E* for 15 years. The lease provides that if, during the term of the lease, *R* decides to sell the property, *E* will have the *first refusal* of the property, that is, the right to buy the property at the price *R* has decided upon as the sale price. The lease is recorded and if R does sell or convey the land to purchase, E will have the right to buy the land from the purchaser at the price he paid for the property.

The few decided cases are in conflict as to the effect of a foreclosure sale.

EXAMPLE: In the example above given, R later mortgages the land to E-2, E-2 forecloses his mortgage and bids the property in at the foreclosure sale for $50,000.00, the amount of the mortgage. Some courts will allow E to buy the property from E-2 for $50,000.00. Other courts will not permit this. 17 ALR 3rd 963.

§ 497. **Defective foreclosures.** Various defects in judicial foreclosures, of greater or less importance, have been cured by legislation adopted in a number of states. Basye, *Clearing Land Titles* § 354. And various remedies have been evolved in case law where a foreclosure has been defective. 73 ALR 612.

§ 498. **Fatal defects in proceedings—rights of highest bidder.** The law is somewhat unclear as to the rights of the highest bidder where, before he makes full payment, a fatal defect in the foreclosure is discovered. Typically in these cases, an outside bidder (not the mortgagor) makes a down payment to the officer who holds the sale. The balance is to be paid when the court confirms the sale. In the interval the bidder orders a title examination. This reveals some fatal error, such as a total misdescription of the property. By the more modern cases the courts will relieve the purchaser from making good on his bid. 50 CJS *Judicial Sales* § 49; 73 ALR 620.

§ 499. **Void foreclosure—attack.** If a foreclosure is void for some reason, the mortgagor will not be allowed to set it aside by court decree unless he offers to pay the mortgage debt. *Satterfield v. Peterson,* 173 Neb. 618, 114 NW2d 376.

§ 500. **Deficiency judgments.** The practice differs from state to state on the matter of obtaining a personal judgment against the mortgagor. The mortgagor, having signed a promissory note, is personally liable to the mortgagee for the debt.

In some states the mortgagee obtains a personal judgment for this debt in the judgment of foreclosure itself. When the foreclosure sale is held, this operates as a *pro tanto* satisfaction of this judgment.

In other states no personal judgment is entered until the foreclosure sale reveals the amount by which such sale failed to satisfy the mortgage debt. A *deficiency judgment* or *deficiency* decree is entered for this amount. Commonly it is included in the order confirming the sale.

A number of states have legislation forbidding the taking of deficiency judgments or decrees on purchase money mortgages. The philosophy here is that the seller sells at a price that is presumably fair to the purchaser and takes back a mortgage for a part of the purchase price that the buyer ought to be able to pay. If a foreclosure ensues and there is a deficiency, it can be inferred that the seller may have, to some extent, over-reached the buyer-mortgagor. These statutes have been interpreted to refer to purchase money mortgages running to the seller of property. They do not refer to purchase money mortgages given by third parties, such as savings and loan associations, banks, or insurance companies. *Childers v. Parkers Inc.,* 274 N.C. 256, 162 SE2d 481.

Other legislation exists limiting or abolishing deficiency decrees. 48 Calif. L. Rev. 705. The significance of such legislation is limited. Statistical surveys indicate that deficiency decrees are seldom enforced, especially in the case of home loans. The public relations problem to the institutional lender is obvious. To garnishee the wages of a man who has just lost his home by foreclosure is definitely not the way to win friends and influence people.

§ 501. Effect of bid at foreclosure sale as reducing insurance coverage. Traditionally the foreclosure sale is viewed as an extinguishment of the mortgage debt to the extent of the amount of the sale price. This poses a problem to the mortgagee with respect to his fire insurance coverage.

EXAMPLE: *R* makes a mortage to *E* in 1967 in the sum of $100,000. Default occurs and *E* brings foreclosure in 1968. In 1969 extensive fire damage occurs. In 1970 *E* bids in the property for $90,000. He now seeks payment of the insurance money and is met with the contention that his maximum recovery is $100,000 minus $90,000 or $10,000. His mortgage has been satisfied to the extent of the bid at the foreclosure sale. *Northwestern Ins. Co. v. Mildenberger,* 359 SW2d 380 (citing several decisions from other states). The same result was reached where the foreclosure was by exercise of a power of sale. *Rosenbaum v. Funcanno,* 308 F2d 680. Not all courts would hold this way. *Malvaney v. Yager,* 101 Mont. 331, 54 P2d 135 (holding the mortgagee's rights to insurance are fixed the moment the loss occurs). But the danger is great. Certainly the mortgagee should arrange to procure new insurance before he bids at the foreclosure sale, insuring his interest as purchaser at the foreclosure sale.

ADDITIONAL REFERENCES ON FORECLOSURES BY VARIOUS METHODS: 28 Dicta 437 (Colo.); 2 Conn. L. Rev. 413; 15 U. Fla. L. Rev. 185; 32 Tal. L. Rev. 555 (La.); 20 U. Miami L. Rev. 18 (Md.); 1950 Wash. L.Q. 423 (Mo.); 4 Mo. L. Rev. 186; 64 N.J.L.J. 141; 44 N.C. L. Rev. 964; 8 Utah L. Rev. 134; 34 Wis. B. Bul. 63; 3 A.B.A. Real Property, Prob. & Tr. J. 416 (state-by-state); Malcolm Sherman, *Mortgage and Real Estate Investment Guide, passim.*

ADDITIONAL REFERENCES: 3 Powell, *Real Property,* § 473 (discussing various state statutes relating to deficiency judgments or decrees).

43

Foreclosure by Exercise
of Power of Sale

§ 502. **In general.** In a number of states non-judicial foreclosure by exercise of a power of sale is permitted. This type of foreclosure rests upon a power of sale clause included in the mortgage instrument. This clause provides for a non-judicial sale conducted after advertising notice of sale as specified in the mortgage. Hence, it is sometimes referred to as *foreclosure by advertisement*. Usually the mortgage document is a deed of trust. This eliminates, at the outset, any difficulty created by the mortgagee bidding at his own foreclosure sale, since the trustee is a disinterested third party, acting for both borrower and lender. Since this is the case, this chapter will discuss the problem in terms of the deed of trust; however, the principles are equally applicable to a mortgage containing a power of sale, except for the matter of conflict of interest above referred to.

§ 503. **Judicial foreclosure—availability.** The existence of power of sale foreclosure in a given state does not preclude resort to judicial foreclosure. 1 Glenn, *Mortgages,* 125, 605, 634. There will be instances where priority of lien is a hotly contested issue and litigation is inevitable. In these cases the mortgagee is well advised to go into equity in the first place and seek judicial foreclosure.

In a number of states the choice is spelled out by statute.

EXAMPLE: In Montana foreclosures involving tracts under three acres in area can be foreclosed by power of sale. This is a substantial advantage, for such foreclosures require only 120 days, on the average, as against 18 months for a judicial foreclosure. *Great Falls Nat. Bank v. McCormick,* 448 P2d 991. In California the mortgagee surrenders his right to deficiency judgment if he resorts to the speedy, effective power of sale foreclosure, but the power of sale foreclosure is free of redemption rights, whereas the judicial foreclosure is subject to redemption. Obviously, judicial foreclosures are virtually non-existent in California. **See** *also* § 539.

§ 504. Comparison with judicial foreclosure. Obviously since the judicial foreclosure involves a court proceeding it will involve more time and expense than a power of sale foreclosure. On the other hand, a judicial foreclosure sale is confirmed by a court. The mortgagor or any other person (a junior mortgagee, for example) must, if he is dissatisfied, appeal from the court's orders. If he fails to do so, the sale stands and never can be questioned thereafter. Osborne, *Mortgages,* 1014.

A power of sale foreclosure on the other hand, is subject to attack on various grounds. It has been said that courts watch power of sale foreclosures with a jealous eye. *Pugh v. Richmond,* 58 Tenn.App. 62, 425 SW2d 789. Realistically, however, this possibility of attack is no more than a mere possibility in most instances. Institutional lenders foreclose only when a genuine default exists. They keep accurate records showing the amount due. Moreover, if a title company is willing to insure the title, or an institutional lender who has purchased at the sale is willing to give a later purchaser a general warranty deed, the risks are minimal.

§ 505. Power of sale clause. At the heart of the deed of trust in states where such foreclosure is permitted is the clause conferring the power of sale. It sets forth the events of default that give rise to the power of sale; specifies the time and manner of publishing notice of sale; the place where sale is to be made; the manner of holding sale; and when deed is to be given. Increasingly, in recent times, the power of sale clause sets forth the recitals that are to be contained in the trustee's deed and states that such recitals are to be conclusively deemed true in favor of the purchaser; for example, recitals that a default exists, that notice was properly published, and so on.

§ 506. Bankruptcy. If the landowner goes into bankruptcy before foreclosure by power of sale is initiated, the foreclosure cannot proceed. This is for the reason that the bankruptcy court acquires exclusive jurisdiction over all assets of the bankrupt to the exclusion of all others. 8A CJS. 377, 386, 387, 391. If the bankruptcy court feels that there is little or no equity in the property over and above the mortgage debt, it will grant permission to proceed with the foreclosure. *See* Chapter 34.

A serious question arises as to the validity of the foreclosure if, despite the bankruptcy, the trustee in the trust deed proceeds with foreclosure. There is some authority for the view that such a sale, if it takes place before the bankrupt has been adjudged a bankrupt, is not void. *Robinson v. Kay,* 7 F2d 576. However, knowledgeable lawyers tend to view such proceedings with suspicion. It is doubtful that many lawyers would regard such a title as marketable. Even if publication of notice for foreclosure has begun before the filing of the petition in bankruptcy, there is authority for the view that the power of sale foreclosure must stop once the bankruptcy suit has begun. *In re Bowden,* 274 FSupp. 729; Collier, *Bankruptcy* § 2.32. *See* § 398.

The language of the corporate reorganization article (Title 11 U.S.C.A. § 548) and the real property arrangements article (Title 11 U.S.C.A. § 906) seems broad enough to bring a pending power of sale foreclosure to a halt. *See* Chapter 34.

§ 507. Foreign corporation "doing business" laws. The power of sale foreclosure enjoys a conspicuous benefit as against the judicial foreclosure in the area of "doing business" legislation. A foreign corporation that has been doing business without a license is, as has been stated (*see* § 77) subject to a defense when it files a foreclosure suit. But statutes denying an unlicensed foreign corporation access to the courts are inapplicable to a power of sale foreclosure, *Flakne v. Metrop. Life Ins. Co.,* 198 Minn. 465, 270 NW 566.

§ 508. Notice of default. In a number of states, the law requres that the trustee file a notice of default in the recorder's office. Thereafter a grace period or interval must elapse, during which the mortgagor may pay the debt. If the debt is not paid, the trustee may proceed to advertise his sale. Nev. Rev. Stats. § 107.080.

In some states notice of default must be mailed to the mortgagor. D.C. Code, P.L. 90–566.

§ 509. Notice of sale. Because sales under a power are liable to abuse, they are jealously watched by the courts and will be set aside on proof of unfair conduct, particularly with respect to the notice of sale. *Pugh v. Richmond,* 58 Tenn. App. 62, 425 SW2d 789. If the deed of trust foreclosed is a junior lien, the notice of sale must indicate that there is a senior mortgage. Otherwise bidders cannot bid intelligently. The office of this notice is to enable outside bidders to make an informed bid.

Where a published notice of sale under a power of sale substantially overstates the amount of the mortgage debt, obviously this has a tendency to chill the bidding, keeping in mind the fact that the holder of the mortgage debt may bid up to the amount of that debt without producing any cash. For this reason, the courts will, on suit by the mortgagor, either restrain the holding of the foreclosure sale or will set the sale aside. *Semlek v. National Bank of Alaska,* (Alaska) 458 P2d 1003; 91 ALR 791.

If the notice describes property other than that being foreclosed upon, the foreclosure will be set aside. Proper bidding at the foreclosure sale requires proper notice. *V.A. v. Ballock,* 180 So2d 610; 59 CJS *Mortgages* § 565e.

Statutes relating to notice of default and notice of sale should be consulted.

In some of the western states (California and Utah, for example) laws exist under which the mortgagor or any junior lienor may serve on the mortgagee or record in the Recorder's Office a request that he be given personal notice of any foreclosure sale, in which case this must be done. But in the absence of such a statute there is no necessity that the mortgagor be given personal notice of the foreclosure sale. *Hodges v. Wellons,* 175 SE2d 690.

§ **510. Payment before sale.** The fact that foreclosure by exercise of a power of sale has been initiated does not prevent payment of the debt by the mortgagor. Such payment may be made at any time up to the actual sale. *Crowley v. Adams,* 226 Mass. 582, 116 NE 241. This is simply an equitable redemption from the mortgage debt. 1 Glenn, *Mortgages,* 665.

§ **511. Defects in foreclosure.** As has been suggested in the opening paragraph of this chapter, the power of sale foreclosure is more vulnerable to attack than the judicial foreclosure. In the judicial foreclosure, the mortgagor and all other persons interested in the property are served with process and are given an opportunity to raise any defense to the foreclosure. The defense raised might be that the mortgagee never paid out any money on the mortgage, that the mortgage debt was paid in full, that the mortgage is void because of usury, or any one of dozens of other defenses. If the court enters a judgment of foreclosure, this means that the court has ruled against all defenses that were raised or that could have been raised. A power of sale foreclosure involves no court proceeding. Hence, even after a foreclosure deed has issued, doubts may persist as to the validity of the foreclosure. In Maryland, however, these doubts are removed by court confirmation of the sale. 1 Glenn, *Mortgages,* 672.

§ **512. Defects in foreclosure—absence of default or payment of mortgage debt before sale.** If, in fact, no default exists or if the mortgage debt has been paid before sale, this invalidates the sale and it will be set aside. *Kyles v. Southern Holding Corp.,* (NC) 168 SE2d 502; *Ladell & Co. v. Carson,* 122 Ala. 518; 26 So 133; *Jackson v. Jackson,* 248 Mo. 680, 154 SW 759.

§ **513. Defects in foreclosure—usurious deed of trust.** In those states where the presence of usury totally invalidates the mortgage, the foreclosure sale will be set aside if, indeed, usury was present. *Wacasie v. Radford,* 142 Ga. 113, 82 SE 442; *Shear Co. v. Hall,* 235 SW 195 (Tex.Civ.App.). *But see* § 514.

§ **514. Defects in foreclosure—miscellaneous defects.** The grounds for setting aside a sale under a power include those that arise from the fiduciary position that the trustee assumes in conducting the sale. A sale may be set aside for fraud or breach of trust, for instance, where the trustee made an unauthorized purchase or acted in a manner that tended to discourage bidding. Gross inadequacy of the price realized has been held to justify setting aside the sale. 8 ALR 1007. But inadequacy of price alone, unless so gross as to raise an inference of fraud or imposition, has been considered insufficient to set aside an otherwise properly conducted sale. 21 U.Fla.L.Rev. 398. Deviations from the statute may be grounds for setting aside the sale.

§ 515. Defects in foreclosure—protective provisions, statutes and decisions.
There are a number of protective rules and devices that insulate a power of sale
foreclosure from attack.

While the original purchaser at the sale may have his title attacked *because
the notice of sale was improper or the sale was made in a manner and at a time
not in accordance with the deed of trust,* a subsequent purchaser from the sale
purchaser is protected against any attack on these grounds. *Gunnel v. Cockerill,*
79 Ill. 79; 59 CJS *Mortgages* § 594(g). Indeed by court decision or statute in
some states any innocent third party who purchases is protected against defects
in the sale procedure. And various statutes have been enacted that in one way
or another bolster the purchaser's title. Basye, *Clearing Land Titles* § 354.

If ownership has passed to an innocent third party, the sale will not be set
aside on the ground of usury. *Tyler v. Mass. Mut. Life Ins. Co.,* 108 Ill. 58;
McCandles v. Inland Acid Co., 112 Ga. 291, 37 SE 419; *Mumford v. Am.Life.
Ins. Co.,* 4 N.Y. 463; *Elliott v. Wood,* 53 Barb. (N.Y.) 285; *Edgell v. Hamm,*
93 F 759.

Moreover recitals in the trustee's deed that all requirements of the deed of
trust were complied with put the *burden of proof* on any one attacking the sale
even where the lender still owns the property he purchased at the sale. 32A CJS
Evidence § 767. The deed of trust may provide that recitals in the trustee's deed
shall be *conclusive* in favor of the purchaser at the sale, and such provisions
are valid and effective. 32A CJS *Evidence* § 767. There are statutes in some
states to this effect. Basye, *Clearing Land Titles* § 43.

§ 516. Injunction restraining foreclosure. Where a controversy exists so
that the holding of a power of sale foreclosure would be prejudicial to the owner
or a person having an interest in the land, a court may issue an injunction halting the sale until the controversy can be resolved.

EXAMPLE: A junior mortgagee disputed the amount due on the first mortgage that was being foreclosed. This controversy made it difficult for him to make
an intelligent bid in protection of his mortgage. Obviously, if there is $100,000 due
on the first mortgage, the first mortgagee can bid that amount without producing
cash, but if the amount due is only $50,000 this reduces to that amount the first
mortgagee's cash-free bid. The court halted the sale pending a resolution of the
controversy. *Carolina Cooling Inc. v. Blackburn,* 267 N.C. 155, 148 SE2d 18.

Sales under a power have been restrained when the mortgage was without
consideration, when the mortgagee failed to properly credit payments on the
notes, when the mortgage was obtained by fraud, or when the notes and mortgage were forged, when the mortgage had been paid in full or a valid continuing
tender of the amount due was made, or when the purpose of the sale was to
intimidate the plaintiff. Neither the fact that an impending sale is harsh or

improvident nor that the mortgagee's motives are questionable will be sufficient grounds for injunctive relief where the mortgagee is clearly acting within the authority given by the power and not acting fraudulently or illegally. 21 U.Fla. L.Rev. 398.

§ 517. Foreclosure by mortgagee—public trustee—sheriff. Prudent lenders tend to avoid the power of sale mortgage. It inevitably places the mortgagee in a conflict of interest situation. The deed of trust is preferable. The trustee can be a disinterested person who holds the sale in a disinterested way. Where a power of sale mortgage is used, the mortgagee must exercise the same good faith and diligence toward the mortgagor that would be expected of a trustee holding the sale. *Silver v. First Nat. Bank.,* 108 N.H. 390, 236 A2d 493.

Where instead of the deed of trust the mortgage form is used in connection with a power of sale, it is best to include a clause giving the mortgagee the right to call upon the sheriff of the county to make the sale. This eliminates the conflict of interest where a mortgagee is holding the sale and also bidding for the property.

In Colorado all sales are held by the Public Trustee, and in Minnesota by the sheriff.

§ 518. Limitations. There is an apparent conflict in the cases as to the effect of limitation laws on foreclosure by exercise of a power of sale. If the law seems to bar *suits to foreclose,* it may not prevent foreclosure by exercise of a power of sale, since such a foreclosure is not a *suit* to foreclose. *National Tailoring Co. v. Scott,* 65 Wyo. 64, 196 P2d 387. But if the limitations law *bars* the mortgage, it also *bars* foreclosure thereof. *Davis v. Savage,* 50 N.M. 30, 168 P2d 851.

§ 519. Effect of foreclosure. Where a power of sale foreclosure is properly conducted, the effect is the same as a foreclosure by judicial proceedings. The mortgagor and all persons claiming through or under him are bound by the foreclosure and all their rights are vested in the purchaser at the sale. *Smith v. Olney Federal S & L Assn.,* 415 SW2d 515 (Tex.Civ.App.).

§ 520. Title acquired. As in the case of judicial foreclosures, title acquired at the sale relates back to the date the deed of trust was recorded, cutting off all junior liens and subsequent ownership interests. *Dixieland Realty Co. v. Wysor,* 272 N.C. 172, 158 S.E. 2d7.

§ 521. Proceeds of sale. If the proceeds of sale exceed the mortgage debt and court costs, the balance is available to retire junior liens, the final surplus going to the landowner. *Nomellini Const. Co. v. Modesto S. & L. Assn.,* 79 Cal. Rptr. 717.

§ 522. Procedure in power of sale foreclosures. When a power of sale foreclosure is to take place, certain procedures should be followed.

1. The trustee must procure the deed of trust or a certified copy thereof. This is the charter of his powers and duties, as to notices to be given, manner of holding sale, etc., and should be carefully studied by his attorney.

2. The promissory note should also be procured. This helps to establish, for one thing, the ownership of the note by the party demanding foreclosure.

3. If there has been an assignment of the deed of trust and note, this should also be lodged with the trustee.

4. The evidence of title should be furnished the trustee. This will be helpful, for example, in establishing whether the deed of trust is a first lien on the land. It is necessary to know this in order to make an intelligent and accurate advertisement of the sale. For example, sale under a junior mortgage normally requires that the notice of sale so state.

5. The holder of the note will have executed a declaration of acceleration of maturity, setting forth precisely the defaults that have occurred. This should also be lodged with the trustee, together with the noteholder's demand that foreclosure proceed. The trustee routinely obtains the noteholder's affidavit that the declaration accurately sets forth the defaults.

6. If the deed of trust or a statute sets forth pre-conditions to foreclosure, *e.g.,* serving of notice on the landowner or junior lienors, recording of notice of default, these preconditions should be met.

7. If after contacting the landowner, the trustee is in doubt, because of controversy between the landowner and noteholder as to the actual existence of defaults, the trustee must at this time determine whether he will proceed with foreclosure (relying, in all likelihood, on the noteholder's agreement to indemnify the trustee against personal liability) or to resign, pursuant to the provisions of the deed of trust. If the deed of trust lacks provision for resignation, the trustee may refuse to accept the trust if he has up to this point given no indication of his acceptance of the trust. The trustee should never forget that he represents both landowner and noteholder, and is trustee for both. If the noteholder is an institution and the trustee is an employee of the institution, it is best for him to resign the moment it becomes evident that foreclosure will be necessary. An impartial trustee can then be appointed by the noteholder under the provisions of the deed of trust permitting this to be done.

8. The trustee should be furnished an affidavit that neither the landowner nor any person interested in the land is in military service, for in such case, power of sale foreclosure is forbidden.

9. The evidence of title should be brought to date. For example, it may show a subordination of the deed of trust, in which case the sale must be advertised as a sale on a junior mortgage. Or it may show a release of the deed of trust in which case, obviously, no sale can be held. Or it may reveal an assignment of the debt to one other than the person demanding that foreclosure proceed. Or it may show a pending bankruptcy of the landowner,

making foreclosure impossible without permission of the bankruptcy court. *See* Chapter 34. Or it may show a federal lien. *See* § 427.

10. Publication of notice of sale should be in strict accordance with the deed of trust and statute. The publisher furnishes a certificate of publication, which remains in the trustee's permanent files. If the deed of trust or a statute also requires posting of notice of sale in several public places, it is customary for the newspaper publisher to attend to this also, and to furnish the trustee a certificate of the posting of notices.

11. Immediately prior to sale, the noteholder should verify that defaults have not been cured and that the landowner is not then in military service. The title search should be brought to date to see that conditions remain unchanged.

12. The sale should be held in strict accordance with the notice, at the time and place fixed in the notice. The trustee should read the notice, including the legal description, and call for bids. If the deed of trust gives the trustee discretion to hold the sale en masse, this may be done, if it cannot prejudice the landowner unduly. It is best, if the deed of trust covers several tracts, to advertise and hold the sale both en masse and in separate parcels, final acceptance of bid to be that bid or bids which produce the highest price, keeping in mind that the trustee is acting both for the landowner and noteholder. The trustee announces the terms of the sale. Usually the deed of trust permits the trustee to adjourn the sale, and he may wish to do so, if controversies arise at the sale; for example, if the landowner announces that defaults have been cured or do not exist or that he has tendered all the balance due. In same areas it is customary for the trustee to have available a current title search, which bidders may examine, but if this is done the trustee customarily states that the sale implies no warranties of title.

13. Normally no problems arise. The noteholder bids up to the amount of his debt, the trustee declares him the highest bidder, and declares the bidding closed.

14. The trustee's deed is then executed and recorded. The deed of trust must be examined at this time to see what recitals it permits. It may permit the trustee's deed to recite that at the date of the sale the deed of trust was a valid and subsisting lien for the amount recited in the recorded notice of default and that such recital is conclusive evidence of such fact in favor of all persons except the noteholder. This is a valuable recital and should be included. The noteholder may, in fact, prepare the trustee's deed, including the recitals, and give the trustee an original and copy, the copy being accompanied by an affidavit as to the truth of these particular recitals. The trustee's deed also recites compliance with all pre-conditions, such as service of notice on parties entitled thereto, recording of notice of default, publication and posting of notice of sale, the name of highest bidder and amount bid, etc. No warranties of title are included.

ADDITIONAL REFERENCES: Glenn, *Mortgages,* §§ 98–112; Osborne, *Mortgages,* §§ 337–345; 3 Powell, *Real Property,* § 468; Wiltsie, *Mortgage Foreclosures,* §§ 837–917; 3 A.B.A. Real Prop., Prob. & Tr. J 413 (1968); Malcolm Sherman, *Mortgage and Real Estate Investment Guide, passim. See* 24 S.W.L.J. 815 (power of sale foreclosure and the federal lien). *See also* references to local articles end of Chapter 42.

44

Foreclosure by Other Methods

§ 523. **Strict foreclosure.** This method of foreclosure, the earliest method of foreclosure as a matter of history, has been discussed briefly. *See* § 5. It is used in Vermont and Connecticut. It is also used in other states, under special circumstances. Its virtue lies in the fact that it eliminates the expense of a judicial sale and also eliminates the statutory redemption period. A study of the restrictive decisions in this area indicates that virtually all of them are of ancient vintage. Resourceful attorneys, impressed by this fact, have taken to using strict foreclosures again in modern times in judicial foreclosure states. The philosophy is simple. Nearly all mortgage foreclosures are default cases. The foreclosing attorney feels he has nothing to lose by asking for strict foreclosure. If all parties default, the judge will usually enter the requested decree, since judges assume that if the defendants do not choose to make a defense, it is not the judge's function to seek or contrive one. If, on the other hand, some party objects to strict foreclosure, the court will, at the least, order a sale, and nothing has been lost. The key to this situation is the concept of jurisdiction and collateral attack. The court always has power to enter a decree of strict foreclosure, in proper circumstances, and any error it makes in deciding that strict foreclosure is appropriate, does not invalidate the decree of strict foreclosure. To be sure, an erroneous decree is subject to appeal to a higher court, but where all parties have defaulted this risk is non-existent.

It has been said that strict foreclosure rests upon the concept of legal title in the mortgagee, with the decree merely cutting off the equitable right of redemption. Therefore, it has been argued, this remedy is unavailable in lien theory states. It fails to vest title, it is said, in the mortgagee. Osborne, *Mort-*

gages § 312. To meet this objection, foreclosing attorneys add to the foreclosure complaint a prayer that the court adjudge and confirm title in the mortgagee. The first decree entered gives the defendants a stated period, often as little as 30 days, to redeem, and provides that if no one comes forward with redemption money, the court will confirm title in the mortgagee. When the specified time has expired, the mortgagee obtains a second decree confirming title in his name. To be sure, this decree may be erroneous, but it is certainly not void. All these suits are brought in equity courts, and all such courts have power to establish and confirm title. Certainly this type of proceeding has been used in thousands of cases, and the only risk run is that a sale will be forced, if some defendant chooses to object.

A further objection that has been raised is that strict foreclosure is unavailable if the mortgage takes the form of a deed of trust, since in these cases, legal title, or some form thereof, reposes in the trustee. This has proved no obstacle to the resourceful mortgagee's attorney, for he makes the trustee party to the foreclosure and inserts in the court decree a provision ordering the trustee to convey title to the holder of the mortgage debt.

A genuine problem exists in states where strict foreclosure is forbidden by statute, or where the statute lists permitted methods of foreclosure, omitting strict foreclosure. Here resort to strict foreclosure is probably not technically fatal to title, since the statute is technically a matter of defense that must be pleaded, and, if not pleaded, is waived. Thousands of lawsuits are open daily to technical defenses based on statutes, but defendants fail to raise the defense and judgment is entered against them. It is unthinkable that such judgments could be considered void. Nevertheless, cautious attorneys might reject as unmarketable a title coming through a strict foreclosure forbidden by state law.

At all events where there has been a defective foreclosure, as where some necessary party has been omitted from a judicial forclosure, virtually all states permit the purchaser in the foreclosure sale to file a strict foreclosure to cut out the omitted party. *Capabianco v. Bork,* 108 N.J.S. 356, 261 A2d 393; 23 Minn. L.Rev. 388; 25 Va. L.Rev. 947.

§ **524. Other methods.** Other methods of foreclosure exist, notably in the New England States. Osborne, *Mortgages* § 314 *et seq.* For example, foreclosure by entry exists in Massachusetts, Maine, New Hampshire and Rhode Island. 1 Glenn, *Mortgages,* 430. In Pennsylvania foreclosure by *scire facias* is common.

45

Equitable Redemption

§ 525. **In general.** Historically, equitable redemption evolved in England as a means of enabling the mortgagor to obtain return of mortgaged land he had forfeited to the mortgagee because of his failure to pay the mortgage debt on the "law day." *See* § 3. It still exists today as a means of compelling a reluctant mortgagee to accept payment of the mortgage debt. Mere default in the mortgage payments cannot be employed as a device to terminate the mortgagor's rights and no clause in the mortgage or other documentary subterfuge will be successful in accomplishing this result. Foreclosure is necessary to terminate the mortgagor's equitable right of redemption, regardless of the mode of foreclosure locally employed.

In point of fact, however, institutional lenders have little desire to snatch mortgaged land from mortgagors. Indeed, they go to great pains to try to work out the problems of a defaulting mortgagor. Payments are reduced and extensions are granted. Institutional lenders want their loans repaid. Foreclosure, for them, is a last resort Hence equitable redemption is no longer a matter of great importance.

§ 526. **Distinction between equitable redemption and statutory redemption.** The distinction between equitable redemption and statutory redemption has been discussed elsewhere. *See* § 7.

§ 527. **Who may redeem.** In general, any person having any interest in the land, whether as owner, part owner, lienor, lessee, and so on, has the right to redeem. Where a necessary party has been omitted from a judicial foreclosure, his right to redeem continues until it has been barred by laches or by the expiration of some period fixed by state law. Where equitable redemption is encoun-

331

tered in modern times, it is usually in this situation. Note that an omitted party seeking to make redemption must pay the entire mortgage debt, not the amount of the foreclosure sale. 1 Glenn, *Mortgages,* 526.

§ 528. Technical aspects of equitable redemption. The procedure for making equitable redemption is simple enough. The traditional bill in equity to redeem is the proper proceeding. However, since this type of proceeding is usually instituted by a party who has been omitted from a judicial foreclosure, he will usually find the mortgagee who foreclosed in possession of the premises. Hence a rather complicated accounting problem is often presented, for the mortgagee will be treated as a *mortgagee in possession.* Osborne, *Mortgages* § 164.

§ 529. Clogging the equity. At times a mortgagee may drive a hard bargain. He may extract something in addition to repayment of debt from the mortgagor.

EXAMPLE: As an inducement to extend payment of the mortgage debt the mortgagee demanded and received an oil and gas lease from the mortgager. When the mortgage debt was finally paid the mortgagor demanded a release of the oil and gas lease. The mortgagee refused. The court ordered the mortgagee to release the lease. This is a "collateral advantage" that the mortgagee is not entitled to. *Coursey v. Fairchild,* (Okla.) 436 P2d 35.

Other examples of illegal clogs on the equity are cases where the mortgagee demands an option to purchase at the time the mortgage is made. 1 Glenn *Mortgages,* 279. Or where the mortgage placed a time limit on the exercise of the right of redemption. Osborne, *Mortgages* § 97.

§ 530. Time allowed for redemption. All states impose some time limit on the exercise of the equitable right of redemption. Ordinarily this comes into play when the mortgagee takes possession in his role as a mortgagee in possession and collects the rents without making any accounting to the mortgagor. In time, the law will bar the mortgagor's equitable right of redemption. *Clark v. Hannafeldt,* 79 Neb. 566, 113 NW 135.

Of course, the equitable right of redemption may be barred in a time shorter than that specified by statute.

EXAMPLE: *E* forecloses a mortgage made by *R* but fails to bring in *X*, a junior mortgage, as a party defendant. *E* bids in at the sale and takes possession. Land values are rising sharply. The court may hold that any appreciable delay by *X* in redeeming will preclude redemption. He is barred by laches. He cannot stand aside, speculating that he will redeem if values go up, but not if they go down. He must act with reasonable promptness. *Walker v. Warner,* 179 Ill. 16, 53 NE 594.

In general any party wishing to redeem may come in and offer to do so at any time before the first bid is made at the foreclosure sale. *People v. Cant,* 260 Ill. 497, 103 NE 232.

46

Statutory Redemption

§ 531. In general. The equitable right of redemption is cut off and terminated by a sale under a foreclosure judgment or decree, since that was the very object of the foreclosure suit. After the foreclosure sale, in many states, an entirely different right arises, called the statutory right of redemption. *Dolan v. Midland Blast Furnace Co.*, 126 Ia. 254, 100 NW 45. Laws providing for statutory redemption give the mortgagor and other persons interested in the land or certain classes of such persons the right to redeem from the sale within a certain period after the sale, varying in different states from two months to two years, but usually one year.

Most statutory redemption laws were passed in a time when America was predominantly agricultural. Most mortgagors were farmers. When the weatner was bad, crops failed, and foreclosures followed. It seemed logical to suppose that next year might bring better weather and good crops. Hence laws created the statutory redemption period, usually one year, and usually with the law so worded that the mortgagor had the right to possession during that year.

At the expiration of the redemption period, if redemption has not been made, the purchaser at the foreclosure sale receives a deed from the officer who made the sale. This deed gives the purchaser such title as the mortgagor had when he made the mortgage. Any rights acquired by any persons after the making and recording of the mortgage are extinguished by the foreclosure.

§ 532. Redemption periods. In *U.S. v. Stadium Apartments Inc.*, 425 F2d 358 (1970), the court attempts to list the various statutory redemption periods. In point of fact, however, it is next to impossible to make any succinct statement concerning state redemption laws. Many of them are quite complex. Owners may have redemption periods different from those given lien creditors. Farmers may have redemption periods different from those given non-farm debtors.

EXAMPLE: In Washington the mortgage must state that the property is "not used principally for agriculture or farming purposes," in default of which the mortgage must be foreclosed judicially and the redemption period is prolonged four months.

In general, one might say that the tendency is to shorten redemption periods. As to business loans (corporate loans, for example), some states have already moved toward substantial elimination or reduction of the redemption period. Businessmen do not need this sort of protection. As the competition for available loan funds continues, one may expect further efforts to bring loan funds into the state by shortening redemption periods and simplifying them.

§ 533. **Efficacy of statutory redemption period as a device to protect mortgagor.** In *U.S. v. Stadium Apartments Inc.,* 425 F2d 358, the court marshalls convincing arguments that the statutory redemption period no longer serves its original purpose. It is a simple economic fact that if lenders find that redemption laws cause them delay and expense, they will refuse to make mortgage laws in the state or charge higher interest rates.

§ 534. **Distinctions between statutory redemption and equitable redemption.** There are a number of differences between equitable redemption and statutory redemption. Historically, equitable redemption was developed hundreds of years ago by the English judges. It provided a means of compelling, by court action, a mortgagee to return the property to a mortgagor who had forfeited it by failure to pay the mortgage debt on its due date. As thus developed, the period of time allowed by the court to the mortgagor to find the funds to pay the debt was entirely up to the judge. It varied from case to case. Since redemption was from the *mortgage,* it was necessary for the mortgagor to pay the mortgage debt and interest in order to redeem. When the technique of foreclosure by public sale replaced the old method of strict foreclosure, it became necessary for the courts to hold that the *equitable right of redemption ended with the foreclosure sale.* Otherwise, the courts surmised, there would be no bidders at the sale. Statutory redemption, as the name implies, exists only by virtue of statutes. In contrast to equitable redemption, *the period of statuory redemption begins with the date of the foreclosure sale* and runs for a specified period fixed by state law. In general, the laws provide that redemption is from the *sale,* rather than from the *mortgage.* Thus, if the foreclosure sale price is less than the mortgage debt, the mortgagor can redeem by paying only the sale price and interest.

§ 535. **Foreclosure with redemption period prior to sale.** In order to avoid the chilling of bidding incident to a sale followed by redemption, a few states have enacted laws providing for a postponement of foreclosure sale for a period of time, during which the mortgagor may pay off the debt. The sale, when held, gives the purchaser immediate ownership without any redemption rights. This device is found in both power of sale foreclosure states and states that require judicial sale. It is commanding more general acceptance in recent times. In many power of sale foreclosure states, however, there is no redemption period. *U.S. v. Stadium Apartments Inc.*, 425 F2d 358. The experience indicates that this type of law, on the whole, produces favorable results for both borrower and lender.

§ 536. Technical aspects of statutory redemption. No field of mortgage law is more replete with outmoded technicalities than the field of statutory redemption. Each state's laws and court decisions must be carefully studied, keeping in mind that this field is in a state of perpetual flux.

Laws vary widely as to who may redeem and what consequences ensue when redemption is made. In some instances the law provides one period of redemption for the owner, the effect of redemption being only to obliterate the foreclosure sale, leaving all liens other than the foreclosed mortgage unimpaired. Creditors of the mortgagor may be given a separate redemption period, redemption in such instance resulting in an acquisition of ownership by the redeeming creditor. Such, for example, is the law in Illinois. Again, it is difficult to generalize because of the wide variations in these laws.

§ 537. United States rights. The United States has thousands of liens on real estate throughout the country, mostly arising from delinquent income taxes. Wherever the United States has a lien or other interest in the land, it has a redemption right from any judicial foreclosure sale, a right existing under federal law. 28 U.S.C.A. § 2410.

Where the mortgage is one in which the United States has an interest, as where the mortgage is FHA insured, VA insured, or a Small Business Administration mortgage, the state redemption law is inapplicable, some decisions hold, and the federal court may order such redemption period as it deems appropriate. *U.S. v. Stadium Apartments Inc.*, 425 F2d 358 *cert.den.* December 2, 1970.

§ 538. Economic consequences of redemption laws. Probably in every state there is a "court house crowd" that makes its livelihood by bidding at public sales. These men know property values, have financing sources, often have regular work crews that make old buildings saleable, and have expertise in marketing real estate thus acquired. They are, however, unwilling to tie up their money unless they can acquire ownership *now*. This the redemption laws prevent. Hence, the court house crowd avoids sales subject to redemption. This leaves the mortgagee as the only bidder and makes public bidding a farce. This is especially true where the redemption period is a year, a rather common period.

Moreover, a mortgage lender must weigh the economic loss involved in waiting an additional year for his money, while the property depreciates in value or incurs the additional expense of receivership.

§ 539. Redemption—elective statutes. In some states the mortgagee can choose a mode of foreclosure that eliminates redemption.

EXAMPLE: In California use of the power of sale bars a deficiency judgment but eliminates redemption. If a judicial foreclosure is used, a deficiency judgment can be procured but there is a redemption period. In Arkansas there is no redemption if a judicial foreclosure is used, but there is a redemption period if a power of sale foreclosure is employed. *See also* § 503.

§ 540. Constitutional aspects. Evidently redemption laws existing at the time the mortgage is executed are considered to enter into the mortgage contract, both for the benefit of the mortgagor and mortgagee. The legislature can neither extend nor reduce the redemption period as to mortgages that take effect under the prior law. 16A CJS *Constitutional Law* § 235: 59 CJS *Mortgages* § 821. However, some decisions permit reduction of the redemption period as to pre-existing mortgages if the law still leaves a reasonable time for redemption. *Mt. Morris S & L Assn. v. Barber,* 17 Ill. 2d 523, 162 NE2d 347; 16A CJS *Constitutional Law* § 391.

§ 541. Rents and possession during redemption. The state laws present a bewildering diversity with respect to the duration of the redemption period and the rights of the mortgagee to rents and possession during such period. Koonts, *Some Problems of Mortgagees,* XIX Assn. of Life Counsel Proceedings 159; 2 Glenn, *Mortgages,* 1116.

§ 542. Waiver of statutory right of redemption. There are few decisions concerning the validity of a waiver in mortgage of a statutory right of redemption. An occasional decision sustains such a waiver. *Cook v. McFarland,* 78 Ia. 528, 43 NW 519. Other decisions hold such waivers invalid. *Beverly v. Washington,* 79 Wash. 537, 140 P 696. *See US v. Stadium Apartments,* 425 F2d 358. An eminent authority contends such waivers should be held valid. 2 Glenn, *Mortgages* § 230. It is difficult to follow his reasoning. The inequality of bargaining power that invalidates any waiver of the equitable right of redemption is certainly operative with respect to the statutory rights. At all events, the practical answer is that attorneys for purchasers are unlikely to approve a title free of redemption rights unless the state court has expressly sanctioned such waivers. Where corporations are permitted to waive statutory redemption rights, one frequently sees deeds made to newly formed corporations that proceed to make mortgages including such waivers. The individual shareholders then guarantee payment. There seems to be no decisional law dealing with the effectiveness of this device.

Index

(References are to sections.)